Between the Enemy and Texas

William Henry Parsons, 1871 (courtesy William D. Parsons, Lake Forest, Illinois).

Between the Enemy and Texas: Parsons's Texas Cavalry in the Civil War

By ANNE J. BAILEY

Texas Christian University Press
Fort Worth
1989

Copyright © 1989 by Anne J. Bailey

Library of Congress Cataloging-in-Publication Data

Bailey, Anne J.
    Between the enemy and Texas: Parsons's Texas Cavalry in the Civil
War / by Anne J. Bailey.
        p.   cm.
    Bibliography: p.
    Includes index.
    ISBN 0-87565-034-1
    1. Confederate States of America. Army. Texas Cavalry.
Parsons's Brigade—History.   2. Texas—History—Civil War,
1861–1865—Regimental histories.   3. United States—History—Civil
War, 1861–1865—Regimental histories.   4. United States—History—
Civil War, 1861–1865—Campaigns.   I. Title.
E580.6.P37B35 1989
973.7'464—dc19   88-31194
                                                              CIP

Drawing on cover and title page by John Groth
Design by Whitehead & Whitehead

For my mother and father

Contents

Illustrations

Preface

There are over fifty thousand volumes that relate to the American Civil War. With so many books already in print one might assume that another could not provide anything new or significant. This is not completely true. When I first became interested in the conflict I wanted to learn more about the participation of Texas troops, particularly those who served on the west side of the Mississippi River. I soon discovered that there were few publications devoted to the common soldier in this region and only a handful related to Texans. Although in the last few years there have been some excellent studies of Texas units published, this is still a relatively unexplored and often neglected field. I hope this book will help to demonstrate that the men who fought on the "other side" of the river encountered many of the same privations and hardships as Southerners serving in Virginia or Tennessee and that their contribution to the Confederacy deserves long overdue recognition.

This book is divided into two parts. The first three chapters recount the organization of the regiments while chapters four through thirteen chronicle the fighting in Arkansas, Missouri, and Louisiana. This was a war characterized by raids and skirmishes but few major encounters. Since much of this account is told by the soldiers themselves, I have kept the original form of their statements, within the limits of readability. As far as possible, I have allowed the troops to tell their version of what happened in their own words and with their peculiar spelling (often in regional dialect) without interrupting the narrative with *sic* or with needless explanation.

A map accompanies each major military action. These are drawn from official military reports as well as descriptions added by contemporary observers. Based on the information available, I have tried to be as accurate as possible, although some degree of error may exist.

In order to emphasize that military history is more than just strategy and tactics I have included, following the narrative, a brief description of the men who commanded the various companies in the brigade. This part is arranged by regiments and is intended to give the reader a feeling for the socio-economic status of each company captain.

Many people gave me valuable assistance while I researched this book. I am particularly indebted to the staff at the Texas State Archives and Barker Texas History Center in Austin for answering all my requests for material cheerfully. Numerous librarians, genealogists, and local historians also guided me toward often obscure information that made the characters in this work come alive.

I owe a special thanks to four good friends. Grady McWhiney read the manuscript, asked significant questions which I tried to answer, then patiently read it again. And two special ladies, Mildred Padon and Mabel McCall, at the Layland Museum in Cleburne, Texas, sparked my enthusiasm and always offered me encouragement and support. Finally, William D. Parsons of Lake Forest, Illinois, great-grandson of the colonel, never failed to share any bit of information he thought might prove important.

I cannot overlook my family—my sister, Lyndal Wilkerson, helped with the maps and never complained when I asked her to add another town or alter the existing layout. And my two daughters, Shawn Marie and Shana Lyn, travelled with me from Missouri to Louisiana visiting site after site when I know they, as teenagers, would have preferred to spend their vacations in other ways.

Finally, I am grateful to all of those who took time to read and comment on all or parts of the manuscript: Alwyn Barr, Norman D. Brown, Perry D. Jamieson, Glenn T. Nelson, Frank T. Reuter, John D. Squier, and Kenneth R. Stevens. At the T.C.U. Press my thanks go to Judy Alter, A. T. Row and Nancy Stevens.

Introduction

Historians analyzing the American Civil War tend to ignore the vast area west of the Mississippi River. Military actions in the Trans-Mississippi Department (Texas, Arkansas, Missouri, most of Louisiana, the Indian Territory or modern-day Oklahoma, and parts of present-day New Mexico and Arizona) did not alter the outcome of the conflict; after the fall of Vicksburg the region was cut off and virtually forgotten. Far more important to Jefferson Davis and the Confederate government was the eastern theater—more specifically Virginia. Even the western theater, which included those Southern states between Virginia and the Mississippi River, demanded more attention. Yet, in terms of fighting, the state with the third most military events (following Virginia and Tennessee) was Missouri.

Men who fought on the "other side" of the Mississippi believed the theater merited more attention. Colonel William Henry Parsons, in a letter to a Confederate reunion in 1878, asserted: "The Texas Regiments of Virginia may have for a time succeeded in keeping the Federal armies out of Richmond, but the army of the Trans-Mississippi . . . did keep formidable Federal armies out of Texas, and never permitted hostile foot to march over her soil." He pointed out that Federal armies occupied much of Arkansas and Louisiana, "but to the alertness and valor of this army whose praises and annals are yet unrecorded, and unrecognized," Texas never suffered the destruction that accompanied an invading army.[1]

Fighting in the Trans-Mississippi was not characterized by stupendous engagements like those at Gettysburg or Antietam, and it never received any acclaim. In 1925 George H. Hogan, a former member of Colonel Parsons's Twelfth Texas Cavalry, complained in an article for the *Confederate Veteran*:

> At our State and general reunions, I often hear remarks by the careless observer that, "you fellows in the Trans-Mississippi didn't know what fighting was. You should have been with us under Lee and Jackson, Joe Johnston; then you could tell what

Flag of Parsons's Brigade (courtesy Hill College History Complex, Confederate
Research Center, Hillsboro, Texas).

a battle looked like." I have refuted these aspersions so long,
and have seen so little in our beloved *Veteran* about "our side
of the river," that I am tempted to come to the front and tell of
some of the operations as witnessed by a "high private" in our
brigade as a refutation that we never saw any service on this
side [of] the river. . . . [2]

The fighting west of the river presented a different kind of war. There
was no Army of Northern Virginia led by a Robert E. Lee nor was

there an Army of Tennessee proudly claiming victory at Chickamauga. There were few major battles, but as historian Norman Brown observed, "The fighting was often as fierce in the Trans-Mississippi Department as in the other two theaters."[3] For Parsons's cavalry, scouting in Arkansas and Louisiana, the conflict was day by day—sometimes boring, sometimes lively, but never-ending. Instead of a clash between armies, it was a contest between men who knew their opponent well—not always personally, but by name and reputation. On both sides, animosity combined with vengeance to produce bitter hatred.

Parsons's Texans reconnoitered along the Mississippi River and its tributaries from mid-1862 until the end of the war, performing an often monotonous but valuable service for the South. Their efforts kept the Confederate hierarchy (headquartered first at Little Rock and later at Shreveport) advised of enemy movements. The troops spent little time in camp; the nature of their service kept them constantly on the move. Unlike infantrymen, who often spent the winters in tents, the cavalry scouted year-round.

Colonel Parsons observed that his brigade served as the "sleepless eye, the good right arm" protecting the Army of the Trans-Mississippi. Further, he asserted, that "whether in the incessant skirmish[es] on the enemy's out-post or lines, or in repeated attacks upon gun-boats on the White, the Mississippi, or the Red rivers," his men had always impressed the enemy "with a conception of number that had no existence in reality." Parsons firmly believed his Texas troops never received the recognition they deserved, especially in 1862, when they shielded the fledgling army organizing near Little Rock.[4]

Parsons's Texans were typical Southerners. They enjoyed drinking, gambling, singing; they were expert horsemen and skillful marksmen. They took orders cheerfully when they agreed with the directive and refused when they thought the order unreasonable. They were better at raiding than performing as traditional cavalry. They lived off the land and fought with the weapons they brought from home. The wide variety of arms complemented the assortment of dress ranging from Mexican sombreros and blankets to coats of Federal blue.[5]

The men of Parsons's cavalry also displayed the Southern trait of loyalty to their leaders. The Texans followed their officers out of personal devotion to them rather than because they were designated military commanders. Over four thousand men fought in the brigade during the war—three regiments, a battalion (later a regiment), and a battery. Two of these regiments, the Twelfth and the Nineteenth Texas, displayed an unusual devotion to Colonel William H. Parsons, even to the point of threatening mutiny after his removal in 1863. The Twenty-first Texas Regiment demonstrated an equally fervent attachment to its commander, Colonel George W. Carter. This affection was reciprocal; both Parsons and Carter led their men in battle and did not hesitate to head a charge as proof they were willing to give their own lives for their men.[6]

This allegiance to an individual leader often frustrated troop efficiency. Throughout the war the fealty the men exhibited toward their particular commander reduced the regiments' ability to work together and destroyed any possibility of true cohesion. Moreover, controversies of this nature plagued the armies throughout the Confederacy. Still, as in the case of Parsons's command, disputes that hampered troop effectiveness in battle did not lessen the Southerners' will to fight.

The Texans were aggressive and preferred to take the offensive. In almost every skirmish from Missouri to Louisiana they struck first. They loved to charge and gained a reputation along the Mississippi River for their wild, impetuous charges and fearless, often violent fighting. In 1862 a member of the brigade noted that the Federals were "afraid even to send out scouts, for fear that we will bush-whack them. . . . [They] have a wholesome dread of the Texans."[7] A Union private noted, "fighting the Texans is like walking into a den of wildcats."[8]

But the men of the brigade did not always fight from the saddle. Parsons taught the recruits in his own regiment, the Twelfth Texas, to fight as dragoons—troops who used their horses for transportation or mobility, yet dismounted to engage the enemy. And the Confederates in the Twelfth Texas Cavalry, originally known as the Fourth Texas Cavalry, often replaced the word "cavalry" with the more descriptive designation "dragoons." Indeed, they often referred to their regiment as the Fourth Texas Dragoons. They learned to fight as proficiently on foot as they did on their horses. But whether mounted or dismounted, the Texans fought with reckless abandon.[9]

Yet this brigade is a study in contrasts. Parsons's Twelfth Texas was composed of men, often young and single, who joined in 1861 anxious to fight for the South. The Nineteenth and Twenty-first Texas consisted of many older men, often with families at home, who joined after the conscript law in 1862 made delaying induction impossible. Charles Morgan's cavalry began as a squadron, increased to a battalion, then by 1865 gained regimental strength. But Morgan's command was a hodgepodge of companies under him in name only, and the men displayed a stronger loyalty to their particular companies than to the regiment. Parsons's Twelfth Texas, on the other hand, presented by far the most disciplined force in the brigade, and it was upon the reputation of this regiment that the troops of the brigade gained fame. In 1863 Brigadier General James F. Fagan wrote that Colonel Parsons "has long commanded a Brigade 'in front' & discharged with great success all the duties & responsibilities of a General Officer."[10]

Although men joined the brigade for a variety of reasons, they held one common belief—the desire to protect Texas from invasion and occupation. A consistent theme throughout much of the extant correspondence is the importance the men attached to defending their homes and families. Moreover, they generally believed that the principles they hoped to preserve were valid and honorable. In 1862 J. C. Morriss of the Twenty-first Texas explained to his wife: "You also said something about hiring a substitute; I do not wish one, I have a pride to do my own fighting. . . . I feel like I am fighting in a just and a glorious cause and that the soldiers, and armys of the Southern Confedercy are under the special guidance of Him who dose all things right. and I have my little family under his protection who never forsakes His trust."[11] Historian Grady McWhiney concluded that Southerners believed "combat was the surest and the best way to protect their rights and their honor."[12]

Fighting west of the Mississippi must be approached somewhat differently from the usual Civil War history. To emphasize only battles would be a mistake. This is a story of men—their values, their actions and reactions in wartime—as well as an account of the military tactics and strategy practiced by a Texas cavalry brigade on the "other side" of the Mississippi.

During the war, the soldiers fighting in the Trans-Mississippi Department felt overlooked and ignored, and that attitude did not change after the war. Even today many historians evaluate much of the fighting west of the river as insignificant and relegate the men who fought there to virtual obscurity. Nevertheless, their "war" deserves a place in Civil War historiography. As Professor Robert L. Kerby has pointed out, the fighting in the Trans-Mississippi "does serve to complement and refine the history of the Confederate States."[13]

Between the Enemy and Texas

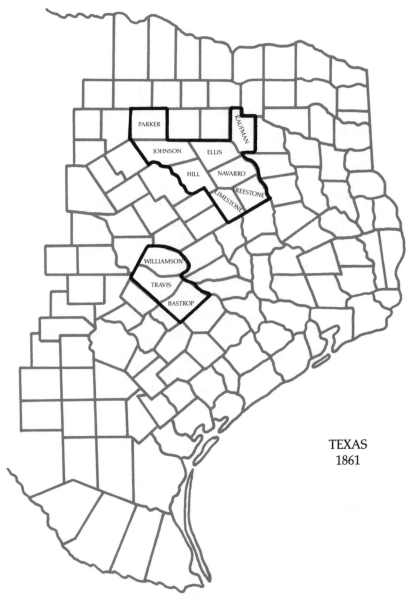

TEXAS
1861

Figure 1. William Parsons raised eight companies in the North Central Texas area. Two additional companies originated in South Central Texas; these recruits rode over one hundred fifty miles to join this regiment.

1.

"A Healthy Bunch of Scrappers"

The campaigns fought west of the Mississippi River seemed "small indeed by comparison with the more imposing and dramatic events of the far east," asserted William Henry Parsons, "but momentous in results to the fortunes of [the] Trans-Mississippi department, and especially to the fate of Texas."[1] As he astutely pointed out, "Our lines once broken, whether on the Mississippi or the Arkansas, or the Red River, would have thrown open the approach to the invasion of Texas, by an ever alert and powerful foe." Parsons strongly believed the Army of the Trans-Mississippi, including his own command, never received the recognition it merited for "again and again foiling the invasion and intended devastation" of Texas.[2]

Parsons had a point; the men who served under him gained scant acknowledgment for shielding Texas from Federal occupation. Yet his troops took part in almost fifty battles (although most were too small to rate a name), and they were responsible for watching Federal operations from Memphis to Vicksburg. For three years the men provided outposts and scouts for the army headquartered first at Little Rock and later at Shreveport. The brigade rarely mustered in full at any single place; instead, the troops generally fought by detachments or regiments. Even during the winter when the infantry retired to camps, Parsons's cavalrymen remained in the field. And, proudly insisted George Hogan: "It was a noted fact that whether fighting as a company, battalion, or regiment, the brigade was never whipped" until the last major engagement at Yellow Bayou during the Red River campaign of 1864.[3]

Parsons's Texas Cavalry Brigade was a veritable collage, described by one Confederate as "a healthy bunch of scrappers."[4] Its nucleus was the Fourth Texas Dragoons (later designated the Twelfth Texas Cavalry), a regiment Parsons raised in North Central Texas soon after the war began. One year later his command included the Nineteenth Texas Cavalry from the Dallas area, under District Judge Nathaniel Macon Burford; the Twenty-first Texas Cavalry mainly from South Central Texas, under

3

Methodist minister George Washington Carter; and Charles Morgan's command, a hodgepodge of companies from throughout the state. Morgan began with a squadron in 1862 but three years later had gained enough companies to attain regimental strength. For artillery, Joseph H. Pratt's Tenth Field Battery from Jefferson in East Texas provided welcome firepower that Parsons used with great efficiency. This amalgamation represented the best of Texas—men from the Piney Woods of East Texas, the Cross Timbers and blackland prairies of Central Texas, and the Gulf Coast of South Texas.

The Confederate Congress never promoted Parsons to brigadier general, although he acted in that capacity for much of the war. Several times he was recommended for field promotion, but the government never granted him a commission. Twice the authorities superseded him with an officer unacceptable to the rank and file. In each instance the troops protested so fiercely that the bureaucracy had to reinstate him. After the war the governor of Texas appointed Parsons a major general of the home guard for services never recognized by the hierarchy in Richmond.[5]

The loyalty most members of the brigade exhibited for Parsons mystified outsiders. The colonel had the ability to inspire affection, to motivate men in order to gain their devotion. If he had one fault, recalled

Lieutenant L. T. Wheeler, "it was in the carefulness of the lives of his men."[6] But even this proved advantageous. The hardheaded and individualistic Texans appreciated his compassion as much as they admired his bravery under fire. Although it appeared that creating a homogenous unit from such an amalgam would prove difficult, through admiration, respect, and mutual trust Parsons molded his brigade into an effective fighting force.

By birth Parsons was a Northerner, by training and preference a fervent, even fanatical, Southerner. Born in 1826 of Puritan stock, William could claim that his ancestors had arrived in the early 1600s on the second voyage of the *Mayflower*. Over the years the Parsons family flourished, and several of William's ancestors fought with distinction in the American Revolution. William's father Samuel was a native of Maine but had married a woman from a distinguished New Jersey family, and it was there that William was born.[7]

William's family moved south when he was a small child, and he never developed the Puritan beliefs of his ancestors. The elder Parsons opened a grocery in Montgomery, Alabama, hired an Irish clerk, and, like most who prospered modestly, purchased slaves. Although Samuel never lost his New England values, his son thrived in an environment that respected a skilled horseman or marksman far more than a scholar. Transplanted Yankees like William often became radical proponents of Southern rights; by the time he reached manhood his political convictions reflected attitudes prevalent throughout the South.[8]

William was typical of restless youths living in a period of increasing tension. In his teens he entered Emory College at Oxford, forty miles east of Atlanta. The institution, chartered by Georgia Methodists in 1836, offered students a conservative curriculum. Parsons acquired the polish of an educated man through a bit of classical learning, a brush with Greek, Latin, and mathematics, and a smattering of geography, astronomy, and chemistry. But at midterm in 1844 the young man quit school—against his father's wishes—and headed for Natchitoches, Louisiana, where he intended to enlist in the army. His father's plans for his formal education ended.[9]

In later years Parsons proudly recalled his military service and noted that he had the distinction of repelling two invasions of Texas, first on the Rio Grande under Zachary Taylor and later on the Red River under Zachary's son Richard. He believed that his skill in sword exercise and field maneuvers learned during the war with Mexico gave him the advantage over other Confederate field commanders drawn straight from civilian life.[10]

After the Mexican War Parsons made Texas his home. In 1851 he married Louisa Dennard, from a prominent family in Jefferson, settled down, and began to raise a family. Texas offered abundant opportunities for an ambitious person. The year after his marriage Parsons joined a stock company, bought a newspaper in Tyler, and at the age of twenty-six became an editor. As his reputation grew, he became known as a well-educated, talented writer whose editorials possessed a rare courage of conviction.[11]

Southern editors were notorious for disputes, and Texans were no exceptions. A disagreement between Parsons and H. L. Grinsted, editor of the *Jefferson Herald*, grew so bitter that Grinsted sent a challenge to Parsons, who accepted. Although dueling was publicly condemned, few men were willing to risk being branded as cowards for refusing to fight. On the appointed day only Parsons showed up, and the two men finally submitted the matter to a Board of Honor. After both parties agreed to apologize, the feud ended without bloodshed. In spite of this, when Parsons visited Jefferson to attend the funeral of his father-in-law, someone shot and wounded him. He claimed he did not see his assailant, but local newspapers speculated that the culprit was a Jefferson printer. Parsons allowed the matter to drop, sold his interest in the *Tyler Telegraph*, and moved to the Brazos River region in Central Texas.[12]

Throughout the 1850s, Parsons lectured and wrote on local, state, and national issues for Texas newspapers. When the Houston *Telegraph* advocated reopening the slave trade, Parsons concurred. When the United States government considered a transcontinental railroad route through the South, Parsons maintained that if Southerners would show "the energy, and the swiftfooted enterprise of our Northern brethren, we would soon cease to complain of Northern political preponderance and commercial supremacy. . . . Let the South take an even start in the race of Empire. We have been outdistanced in our north-western territories; should we now supinely yield territory, legitimately our own without a struggle?" His writing indicated a strong devotion to his adopted state. "Give Texas all she now needs," he advocated, "to make her not only the empire state of the South, but of the nation." While he spread his political rhetoric throughout Central Texas, he insisted, "there has been a tendency upon the part of some of the Texas, and Southern press, to discourage Southern emigration, and to disparage the resources of these new fields of adventure and enterprise."[13]

Parsons needed a mouthpiece for his increasingly radical convictions; in 1860 he founded his own pro-Southern newspaper in Waco. In October he issued the first edition of the *South West*, a weekly newspaper devoted to supporting Southern rights. The Houston press soon called it one of the best papers in the state. Although one old resident recalled, "Parsons made the sheet a red-hot one," the content is impossible to verify because only three copies still exist.[14] In the first issue Parsons stated that he supported "co-equality of rights in State and Territory; and the maintenance of the present social relations of the races in Southern society"[15]—although he owned no slaves himself, and his wife Louisa possessed only "Aunt Esther," more part of the family than servant.[16] Parsons professed that his paper would not support any party, for "we care nothing for men, nor mere party; but principles have indistructible essence." He did suggest, nevertheless, that Texans arm themselves for a possible conflict if Abraham Lincoln won the presidential election.[17]

Parsons correctly predicted his state's reaction. As word of Lincoln's election spread throughout Texas, radicals called for a secession convention. While politicians squabbled over the state's position, a number of diehard Texans seized the initiative by lowering the United States flag from above the Alamo. The Secession Convention, which convened in January 1861, began to prepare for war. All three future colonels in Parsons's brigade travelled to Austin to support the work of the legislators.[18]

After the convention announced that Texas was no longer a part of the Union, Federal troops evacuated the western forts, leaving the fron-

tier at the mercy of roaming Indians. Many of the men eventually joining Parsons's brigade originally enlisted in companies providing local defense, but the outbreak of war quickly transcended problems along the
frontier. As soon as the Confederate government began to request soldiers, Governor Edward Clark authorized prominent citizens to raise
troops for state service. Parsons was among those commissioned.[19]

The Texans' preference for mounted service exasperated the governor. Most wanted to join the cavalry and refused to have anything to do
with the infantry. Clark observed that the Texans' disinclination to become foot soldiers was founded "upon their peerless horsemanship."
They were "unwilling, in many instances to engage in service of any
other description, unless required by actual necessity."[20] Even English
Colonel James Fremantle noted that when the war began "it was found
very difficult to raise infantry in Texas, as no Texan walks a yard if he
can help it."[21]

While Governor Clark tried desperately to fill the Confederate War
Department's request for infantrymen, Parsons had little trouble enlisting horsemen. By December 1861, the cavalry leaving the state outnumbered the infantry by twenty-four to one. Texas produced far more than
its fair share of mounted troops, while neighboring Louisiana claimed
thirty foot soldiers to every mounted one. (Estimates for the entire area
west of the Mississippi for this period suggest that infantry outnumbered
the cavalry by a slim margin of one and one-fourth to one.)[22]

Enlisting recruits was an informal process. Prominent men who decided to raise their own companies competed with one another to fill
quotas. Although minor details varied, the procedure was generally the
same throughout Texas. A typical example was that of Jeff Neal, a young
lawyer who set out to raise a contingent to join Colonel Parsons. In
Buchanan, seat of Johnson County, Neal appealed to the men's sense of
loyalty while he provided them with free liquor. At the proper time he
mounted a big box he had placed in the center of the square and called for
volunteers. "All that waat [want] to go away in my company just form a
line right out in front of me," he shouted. Nearly fifty citizens, spirits
stimulated by the free whiskey, came forward. "Now gentlemen," Neal

charged, "raise your right hand, pull off your hats and I will now administer the oath to you or muster you into service."[23] Men lined up next to their friends, the liquor continued to flow, and the next morning many discovered they had joined the "Johnson County Slashers." To commemorate the event the townspeople threw a barbeque on the "great glorious and never-to-be-forgotten Fourth of July."[24]

Eight companies from North Central Texas and two from the region near Austin (Figure 1) eventually rendezvoused in Ellis County, where Colonel Parsons opened a camp of instruction early in July. These troops formed the Fourth Texas Dragoons (later designated the Twelfth Texas Cavalry), the unit that became the backbone of Parsons's brigade. Few men paid much attention to rank. Lawyers, doctors, bankers, merchants, college graduates, and sons of prominent families enlisted along with farmers and stock raisers. The majority were eager young men anxious to fight Yankees and unconcerned with the political issues involved.[25]

Throughout the hot summer Parsons drilled military training and discipline into the raw recruits. Those who could not endure the hard life left; those who remained learned essential military skills. Lieutenant George Ingram wrote his wife: "We rise at daybreak and drill from 7 oclock A.M. until 11 oclock A.M. and from 2 until 5 oclock P.M. We are improving very fast." The majority seemed proud of their accomplishments, and Ingram added that all of the "companies here are learning the art of war quite fast and all hands seem to take a great interest in the drill."[26]

The person immediately responsible for the training was usually the company captain. Although each group had a distinctive nickname and a letter for proper designation, companies often went simply by the name of the captain. The average age of the original ten captains was thirty-five, while the average age for the rank and file was twenty-five. Deaths and resignations changed the company officers during the war, and of the ten men selected in the summer of 1861, only half persevered until the war's end.[27]

The office of captain carried considerable prestige, but a man might easily yield it to another if offered a higher rank. When Captain John

Mullen of the "Williamson Bowies" was elected lieutenant colonel, he passed the captain's position on to Wiley Peace. Mullen, a fifty-year-old farmer from Delaware and a veteran of the Mexican War, was an expert on infantry tactics as well as cavalry drills. He elicited respect for his sound judgment and coolness under fire—a trait frequently lacking in officers at the outset of the war. Many thought Mullen should have allowed them to enter his name for colonel; indeed, he was the only real competition Parsons ever had in his own regiment. Yet Mullen served as lieutenant colonel only until 1862 when, because of his age and personal commitments, he resigned and returned home.[28]

His replacement as lieutenant colonel was the former adjutant, Andrew Bell Burleson. The Burleson name carried prestige in Texas. All of the troops knew that Bell's uncle, Edward Burleson, had served as vice-president for the Republic of Texas and that Bell's father and uncles had fought in the Texas Revolution. Although personally brave—despite his exploits he miraculously escaped injury during the war—Bell drank too much. By late 1864 he was in trouble with his superiors for insubordination and probably escaped serious military discipline only because the war ended.[29]

As with all elective offices, the selection of major revolved around personalities. The large contingent from Ellis County was able to elect one of its own, Emory W. Rogers, the proprietor of a local hotel. Rogers, who had migrated to Texas not long after the war for independence, settled in the area that became Waxahachie around 1847 and donated the land for the original townsite. A family history describes him as a "loveable, impulsive, generous Irishman." He declined reelection at the reorganization in 1862 because his four sons and a son-in-law belonged to the Confederate army and he believed he should return home to take care of his family.[30]

Lochlin Johnson Farrar, a young captain whose small company had abandoned the camp of instruction, replaced him. Farrar contrasted with his predecessor in a number of ways. Whereas Rogers had helped establish the town of Waxahachie, Farrar was a newcomer. He had arrived in the state in 1858 and settled the following year at Springfield in Limestone County, where he opened a law practice. In 1860 Farrar lived in the local hotel; he had no land and reported only three hundred dollars in personal possessions (probably indicating the ownership of one or two horses).[31]

For the first few weeks in state service, Parsons depended upon each of his officers to help him gain the confidence of the troops as well as to teach the obstreperous Texans the rudiments of war. A mutal confidence evolved between the colonel, officers, and enlisted men and became the secret of the regiment's success. Although Parsons rigorously drilled the recruits, they cheered whenever they saw him.

The formal election of officers took place at Camp Beauregard near Waxahachie in September. W. H. Getzendaner, who belonged to an Ellis County company, described the ceremony: "Early in the morning the people began to pour in, . . . until the entire place was thronged with men, women and children." When the bugle sounded the companies formed a "hollow square" and Parsons, "a proud form on as proud an animal glided into the open space," where he delivered a brief speech equal to the "novelty and magnitude of the occasion."[32]

After several weeks in North Central Texas, the colonel received orders to march for Hempstead near Houston, where a mustering officer would transfer the entire command into the Confederate service. Hoping his men would prove loyal to the cause, Parsons requested those willing to fight for the South to follow him. An observer recalled that company after company "marched off shouting for the Confederacy."[33] James J. Frazier of the "Johnson County Slashers" informed his mother that out of some twelve hundred troops only "some 50 or 60 refused to be mustered." But, he proudly noted, none came from their county.[34]

The trip south was an event the men never forgot, since many of the young recruits had never seen a large town. Henry Orr recalled that when Parsons arrived by railroad at the new camp, pandemonium broke out. "Such cheering and shooting of pistols, I never before heard," wrote Orr. "This was a day long to be remembered by many of the boys from the interior of the state, who here saw for the first time the Iron Horse." Indeed, the railroad proved an awesome novelty. The troops camped where they could watch "the 'Iron Horse' come snorting by every day," observed Orr. "When the boys hear this deadly tread, they break for their lives, whooping and yelling, 'Run here, everybody!' and when it is passing they huzzah and wave their hats and take after it."[35] But the men soon lost their excitement over locomotives when ordered to guard both rail and telegraph lines. And upon discovering that soldiers could ride the train free of charge, they frequently passed back and forth between the camp and the bright lights and bustling life of Houston.

Although the troops generally heeded orders, there were instances when discipline faltered. Lieutenant Colonel Mullen issued orders permitting no enlisted man to leave the vicinity of the camp except with a commissioned officer. But many captains ignored instructions and allowed their troops to stray. While celebrating their October 28 induction into the Confederate army, several carefree young men filled with too much whiskey terrorized local citizens. Even though the culprits did little damage and authorities soon arrested them, a much-exaggerated account appeared in Texas papers. James J. Frazier summed up the affair to assure his family that it was only an isolated incident. Some of the "boys got drunk," he explained, and "run thrugh town firing off pistols & broke into a grocery & took the mans whiskey & done other things unbecuming to a sivalized soldier."[36]

Troublesome incidents like this rarely occurred, but mischievous antics abounded. Harper Goodloe, a private from Ellis County who later became Parsons's aide-de-camp, recalled that the prosperous German farms around Hempstead proved too tempting for the young soldiers. "The beef issued to us was very poor," related Goodloe, "and these Germans had fine hogs running in the woods; so our boys slipped across the bayou and killed a fine shoat occasionally." After the Germans lodged official complaints to headquarters, the colonel ordered the foraging stopped. But, confided Goodloe: "The boys slipped a fine ham to the colonel's cook, and no arrests were made." The Germans nevertheless demanded compensation, and Parsons "ordered the commissary to pay when the skins and ears were presented." The men called this "chaparral bear meat."[37]

But the citizens generally did their best to accommodate the new Confederate soldiers, and frequent social events kept the young recruits occupied. In November local residents planned a concert, complete with brass band, to benefit the regiment. But it was soon "ascertained that the instruments had been used in casting a brass cannon for home defense in the county," and the event had to proceed with substitute music. Still the receipts exceeded expectations. During the evening Colonel Parsons thanked the townspeople for their interest "in a language glowing with patriotic fervor and eloquence. . . . His address was one long to be remembered, abounding in imagery of poetic beauty, thrilling you at times with the depths of its pathos, and firing you with the zeal that flashed from his own burning words."[38]

Although pleased with the progress of his regiment, Parsons became impatient for action. Inactivity was beginning to tell on everyone, and he looked for ways to occupy the men while at the same time teaching them the basic skills of warfare. He challenged other regiments to a trial drill, the prize was a horse and equipment worth not less than $1,000. Another idea he concocted was more dangerous: telling his recruits it was necessary for them to train their animals to jump, he provided an obstacle course, then ordered all to practice clearing the bars. The less skillful horsemen took some ungraceful spills attempting to coax their mounts over the four-foot high fence, and when they tried to force their horses to cross a five-foot ditch, many obstreperous animals refused to comply.[39]

This training, nevertheless, proved invaluable. Parsons believed that the men's eventual proficiency in drill helped his regiment remain mounted throughout the war. In January 1862 James J. Frazier informed his family: "General [Paul O.] Hebert reviewed our regiment last week . . . he complemented the Col verry nicely" and said, "Col I congratulate you on the efficiency your men hav attained in cavalry drill." Frazier bragged, "I understand that he sayed that this was the finest cavalry regiment in the Confederate Service."[40] Colonel Parsons recalled that "in the United States regular cavalry I acquired the experience and proficiency that eminently qualified me to impart to the 1200 splendid horsemen . . . a thorough knowledge of cavalry tactics." This expertise, he added, had prompted General Hébert, who commanded in Texas, to comment, "You lack but one thing to make you perfect dragoons—sabers."[41]

Despite the colonel's best efforts, lethargy prevailed in the camp as 1861 drew to a close. The men had become tired of drilling and making cartridges; they were impatient for a fight. A member of the "Slashers" reported: "Surely we are as contented as any body of soldiers," but lamented, "all that troubles us is the fear that the Yankees will not give us a chance to flog them outright decently."[42]

The listlessness gave way early in 1862, when reports of Federal vessels sighted near Galveston stirred sudden activity. Although it proved a false alarm, many of Parsons's men worried that authorities might order them to defend the island. Colonel Parsons, aware that most of them preferred service across the Mississippi River, assured his troops that he would not allow anyone to station them permanently near Galveston. He urged his "boys" to be patient, then left for Houston to meet with Hébert. Following the conference, Parsons returned to the regiment with welcome news—he had orders to take his command to either Kentucky or Missouri.[43]

This announcement delighted the men. Parsons delivered a speech in his "usually warm, impulsive style," then authorized the troops to ride by their respective homes and rendezvous at the Red River rather than proceed there as a unit. The reaction, according to Henry Orr, was "universal approbation, and many of the boys fairly made the 'welkin ring' in applauding the Colonel for granting them this privilege."[44]

Parsons knew this action would inspire loyalty even if it did not follow military regulation. Henry Orr astutely noted, "The Colonel plays much on the sympathies of his soldiers."[45] This was the secret of Parsons's success: he never placed himself above his men but treated them as equals rather than subordinates. In fact, Richard Taylor later noted of the Texas cavalry under his command: "Officers and men addressed each other as Tom, Dick, or Harry, and had no more conception of military graduations than of the celestial hierarchy of the poets." Although Taylor did not refer directly to the troops under Colonel Parsons, the description could fit many Texas cavalry units. "The men were hardy and many of the officers brave and zealous," recalled Taylor, "but the value of these qualities was lessened by lack of discipline. In this, however, they surpassed most of the mounted men who subsequently joined me, discipline among these 'shining by its utter absence.'"[46]

Parsons eventually commanded two regiments, the Nineteenth and the Twenty-first, whose inexperienced recruits had little knowledge of the fundamentals of war that Parsons had so carefully imbued in his own troops. But his dragoons, who eventually were known as the Twelfth Texas, were a proficient fighting force as they marched north. All the months spent drilling, all the spills while training their horses to jump, paid off. The troops in Parsons's regiment had another major advantage over those who entered the war later: recruits leaving in 1861 rode the best horses they could afford, but a year later comparable mounts had become difficult if not impossible to find at any price.[47] Not only did all of Parsons's men leave Texas mounted, but he had inculcated the rudiments necessary for survival. They were as skilled a cavalry force as any serving in the Trans-Mississippi Department.

During the war these Texans worked well together. For their fine preparation the men of Parsons's Twelfth Texas could thank their colonel. One observer believed his secret was "just enough of *red-tape-ism* to render him, in our estimation, the type of man for the times."[48] L. T. Wheeler later penned: "As a horseman I can say he had no superior in the Confederate army; proud, well equipped, he looked a very knight of chivalry; brave and of commanding voice, which could be heard above the din of battle, his white plume could always be seen in the front of the battle; with true military genius he was always quick to take advantage of the enemy's mistake; resolute and self-confident, and confident of the valor of his men, he often turned what seemed to be defeat into victory."[49] But it was Parsons's brother-in-law, A. J. Byrd, who summed up the colonel's nature. He was, Byrd believed, "as vain as a peacock, through as brave and dashing as Richard the Lion hearted."[50]

One advantage that Parsons had over the other colonels in his brigade was the military experience he acquired while fighting in Mexico. Although his service with the United States Army had been brief, it had given him valuable training. Few commissioned officers could claim military background, and for many of the men serving as leaders with Parsons, this lack of knowledge proved a disadvantage. A good example was George Washington Carter, a Methodist minister who turned soldier at the outbreak of the conflict. Although Carter initially hoped to lead his own brigade, he and part of his command eventually joined Parsons in Arkansas. His inexperience in military matters would at times seriously hamper the effectiveness of the unit, while his overconfidence in his abilities produced a conflict with Parsons that endured throughout the war.

2.

A Fightin' Preacher and His Unruly Flock

As Parsons's troops rode out of Texas, events far from their homes were helping to shape other units that would eventually join Parsons's brigade. "All we hear is the call for more troops, more troops, war, war, war," wrote Susan Anna Good from Dallas to her husband John Jay Good, captain of a Texas battery stationed in Arkansas, in April 1862. "God only knows when it will cease."[1] Even Abraham Lincoln and Jefferson Davis had assumed that the conflict would end quickly, but the events of the past year had proved them wrong. The war, which both had hoped would be brief and limited, still raged. In the East, Union forces began to approach Richmond; across the Mississippi, the situation became equally critical when the Confederate army abandoned much of Missouri, Arkansas, and southern Louisiana to meet the Federal threat in Tennessee and Mississippi, just as the twelve-month enlistments neared expiration.

Davis feared that his army would disintegrate at the moment he needed it most. Consequently, the Confederate government enacted the first conscription law in American history, making every white male between eighteen and thirty-five subject to military service. Davis thus could hold his army together by encouraging more enlistments—volunteers could choose their regiments and officers, those drafted could not. The law compelled many who had hoped to delay military service to answer the urgent appeal. Texans, quite naturally, hastened to enlist in the cavalry before the government assigned them to infantry service. Men travelled far from their homes to enroll in mounted regiments. The highly publicized "Texas Lancers," organizing in South Central Texas under noted Methodist minister George Washington Carter, became a popular choice. But even though these often reluctant recruits hurried to sign up, the law was not as severe as it seemed; it exempted a number of professions ranging from druggists to high government officials—as well as teachers, professors, and ministers.

The Reverend Carter, whose regiment would eventually unite with Colonel Parsons in Arkansas, never claimed this exemption although he was both a clergyman and head of a thriving college for young men. Carter was an enigma. One acquaintance later described him as "an engaging and prepossessing man, of very fine education" who "was one of the most gentle, simple, and attractive men that I have ever known . . . gifted with a remarkable ability to state and illustrate a proposition." But Carter was ambitious and let nothing stand in the way of obtaining whatever goal he set. The same acquaintance who praised the preacher's virtues also claimed "that this mild-mannered, able, and accomplished man" had not only "developed a fondness for drink" but was also "dishonest, faithless, and in a position where he could do great harm."[2] A Texan who served under him drew a similar conclusion. Private J. C. Morriss related to his wife Amanda that Carter "is certainly a good preacher whether a good man or not."[3] The former clergyman's personality generated strong devotion from his followers and vehement dislike among his enemies.

Born in Virginia in 1826, Carter had been admitted to the Methodist Church when he was twenty-one years old and he ministered to congregations in the Richmond, Petersburg, and Fredericksburg districts of Virginia. Four years later the church ordained him an elder, and in 1858 he was appointed professor of ethics at the University of Mississippi and moved to Oxford.[4] In January 1860, while he was living in Mississippi, the Texas Methodist Conference invited Carter to become president of a promising new school, Soule University, located at Chappell Hill between Austin and Houston. The academy seemed a propitious assignment for the ambitious clergyman. The Texas conference had taken preliminary steps to create Soule in 1854, but two years passed before the school became operational. The financing, Carter soon learned, had come from wealthy and prominent men who donated as much as twenty-five thousand dollars to endow various departments. The main building, constructed in 1858, had cost an estimated forty thousand dollars. The trustees also authorized a law department to open in Houston and a medical facility for Galveston.[5]

Carter, who arrived at Soule in May 1860, promised to introduce sweeping reforms. The trustees agreed to expand the curriculum, restructure the faculty, and add a number of departments. Knowing the recalcitrant, undisciplined nature of Texas youth, an earlier administration had instituted rigid rules of conduct and demanded a signed statement requiring obedience, punctuality, and application to study. One pledge required that the young "gentlemen" relinquish their "concealed weapons" to the president.[6]

Carter had hardly settled in Texas before volatile political affairs terminated his programs and touched off a crisis at the university. Much to the dismay of conservatives at Soule, Carter was among the first to advocate disunion, and his speeches fomented ardent secessionist sentiment.[7] Although not a large slave owner, he possessed four servants and firmly believed that the Federal government was tramping on Southern rights.[8] Scarcely days after his native state seceded, Carter resigned his position and left for Richmond to offer his services to the Confederate government. Before he left, he urged his students to leave the academy and join the Confederate army. Although moderates argued against students leaving college, few young men listened. Reverend W. A. Parks of Fayette County mourned the insurgent attitude in both his congregation and the clergy in general. "The people are so absorbed in the 'Crisis' that it seems that many have forgotten that they have souls," he warned. "The apathy of the church and the carelessness of sinners cause me much anxiety and solicitude."[9]

Soule began to decline. One faculty member placed the burden for the school's deterioration directly on the management, including Carter, rather than the military emergency. A letter he wrote in March charged "the proceeds of too many scholarships have found their way either into the stone walls, or attendant expenses."[10] The administration had to abandon plans for the branches in Galveston and Houston. Then, with-

Figure 2. By 1862 attitudes toward enlisting in the army had changed. Pressured by the conscription law, the men in the Twenty-first Texas left their homes to join Carter's Lancers. Although there was a sense of county pride, it was not as evident in this command since recruiters had to cross county boundaries to find enough men for a full company. This map represents those counties contributing the majority of troops.

out students or funds, Soule University could not continue to operate. Soon after Carter left for Virginia the main building became a Confederate hospital.

Carter's first assignment upon reaching Richmond came directly from the war department. There was very little artillery in the Confederacy, and the South had few machines capable of producing weapons or workmen skilled in armament manufacture. Carter was to arrange for the construction of an improved wrought-iron gun, although the project was hampered by a lack of capital as well as shortage of proper equipment to construct the weapon. His diligence finally paid off, however, when he contracted for the gun's manufacture in both Norfolk and New Orleans. Carter returned to Texas in October with a colonel's commission authorized by the secretary of war.[11]

While in Virginia, Carter had been authorized to raise a regiment. He was an unlikely candidate for such a position since he had no military background. An acquaintance later wrote that it was impossible to feature the gentle preacher as the same "bold, bloodthirsty man" who had led a regiment of Texans known for their "sanguinary spirit."[12] Indeed, Carter apparently had little experience with weapons. At least following the war when he engaged in a duel, with rifles at sixty paces, both he and his opponent missed. The New Orleans *Daily Picayune*, which reported the affair, observed that neither "of them could hit a barn unless they were to go inside and shut the door."[13]

But Carter did not plan to organize just another cavalry force for the Confederacy; he proposed to mount a body of lancers. In November the *Texas State Gazette* announced, "this will be the only Regiment of Lancers in the service, and Lancers are the most formidable cavalry in the world. . . . The lance simply takes the place of the sword in a charge, and is much the more terrible weapon."[14]

The use of lances was not as novel as many Texans thought. Confederate General Joseph E. Johnston favored increasing Southern cavalry and alleviating the shortage of arms by "equipping a large body of lancers."[15] Even Union General Henry W. Halleck emphasized that in a charge the lance or saber often proved superior to a pistol or carbine. "In a regular charge the lance offers great advantages," observed Halleck, "in the mêlée the saber is the best weapon; hence some military writers have proposed arming the front rank with lances, and the second with sabers."[16] And Confederate cavalry commander Joseph Wheeler, in his widely read manual on tactics, included instructions for defending oneself against the lance. Noting it was the common weaponry of Indians, he maintained that defense "depends much upon horsemanship, the judgment of the rider." Successful maneuvers, he contended, were similar to those used for the bow and arrow.[17] Thus Texans should be extremely proficient in this type of warfare.

Becoming a lancer appealed to many, but not on the terms Carter offered. His orders authorized him to enlist troops for three years or the duration of the war, while other recruiters offered one-year enlistments. Carter therefore had trouble convincing men, after joining, to commit themselves for the extended period. In December 1861 Carter requested General Paul O. Hébert to send him a mustering officer at once. "I have now the full complement of companies in the regiment," reported Carter, but "such is the restlessness of Texan volunteers, that I fear the companies now ready, may disband if delayed until all are prepared for muster." Postponing official induction, he warned, would give many Texans time to change their minds. "Such result has already followed delay in two instances."[18]

The problem, of course, was that many of the volunteers had second thoughts about enlisting for the longer term in service. Governor Francis R. Lubbock explained to Secretary of War Judah Benjamin why Carter repeatedly had to delay official organization: "Colonel Carter met with much difficulty in raising his regiment, because of the interference of colonels who were raising men for shorter periods than the war. He raised forty companies before he could induce ten to stand to be mustered in as a regiment for the war. As fast as he would raise companies twelve-months' colonels would take them or cause disorganization."[19]

Captain Oscar M. Addison, a Methodist minister authorized to enroll men for Carter, recalled: "I found a reaction among the people, and but few were disposed to enlist. There were many recruiting officers in the field, calling for 12 months men, who met with but little success. This being the case men for the war (these I desired) could scarcely be obtained on any terms, and feeling disgusted with the apathy of the people, I gave up the business and returned home."[20]

In spite of this indifference, Carter's command finally filled to overflowing. Loyalty to the Southern cause had little to do with the change; passage of the conscription law in April 1862 brought many closet patriots into the open. Newspapers constantly encouraged citizens to enlist. The *Bellville Countryman* reminded Texans that becoming "honorable volunteers" was preferable to induction. "Now boys," the paper urged, "is perhaps the last chance you will have to go into [the] service on your own terms. Who responds?"[21]

Carter, alert to the increasing prominence of his Lancers, took the opportunity to make some drastic changes. Ordered to Richmond in February, Carter assured uneasy Texas authorities that his only reason for the trip was to report his command. Yet while in Virginia he persuaded the war department to increase his maximum force from ten companies to thirty. He also obtained commissions for his lieutenant colonel, Franklin C. Wilkes, a minister from Chappell Hill, and his major, Clayton C. Gillespie, who had edited the New Orleans *Christian Advocate*. The three regiments thus created became the First, Second, and Third Texas Lancers, later designated the Twenty-first, Twenty-fourth, and Twenty-fifth Texas, commanded by Carter as senior colonel.[22]

Although Governor Lubbock had initially supported Carter's recruiting efforts, this action changed his mind. The governor shot off a hot letter to Judah Benjamin: "I am this day in receipt of letters informing me that recruiting officers are issuing authority for the raising of cavalry companies so as to increase Colonel Carter's command to a brigade. I wish to be advised as to the facts." Lubbock quite naturally desired his office to receive recognition for all Texas troops, and the Richmond hierarchy had not requested more cavalry. The governor, who found himself pressed to send fifteen additional infantry regiments, complained, "If it be so that such authority is vested in Colonel Carter or others I can only repeat what I have already said, that it will defeat every effort I can make to raise infantry." He added that he could not "understand why individuals should be placed on a more favorable footing in the raising of men than the State authorities. If cavalry is wanted I could fill your requisition in twenty days" and if "permitted to act independently of gentlemen having roving commissions my efforts would be successful."[23]

Carter ignored the governor's protests and continued recruiting cavalry. As soon as he had thirty companies he initiated an unusual method of allotting the troops between himself, Wilkes, and Gillespie: they drew lots. When he found one of the groups exceeded the number of men allowed, he formed the excess into a small company which he attached to his own command, the Twenty-first Texas. These recruits were frontiersmen, Indian fighters from the western fringes of settlement. Their practical experience made them too valuable for Carter to turn away in a state where every male citizen considered himself a proficient horseman.[24]

This preference of Texans for cavalry service had plagued state authorities since the beginning of the war. When the conflict failed to end quickly, the Confederate government requested fewer and fewer cavalrymen, and Richmond pressed Texas authorities for additional infantry. Passage of the conscription act prompted those men who had not joined a mounted regiment to do so before induction into the infantry. Under the law, persons liable for military service could volunteer in any corps authorized by either the secretary of war or by the states. As an additional incentive, volunteers could collect a bounty and elect their own officers, provisions not allowed draftees.

Because much of Carter's force was composed of Texans hoping to avoid infantry service, it had a wide variety of enlistees—young and old, rich and poor. Although the recruiters tried to meet basic requirements, volunteers walked into camp with the expectation that they would be able to buy a mount or ride a horse the government provided. The initial returns of the Twenty-first Texas suggest a shortage of horses in 1862, and the men often obtained mounts that were unsuited for cavalry. Replacing horses was also difficult; after Carter's Lancers left for the field, resupplying the troops hundreds of miles away became a logistical problem.

Recruits joining Carter generally lived in South Central Texas, although he did draw some from the extreme eastern and western regions (Figure 2). One company, whose men had ridden almost two hundred miles from Beaumont, drew about twenty percent of its members from the east side of the Sabine River in Calcasieu Parish, Louisiana.[25] Carter also enlisted frontiersmen who had ridden equally far to join him rather than enter infantry companies organizing near where they lived.

Volunteers riding long distances anxiously anticipated the bounties promised by recruiters. Unfortunately, the money never materialized, and without this incentive, efforts to enroll men often failed. G. R. Freeman, who raised a company in Bell and Milam counties, complained that he enlisted and swore in sixty men, including himself, but thirteen had refused to report. He had heard that these men joined another company and believed they should be considered deserters.[26] Naturally, cash payments gave tremendous advantage to those recruiters able to offer the most. Many men simply went into the bounty business, and a large number of those listed on the rolls as deserters were bounty jumpers. Freeman's absent recruits probably never intended to become lancers and quite likely joined one of the numerous organizations that paid its men at the time of enlistment. Carter's men, as the recruits soon learned, would have to collect their bounty from Richmond at some future date.

Since the secretary of war had accepted the regiment into the service, Carter's orders came directly from Richmond.[27] He made it a point to keep his organization separate from those under state control. With well over two thousand men to train, he needed two camps of instruction. One, designated Camp Hébert, honored the commander in Texas; the other, Camp Carter, recognized the brigade commander. The camps, located in Austin County near Hempstead (now Waller County), were contiguous to other Texas forces yet detached by reason of their unique status.

To avoid trouble with Texas authorities, Wilkes, who commanded the brigade during Carter's frequent absences, honored most of Hébert's requests, but the distinction between troops under state authority and those under orders from Richmond frequently produced discord and hindered cooperation.[28] George Flournoy, colonel of the Sixteenth Texas Infantry, complained to Samuel Boyer Davis, the assistant adjutant general, about the presence of a "military organization purporting to be 'Carter's Brigade' in the Confederate States service." He pointed out that the brigade officers refused to follow correct channels in their communications and orders and never filed required reports with the "superior military commanders." The officers, furthermore, were making large purchases in the name of the Confederacy which, Flournoy suggested, might be without proper authorization.[29]

Flournoy was correct; Carter's commissary bought numerous supplies that enabled the troops to live in some comfort. J. P. Blessington, a private in the Sixteenth Texas Infantry who visited Carter's camp, recorded that he watched the colonel and his staff dine upon stewed beef, boiled ham, mashed potatoes, and chicken. This feast, Blessington believed, "some of the Austin County housekeepers were kind enough to raise for them—*at least the officers' servants thought so.*" The dessert included "a couple of bottles of old rye" furnished by the local planters and served by a "respectable force of negro waiters." As for the rank and file, Blessington speculated they ate turkey or chicken. Indeed, Blessington mused: "This is the way the cavalry lived at 'Camp Hebert.'" But how did the officers provide all this? "They will tell you," answered Blessington, "that their commissary furnished them. Follow their career through Arkansas and Louisiana, afterwards, and ask the ladies of those States about their chickens, when Carter's Cavalry was in their neighborhood."[30]

Life was easy in the two camps of instruction. Many of the men "were wealthy and brought into camp black servants whom they sent out to purchase such dainties as the government did not supply," recalled Private William Zuber. While Carter was away, Wilkes tried futilely to drill the recruits regardless of social standing. To practice actual battle-field tactics in "sham fights," the men divided into two groups, one representing cavalry, the other infantry. Zuber recollected: "In these, we shot paper wads at each other, recklessly wasting powder. Several men were accidentally hurt, and some of them were disabled for further service during the war."[31] Though Blessington said these men had "the appearance of warriors" with "bell-spurs" on their boots and huge knives dangling around their waists, they were untrained and poorly disciplined recruits ill-prepared for war.[32]

Although Carter's command had inspired envy in the camps of instruction around Hempstead, that was to change. Carter returned from another trip to Richmond soon after his troops had left for Shreveport and joined his men en route. When he did not produce the expected bounty and back pay, frustration and resentment quickly spread through the ranks. As the three regiments slowly progressed northeast with a force of between two and three thousand, the discontented soldiers vented their ire upon the unlucky citizens along their path. They remained in each neighborhood just long enough to ravage corncribs and smoke-houses. W. W. Frizzell, who lived at Alto in Cherokee County, reported to his friend and neighbor, Confederate Postmaster General John H. Reagan, that "even the defenseless widow meets with no mercy at their hands." While the men did offer to pay for their rations, Frizzell charged that the drafts were on an unknown individual at Houston and probably worth nothing.[33]

Frizzell questioned the authority of the officers to appropriate supplies in the name of the Confederate government. He complained "that notorious outrages are at this time being practiced in the way of plunder (through this section) from good citizens by an armed party of the citizens of Texas, professing to be Confederate soldiers and under the command of one Colonel Carter." No one, he believed, was spared. "They on yesterday made their boasts that they found an old widow lady in possession of only 280 pounds of bacon," angrily charged Frizzell, and "they took half." He added, "while I write I have seen them prowling about from house to house, evidently seeking whom they may devour next."[34] Reagan referred the letter without comment to the secretary of war, whom he considered responsible for the actions of the troublesome brigade.

Texans began to question Carter's character as well as his qualifications for a military position. Rumors circulated throughout the state that Carter "had been lying drunk for several days at a time, when on his way to Shreveport, both at Alto and Crockett," totally unfit to command. A newspaper correspondent in Texas believed the slanderous stories probably originated from "some disappointed aspirant for office," who was upset with Carter's commission from Richmond. Yet the Marshall *Texas Republican* investigated and reported the accusations "wear a very serious aspect." Witnesses, some very reliable, made statements as to Carter's "continual drunkenness" and verified that "the bad men under his command" had harassed the neighborhood. The *Republican* concluded that Carter had "either acted very badly" or was "grossly slandered."[35]

Carter threatened retaliation when he heard the allegations. Not only was his military competence in question, but the *Texas Republican* had suggested a church inquiry into the matter.[36] Carter insisted the stories were "unmitigated and gratuitous lies" and warned: "When I return to the State, I will hold to a strict personal accountability any persons (worthy of notice) whom I may ascertain to have been engaged in this cowardly and slanderous work." The editor of the *Telegraph* in Houston was incredulous that anyone could slander such an "estimable and honorable gentleman, patriot and christian" as Colonel Carter.[37]

Carter maintained that his men had no reason to forage and pillage needlessly as he had provided ample provisions for the trip to Shreveport. He reported that his cumbersome assemblage included a herd of cattle and several supply wagons carrying enough salt to preserve all the beef.[38] But when the brigade reached Alto, J. C. Morriss complained, "we have seen nor heard nothing of Col Carter since we arrived at this place." And, charged Morriss: "He had made no provision for our subsistance, and if we had not provided for our selves we would have been compelled to suffer. but through the exertions of our officers we have plenty of meat and bread and corn for our horses."[39]

It was on this march toward Shreveport that the men of the Twenty-first Texas formally elected officers. Carter, without opposition, became colonel. DeWitt Clinton Giddings was raised to lieutenant colonel from his previous rank as a company captain. Giddings could be impetuous at times, but he bore a respected name and proved an able, efficient officer. He quickly overcame the fact that he was a Pennsylvanian by birth and had initially opposed secession. The troops also selected Benjamin D. Chenoweth, a young lawyer who was originally from Virginia, as major.[40]

Although Carter's commissioned officers were about average in ability, they had no training or background to prepare them to lead unruly troops. The trip across the state tested the patience and tolerance of the officers, for the Texans disliked both drill and discipline. When the three regiments arrived at Tyler, Brigadier General Henry E. McCulloch, in command of the Eastern District of Texas, closed all the liquor shops and issued orders holding the officers personally responsible for the actions of their men. McCulloch wisely did not allow Carter's regiments to camp near the town, but he did enjoy a Sunday service performed by the well-known and eloquent preacher.[41]

Although Carter kept the Twenty-first under tenuous control, Wilkes and Gillespie had serious trouble with their commands, the Twenty-fourth and Twenty-fifth Texas respectively. The reports of pillage intensified after the troops reached Shreveport. Gillespie, reported the Marshall *Texas Republican*, was "charged with continual drunkenness and other improprieties, and it is stated had a fight in a grog shop at Shreveport with one of his own men."[42] Governor Thomas O. Moore of Louisiana complained to Secretary of War George W. Randolph that part of Carter's command, under orders from Wilkes, had terrorized his state. The party, the governor claimed, had "seized private property, entered houses of private citizens, brutally practiced extortion and outrage, and with bullying and threatening language and manner spread terror among the people." Their mission, to requisition supplies for the army in Arkansas, had angered the people of Louisiana. Believing that he was "forced to self-protection," Moore ordered the militia to Alexandria to prevent similar raids. He warned Randolph: "You can refuse to dismiss them (the captain and the colonel), but my marksmen may save you the trouble if they come again. There is a point to which patient endurance can extend no further."[43]

The governments of both Texas and Louisiana had received complaints about Carter's Lancers. Hébert, trying to absolve himself from responsibility, pointed out to Randolph "that it has been found impossible to control these independent corps, raised by persons under direct authority from Richmond and with orders to report to some command or general outside of the Department of Texas." As if to place the responsibility upon the war department, Hébert proudly boasted: "No charges of the kind have ever been preferred against the troops proper of the Department of Texas."[44] As a result of the incident, Hébert issued orders providing for the arrest of any officer violating the law.[45] This gesture, however, proved academic, for by the time the proclamation became effective Carter's command was far from Hébert's reach.

Carter's own regiment, the Twenty-first Texas, managed to stay out of trouble in Louisiana, although his men encountered some tense moments with citizens in Shreveport. J. C. Morriss told his wife the troops seized "three Steamboats one loaded with salt and one with coffee all of them trading with the federals and confiscated their cargoes."[46] The officers issued the coffee to the Texans, but Carter ordered Lieutenant Buck Walton to accompany the vessels, filled with supplies from the Shreveport area, to Pine Bluff, Arkansas. Walton followed the Red, Black, and Washita rivers as far as they were navigable, then transported the provisions overland to their destination. Since most of the cargo had belonged to Louisiana farmers until commandeered, Walton was not surprised when Governor Moore's state militia detained his expedition at Alexandria. After twenty-four strained hours for the inexperienced Walton, the militia released the consignment. About sixty miles below Alexandria Walton found the river blocked by a gunboat. Again the two sides entered heated negotiations. Fortunately, Walton's cool head and good manners prevailed; after intense deliberation and hasty consultation with Governor Moore, the state authorities released Walton's charge, and he delivered his cargo to the commissary at Pine Bluff in good condition.[47]

In Arkansas, the fragile bond between Carter, Wilkes, and Gillespie reached a breaking point. Carter received instructions to arrest any officers connected with the misdeeds in Louisiana. Governor Moore had requested Wilkes's removal, and the charges also implicated Gillespie. Although Carter apparently disregarded the order, the tenuous alliance of three Methodist preachers was about to end.[48] Wilkes, who had gone to Richmond to draw the back pay and bounties due the men, informed authorities that the brigade did not exist and returned to Arkansas with orders showing that he and Gillespie commanded unattached regiments. After appropriating the money he had obtained in the Confederate capital for his own troops, Wilkes removed his men from Carter's camp.

But Wilkes and Gillespie had a surprise awaiting them. Orders from General Theophilus H. Holmes, who commanded at Little Rock when they arrived, instructed the cavalry to dismount and turn their horses over to the local quartermaster. Wilkes and Gillespie, although reluctant, followed Holmes's instructions to the letter. Thus, after trying so hard to become mounted lancers, the Twenty-fourth and Twenty-fifth Texas became dismounted cavalry.[49]

Lieutenant Colonel Giddings, commanding the Twenty-first while Carter was absent, had other plans for his regiment. He carefully avoided reading any of the notices even though Holmes had them posted on every street corner. When Giddings received a special order from the general instructing him to dismount the men, he put the dispatch into his pocket—unread. He knew, as Private William Zuber recalled, "This was an unreasonable demand, for throughout the Trans-Mississippi Department every cavalryman's horse was his private property and many of the dismounted regiments were permitted to send their horses home by men detailed to conduct them." Instead, Giddings wrote to Colonel Parsons requesting that his regiment join the Twelfth Texas, thus enabling Parsons to form his own brigade. Parsons responded favorably and asked Holmes to order the Twenty-first to proceed immediately to his camp. Colonel Giddings, wrote Zuber, chose to read and obey this order.

"Thus he saved our regiment from being dismounted."[50] This did not go unnoticed by the Texans. J. C. Morriss observed: "It is rumored in camp that Lt Col. Giddings is promoted to Col of the Regiment I hope it may be so for col Giddings is very popular."[51]

The agreement between Giddings and Parsons, consummated without Carter's knowledge, would prove vexing. The unofficial brigade now had two colonels, and neither wanted to be subordinate to the other. Carter argued that his commission, which came directly from the secretary of war, antedated Parsons's commission. Carter's authorization, dated the summer of 1861, had enlisted men for three years by the authority of the war department. Parsons also had a commission dated in the summer of 1861, but it was to raise state troops; he did not muster his men into the Confederate service until October. Carter applied to Richmond for recognition as Parsons's senior. But the case, referred to a committee, would not be settled for almost two years. In the meantime, Carter preferred not to camp his men with the Twelfth Texas, and Parsons tried to accommodate him by locating the Twenty-first far from the other regiments when the brigade was together.[52]

Carter never pressed the issue even though he knew he had the backing of his own men. He realized that if he should assume authority over the brigade, the Twelfth Texas would mutiny—as indeed they almost did each time Parsons was removed from command. Instead, Carter had to comfort himself with the recognition accorded him by his own soldiers. Lieutenant Buck Walton recalled that Carter "was as simple hearted and credulous as a child—yet brave and fearless as a lion."[53] Even when he castigated his troops they listened. "There were men there who could have shot off any button of his uniform, and who knew not the word fear," claimed Walton, "but they simply did not wish to have any difficulty with him." The rank and file, he believed, "loved Col. Carter."[54]

Carter tried hard to create the image that Texans expected from a commanding officer. A newspaper correspondent from Galveston reported that "with his coonskin cap, his tiger blanket and top boots," he was an impressive figure. Indeed, "one would hardly recognize the gifted and eloquent preacher of the Gospel in Texas." Moreover, the reporter

noted, Carter was "a most invaluable officer, always in the saddle, watchful, energetic and perfectly fearless." Of the dispute with Parsons, the paper noted that Carter and Lieutenant Colonel Giddings, "with their excellent regiment of cavalry, have contested the palm with Parson[s]'s, and deserve equal praise."[55]

If Carter was an enigma, his men were only typical Southerners. They drank too much on duty; they ate too well on food that belonged to others; they gambled among themselves; they loved to fight impetuously at a moment's notice. And they hated discipline. Lieutenant Buck Walton recalled that when Carter threatened to give lashes to anyone caught stealing, the troops became almost mutinous. "The idea that a soldier, a volunteer soldier, would be publically whipped by stripes on the bare back—was not to be considered—no matter how many hogs and chickens, ducks and turkey he stole. They were free men—if they were soldiers—and no such punishment should be held over them." Yet their loyalty to Carter was strong. "He was," observed Walton, "an excellent man & officer—genial, sun shiny—and lovable."[56] Most would have followed him anywhere.

But Carter never quite reached the point he wanted. His brigade had dissolved when the lances failed to materialize; Wilkes and Gillespie had taken their regiments and gone their separate ways. This left Carter with just one regiment, the Twenty-first, full of headstrong, impetuous, independent Texans who followed his orders not out of military necessity but because of their strong devotion to the ex-Methodist preacher. They became part of Parsons's brigade for much of the war, but they looked to Carter for leadership. The two regiments, each fiercely loyal to the officer that organized it, would seldom work together, and rivalries between the two colonels would arise at inopportune moments.

3.

"If You Want to Have a Good Time Gine the Cavalry"

"We was dismounted on the 13th & horses sent home," wrote Captain Bryan Marsh of the Seventeenth Texas to his wife in July 1862. The men "unanimously objected," he observed, "but under the circumstances we could doo no better—our horses was starving for feed—scarcely half of them being fit for duty."[1] Certainly forage gave out quickly as hundreds of troops arrived daily in Arkansas; the Confederate authorities had no choice but to send many horses home. But Frank M. Files had a different explanation. "You know," recalled Files, "it was almost impossible to get a Texan to join the infantry." The method that the Confederate government used "was to organize a cavalry troop and then dismount them," though the boys "sure did kick when they found they had been tricked."[2] Men like Files of the Nineteenth Texas, which was exempt from the dismounting order, counted themselves lucky. But often it took more than just good fortune; a commander with a reputation helped as did connections in the right places.

The commanders of the last two regiments to join Parsons's brigade

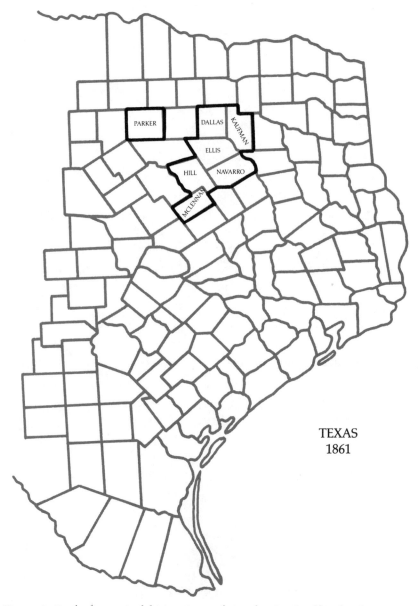

Figure 3. Burford recruited his regiment from the Sixteenth Judicial District, which embraced Dallas, Kaufman, Navarro, and all of those counties and territory to the west.

were well-known by the spring of 1862. Both could boast of excellent records in the Confederate service from the previous year and used this to help them maintain command of a mounted force. Charles Leroy Morgan, who led a battalion for much of the war, had impressed his superiors by his skill and daring. Nathaniel Macon Burford, colonel of the Nineteenth Texas Cavalry Regiment, had gained respect from his previous service with Ben McCulloch. Burford had the added advantage of connections in Richmond: the postmaster-general of the Confederate States, John H. Reagan, had once been his law partner.

Burford had little to recommend him for the job as commander of a cavalry regiment. He was of slight build, scarcely five feet seven inches, with dark brown hair and soft gray eyes. Remembered by a friend as "an affable, genial man, generous to his own detriment, . . . and though not a poet, has much of poetry in his nature," Burford lacked many of the steel qualities that made a good commander of men.[3] Yet he was popular in Dallas and surrounding counties; the citizens of the blackland farms in the Trinity and Brazos river bottoms knew that Nat Burford, the district judge, would take care of their boys just as he had always understood the needs of the farmers in his judicial district (Figure 3).[4]

Burford's background was much the same as the folk he represented and the men he commanded. Born in middle Tennessee in 1824, Burford had hoped to become a lawyer, but his father was unable to provide for his education. At seventeen Nat began teaching at a country school; by twenty-one he had graduated from Irving College and Lebanon Law School. When the Mexican War began, he gave up his fledgling law practice in east Tennessee and volunteered for service, but by the time his company reached Knoxville, the state had filled its required quota. Not to be left out of the conflict—his brother William had left for Mexico City with Winfield Scott—Burford set out for Texas with the intention of joining the army.

Burford's early years in Texas were uneventful. Short of funds, he had to work his way to Shreveport, Louisiana, as a deck hand. From there he walked to Jefferson, Texas, where he arrived with three dollars in his pocket. But he was out of money and never made it to the fighting in Mexico. Instead he took a job as deputy clerk of the district court, planning to save a little cash so he could move further west. As soon as he had thirty dollars he spent twenty-five for a pony and, carrying all his earthly goods (his clothes and five dollars in coin), he left Jefferson and arrived at the village of Dallas in October 1848. As the little hamlet on the banks of the Trinity River grew, so did Burford's law practice. His name did not appear alone on his shingle long; he soon formed a partnership with another Tennessean, John H. Reagan.[5]

Burford and Reagan prospered. Dallas residents elected Burford district attorney two years after his arrival, a post he held for several years. Reagan served as district judge in East Texas, while Burford became district judge of the newly created Sixteenth District covering the area surrounding Dallas. After dissolving their partnership in 1856, Reagan gave his landless friend one hundred acres in Dallas. This was not the last time that Reagan's friendship would prove valuable to Burford.[6]

As Burford's wealth increased, so did his popularity in his district. He was known for his infinite good humor. Major A. J. Byrd, brother-in-law of Colonel Parsons and member of the brigade staff, recalled an incident that he thought described Burford quite accurately. While holding court in an "old rickety box house" in Johnson County, the Judge had found it difficult to keep warm; a Texas "blue norther" blew through the cracks and crevices in the tiny structure. Burford ordered a halt to the proceedings at the bar until the bailiff could fuel the fire. During the recess the Judge fell asleep only to be awakened by the bailiff shouting to "wake up and get out of this old barn, for its all ablaze and will soon burn to the ground." Burford drowsily opened his eyes, surveyed the situation, and replied, "let her burn, and may-be we will all get warmed up."[7]

Although complaisant in his dealings with the public, Burford nevertheless strongly supported states' rights. At least, as a politician reflecting the views of his Southern constituents, he campaigned against a strong United States government. At a meeting in Dallas in February 1860, Burford spoke for well over an hour in support of slavery (although he only owned one young woman with two tiny children). Furthermore, Burford believed that all people had the right to take their property into the territories belonging to the government. Along the same lines he urged local citizens to pass resolutions reinforcing the legality of slavery.[8]

When the war began Burford promptly enlisted in a battery recruited at Dallas. He did not take advantage of his recognized political position to request a commission, but instead took the oath of allegiance to the Confederacy as a private and joined the First Texas Artillery under the command of John J. Good. Good, a local political leader, had become the judge for the Ninth Judicial Circuit in 1857, when Reagan resigned to run for a seat in the United States Congress, and was Burford's friend as well as a fellow member of the bar. Good firmly believed that Burford's background recommended him for higher rank.[9]

Burford was the model soldier. In July 1861, as Good's battery marched to Arkansas to join General Ben McCulloch, Good confided to his wife: "The judge [Burford] does his part like a man and is now one of the finest specimens of a cornfield hand you ever saw." In fact, Good amused his wife by writing that she and Mrs. Burford would "laugh heartily" over some of his efforts to blend into the rank and file. "Just imagine our District Judge," he wrote, "in his shirt sleeves standing over a mess kettle washing out a shirt or pair of drawers." Pleased with his friend's performance and distressed that he was inferior in rank, Good recommended Burford for a staff appointment. McCulloch agreed and offered Burford a horse, saddle, and bridle to accept the position. Burford, however, refused to leave the artillery company.[10]

By the end of 1861 Good considered Burford one of his finest soldiers and worked to have him promoted in a form that he could not refuse. "He never fails to do any duty required of him day or night," observed Good. When McCulloch visited Richmond in the winter he asked Reagan to secure a commission for Burford as a colonel, with permission to raise a regiment.[11]

The news of Burford's promotion did not please everyone. Governor Francis R. Lubbock again vented his frustration to Judah P. Benjamin in a March letter: "I have just learned that Judge Burford has authority to raise a cavalry regiment. . . . I believe this mode of obtaining men is all wrong, and I feel satisfied that if persons are thus permitted to raise troops in our State it will greatly interfere with the raising of the fifteen regiments proposed . . . in Texas."[12]

Burford replied in a letter published by the Texas press. He pointed out: "I did not seek the position, but felt in honor bound to accept the position, when tendered; and as this is the first instance where a Government has authorized a private soldier to leave the ranks to raise troops, I hope the expectations of the Republic will not be disappointed." Further, he insisted, this had not been his idea, as the "Secretary of War ordered me to be discharged and sent home for the purpose of raising a regiment of cavalry to serve during the war."[13]

Recruiting a regiment was not as easy in 1862 as it had been earlier in the war, and several officers visited the Dallas area enlisting men. Burford's leading competitor was not an outsider, however, but Trezevant G. Hawpe, a local resident. Colonel Hawpe, a wealthy farmer, apparently resented Burford's arrival, especially since Burford began recruiting much later than Hawpe but reached his quota much quicker. Burford's regiment filled by April; Hawpe's did not muster in until May. Sue Good confided to her husband that Burford suffered at the hands of the hot-headed Hawpe: "I guess there may be some misunderstanding and hard feelings existing between them."[14]

Hawpe's criticism seems to have had little impact on the popularity of Burford, who modestly refused to exercise the authority given him by the secretary of war. He joined the regiment, like any other recruit, as a private in the company of Allen Beard, a former Dallas sheriff. But Burford remained in the ranks only about two weeks; at the regimental elections, the troops selected him colonel.[15]

Burford may have been well connected and unassuming, but he did not have the qualities necessary for his position. The regiment seldom suffered, however, because the second-in-command, Benjamin Watson, was an able officer. Watson, as a member of the brigade recalled, "displayed considerable genius in military affairs, and was always ready for service, generally commanding the regiment in trying moments." He was popular with his men and "distinguished himself by his coolness in action . . . and his gallant conduct."[16]

The man elected as major soon demonstrated that he, like Burford, was not cut out to be a soldier. Joel T. Daves, a young Methodist minister, never felt comfortable holding a weapon, and in 1863 he resigned and returned to his congregation. The commanding officer, Major General John G. Walker, sarcastically noted on the outside of Daves's request: "The reasons offered for this resignation are insufficient, but as it seems to be a case of conscience I recommend its acceptance." Replacing Daves was John B. Williams, a merchant from Hillsboro, who had come to Texas from Georgia around 1850. Williams, who was twenty-eight years old when he enlisted, proved to be an outstanding and popular officer.[17]

Some men became disenchanted early with the new colonel. Burford "stays at Dallas [and] drinks whiskey," complained Private William J. Simms in June. He "never comes to camps and will not let us move." As a result, observed Simms, "there is a good deal of grumbling at him."[18]

Perhaps Burford did drink too much, but the fact that his regiment had to delay leaving Texas was not his fault. The colonel had repeatedly asked the Texas authorities for permission to move, but in a letter to P. O. Hébert, he pointed out that his men were almost totally without arms or tents. Hébert replied that he had "no orders in regard to Independent regiments raised by direct authority from Richmond." Further, "the regiment would be of more service *dismounted* as the Government needs *Infantry*."[19]

Exactly how Burford managed to join Colonel Parsons remains unclear, especially since Hébert had recommended the regiment's transfer to infantry.[20] One can only speculate that Burford's supporters in the Confederate Congress as well as his long-standing friendship with the postmaster general proved invaluable when he needed a special favor.

But Burford had not prepared his men for war. When the Nineteenth Texas reached Arkansas, their lack of training was so evident that Parsons ordered Burford to institute daily drills. William J. Simms complained, "we are no nearer ready for service now [than] 6 months ago [and] we have not drilled any." Simms announced that Burford had sent to Richmond "to get what he ought g[ot] when he was there." Further,

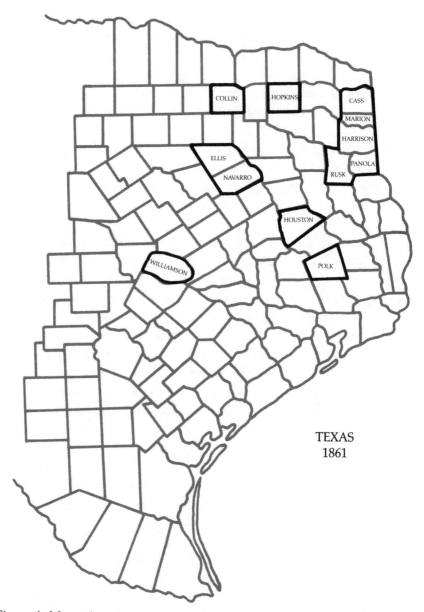

Figure 4. Morgan's regiment was an assortment of companies from all over Texas. The troops did not represent any one area of the state and they seldom operated together as a unit.

he grumbled, "we are sorry that there ever was such a man as Bufford."[21] In October Henry Orr of the Twelfth Texas wrote home that Burford was in serious trouble with authorities in Arkansas for drinking too much and disobeying orders.[22] Moreover, he added soon after the regiment joined the brigade, Colonel Burford was "not very well beliked" by his men.[23]

If Burford received little praise as a commander, the same cannot be said of Charles Morgan, who was the only native Texan to serve as a regimental commander in Parsons's brigade. Ambitious and aggressive, Morgan was an exceptional young man who commanded an unusual combination of companies—first as a squadron, then as a battalion, and finally as a regiment. Most of his officers and many of his enlisted men, like Morgan himself, came from organizations mustered into the Confederate service in 1861, which for one reason or another had become detached by the time of the major reorganizations of 1862.

Charles Morgan, whose family had arrived in Texas in 1839, the year before his birth, enlisted when the war began in the Eighth Texas Cavalry, better known as Terry's Texas Rangers for its first commander, Benjamin F. Terry. Elected first lieutenant of Company D when he was only twenty-one years old, Morgan accompanied the Rangers to Kentucky and was in the fighting when Colonel Terry fell. But Morgan resigned, citing a disability, and returned to Texas in December 1861.[24]

His career, however, was just beginning. In March 1862 he joined the Eighteenth Texas Cavalry, a regiment in which his older brother Hiram commanded a company from Bastrop. Charles Morgan, already known for his exploits with Terry's Rangers, was elected major. Although it is difficult to follow his movements in 1862, as early as September he commanded a squadron of about one hundred fifty men operating around Little Rock.[25] In January 1863 the Eighteenth Texas, ordered to dismount and report to Fort Hindman, surrendered to a Federal army when Arkansas Post capitulated. Union troops captured almost all of the regiment, including Morgan's brother, and transported the Texans to prisoner-of-war camps in the North; most never returned to Arkansas. As luck would have it, the younger Morgan was not at the post when it fell. He remained in the Trans-Mississippi, where in 1864 a member of his regiment meeting him for the first time noted: "The boys are highly pleased with our new commander, he is a dashing young officer, and will make his mark."[26]

The formation of Morgan's command is difficult to chronicle. Surviving muster rolls indicate that in November 1863 Morgan headed a battalion consisting of seven companies from his own squadron, Captain Benjamin D. McKie's squadron, and Captain William B. Denson's squadron of Louisiana and Texas cavalries. Three other companies, added at various times, increased the unit from battalion to regimental size, but the war ended before this became official.[27] Moreover, the command never developed a unit pride since the companies, which originated in different regions of Texas, seldom fought together (Figure 4), and each had its own unique history. Troops never utilized their designated company letters but were generally known by their captain's name.

Two of Morgan's officers deserve special attention. The first, B. D. McKie, a wiry thirty-four-year-old native of Tennessee, was renowned for his personal courage. He had military experience, too: while fighting in the war with Mexico he had been hit twice by enemy fire. After the war ended he stayed in Mexico for a while, then moved to Arkansas and finally to Navarro County, Texas. In 1861 McKie organized the Navarro Spies, which became the Independent Mounted Rangers in August 1862. By 1863 he was a major commanding his own squadron under Morgan. He was always at the head of his men in a charge and appeared unconscious of his personal safety. Twice wounded, he refused to abandon his characteristic fighting style until a third bullet forced him to return home to recuperate.[28]

The second officer, Alf Johnson, commanded a spy company from Collin County. Johnson had earned an almost legendary reputation in Arkansas by the time Colonel Parsons arrived with his regiment in the spring of 1862. As the Houston *Telegraph* aptly pointed out in late June, "everybody in Texas knows Alf Johnson"[29] for his daring exploits while serving under Ben McCulloch. A. S. Graves, a private in the company, recalled that his captain was "one of the gamest and best scouters" west of the Mississippi. With McCulloch near Springfield, Missouri, Johnson and another scout rode alone into the town to learn the number of soldiers with Federal General John C. Frémont. When the two men found themselves in a house completely surrounded by Union soldiers, according to Graves, "Capt. [Hinchie P.] Mabry went out the door fighting like a wildcat. Capt. Johnson ran to the window, threw the curtains aside, raised the window and jumped out. No sooner did he hit the ground than he let both barrels of his shotgun go off into the Yankee lines." After their daring escape, the two men raced their horses to McCulloch's camp to deliver their information as well as to receive surgical attention; "both were badly wounded."[30] Captain Good, under whom Burford served at the time, wrote his wife that the two men "had a little frolic with the Federalists in which Capt Mabry was shot through the hand and Capt Alf Johnson through the leg." But, noted Good, "There has been no *official* report of this unless it came in today."[31] Johnson nevertheless was "soon in the saddle again," with a commission to raise a "spy company" for General McCulloch's army.[32] Johnson's company was the only Texas cavalry in Arkansas when Parsons arrived in the spring of 1862.

Both Johnson and McKie, leading independent commands, excelled at the hit-and-run raids that gave the Confederate cavalry an edge early in the war. Both loved the charge, and both played a prominent part in defending Arkansas in 1862. But neither made it to the war's end. McKie, who never fully recovered from his wounds, could not return to combat, and Johnson, among the Confederates captured at Arkansas Post in January 1863, died en route to Federal prison.[33]

Finally, Colonel Parsons completed his command with one of the best artillery companies then in Arkansas. Joseph H. Pratt, a railroad builder from East Texas, raised his force from Harrison, Marion, and Cass counties. A member of the battery, R. J. Oliphant, claimed that of the original seventy-two who joined in Jefferson, only seventeen surrendered in 1865.[34] One hundred seventy-one names appear in the records of the unit officially known as the Tenth Field Battery, but at one point during the war Pratt lost so many men that he had to borrow from the cavalry. Captain Frank G. Lemmon's company, a unit raised in East

Texas, had to temporarily turn in their horses and man the guns.[35] Before the war ended, Pratt was promoted to major and commanded the Second Horse Artillery Battalion, consisting of his own Texans under H. C. Hynson, one battery from Arkansas, and two from Missouri.[36]

In the spring of 1862 Pratt's battery, the Nineteenth Texas under Burford, Carter's Lancers, and all of the companies that eventually joined Morgan (except Johnson's Spy Company) were in Texas awaiting orders to march north. Earl Van Dorn's Confederate army desperately needed reinforcing to prevent the capitulation of Little Rock; indeed it was possible that all of Arkansas might fall, leaving Texas open to invasion. But forwarding troops to Arkansas took time—too much time. The defense of Little Rock would depend on the few scattered regiments that arrived first.

As Parsons led the Twelfth Texas across the Red River, he had no idea that his troops would play a pivotal role in defending Arkansas. He also could not know that the reputation he would gain in the next few weeks would be the reason his regiment retained its horses when the Confederate hierarchy dismounted all others. Just as Lieutenant Colonel Giddings of the Twenty-first Texas sought out Parsons in order to save his regiment's horses, both Burford and Morgan would soon discover the advantages of joining Parsons's command.

4.
"The Yankees Are as Afraid as Death of the Texans"

C hecking the Federal advance toward Little Rock in 1862 seemed "small indeed by comparison with the more imposing and dramatic events of the far east," noted William H. Parsons, "but momentous in results" to the security of the Trans-Mississippi Department.[1] Not only was the possession of Arkansas at stake, declared Parsons, "but for immediate results to the fate and fortunes of Texas, few successful movements can be recorded of graver and more decisive" significance than those first campaigns which arrested the Federal drive south.[2] The timely arrival of the Texas troops prevented the fall of Little Rock and deterred Federal occupation of the state. Parsons's own regiment, the Twelfth Texas, played an important role in defending Arkansas, and a hastily organized handful of Confederate cavalrymen, feigning a show of force, prevented any Federal move toward Texas.

The Federal threat to Little Rock in the spring of 1862 was critical. Although the situation in Arkansas had seemed promising at the beginning of the war, it had rapidly deteriorated. Ben McCulloch, a flamboyant, aggressive, and headstrong brigadier general commissioned in May 1861, had assumed command of the forces gathering around Fort Smith in northwest Arkansas. He earned distinction commanding the Confederates in their victory at Wilson's Creek, Missouri, in August. But instead of pursuing the initiative, McCulloch argued with Missourian Sterling Price over future strategy; neither would compromise, and they could not agree upon any concerted plan to defend Missouri and Arkansas. To alleviate this impasse, the War Department placed both men under Major General Earl Van Dorn. Price and McCulloch paid heavily for their differences: their early success faded as a Federal force of over eleven thousand moved steadily through Missouri into Arkansas, and during Van Dorn's loss at Pea Ridge in March 1862, McCulloch was killed.

As the Federal army under Samuel Ryan Curtis took possession of northwest Arkansas, General Albert Sidney Johnston, then commanding the Confederacy's Western Department, ordered Van Dorn to join him. But bad weather, poor roads, and swollen streams hampered Van Dorn's movement. By the time he concentrated his army at Memphis in mid-April, General Johnston had been killed in the battle at Shiloh, and his successor, General P. G. T. Beauregard, had withdrawn to his base at Corinth, Mississippi. Van Dorn's men, mostly Arkansans and Missourians, pressed on to unite with Beauregard, leaving behind only a nominal force to defend Arkansas. Few troops remained between Curtis and Little Rock; Alf Johnson's Spy Company was the only Texas command there.

Van Dorn's actions forced state officials to rely upon their own ingenuity. Following Pea Ridge, Curtis had marched the Federal army along the White River into north central Arkansas, halting at Batesville. With Union scouting parties only miles from the capital, Governor Henry M. Rector moved the archives to Hot Springs and let it be known that he thought the Confederacy had sold his state down the river. The *Arkansas True Democrat* critically noted, "The flight of Gov. Rector was an invitation to Gen. Curtis to come to the Arkansas river, because it showed a weakness and a want of nerve calculated to assure an easy conquest."[3]

But Arkansas did not prove simple to subdue. The commander of Arkansas's scattered troops, former governor John Seldon Roane, had orders "to harass the enemy 'in his flanks and rear, to cut off his trains, and destroy his supplies,' and 'defend the crossings of the Arkansas river to the last extremity.'"[4] He declared martial law and, with Beauregard's permission, stopped all Texas cavalry en route to join Van Dorn and diverted them to Little Rock.

Squadrons of Parsons's Twelfth Texas riding to reinforce Van Dorn were unaware of the perilous situation in Arkansas, but their orders changed several times as Van Dorn's Confederate army moved east. First the Texans were told to rendezvous at Fort Smith, on Arkansas's border with the Indian Territory; then the destination changed to the sparsely

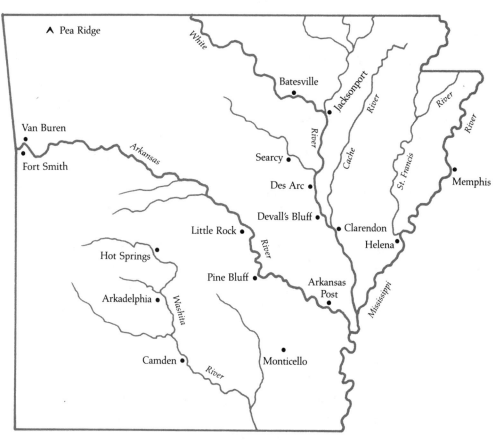

settled region north of Little Rock; finally the troops headed for Pine Bluff, where they would find transport down the Arkansas River, then up the Mississippi to Memphis.[5]

After almost one year in the Confederate service, the Texans were impatient for a fight. Colonel Parsons and his advance squadron travelled rapidly by steamer to Memphis, where they heard for the first time that General Curtis's Army of the Southwest threatened Little Rock.[6] Two companies, the Freestone Boys and the Ellis Rangers, reached the city soon after Parsons. Henry Orr reported that the Rangers had "arrived safely at Memphis on last evening [May 8] after a voyage whose pleasantness was only marred by fears that we might [not] be able to get [here], owing to New Orleans being in the possession of the Yankees [New Orleans fell April 29]. . . . Col. Parsons came to us while we were landing and was almost overjoyed at meeting us."[7] Learning that Beauregard had retreated to Corinth, the Texans anxiously awaited orders to join the main army where they might finally meet the enemy.

The situation in Arkansas necessitated yet another change in plans. When Beauregard learned of the Federal movement toward Little Rock, he immediately countermanded instructions for transporting the remaining Texans to Memphis. Instead he directed Colonel Parsons, who visited Beauregard at Corinth, to return with his advance to Little Rock. Parsons remained east of the river only long enough to get permission for his troops to continue as cavalry and to obtain the funds to pay his regiment and supply the bounty of fifty dollars per man.[8] He then hurried back to Arkansas's capital, where he expected to become senior colonel in command of all Texas cavalry. Upon hearing this good news, Lieutenant George Ingram of the Hill County Volunteers jubilantly reported: "Hurrah for Parsons."[9]

Parsons's men had not stayed idle while their colonel visited Beauregard; those who had not yet boarded the transports bound for Memphis headed for Little Rock instead. Arriving in the capital in mid-May, the Texans found the citizens discouraged and downcast. With the exception of Alf Johnson's Spy Company, there were few regular soldiers to defend the city. James J. Frazier of the Johnson County Slashers wrote his family, "every thing was gloomy all the patryots about Little rock looked dispondent & full of fears & appryhensions of eavil." An aged Arkansas gentleman questioned Frazier's captain, Jeff Neal, "how long before the enimy would be their?" Neal confidently swore: "Never! We will whip them back." The old man, much surprised at such a cocky answer, asked Captain Neal where the means of defense was, since only a meager number of Texans now occupied the capital. Neal, looking around him, boldly stated that the forces in Little Rock would keep the enemy at bay until reinforcements arrived.[10] The brash young captain's prediction proved true, but he would give his life in the effort.

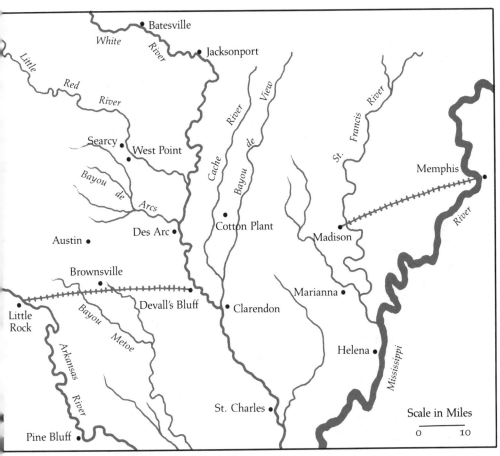

The impetuous Texans quickly took charge in Little Rock. George Ingram wrote his wife that there was no Confederate flag flying on the capital, "but tomorrow we will hoist one on the dome. . . . Hurrah for the Texans." He claimed that apathy had struck the local citizens: "These Arkansawyers were just about to give it up before we got here, and there are many union men in this place."[11] On the same day David N. Shropshire, a private in the Slashers under the command of the dashing Captain Neal, repeated identical plans: "Col. Mullens [Lt. Col. John Mullen] says he is going [to] hoist the Confederate flag tomorrow on the

Capital. It has never been hoisted yet." Again he attributed the lack of a flag to indifference. The people, observed Shropshire, "have been afraid for two thirds of the citizens is said to be Union men."[12] Roane was so excited about his enthusiastic reinforcements that he told Beauregard "he was holding four companies of Parsons' Texas cavalry, and 'thought with the Texas troops and such others as I could raise in the State, I could hold the enemy in check until you could whip the Federals at Corinth.'"[13]

One group of Texans was raising havoc in Federal camps already—Alf Johnson's Spy Company, probably the best known of the Texas troops. Newspapers from Little Rock to Galveston carried stories of its latest exploits. A few days before Parsons's command arrived, the Little Rock *True Democrat* reported: "A portion of Capt. Alf. Johnson's company of mounted Texans brought in a Dutch Captain and a private on Tuesday last. . . . Three or four were killed or drowned in crossing [Little] Red River. . . . Capt. Johnson's men are good fighters and gentlemen in all their intercourse with the people."[14] George Ingram wrote his wife that the spy company had "discovered 8 Federals that had taken a pleasure ride out of Camp. Johnson's men made a charge on them, and Captured two. The others plunged into the River to swim across to their camps but 3 of the rascals drowned in the attemp[t]."[15] David Shropshire related to his family much the same tale: "Johnson and two of his men met up with a federal Capt. and six privates, killing three, capturing the capt. and one private. The others plunged into White River and drowned."[16]

As these tales spread and the number of Texans increased, the morale of Arkansans greatly improved. "Our gallant Texas friends continue to arrive," observed the *True Democrat*, "and enough of them will be here in time to accomplish the purpose for which they come. . . . Gen. Curtis is likely to have a livelier time capturing Arkansas than he anticipated."[17] The paper predicted: "The gallantry of the Texans now with us, and the patriotism and spirit of our own people, will enable him [Roane] to make short work of all their hopes as soon as his preparations are completed."[18]

Parsons's men scarcely had time to acquaint themselves with Little

Rock before they received orders to march north and ascertain the strength and disposition of the enemy. Over four hundred troops of the regiment left for the Little Red River, south of Curtis's headquarters at Batesville, while Colonel Parsons was en route from Memphis to Little Rock. Major Emory W. Rogers led the force from the state capital early in the afternoon on May 17; his command travelled twelve hours before stopping to rest near Austin, Arkansas. After proceeding to within six or seven miles of the enemy's camp near Searcy, Rogers was joined by Captain Francis M. Chrisman, an Arkansan whose home was nearby and who was to guide the Texans through the forest-crossed farmland. In a skirmish on the Little Red River just before he joined Rogers's force, Chrisman had captured five wagons and over twenty mules belonging to the Federals. Now he was to help Rogers determine the direction that the Federal army was moving.[19]

Curtis, in fact, planned to march his army directly into Little Rock to ease Federal supply problems. Detachments of Federal cavalry from Batesville already had raided the counties bordering on Missouri, and as forage in northern Arkansas gave out, Curtis turned his attention toward the fertile land above Little Rock. His situation had become critical, and he ordered new expeditions to scour the countryside and collect supplies from the local farmers, who had heard reports of Yankees burning homes and stealing crops, horses, mules, and slaves in the counties near Missouri.[20]

The Federals' decision to send a foraging party across the Little Red River east of Searcy launched the first battle involving the Twelfth Texas. Although the action was just a skirmish, the Confederate troops would proudly recall their victory near Searcy or, more specifically, in Whitney's Lane.

On the morning of May 19, three companies of the Fourth Missouri Cavalry, Frémont Hussars, under Major Eugene Kielmansegge, and three companies of the Seventeenth Missouri Infantry—Company F, commanded by Second Lieutenant August Fischer; Company G, under Captain F. Wilhelmi; and Company H, under Second Lieutenant Henry Neun—headed down the main road from Searcy to West Point to guard the Federal foraging party. These Northern troops, part of Curtis's army, belonged to Peter J. Osterhaus's division and, as their names indicate, were of German ancestry; the Texans called them "Hessians" or "Dutch Conscripts."[21] Their orders were to empty cellars and clear the fields of all foodstuff. Their only opposition seemed to be the White County home guard, which threatened to meet the invaders with shotguns and hunting rifles.

The Federal foraging party deployed along the main road about three and one-half miles from their camp near Searcy Landing. Fischer's company moved down the main road to a farm owned by a man named Whitten; Wilhelmi's company took its wagons about a half-mile up Whitney's Lane to Hopper's farm, and Neun's company remained at the junction of the lane and the main road to keep open their line of retreat toward Searcy. The cavalry accompanied the party to Whitten's farm, which was separated from the lane by a field enclosed with a common rail fence. The Federal detachments were in a triangular formation around the field.[22]

Major Rogers had no intention of engaging a Federal force; he left his camp with only a small detachment of about one hundred men. But about halfway to the enemy's position, his advance scouts informed him that a foraging party supported by infantry and cavalry, three hundred strong, was ahead. Rogers halted and quickly ordered a man to return for the main body of Texans. While waiting for reinforcements, the small detachment concealed its movements in the brush and moved to within a mile of the foragers. Rogers and Chrisman, unmindful of their personal safety, rode on. They had hidden themselves in the woods about four hundred yards from the Germans when some Texans arrived to inform Rogers that the enemy wagons were assembling along the main road. Rogers hastily returned to his men, but the Confederate reinforcements were nowhere to be seen. Rogers knew, however, that any delay would allow the wagons, filled to the top with food, to join the Federal detachment stationed at Searcy Landing.[23]

Rogers deliberated, but only momentarily. While he analyzed his options, about sixty mounted Arkansans under Captain Howell Hicks

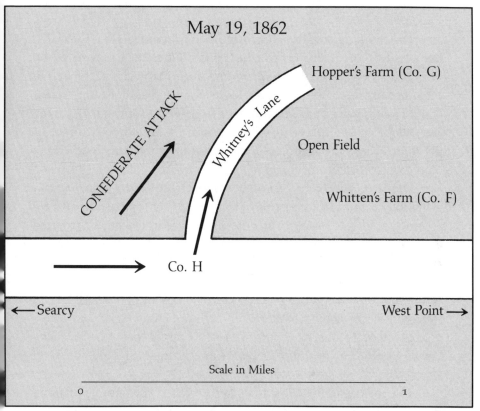

THE BATTLE OF SEARCY OR WHITNEY'S LANE

May 19, 1862

CONFEDERATE ATTACK

Whitney's Lane

Hopper's Farm (Co. G)

Open Field

Whitten's Farm (Co. F)

Co. H

←— Searcy

West Point —→

Scale in Miles

0

1

joined him. This brought the little force up to about one hundred and sixty Confederates. Since his orders had been to cut off the enemy if possible, Rogers concluded: "I had no choice left but to fight, notwithstanding the odds."[24]

Though time was short, Rogers carefully planned the attack. He divided his force into three units under Lieutenant Dan Grady of the Bastrop Cavalry, Captain William J. Stokes of the Ellis Blues, and Captain Hicks with his Arkansas troops. Knowing how the Federals were deployed, Rogers ordered a charge up the main road from the direction of Searcy to cut the Federals off from their camps and reinforcements.[25]

The attack came as complete surprise to the unsuspecting Germans. Just as two Frémont Hussars who had been scouting the perimeter of the Federal position came rushing down the main road yelling, "They are coming; they are coming,"[26] Major Kielmansegge "heard the war-whoop of the Texas Rangers, and saw them in a large body advancing toward me at a gallop."[27] He quickly ordered the infantry to form in the corners of the fence where the lane joined the road, and there the Southerners "soon approached in full charge."[28]

The Texas version of the action was much the same. "When within half a mile of the lane, Lieutenant [Dan] Grady, of the Bastrop cavalry, at the head of the Texans, was ordered to make the charge," reported the Houston *Tri-Weekly Telegraph*. The letter published in the paper bragged that the charge "was done in the most gallant manner, the boys yelling and spurring their horses, as only Texans can."[29] Henry Orr, whose company had not returned from Memphis in time to take part in this scout, wrote home what he heard in camp. Using an analogy easily understood by Texans, he wrote: "The boys charged them [the Federals], yelling like Indians, which confused them very much and used them up very badly."[30]

The men executed Rogers's plan perfectly. Because his troops, armed with double-barrel shotguns, had to ride in close to be effective, Rogers ordered a flank movement on the left of the lane, then led an attack up the main road. As he turned to charge up the lane, Rogers's horse fell, struck by a bullet. The animal recovered sufficiently to race on, but in a minute or so, he was shot again. Rogers, from the ground, urged his men forward shouting, "Give 'em hell, boys." Quickly throwing down the fences, the Texans drove the Germans back across the field. At the same time, Chrisman observed Federal infantrymen fleeing through the corn and ordered a charge around their right flank. The Germans hastily began to retreat.[31]

This attack introduced the Texans to the cruelty of war. Second Lieutenant N. Brown McDonald, an amiable young lawyer from Ellis County who had contested with Rogers for the rank of major, took the lead. He was racing nearly one hundred yards in advance of his comrades when he spied the enemy and yelled, "here they are, boys, follow me!" Waving his revolver over his head, McDonald dashed into the lane and began firing. The defenders discharged a volley which killed him instantly. McDonald was the first man the Texans had seen killed in combat. They were shocked, then enraged, and immediately struck the Germans, "shooting and cutting like demons—the powder from their pistols burning the faces of their foes."[32] Then another Texan fell: Montgomery (Gum) Lowery, whose friends last saw him dismounted. His body was not found for several days; when it was, Lowery had a single bullet through his leg, but his head had been "split open with his own sabre."[33]

After the initial charge the fighting became man against man. As about twenty-five Federals headed across the field, Captain Chrisman and his Arkansans (a number of whom had farms near Searcy) cut them off, drove them into the bushes, and killed several. Neun reported: "I saw the rebels cutting Private Wurges, of my company (H), over the head with a bowie-knife after he had surrendered, and heard the rebels crying out, 'D____n you, we want no prisoners.'"[34] But Rogers recalled: "Many of the enemy fought bravely, refusing to surrender and fell while busy reloading."[35]

As battles go, the affair in Whitney's Lane was not a major one; it was not even much of a skirmish. It lasted scarcely three quarters of an hour before the Texans, unable to organize a rally, had to fall back in the face of reinforcements. Rogers reported one killed, McDonald; one missing, Lowery; and one slightly wounded. Chrisman counted two Arkansas troops killed. The division commander, Peter Osterhaus, informed Curtis that the Federals had lost fifteen killed, thirty-two wounded, and two missing. But the most devastating damage was to Company H, Seventeenth Missouri Volunteers. When Captain John Kaegi arrived at the fighting he found ten dead and fourteen wounded lying in the lane—his entire command still on the field.[36]

The significance of this battle was not its size, but the hope it gave to Arkansans. News of the Confederate victory produced euphoria in Little Rock. Rogers was a hero, the Texans had accomplished "one of the most daring and brilliant feats of the war,"[37] and the people had renewed confidence in the Confederacy. Parsons, who arrived at the capital just as news of the battle broke, claimed that the affair at Whitney's Lane and other demonstrations by the handful of Texans "so successfully impressed Curtis with the conviction that his further advance was opposed by a newly arrived army, that he precipitately fell back." Curtis was more correct, however, when he noted that his planned movement toward Little Rock had stalled because of food supply problems.[38]

Reverberations from this skirmish travelled all the way to Texas. In San Antonio the *Herald* printed: "The campaign in Arkansas will be looked to with much interest by the people of Texas, as it is generally understood that the Federals now in that State are trying to work their way through to Texas to 'wipe us out.'"[39] Henry Orr summed up current sentiment when he wrote his sister Mollie: "It does me good to know that we will be placed between the enemy and Texas."[40]

With all Civil War battles, legend often becomes part of the story, and this one is no exception. According to the Houston *Telegraph*, when John Henry Brown accompanied Ben McCulloch's body to Austin after the general's death at Pea Ridge earlier that spring, Brown met a regiment on its way to Arkansas. He gave McCulloch's sword and pistols to young Alexander McCulloch, the general's nephew and a member of Parsons's Twelfth Texas, who asked Brown if he might take the weapons with him to Arkansas. Alexander kept one pistol as he had received it, still loaded, until the battle near Searcy. During the fight, the *Telegraph* claimed, Alexander killed five men, including a colonel, before a Federal lieutenant leveled a pistol at the young Texan's head. He fired, but the pistol only snapped. Alexander took careful aim and discharged his weapon, killing the man instantly. Thus, the paper announced, the general's own pistol, "loaded by himself, avenged his death by destroying six of his enemies."[41] Although young McCulloch probably had received his uncle's pistol and did take part in the battle, there was no report of a Federal colonel killed and Osterhaus did not indicate a loss of any officers.

Elation from the victory at Searcy had barely subsided before the men of the regiment suffered their first disappointment. Major Rogers, who was nearing fifty years old, took advantage of his exemption under the conscript law and declined reelection when the regiment reorganized a few days after the skirmish. Lieutenant Colonel Mullen did the same. This loss was great, but the men's replacements, Bell Burleson as lieutenant colonel and Lochlin Farrar as major, would prove good choices. In addition, and a surprise to no one, the men reelected Colonel Parsons by acclamation.[42]

On May 28, soon after the regiment had reorganized, the colonel took command of all the Confederate troops north of the Arkansas River. He moved the Texans forward to establish a line of defense west of Des Arc. From there foraging and reconnoitering parties harrassed the Federal army's every movement, causing Curtis to recall his men from their line of operation on the Little Red River and retreat north. Colonel Parsons then based his operations at Searcy, concentrating the cavalry there. A few days later, Brigadier General Albert Rust, who arrived in Little Rock and assumed command, agreed with Parsons's strategy and continued to support the existing lines.[43]

Rust would prove a better congressman than a soldier, and the Texans were not at all happy to be commanded by an Arkansan. Colonel George Sweet of the Fifteenth Texas Cavalry observed: "Brig. Gen. A. Rust commands us at this time [June 11], a clever gentleman and good officer; but the boys are quite clamorous for a Texas Brigadier and Major General to command them—a very natural feeling of State pride, but I have no doubt they will do just as good fighting under any other man."[44] Not all officers agreed. George Ingram wrote his wife: "Great dissatisfaction prevails throughout our Brigade in relation to the management of our generals. Our Brigade is commanded by Gen. Rust who is an Arkansawyer."[45]

For the moment, however, who was to command became less important than other considerations. Colonel Sweet reported: "The weather has been extremely unpleasant, rain! rain! rain! The whole State is a mud-puddle."[46] Moreover, the bad weather that inconvenienced Confederate troops was a severe blow for the Federals. A few days after the fight at

Searcy, Curtis lamented that a rain of thirty-six hours created an impossible situation: the rivers, swollen out of their banks, had cut his supply line. He observed: "The ox-train had brought me a supply of seven or eight days, and on this I hoped to reach Little Rock. Now dry creeks are impassable and several days will transpire before I can cross streams, and during this time my bread supplies will probably run short. The country here and below cannot furnish flour, and I must depend mainly on the trains for bread."[47]

This news brought rejoicing to Arkansas. The *True Democrat* proudly declared: "The enemy are in starving condition, and must fight or run without delay. In either event we shall be rid of them."[48] Confidence and patriotism restored, a San Antonio newspaper reported: "They speak yet of their visit to Little Rock, but we are still of opinion they will never accomplish that march."[49]

The Confederate government also finally did its part to aid Arkansas. General Beauregard ordered Brigadier General Thomas Carmichael Hindman, a former lawyer who had commanded a division at Shiloh, to assume command in the Trans-Mississippi Department. Hindman reached Little Rock on May 30 and immediately began to organize a defense. He knew he must mold the multitude of Texans into an effective army if he was to be successful.[50]

The Texans quickly developed a strong dislike for the new commanding general. When Hindman ordered all equipage reduced to what the men could carry on their horses, allowing only one wagon to the company and no tents or surplus clothing, many enlisted men resented this intrusion into their affairs. Lieutenant George Ingram grumbled: "The Texans are treated with disrespect on evry occasion," and he supported suggestions to return the army to Texas: "5,000 Texans will not be run over rough shod by a few Arkansas gentleman and we are all a unit in this move."[51] In another letter he reported, "The Texans are not appreciated here by the Arkansas Generals. If Gen. Hindman dont keep himself very close some of them will kill him." Even the colonels, he noted, were "treated contemptuously." But Colonel Parsons "says that no man in Arkansas shall impose on his Regt. Col. P is the most popular man in the State. . . . The longer I am with him [the] better I like him."[52]

But the threat of mutiny came to nothing. Instead of returning to Texas, the men obeyed orders to move upon the flank and rear of the Federal army in the mountainous country northwest of Little Rock. On this scout Parsons ranked as senior colonel in command of the cavalry. Complaints changed from who was in command to how the Confederacy treated enlisted men. Henry Orr observed: "We get from ten to fifteen ears of corn per day."[53] Gil McKay of Taylor's regiment was more specific: "The Quartermasters were ordered to issue our rations, which consisted of ten ears of corn to the horse, and *four to the man*. The horses took theirs raw, and the men parched theirs."[54]

Food for men inexperienced with long campaigns became a real problem. "The idea of weighing out a certain quantity of meal and meat for *white men*, say three-quarters of a pound of meat, and a pound of meal or flour a day, for each man, struck me with considerable force," adjudged McKay. "It reminded me of what I had often seen overseers do on plantations in Texas." This was a striking change to the rather easy life the Texans had enjoyed before the scout began. "On the second or third day out," recalled McKay, "some messes were short of bread, others of meat, and some of both bread and meat—in fact, before the end of the third day, we had consumed all our provisions. We never did return to Little Rock, and were absent ten days from the camp."[55]

Throughout June the Confederates were in constant contact with Federal pickets. One Texan bragged, "The enemy could not stand the Ranger's war-whoop,"[56] and Henry Orr boasted, "The Yankees are as afraid as death of the Texans and curse us for everything they can think of, for 'bushwhacking' them."[57] This was probably true. McKay colorfully described a charge from a distance of about four hundred yards upon a group of Federals: "our men commenced yelling, and for five minutes there was one of the most unearthly screams that I ever heard—it was fearful." The "Feds *skedaddled*"—a term he explained meant "*to cut dirt*"—once they had ascertained who their opponents were. "When the enemy first saw us," mused McKay, "they thought we were 'Arkansawyers' and intended to fight them to the last, but when we raised the yell, their commander told them that 'they were the d—m Texans, to look out for themselves.'''[58] A Union private wrote, "fighting the Texans is like walking into a den of wildcats."[59]

The Texas regiments under Parsons harassed and annoyed Curtis's army with hit-and-run raids. "Our (Texas Rangers, as they call us) cavalry is a terror to them," boasted McKay.[60] And the feint worked. Believing Little Rock had received reinforcements that would preclude a successful campaign against the capital, Curtis looked for another solution to his problem of dwindling supplies. The surrender of Memphis on June 6 seemed an answer to his prayers: he could receive reinforcements, the Mississippi was in Federal hands from Saint Louis to Vicksburg, and he would soon give these Texas upstarts a good thrashing.

But the Texans had other ideas. A member of the Fifteenth Texas, R. M. Collins, observed: "The service we were doing for the Confederacy was too tame for our hot Texas blood, and the boys were clamorous for a set-to and a closer acquaintance with the Yankees and their prowess in battle." Collins observed: "Something had to be done. We were fat, sleek and full to running over with fight." Colonel George Sweet predicted battle was imminent, "even if we have to go right into Batesville and pull old Gen. Curtis' beard till he gets mad enough to entertain us in a war-like manner."[61]

But that was not necessary; Curtis was ready to accommodate the Texans. On June 16 a Federal fleet of gunboats and transports appeared in the White River, headed toward the heart of Arkansas carrying reinforcements and supplies for the hungry soldiers. A few days later Curtis began to move his long-stagnant army toward the vessels. He had abandoned any thoughts of capturing Little Rock from the north. Colonel Parsons later claimed that although "terror reigned at the capitol," the handful of Texas cavalry had successfully deceived Curtis and prevented a movement on the city from Batesville.[62]

Although the danger of a campaign from the north had ended, Curtis had not given up hope of occupying part of the state, and the threat to Confederate Arkansas was not over. As the Federal Army of the Southwest marched to join the fleet, Texans would have to continue tricking Curtis into believing that they were a much larger force than their actual number and thus compel him to retreat to the Mississippi River. If the Texans proved unsuccessful, not only would Curtis control much of Arkansas, but Texas would be vulnerable as well.

WHITE RIVER EXPEDITION

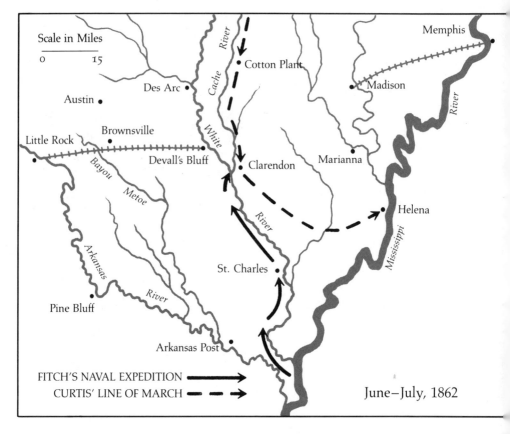

Scale in Miles

0   15

Memphis

Cache River

Cotton Plant

Des Arc

Madison

Austin

White

Brownsville

River

Little Rock

Devall's Bluff

Clarendon

Marianna

Bayou

Metoe

River

Helena

Arkansas

Mississippi

River

St. Charles

Pine Bluff

Arkansas Post

FITCH'S NAVAL EXPEDITION ➡

CURTIS' LINE OF MARCH ⇢

June–July, 1862

5.
The Swamp Fox Regiment

"If a juncture had been permitted between Curtis' really wearied and exhausted army," noted Colonel William H. Parsons, "and the ascending fleet of iron-clads and transports under Colonel [G. N.] Fitch, a base of operations would at once have been established on White river within forty miles of the Capitol of the state, with an all rail prairie route to this heart of the valley of the Arkansas."[1] The combined forces could have occupied the fertile lowland of the Arkansas River, and, as Thomas C. Hindman, commander of the Confederate Trans-Mississippi Department, reported: "Any hesitation or serious error would inevitably result in the capture of Little Rock and the loss of the remainder of Arkansas to the Confederacy. . . . Such calamities could not be averted without an army."[2] Yet in June of 1862 Hindman had no army; his command consisted of a few Arkansas troops and the handful of Texas regiments. Although the scattered Confederates constantly harassed and annoyed Curtis's numerically superior force, Hindman needed a miracle, or at least exceptional good luck. Most of all he hoped his Confederates could successfully thwart Curtis long enough for reinforcements to arrive from Texas. Parsons's regiment again became the focal point of this resistance. "Time was thus secured," as Parsons later bragged, "to organize a new army at our rear."[3] But the Texans paid a high price for this precious time. Before the Confederates secured Arkansas, Parsons's men would know both disaster and great victory.

In late June, when the Federal army began marching from Batesville down the White River, Hindman hastily took steps to cut Curtis off from reinforcements. The Confederate commander ordered General Albert Rust to move his cavalry across the river at Jacksonport, deploy in Curtis's front, and stop him. When Rust informed Hindman that it was impossible to ford the river, Hindman ordered the cavalry south; all of Parsons's regiment except one company headed downstream. After a forced march of three days and two nights the Texans halted at Devall's Bluff.[4] D. N. Shropshire, writing to his sister of the impending fight, observed: "No man is allowed to leave camp, and when we go out to graze our horses the whole command goes together with our arms and ammunition." The gunboats, he pointed out, were only ten miles below. "We have to sleep with our saddles under our heads and guns either in our arms or beside us," sighed the exhausted soldier. "We are nearly all wore out. During our force[d] march we only got two meals during the march, and six ears of corn for our beloved horses, but if we have the chance we will give them a good fight."[5]

Curtis, in fact, had originally planned to fight all the way to Little Rock. The easiest route lay down the White River to Devall's Bluff, where the railroad from Little Rock terminated only sixty miles from the state capital. Devall's Bluff was less than two hundred miles by river from the Mississippi, and since the White River afforded ten feet of water for the gunboats and transports, the fall of Little Rock seemed imminent.[6]

Hindman tried to obstruct the White River and harass Curtis's movement. He ordered Francis M. Chrisman, with a detachment of Texans and Arkansans, to slow Curtis and give the main cavalry time to prepare. The Hill County Volunteers of Parsons's command remained upriver with Chrisman. Early in July George Ingram, in charge of the company, engaged the Federals floating downstream; the Confederates hidden in the brush along the riverbank exchanged shots with the Federal soldiers on the boats. Neither side inflicted any damage, but Ingram reported: "The minnie balls came thick and fast from behind the cotton bales and rattled through the cane like hail but none of our boys were hurt. . . . So you see that we celebrated the fourth of July in a different manner to what we did in the days of yore."[7]

While Rust's main cavalry force tried to prevent Curtis from moving south, other Confederates were to stop Federal reinforcements coming up the White River. One detachment, under the command of Charles Morgan, held the enemy near Clarendon. A regiment of Federal infantry landed on the west side of the river but advanced only about five miles before Morgan and his Texans, aided by some Arkansas troops, forced the enemy to return to their transports. Hindman delightedly reported the Federal loss at fifty-five killed or captured.[8]

Alf Johnson and his Texans were also busy operating against the Federals. The Houston *Telegraph* reported late in June that Johnson's Spy Company "had been in the Valley for several days, and though it numbered less than one hundred men, it annoyed the enemy seriously, cutting off their foraging parties, killing their pickets, etc."[9] Hindman verified that Johnson's feats were no exaggeration of an over-enthusiastic Texas press. In his official report he noted: "Capt. Alf. Johnson, commanding an unattached company of Texans, inflicted frequent defeats upon Federal scouting parties and won much distinction as a brave and skillful partisan. Upon one occasion he literally destroyed an entire Federal company."[10]

In spite of all these efforts, the two Federal armies moved closer and closer. Although Curtis's Army of the Southwest outnumbered his own force, Hindman ordered Rust "to resist the enemy to the last extremity, blockading roads, burning bridges, destroying all supplies."[11] In fact, the Texans had scarcely rested before Rust ordered them toward the Federal army. Leaving Devall's Bluff, the force crossed the White River where it turned east at Des Arc. Fording the Cache River late in the evening of July 6, the Texans camped within miles of Curtis's advance guard.

The reports of subsequent events are contradictory and confusing. Even Federal commanders disagreed about specifics. But all of the participants concurred that when Rust's Confederates engaged the enemy near Cotton Plant, the Texans rode into an ambush and had to retreat. Even Hindman could not verify what happened. He later informed Richmond authorities: "No report of this affair was ever received, though often called for; consequently I am not able to give any of the details."[12]

The ultimate responsibility for the Confederate rout belonged to General Rust, who ordered the cavalry forward early on July 7. Colonel Parsons led the way with his own regiment, followed by James Taylor's Seventeenth, William Fitzhugh's Sixteenth, Nicholas Darnell's Eighteenth, then George Sweet's Fifteenth Texas cavalries, as well as scattered Arkansas units. The Texans had ridden only a few miles before their scouts warned of a large Federal force ahead. Without waiting to ascertain the position or strength of the enemy, Rust ordered Parsons forward. Just as the colonel and his regiment entered a creek bottom covered with thick underbrush, a hail of shot and shell rained down upon them from the front, right, and left—it was a hastily concocted trap. A withering fire poured into the regiment; as George Ingram later reported: "Heavy firing was opened on them on three sides and nothing but the smoke of the guns could be seen."[13]

The Texans had encountered a Federal force under the command of Charles E. Hovey, colonel of the Thirty-third Illinois Infantry. With him were several companies of the Eleventh Wisconsin Infantry and one small steel gun of the First Indiana Cavalry. After Hovey heard the firing in his front, he deployed his skirmishers along the road. "As the rebels came charging at full speed," observed Hovey, "the infantry fired. The rebel column hesitated, but moved on. Another volley, and the ground was covered with their dead."[14]

Parsons immediately formed his men into a line. But the mounted attack was not effective against the concealed force. "Charge!" the Federals heard, "Charge on the corn field!"[15] Henry Orr pronounced: "We charged through a very bad cypress swamp up near them, although we could not see many of them for the bushes, and fired upon them and fell back and formed on the left. The several companies did likewise and were followed by Col. Fitzhugh's Regiment."[16] Another participant confirmed that the Texans stormed across "the worst swamp he ever saw."[17]

During the confusion few knew exactly what happened. Reports from the scene credited Parsons with capturing a Federal cannon, but without support he had to fall back and abandon it. The colonel's horse was killed, but he had another brought up and mounted it in the midst of the smoke. Ingram wrote his wife: "All that I have heard has been from persons coming from that direction and the reports are very contradictory but all agree that our regiment fought like tigers."[18] Orr confirmed that the Texans had pushed back the Federals: "We held the field as long as we contended for it but we finally withdrew, and the soldiers engaged all say that it was about an even quit-off."[19]

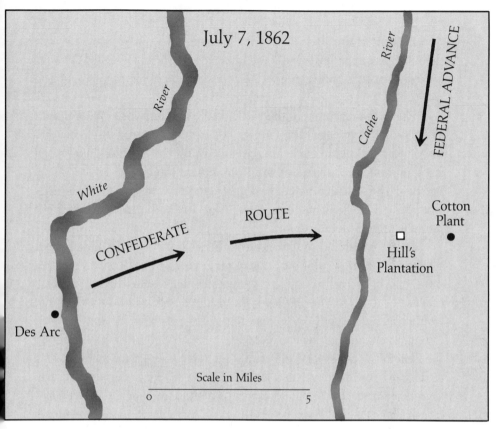

As Federal reinforcements arrived—a battalion of the First Indiana Cavalry and two more steel guns—the artillery poured canister into the Texans' front and shell into their rear, inflicting heavy damage. But the Texans came again. They raced forward, reported a Federal newspaper account, "with extended wings in the form of a V, the concave side facing toward our men."[20] The dashing Captain Jeff Neal fell, gravely wounded by a bullet in the groin. After brashly promising to keep the Yankees out of Little Rock just a few weeks before, he became one of the casualties of that defense. Two privates of Neal's company died instantly, and four more fell from their horses, three severely wounded, one missing. Henry Orr assessed the situation much as Captain Neal must have felt: "I was not impressed with a sense of danger I was in, and I think but few were." Most of the shots missed their marks. "The enemy turned loose their artillery upon us, firing some forty or fifty times," recalled Orr, but for the most part "it was not well directed and went tearing through the tree tops."[21]

Rust's management of the battle nearly cost him his army. As soon as Parsons had engaged the enemy, the general ordered Taylor's regiment, next in line, to circle around and cut off the Federals' retreat. At the same time he ordered Fitzhugh's regiment forward to assist Colonel Parsons. The scathing fire cut into the Sixteenth Texas, and a shell badly wounded Fitzhugh in the arm. Moreover, Taylor's regiment rode right into a waiting Federal column.

Rust's command to Colonel Taylor not only proved a blunder but resulted in a rout. Taylor's unit, marching second in the Confederate column, had halted at the edge of the bottom, where the Texans received orders not to go to Parsons's aid but to move back and take a road that would lead by way of Cotton Plant to the enemy's rear. Henry Orr critically pointed out that instead of engaging an isolated force, Taylor found the Federals "to be very numerous. In fact, [they] saw them rise up at the tap of a drum over two large fields like blackbirds; so they had to save themselves by flight."[22] Bryan Marsh, a member of the Seventeenth, later joked: "Then began the rases with our Regimen for fifteen or twenty miles to prevent being cut of[f]. Siveral horses fell from exaustion. Price hors fel and the boys say he out ran any horse in the company being first to the river."[23] Taylor's position was such, noted an observer, "that for the obstinate stand of Parson's Regiment, he must have been cut off and sacrificed."[24]

Both sides claimed success. Rust reported the battle a "great victory" and heaped praise upon Parsons and his men,[25] assuring the colonel that he had "covered himself, his regiment and his State all over with glory."[26] On the other hand, Bryan Marsh, whose Seventeenth Texas had barely escaped capture, believed the Yankees had "jenteely whipped" Rust's force.[27] Federal Brigadier General Frederick Steele reported the "enemy was defeated and totally routed, with heavy loss on his part and comparatively small loss on ours."[28]

For the Confederates the engagement was a disaster; poor planning, inadequate reconnaissance, and faulty execution almost obliterated the small Southern army. Rust's actions brought nothing but criticism. "I dare say," declared a member of Allison Nelson's Tenth Texas Infantry, "that if Col. Parsons had held, the command that morning from the beginning he would have gained a signal victory. I reiterate that if Col. Parsons had had the command early in the morning, he would have captured the last mother's son of them." To this infantryman the answer seemed simple: "Curtis out-generaled us on the 7th, and was soon out of danger, for I heard on the 10th that he was drinking champagne toasts with the other Generals on his return to Memphis."[29] Henry Orr also sharply criticized Rust: "Upon the whole, it was a badly managed affair."[30] But perhaps the unlearned prose of Thomas Green revealed the most insight when he observed that the Texans "were drawed into a trap but the managers was not quite smarte a nufff to close the dore quick a nuff." Even at that, however, the Texans "had to sift sand fast till they got out of that place."[31]

If Rust drew sharp words from the Texans, their own commander received warm praise. Henry Orr, who had watched Colonel Parsons during the battle, attested that the colonel "acted very cooly though brave as a lion; indeed I never saw him more composed and more at himself."[32] George Ingram alleged: "Gen. Rust went to the rear as all supposed to bring up the Infantry but never returned again."[33] A member of Nelson's Tenth Texas Infantry Regiment corroborated Ingram's complaint: "The intrepid Parsons then, with a mere handful of Texans, was left to fight his way through."[34]

Not all the Texans made it through; seventeen were killed and thirty-two wounded out of the four hundred members of Parsons's regiment at Cotton Plant. The three companies from Ellis County accounted for seven of the dead and eleven of the wounded.[35] One of those wounded was young David C. Nance, a nineteen-year-old youth who had gone into the battle on a fine Morgan horse his father had given him when he left home. Nance later penned: "I called him 'Morgan' . . . , and in the army everybody wanted him—but he was mine. This was the horse that was killed in the battle . . . , And I know if I had not been so nearly killed too, I should have cried bitterly at his death at the time."[36]

Nance had quite a story to tell after the battle. Wounded and without a mount to escape, he surrendered. The blood flowed freely from an injury on his head, so the young Texan convinced his captors he was mortally wounded. When he asked permission to hide behind a tree "for protection from the shots of his friend[s]," they yielded. One of his comrades, B. F. Marchbanks, in relating this tale in later life, remembered that Dave, "being hid from the enemy by the thick under growth, kept hunting a better tree, and finding one that suited him he hid his pistol [a Whitney he had purchased in Dallas when he joined the service], and money under it and finally reached his Company and was taken to Des Arc from there to our hospital at Little Rock."[37] After Nance recovered he rejoined his command, which at that time was camped near the location where he had received his wound. Nance, with some friends, rode to the swamp and found both his money and pistol still buried.[38]

Although the Federal officers had won the day, they disputed among themselves which commander should receive the credit. Colonel Hovey objected to Lieutenant Colonel William F. Wood's report of the conflict because it accorded too much credit to Wood's reinforcements and not enough to Hovey's initial stand. Wood took offense and demanded a court of inquiry; Colonel Conrad Baker, commander of the Fourth Brigade, concurred that "the imputation cast upon him is both unkind and unjust, and entirely inconsistant with the strong words of congratulation and approbation spoken by Colonel Hovey to Lieutenant-Colonel Wood in the presence of other officers immediately after the engagement."[39] The division commander, Brigadier General Frederick Steele, refused to hold a court of inquiry; he informed Curtis that the "interests of the service would not be benefited" by such an investigation.[40] Instead of rebuking Colonel Hovey, Steele promptly requested the secretary of war to promote the colonel to brigadier general. In August Edwin M. Stanton approved the appointment.[41]

Curtis allowed the promotion to pass his desk, but he commented upon the conduct of his officers during the battle near Cotton Plant. Curtis pointedly stated that Hovey's complaints about Wood did "great injustice to superiors as well as himself" and that Hovey seemed "to impeach the veracity of associates who certainly shared with him gallant service."[42] With that said, the Federal commander closed the controversy.

Although the Confederate force fell back across the White River and evacuated Devall's Bluff as the Union army advanced, Curtis could not take advantage of the situation. He and Fitch missed connections at Clarendon by only a few hours, but lacking supplies, Curtis had to continue on toward Helena where relief awaited his exhausted men. Curtis realized he had lost a rare opportunity. He complained to his superior, Henry W. Halleck: "Only needed three boats to assist me in crossing White River and a few days' rations to enable me to drive the enemy beyond Little Rock and out of harm's way."[43] Instead, the immediate threat to the Arkansas capital had ended.

The shortage of supplies was the primary reason Curtis evacuated the state, but many Confederates believed he had another motive for postponing his march to Little Rock. Hindman had cleverly sent spies to inform the Federal commander that large numbers of reinforcements from Texas had reached the capital. Although by late June this was partially true, at the time Curtis decided to move his army to his new base on the Mississippi, scarcely a handful of Texans had arrived. Henry McCulloch, who coordinated movement from Texas to Arkansas, had over 13,000 Texans still near his headquarters at Tyler in East Texas. His aide, Captain E. S. C. Robertson, estimated that 7,400 Texans were in Arkansas.[44] McCulloch dispatched men daily, but the trip to Little Rock was long and many of the men sick. Curtis, however, based his decision on the faulty reports, and as William Parsons later maintained, for "the second time was he foiled in this intended movement on Little Rock."[45]

The Texas cavalry had saved Arkansas's capital, but they were powerless to do the same for their cherished horses. Hindman, who needed more infantry and lacked forage for the rapidly growing number of mounted Texans, ordered nearly all the troops to dismount. "Among those to be dismounted, there is a great dissatisfaction," observed Henry

Orr, whose Twelfth Texas was the regiment selected to retain its mounts, and "some of them have started home."[46] Why did Hindman choose Parsons's command from among the many Texas cavalry units? A member of the Twelfth bragged that Parsons's men had an "enviable reputation" born of hard campaigning and could credit the selection to "its fine drill and fighting reputation."[47] Another reason probably came from Parsons's personal visit to Beauregard in May; there the colonel had received assurances that his troops would remain cavalry.

Yet the scarcity of forage forced even Parsons's cavalry to tighten up. Hindman allowed each company only seventy-five men, and an official committee headed by Rust inspected all the mounts. "Most of the horses are dead on their feet," noted John W. Truss of Company D. Nevertheless, he boasted, the committee "announced my horse one of the best horses in the regiment."[48] Henry Orr added that few of Parsons's men had their horses rejected, and those that did had bought others.[49]

With the threat to Little Rock temporarily relieved, Hindman began to organize his army. He gave Parsons command of the First Brigade, First Division, Army of the West, and rumors circulated that the colonel had become a brigadier general. His men thought the rank well deserved since Parsons had commanded the cavalry much more efficiently than Rust.[50]

The report proved false; instead of a promotion the colonel received the first challenge to his authority. While the Twelfth Texas camped near Brownsville, Carter's Twenty-first Texas arrived under the command of its lieutenant colonel, DeWitt Clinton Giddings, who speedily attached the regiment to Parsons's command. This pleased Colonel Parsons because he could fill out his brigade, but Colonel Carter (who had not accompanied his men to Arkansas) was furious. The former clergyman, who had only recently lost his own brigade, now found himself under another colonel. As soon as Carter arrived he argued that his commission, which came directly from the secretary of war, superceded any authority Parsons might have. Rather than feud, on August 4 Parsons ordered the newly arrived Texans to a camp on Bayou de View, a safe seven miles from his own regiment, on the pretext it should scout independently.[51]

Although Carter objected, Parsons remained senior colonel because Hindman needed a commander experienced in reconnaissance. Federal troops still lingered in the state, and this was not the time to trust a Methodist preacher with the safety of Little Rock. While all the newly dismounted Texans were ordered to camps of instruction near Austin, Arkansas, Parsons turned his command toward the Mississippi River. Almost daily scouting parties brought in prisoners. Henry Orr, proud of this new responsibility, wrote his family: "Texas soldiers seem to know no fear." Yet the Yankees, he believed, held Parsons's troops in awe. "The prisoners," he asserted, "said they had long heard of our regiment and had wished that they might never come in contact with us."[52]

The colonel planned to avenge the loss his troops had suffered near the Cache River. Scouting independently, he had to answer to no one except Hindman, who gave him permission for a daring raid. During the last week of July Parsons left his camp near Cotton Plant with a detachment of over three hundred of the Twelfth Texas and forty from Johnson's Spy Company. The Texans rode toward the Mississippi until they were within thirty miles of the Federal camps on the St. Francis River. Parsons carefully concealed his own force and watched the enemy's movement until he planned his strategy.[53]

Indeed, the Union officers had no idea there were any Confederate cavalry nearer than the White River, and Parsons found that they had relaxed normal precautions. Seeing his chance, Parsons marched his men all day and into the night of August 2 until they were within a few miles of a Federal camp. Careful reconnaissance assured Parsons that he was near a supply train headed for Helena; the main body was eight miles ahead across the L'Anguille River near Marianna. The Federals were confident that no one would attack the force so near to the main army base at Helena, so Lieutenant Colonel Oscar H. La Grange had separated his two detachments by almost a day's march.[54]

Parsons was watching men commanded by Henry S. Eggleston, a major in the First Wisconsin Cavalry; they were part of a larger force that had headed south from Missouri to assist Curtis as he moved across Arkansas. But Eggleston's unit had not arrived in time to do Curtis any good, and many of his one hundred thirty men were sick. With twenty-seven wagons and about one hundred horses and mules, Eggleston had left Madison on August 2 heading for the ferry on the L'Anguille River. When he arrived at the crossing he received orders not to proceed, but to remain in position until issued other instructions. He did not question his commander's change in plans, nor did he think that it might have something to do with the presence of enemy troops in the area. He took no special precautions but camped his wagon train about a half-mile from the river and detailed twenty-four men as pickets and guards.[55]

Colonel Parsons's plan was simple. He divided his force into five squadrons. He and Major L. J. Farrar would lead four squads while Lieutenant Colonel Bell Burleson and a fifth squadron would circle around the enemy and cut off any retreat. Lieutenant W. N. Kenner of Ellis County would lead the advance. The men had rested scarcely an hour before Parsons ordered them to mount; at one in the morning they headed for the unsuspecting Federal encampment.[56]

Darkness helped to conceal the Texans, but it also made movements hazardous. Nearly a fourth of the horses lost their riders while crossing the boggy river; on the other side a narrow trail snaked through the swampy woods. The horses stumbled over bushes and sank into bogs. Unable to see anything but the rider in front, and fearing detection at any moment, the Texans kept their pistols in one hand, their reins in the other. They were also uncertain of the patriotism of their Arkansas guide, and they did not relax until sunrise.[57]

The plan had been to attack at daylight, but the march had taken much too long. Parsons feared that Burleson's squadron, which had taken another route to the rear of the camp, might be in danger; if the main body failed to come up as scheduled, the Federals might discover Burleson's small group. Parsons ordered the squads into columns of four and hastily charged the men to cap their guns. He then spurred his horse into a sweeping gallop in the direction of the wagon train.[58]

Parsons's gamble paid off. The Federal soldiers had no idea that a Confederate force was anywhere near. One lieutenant recalled: "At sunrise the next morning—a quiet, beautiful Sabbath—while the wearied soldiers were still asleep, a single shot was heard up the road along which

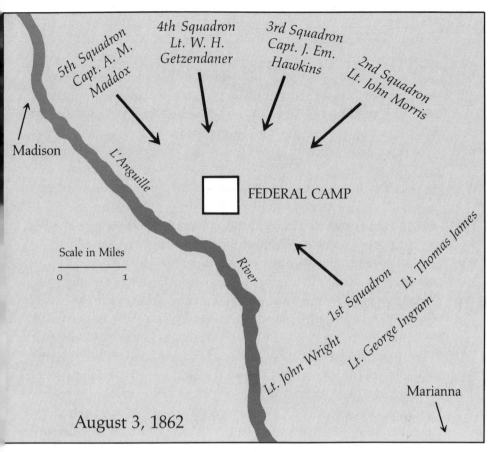

the train had come the day before." But no one paid any attention to the sound. The lieutenant, like most of the men busily preparing their breakfast, assumed it was an early forager shooting a pig for his mess. Instead, the half-dressed soldiers continued to move lazily around their wagons in perfect calm.[59]

The shot that no one heeded was indeed a warning. Parsons, anxious for the safety of Burleson's detachment, had raced toward the camp. But just before coming into view of the pickets, he had stopped. The column moved slowly and deliberately down the road toward the guards stationed about three hundred yards from the main camp. Only one was awake; three pickets slept secure in the belief there was no enemy near. The man on duty was so confident that the approaching column was one of his own that he did not wake his comrades. He realized his error when the horsemen halted twenty yards in his front and aimed their guns at him. He surrendered at once, but another, aroused from his slumber by the commotion, realized the mistake and fired his gun.[60]

In the rear, Burleson waited for a sign. "But, hark," recalled Ingram, "a gun fired. It was the Fed pickets. We were now in breathless suspence but for only a very few seconds. The charge was commenced by Col. Parson's command and evry Texan began the Comanche yell." Then, "the report of the double barrell guns were the signal of action for us." As the bugler blew the charge, Burleson's men took off yelling.[61]

The Texans displayed the perfect training that had become their trademark. Forming a line within a few yards of the enemy's camp, they charged through the tents and campfires. "The rangers were well disciplined," pronounced the Federal lieutenant. "As one fell from the saddle his horse moved forward in the rank as steadily as before." The shocked Wisconsin soldiers heard the bugle sound and saw "six hundred rangers, yelling like devils," advance. There was no escape; their own horses were hitched to the trees, unsaddled. The fighting was hand to hand. As a Federal officer later wrote, the Wisconsin troops were accustomed to fighting only guerillas, "who, cruel as death to captives, had never dared to face us in a fair fight."[62]

Confusion filled the camp. Refugee slaves ran in every direction from the wrath of the approaching Southerners. Eggleston, among the sick, rose from his bed and unarmed, with coat unbuttoned and hand tucked in his pocket, stood in the center of the camp quietly looking on. "An order," asserted a Wisconsin lieutenant, "would have been foolish." Men were fighting among the wagons and trees. As Burleson's rear guard advanced, a volley of ball and buckshot hit the camp from the south, the noise becoming an incessant roar. Trees no longer provided protection. Horses and mules, wounded from the buckshot, reared and fought to escape their halters. Federal soldiers found themselves under the feet of the frightened animals.[63]

Surrender was impossible, although Eggleston later assured his superior that such an idea never crossed his mind. Parsons had hoped that the men would succumb without a fight, but the screams of the blacks made any communication impossible. Parsons had ordered the first volley fired over the heads of the enemy, since most were almost in a nude state and many still in their beds. But the Federals, without instructions from Eggleston, had grabbed their Belgian rifles and Springfield muskets and contested for every inch of ground against the mounted Texans' double-barrel shotguns loaded with buckshot.[64] Henry Orr wrote home: "They fought bravely for a few moments, thinking we were Missouri troops. But they couldn't stand Texas." After a fight of about thirty minutes, all was quiet. "It was a glorious little affair," bragged Orr.[65] Many soldiers fell back into the woods, leaving the camp in the possession of Parsons's men. "There was no surrender," noted the Federal lieutenant. "Perhaps no one knew how to indicate such a desire if he had been so disposed, for hitherto no portion of the Regiment had ever been defeated."[66] Yet many escaped, including the officer who later carefully recorded his recollections of the battle.

A Wisconsin soldier claimed: "The rebels, now that resistance had ceased, took possession of the camp, and with the most fiendish barbarity murdered many negroes, both men and women, plundered and burned the train, and then with forty-seven prisoners besides negroes, returned, as rapidly as they came, toward Little Rock."[67] Indeed, the Federal loss was devastating. Eggleston reported that the Confederates took seven wagons and all the horses and mules and burned or destroyed everything they could not carry with them. The Little Rock *True Democrat* listed Parsons's booty at three wagons of ammunition, one of arms, two ambulances and one commissary wagon, with over fifteen wagons destroyed. The property loss for the United States Army was almost half a million dollars. Federal accounts differ about the number killed, wounded, or captured. A safe estimate would be thirteen or fourteen soldiers killed, nearly fifty captured, and around forty wounded. In addition, an estimated forty blacks were killed and over one hundred taken captive. Parsons, on the other hand, lost two killed and about ten wounded.[68]

The Confederates completed the raid with precision and skill. But Parsons knew his little force was too close to Helena for safety, even though the balance of his regiment arrived at the scene that evening. After burying the dead and caring for the wounded, he ordered the wagons to move out. As the Confederates headed back toward the Cache River, time again was of the essence. Despite the burden of wagons and prisoners, the Texans made the march of nearly ninety miles in less than sixty hours. The advance arrived back in camp in fifty-two hours, with only a five-hour rest and no food for the men or horses.[69]

L'Anguille was a great victory at a time when the Confederate hierarchy in Arkansas desperately needed a morale booster. Hindman lavished praise on both Parsons and Burleson.[70] Henry Orr bragged that although the Federals "were very wrathy and swore they would avenge themselves," they would "never catch us a-napping." He and other members of the regiment were proud of the publicity. The Yankees "call us murderers, the 'Swamp Fox' Regiment," he boasted, "the latter I think tolerable appropriate for we lie in the swamps in daylight and travel at night. We have done more to keep the enemy out of this country than all the balance of the troops combined."[71] The Houston *Telegraph* reported that the Federal soldiers in Arkansas "have a great deal more fear of Texas Rangers than they have of the devil."[72]

But cavalry service was hard. It was difficult for the authorities to provide for both men and horses. Orr told his parents: "We have traveled a rough road since we've been in this state while all other soldiers have been lying at ease."[73] The usual number of sick in the regiment averaged over one hundred. Without a hospital fund, they had little medicine, few nurses, no bandages, and no ambulances to convey the ill.[74] As winter approached the men longingly recalled the clothing and tents they had discarded when they had become light cavalry.

Still, they could be proud of their accomplishments, as Colonel Parsons succinctly summed up in his letter to the brigade's reunion in 1878. The Twelfth Texas, wrote the colonel, "won the high honor a month after reaching the theatre of war in Arkansas in 1862, when all other cavalry commands then at the front were dismounted, of being specially selected . . . to remain mounted" and "act as advance guard and cavalry arm of the new army then organizing in our rear."[75] This was true, for after the battle at L'Anguille River the enemy confined its actions to the vicinity immediately around Helena. "Parsons' command," asserted Hindman, "was left to watch that line, and the remainder of my troops were put in camp near Little Rock and their organization and instruction commenced."[76]

6.
"They Dont Like Our Mode of Fighting"

"Col. Parsons, of your State, is doing the country an immense service," asserted a letter to the editor of the Houston *Telegraph* in the autumn of 1862. "He rarely ever has an encounter with the 'Feds' but what he puts them to flight. He is frequently down within a few miles of Helena, and is continually cutting off the enemy's foraging parties and driving in their pickets."[1] The *Dallas Herald* also cautioned that the Yankees entrenched behind their fortifications "had better keep a sharp lookout for one Parsons and Alf Johnson, who seem to have a peculiar feeling for their foraging trains and niggers."[2] Moreover, the colonel had "annoyed them to such an extent," according to one observer, "that they are fulminating all kinds of threats as to what they will do with him *when they catch him.*"[3]

Indeed, Parsons's orders directed him to harass scouting parties emanating from the Mississippi River region and to keep the Federals at a safe distance from Arkansas's capital. It was vital that the cavalry shield the true situation in Little Rock until the Confederate hierarchy had time to prepare a defense. Throughout the remainder of 1862 the Texans harassed Federal scouting parties scouring the marshy river bottoms of eastern Arkansas. With each success his reputation grew. "Parsons is a trump," bragged Captain Elijah P. Petty of the Seventeenth Texas Infantry. "The feds never make a play but he catches them. They hate him as the devil."[4]

Parsons's instructions to harass the Federals came from Theophilus H. Holmes, who had succeeded Hindman as commander of the Trans-Mississippi Department in August. Hindman, relegated to commanding the district of Arkansas, Missouri, and the Indian Territory, turned his attention toward Fort Smith. Holmes, a West Point classmate of Jefferson Davis whom the troops surreptitiously called "Granny," also was not the commander the Trans-Mississippi needed. He proved hesitant and weak when faced with critical decisions, and he never devised a strategy to defend his department. He spread his army thin, hoping to protect the entire area from the Indian Territory to the Mississippi River, and therefore he could neither adequately aid Hindman, whose tenuous hold on northwest Arkansas constantly needed reinforcing, nor successfully protect Confederate forces in the extreme southeast.

Late in September Holmes reorganized the army. He ordered several regiments to join Hindman but kept most Texas soldiers near Little Rock. He divided sixteen Texas infantry and dismounted cavalry regiments into two divisions, assigning eight to Brigadier General Henry McCulloch, who had arrived in the state early in the month, and the remainder to another Texan, Allison Nelson, a newly appointed brigadier general. Much to the consternation of Colonel Carter, Parsons, although not promoted, received command of a cavalry brigade consisting of the Twelfth and Twenty-first Texas as well as Francis M. Chrisman's Arkansas battalion. Joseph H. Pratt's battery from Jefferson provided welcome firepower which Parsons utilized with great efficacy along the Mississippi River.[5] In addition, several autonomous commands generally camped with the cavalry brigade. These included Alf Johnson's Spy Company, Charles Morgan's squadron of Edward Vontress's and Frank Lemmon's companies, and at times Benjamin D. McKie's squadron of his own company and that of Milton M. Boggess.[6] Although the authorities eventually consolidated the squadrons into a battalion assigned to Parsons, in 1862 Holmes allowed each to operate independently.

Parsons needed more men. With only two regiments, and both debilitated by illness, he hoped to augment his strength with another regiment. The scarcity of forage made mounted troops difficult, if not impossible, to secure as Holmes continued the unpopular practice of dismounting cavalry. Although Nathaniel M. Burford's Nineteenth Texas, which had recently reported to Little Rock, escaped that fate, Holmes ordered it to northwest Arkansas.[7] Parsons nonetheless hoped to convince the general that he might better utilize Burford's troops near Helena. A private under Parsons noted, not realizing how accurate a statement he made, that General Holmes "always granted the requests of the latest callers—even if by so doing he revoked his last previous order."[8] Perhaps the eloquent Parsons and the politically well-connected Burford could persuade Holmes to change his mind. Such a merger would do more than just add names to Parsons's muster rolls. The two colonels had enjoyed an agreeable professional relationship prior to the war, and their friendship might give Parsons the edge over Carter when the touchy matter of seniority arose. Burford discerned qualities of leadership in Parsons that he saw lacking in both himself and Carter. Certainly Parsons perceived these advantages even though he recognized that initially Burford's cavalry would probably prove a liability.

With only rudimentary and ephemeral military training, Burford's troops exhibited the defects of men drawn straight from civilian life. In addition, they possessed few arms and not all arrived in Arkansas mounted, since many had hoped to procure horses at Little Rock. The affable Burford, with no military background, had little inclination to drill or discipline his men beyond the absolute minimum. As a result, William J. Simms, a private from Ellis County, complained that the troops were not "ready for service," had "not drilled any," and had already "forgot what little we knew." Since the former judge seldom reprimanded his soldiers, Simms sarcastically observed, "the boys of this regiment is as bad as they can be, bee gums, hen roosts, & negro kichens is in danger wherever we go, there is more mean men in this world than I had any idea of." The Nineteenth Texas, like the Twenty-first, had to rely upon its lieutenant colonel for those qualities the colonel lacked. Benjamin Watson, elected to that office, attempted to remedy some of the discipline problems by taking drastic measures; he ordered night guards over the Texans with instructions to shoot anyone whose movements appeared suspicious.[9]

Poorly prepared troops under nonprofessional field officers vexed Holmes; these men constituted much of the army he depended upon to defend Little Rock. Early in October he ordered McCulloch's division, with Parsons's command as advance guard, to Devall's Bluff on the White River to discourage a possible offensive from Helena. Instead of sending Burford's cavalry west as planned, Holmes detailed it to scout for the Sixth and Tenth Texas infantries camped near Clarendon. But Colonel Burford did not accompany his men. According to Henry Orr, the colonel was "under arrest at the Rock for getting drunk and stopping his command out of the rain while on a forced march, on orders signed by Gen. Holmes."[10] Private Simms, disturbed with the colonel's conduct, grumbled that even Burford's own men had begun to fault him.[11] Indeed, Holmes seemed to agree with their assessment. He complained to Richmond that most of his colonels, including Burford, were unfortunately "not qualified to command a regiment."[12]

Burford was an excellent example of a practice plaguing both sides during the war; he had received his commission not because of military expertise but because he had powerful friends in both Texas and Richmond. Holmes knew this. Not only was Burford's incarceration brief, but when the anticipated advance from Helena failed to materialize and the general ordered the infantry back to camps of instruction, he sent the Nineteenth Texas to join Colonel Parsons.[13]

This decision to attach Burford's troops to the brigade could not have pleased the men more; eight companies of Parsons's Twelfth Texas originated in North Central Texas, while all ten companies of Burford's regiment came from the Dallas area. Friends greeted friends; relatives anxiously sought cousins or brothers and absorbed long-awaited news from home. Henry Orr was delighted when the new addition to the brigade rode into camp under the command of Lieutenant Colonel Watson, a fellow Ellis County resident. Orr observed: "They are a fine looking body of soldiers," reserving his only criticism for the colonel who, he adjudged, had gained scant approval from his men.[14]

The Nineteenth Texas filled the brigade, but it must have seemed to Parsons that as soon as he solved one problem, others arose. Upon reaching his headquarters at Cotton Plant he learned that Jeff Neal, captain of the Johnson County Slashers and a friend who had served under him from the beginning of the war, was seriously ill. Neal's quintessential devotion to the Confederacy had earned him the esteem of his men, and his courage and coolness under fire had the respect of his colonel. But the captain, wounded while leading a charge on the Cache River in July, died in October.[15] This was more than just a personal loss for Parsons; few of his officers inspired the men as Neal had done. Moreover, with the inclusion of Carter's and Burford's regiments in the brigade, Parsons would need more officers of Neal's caliber.

The troops in both the Nineteenth and Twenty-first Texas were novices at scouting. Burford's men knew nothing about fighting, and although Carter's had been in Arkansas for over two months, they had not yet mastered the rudiments necessary to survive in the Arkansas marshes. Just days before Neal's death, Parsons learned that Northern troops from Helena had given Carter a rude introduction to war. Much to Colonel Carter's embarrassment, Federal cavalrymen had captured over twenty men of his command, including two commissioned officers and, more important, the lieutenant colonel.[16]

The Texans had a skillful adversary in Helena—Major Samuel Walker of the Fifth Kansas Cavalry. Lieutenant Buck Walton, a scout for the Twenty-first Texas, evaluated Walker as a "daring, and vigilant" officer.[17] The major made an indelible impression upon many Confederates, and by the war's end his ability had earned him a brevet to brigadier general. But many Texans thought him callous and cruel. William P. Zuber, a private in the Twenty-first, insisted: "This fiend has been the author of nearly all the house burning that has been perpetrated in Philips and adjoining counties," and he called the troops of the Fifth Kansas, "a band of thieves."[18]

Yet in the autumn of 1862 war in Arkansas still seemed a game in which the craftiest won: proficiency in frontier cunning was more valuable than all the West Point training. New recruits had to serve an appenticeship, and both sides waited patiently for those men lacking experience to perform ineptly. Late in September, when some men of the Fifth Kansas dropped their guard, a detachment under Lieutenant Buck Walton captured nearly thirty. Such a blow deserved repayment. As Walton and Walker met under a flag of truce a little over a week later, the Federal major promised the Texan he would "get even." Before long he partially kept his word.[19]

Walker's first retaliation followed within days. Walton, who had left on a scout with thirteen men, planned to surprise and capture some pickets near Helena. With six men he rode toward the river port to reconnoiter; he left seven behind with Lieutenant Alfred P. Luckett, who had strict orders to watch for enemy cavalry. Luckett, feeling secure in his position, disregarded Walton's instructions. When an old friend invited him to visit his home, he yielded to the temptation of a hot meal and, leaving no picket on duty, ate his dinner unaware that enemy scouts had discovered not only his presence but also his carelessness.

When a detachment of the Fifth Kansas surrounded the house, three Texans tried to escape on foot by running across a cornfield into a small woods. Eighteen-year-old James Townsend was shot immediately and fell as he headed for the fence; Dunk McClennan and Napoleon Kelly continued at full speed. McClennan stopped when he spied shelter in a peach tree blown down by a wind, but Kelly ran right into several mounted Kansans. One of the soldiers took three shots at him, missing each time, before a Federal officer ordered the man to stop firing and Kelly surrendered. Major Walker had exacted revenge. McClennan, who did not come out of hiding until the cavalrymen had left with their prisoners, brought the wounded Townsend back to the Confederate camp and reported the affray.[20] "The loss of the men were charged to me," lamented Lieutenant Walton, "and it somewhat cast a shadow on me for the time."[21]

A second Federal tour de force a week later quickly eclipsed Walton's misfortune: the Twenty-first Texas lost Lieutenant Colonel DeWitt Clinton Giddings. Clinton and his brother Francis, both natives of Pennsylvania who had joined their brothers in Texas ten years earlier, had rapidly absorbed Southern customs and culture. Four of their brothers already possessed noted reputations in the state. Giles had died from wounds received at San Jacinto; Jabez Demming helped to found the town of Brenham in Washington County and served on the Board of Trustees of Soule University; James was a civil engineer, and George a Confederate colonel.[22]

Clinton, a man of firm conviction, seldom changed his mind once he had reached a decision. When Lieutenant Walton heard that Giddings planned a scout near Helena, he visited his commander to share his recent experiences. The interview proceeded well until Walton began to offer some hints; instead of acknowledging his gratitude, Giddings superciliously dismissed his subordinate. Walton later wrote, "he did not seem to take my cautions in the spirit they were tendered—and we soon separated, I to go my way, & he his."[23]

Giddings's scout started well enough. Late in the evening on October 11, he rode upon a party of the Fourth Iowa Cavalry heading for Helena. About fifty troops, returning from a scout fifteen miles west of their base, had carelessly stretched out their line. Since the tired Iowans were only three miles from the town, Major Benjamin Rector neglected normal precautions. The detachment made a tempting target for the Texans, and Giddings quickly planned his strategy. He waited until the enemy entered a lane (about one-fourth mile long with fences on both sides), then ordered his men to charge. The unexpected yells of the Texans caused the Iowans to panic. Major Rector rode to the end of his column to rally his surprised, disordered, and frightened men, but hemmed in by the fences he could do little but surrender. Giddings's men killed three, wounded two (one died later), and captured fifteen Federals. After dispatching part of his force back to camp with the captives, Giddings and part of the detachment continued on looking for more prey.[24]

Here his luck ended. Federal troops in the area had heard the noise; Lieutenant George B. Parsons and forty men of Company B headed in the direction of the engagement. According to William Forse Scott, adjutant of the Fourth Iowa, Lieutenant Parsons captured Giddings and eleven of his men. In the affair Parsons had four soldiers wounded, including himself, and two more captured.[25]

Other accounts did not credit the arrest to the Fourth Iowa. A newspaper article among the private papers of Clinton Giddings gave the honor of his capture to a detachment of the First Missouri Cavalry under Captain Barbour Lewis. A Federal paper reported: "This body put themselves into line of battle and received the Rebels with well-aimed revolving carbines, unhorsing several of them, causing the main body to fly in confusion." A third source attributed Giddings's capture to the First Wisconsin Cavalry.[26]

After the affray, which the Federals called the engagement at "Jones's Lane" or "Lick Creek" and the Confederates the battle of "Shell Creek," Henry Orr informed his family: "The boys say their regiment will be broken up almost without him, as Col. Carter is not of much force."[27]

Apprehending Giddings was not enough satisfaction for the loss suffered by the Fourth Iowa, and Federal retaliation quickly followed. Major Walker of the Fifth Kansas ordered his men to burn at least two homes he claimed belonged to Southern sympathizers. Walker also directed his wrath toward Clinton Giddings's nephew, seventeen-year-old Edmund T. Giddings, who sent word to Walker that he planned to avenge his uncle. Walker threatened personal retaliation, and Private Giddings answered that the only way to stop him would be "to bury him."[28]

This dare presaged a personal feud lasting for over three months. Early in January, when Parsons's command left northeast Arkansas, Private Giddings was on a scout and not apprised of the departure. But Giddings's desire to avenge his family honor (most likely his own, since by this time his uncle had secured a release) kept him near Helena. Walker, for his part, did not plan to wait for the young Confederate to find him. He knew that Giddings was a loner who seldom mingled with local citizens and therefore would not be easy to trap. But late in January Walker encountered the perfect opportunity. Giddings, in a rather unusual move, accepted an invitation to a party at La Grange. Although warned the affair might be a trap, the young man departed from his characteristic wariness and decided to attend. In a bitter letter to the Houston *Telegraph*, W. P. Zuber reported that during the evening "Walker dashed into the house leading, a band of his jayhawkers." Although Giddings fled outside, Walker's men surrounded the teenager and killed him instantly.[29] When news of this fight reached the Confederate camps, the circumstances surrounding his death enraged his friends.

The fates of Edmund Giddings and his uncle typified the mutual hatred prevalent in Arkansas. The practice of exchanging prisoners was fairly common in 1862 and Lieutenant Colonel Giddings expected a parole after his capture. But such was not the case. E. A. Carr, the Federal commander at Helena, believed Holmes planned to hold Major Rector (whom Giddings had captured) for ransom. Moreover, Carr was angry about reports that troops in the Twenty-first Texas had murdered an Iowa private captured at Shell Creek for refusing to trot. He retaliated by transferring his prisoners to Gratiot Street Prison at St. Louis. Giddings complained the conditions there were "suffocating." He wrote home that his makeshift cell held 1200, but "was scarcely large enough to hold 100 comfortably."[30]

Yet after his capture Giddings tried to make the best of his situation. Sociable and gregarious, he made a favorable impression upon his captors while at Helena. A Federal paper called Giddings the "inveterate Rebel" and described him as "a tall, fine-looking man, over six feet high," and "a brave officer." He enjoyed talking about the war but insisted that the South would not be subdued, and he was "thoroughly devoted to the cause of the Rebellion, believing firmly in its ultimate success."[31]

While confined in St. Louis, Giddings continually petitioned for release for himself and his men. He bombarded Samuel Curtis with letters and even requested a personal interview. When turned down he complained: "Why is it that when my Government observes the cartel that I and my men are denied the benefits of it? I again, in behalf of myself and members of the Twenty-first Texas Cavalry, demand our exchange or parole in accordance with the terms of the agreement between the two Governments." Not only did he apply to the Federal authorities for release, he also persuaded them to approve the transfer of nineteen-year-old Jerome Alexander, who had developed typhoid pneumonia, to the hospital. But in spite of Giddings's efforts, the young man soon died.[32]

Although he heard no response from Curtis, Giddings had a valuable friend on the other side. While in prison he received a letter from John N. Noble, Curtis's aide-de-camp, who had become acquainted with Giddings early in September, when Noble had conducted Confederate prisoners to Little Rock for exchange. Giddings had learned of a party passing near his regiment under a flag of truce and had offered to accompany it to the capital. General Holmes had severely reprimanded Giddings for allowing the party to pass the pickets without permission, and during the interview with Holmes, Giddings had interceded for Noble and drawn a further upbraiding upon himself. The Federal aide had not forgotten, and he promised to assist Giddings all he could, although Holmes's actions against the prisoners under his charge had angered Curtis. Noble warned Giddings not to become too hopeful; he believed Curtis planned to transfer him to Alton, Illinois. By mid-November, however, the acrimony between the two department commanders abated, and Curtis was ready to exchange the lieutenant colonel and sixteen of his men. The Texans returned to Arkansas December 1, almost two months after their capture.[33]

Six weeks in prison had not moderated Giddings's impetuous temperament. Both he and the Federal major had requested the return of their horses and rigging as well as weapons. But at the exchange point in Helena, the Texan discovered that his saddle was not among his possessions. Saddles were difficult to procure, but he complained to no avail. When he arrived at Henry McCulloch's camp on Bayou Metoe he was still seething and told E. S. C. Robertson, the general's aide-de-camp, that he would "kill the fed that has it, if he can find [him] & if not that one, some other."[34] Although he apparently located his saddle, he did attempt to exact revenge, leading a party of twenty Texans toward the Mississippi River, where he attacked and captured twenty-six cavalrymen only two miles from Helena and one-half mile from their camp.[35]

Yet Giddings's fervent enthusiasm could not replace the practical experience of those Texans who had served in Arkansas for months. Alf Johnson epitomized the excellence that only time in the field could teach: he carefully picked every man who joined his company and expected the same meticulousness from them that he required of himself. A week after Giddings's capture, Captain Johnson, joined by two companies of Chrisman's Arkansas battalion under Captains Samuel Corley and George W. Rutherford, successfully assaulted a foraging party of twenty-two wagons and over two hundred soldiers. In a short skirmish Johnson captured seventy-seven prisoners, all the wagons, and over one hundred horses and mules. A Federal account described this as a "bold attack" within a few miles of the cavalry camp. "This time," wrote Adjutant

William F. Scott of the Fourth Iowa, "it was the Fifth Kansas that suffered, losing a number of men and a large wagon-train filled with forage which they were bringing in."[36] The Confederates counted only one serious casualty. "My fine old war horse, Copperhead," grieved Captain Johnson, "was shot dead from under me."[37]

Experienced counted. Parsons could always rely on Johnson as he did his own troops; the Twelfth Texas was still the undisputed cadre of the brigade. Scouts from the Twelfth brought in one or two prisoners daily with scarcely any loss on their side. Captain E. S. C. Robertson reported: "Our men are having a fight, what might be called pretty heavy skirmishing every week, in the neighborhood of Helena—in all of which they get the better of the federals." Yet he pointed out: "Our men are cautious, but when they make a fight, they fight like devils. The Yankees, call them *Hell Yelpers*, from the fact that they allways raise the war whoop when they fight."[38] And J. C. Morriss of the Twenty-first Texas concluded that the Feds "have a wholesome dread of the Texans— they dont like our mode of fighting. I believe the Texans mode of fighting is to hurt somebody no matter how that is."[39]

Skirmishing continued daily. At times the Federal cavalry won; in other engagements the Texans came out victorious. A strange friendship based on mutual respect evolved between many men in the two armies. Despite their retaliations against one another, Texan Buck Walton and Kansan Samuel Walker developed an unusual relationship. "Personally," recalled the Texan, "we became great friends, though we fought fiercely against one another in the field." When they had occasion to meet under a flag of truce they generally tried to stay the night together. The Federal major brought his friend such coveted items as whiskey, cards, or sardines and always gambled his greenbacks against Walton's near-worthless Confederate money. One time the major brought Walton a pair of cavalry boots, and the Texan fondly remembered: "Did I take them, Yes—for I was nearly naked."[40]

In fact, United States Army supplies often reached the Texans stationed in the vicinity of Helena. Since the Confederate commissary firmly believed cavalry could subsist by foraging, requisitions for food and clothing often went unfilled. Spies from Parsons's command rode in and out of Helena almost at will, and every time there was a prisoner exchange the Confederates returned from the port with wagon loads of goods purchased there. James J. Frazier of Parsons's Twelfth Texas promised his mother that on his next outing he would send into the city and buy her a pair of cotton cards.[41] Ed Rundell, a thirty-year-old sergeant from Washington County, successfully passed in and out of Federal camps under the name of Ed Wallace until his capture with Lieutenant Colonel Giddings, when the authorities shipped him to the Federal prison at St. Louis.[42]

Interminable shortages forced the Texans into the contraband trade. Supplying cavalry mounts, always a vexing problem, had become extremely difficult. The land west of the White River was devoid of forage because a drought the preceding spring had destroyed most of the crops. The commissary procured corn from the bottomlands of the lower Arkansas and shipped it by water to Little Rock, but the river became too low to navigate, even for shallow-draft boats. This forced the cavalry to camp east of the White and Cache rivers where grass grew more abundantly.[43] Moreover, John W. Truss complained that the unusually frigid weather was harsh on the troops, most of whom had left their bedding and clothes early in the summer when Hindman had ordered them to become light cavalry. Truss had lost his large overcoat and comforter, and since the men had not received any pay, they could buy no more. "I think," Truss mused, the authorities "are afraid to pay us off now for fear the boys will go home."[44]

Adding to the strain, Richmond requested more men from the Trans-Mississippi Department. When General Samuel Cooper, head of the adjutant and inspector general's office, instructed Holmes to send seven regiments to the army in Virginia, Holmes countered with an appeal that the Arkansas regiments east of the river be returned to Little Rock. A disagreement soon developed between President Jefferson Davis and Secretary of War George Randolph over who should hold the ultimate responsibility for the disposition of Holmes's troops. As a result, an angry Randolph tendered his resignation.[45]

Nevertheless, problems in the administration did not stop the government from pressing Holmes for more men. Holmes received another order from Cooper, this time requesting ten thousand reinforcements for Lieutenant General John C. Pemberton at Vicksburg.[46] Holmes, however, claimed he had no soldiers to spare. A. P. Hovey, the new Union commander at Helena, had just attempted an assault on Fort Hindman, the uncompleted bastion at Arkansas Post. Fortunately for the Confederate defenders, the gunboats drew too much water and a mix-up in communications compelled Hovey to order their withdrawal.[47]

Still, Holmes was thoroughly alarmed and began to prepare for invasion. He ordered one of the brigades with McCulloch to reinforce the post, where Brigadier General Thomas J. Churchill had assumed command. With McCulloch's three remaining infantry brigades and Parsons's cavalry, Holmes sought to defend the fertile Arkansas valley, an expanse of rich farmland vital to the subsistence of Arkansas and northern Louisiana.[48]

Rather than accede to Richmond's demand for more men, Holmes stalled. Writing to General Cooper, he pleaded for the safety of Arkansas. To abandon the valley would open it to almost certain occupation, and for any troops to reach Vicksburg would take at least thirty days even under the best conditions. Vicksburg, over three hundred miles away, was too distant for troops unaccustomed to marching. This, coupled with the facts that the river had risen and forage was scarce, made it almost impossible for Holmes's troops to reinforce Pemberton.[49]

The apparent disregard of orders generated some concern in Richmond. A few days later Holmes received a terse message from Cooper: "The President reiterates his orders that you send without delay sufficient force from your command to General Pemberton."[50] Holmes replied immediately that McCulloch's was the only division available, and to remove it would leave the country around Helena almost undefended. "Solemnly, under the circumstances," answered Holmes, "I regard the movement ordered as equivalent to abandoning Arkansas."[51]

At the same time Holmes hit an impasse with the authorities in Richmond, he inadvertently created a dilemma for his Texans. He replaced Colonel Parsons with a Kentuckian, Brigadier General James M. Hawes, who had received orders to report to Little Rock late in September.[52] Holmes planned to place Hawes over the cavalry in front of Helena, a logical decision since the Kentuckian had at one time commanded the cavalry in Albert Sidney Johnston's Western Department.[53] But as a regular army officer, graduate and instructor at West Point, Hawes believed in strict discipline and enforced military law to the letter. No one could even visit town without written permission. Naturally many men resented this rigorous adherence to regulations. Henry Orr observed: "some of the boys are put under arrest most every day . . . but the offences are trifling—no one has been punished yet . . . some of the command dislike him—I have found no fault with him yet."[54]

All agreed that Hawes handled the brigade proficiently. Lieutenant George Ingram evaluated him as "a good disciplinarian and an unasuming gentleman. . . . He is a Kentuckian but claims to be a Texan."[55] William Zuber of the Twenty-first Texas thought Hawes "an approachable and courteous gentleman and an able commander, though his command of the brigade was brief."[56]

Parsons had required his troops to excel in drill, but he seldom enforced military regulations except in extreme cases. In one instance when the colonel had decided to punish foragers, Henry Orr had found himself among the accused. Therefore, when Hawes became the commander, Orr, apparently still bearing resentment over his embarrassment quipped: "So Col. Parsons comes to his retirement. I judge he *does not feel so elevated as he has been feeling.*"[57]

But Hawes's efficiency could not override loyalty to Parsons, and the majority of the Texans objected to their new commander. Early in December a group from the Nineteenth Texas serenaded Hawes in what Private Henry Orr termed "a disrespectful manner . . . which created a sensation." Although little is known of this incident, Hawes issued a special order on December 9 which read that the general commanding "is much gratified to know that the 12th and 21st Texas Regts & Pratts Battery were not engaged in the disgraceful & mutinous scene of last evening."[58]

Discontent spread though the brigade. The commissioned officers of the Twelfth Texas, to the surprise of no one, petitioned General Holmes for permission to return to Texas, where Colonel Parsons had gone. The colonel spent little time visiting his family, however; instead he worked for authorization to detach his regiment from Hawes and have it join him south of the Red River. At the same time some of the leading men in the brigade tried to have the unit headquartered at Shreveport, just in case Parsons's efforts proved unsuccessful.[59]

Any chance of returning home ended in December, however, when the situation in Arkansas suddenly changed. Disturbing reports filtered to Holmes at Little Rock that large numbers of troops had left Helena, heading toward Vicksburg.[60] Hindman, retreating down the Arkansas River after his defeat at Prairie Grove early in the month, also needed reinforcing. The general faced a predicament. Should he send the Texas cavalry to Hindman's assistance or should he hold the brigade in reserve east of Little Rock? Holmes, unfortunately, did not have the freedom to contemplate long. Instead Federal movement up the Arkansas River dictated his course of action. As 1863 opened, the frailty of Arkansas's meager defenses became readily apparent.

THE BATTLE OF ARKANSAS POST

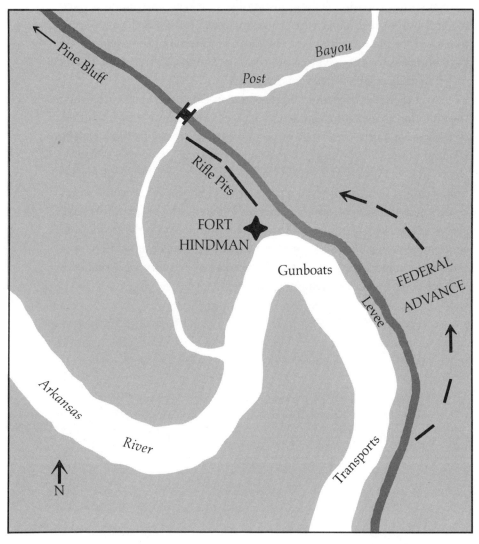

7.
The Race to Arkansas Post

"Yesterday was a busy time in camps," George Ingram wrote to his wife on January 2, 1863. "Night before last we received orders to take up the line of march for Hindman's army. Yesterday was spent in making preparations for the trip but last night the order was countermanded."[1] Holmes had planned to send Parsons's brigade to reinforce the Confederates retreating from Prairie Grove, but he abruptly changed his mind. A Federal army was poised at Milliken's Bend just above Vicksburg, and he feared a possible offensive from the southeast. Although the situation all across Arkansas appeared serious, Ingram observed, "our leaders do not seem to be alarmed. In all probability they are drawing the Feds in a trap."[2] In fact, Holmes had concocted no stratagem. While he wavered, a massive force from Grant's Vicksburg expedition headed for Arkansas Post with plans to destroy the menacing enemy base located there.

Holmes had almost five thousand men—mostly Arkansas and Texas soldiers—at Fort Hindman, the Confederate bastion on the lower Arkansas River. Among the Texas regiments under the command of Brigadier General Thomas James Churchill were two from Colonel Carter's old brigade of lancers, Franklin C. Wilkes's Twenty-fourth Texas and Clayton C. Gillespie's Twenty-fifth Texas, now both dismounted. Holmes also ordered the Fifteenth, Seventeenth, and Eighteenth Texas—three of the regiments that had lost their horses in July after the battle near Cotton Plant—to the fortification. Churchill had only two regular Texas infantry regiments, the Sixth and Tenth Texas. For cavalry, Samuel J. Richardson's company from Marshall arrived early in December and joined the Louisiana companies of L. M. Nutt and W. B. Denson on picket duty.[3]

Many Texans at Fort Hindman, about forty miles from the Mississippi River, regarded their position with foreboding. Captain Gil McKay of the Seventeenth Texas, a friend of Sam Richardson, believed the fortifications totally unsuitable. Arkansas Post was, in his opinion, "Ft. Donald-son No. 2."[4] A second member of the Seventeenth Texas, Marshall S. Pierson, agreed: "It was my impression that we could not hold this position."[5] Lieutenant Flavius W. Perry of the same command joked: "This county was never made I don't think for white people to live in, nothing but frogs and craw fish can live here long. . . . I don't think the Yankeys would have it if they could get it."[6]

Perry was correct. The Union commanders had no intention of taking and holding Arkansas Post. But reducing the Confederate garrison would be a practical rehearsal for the more than thirty thousand Federal troops waiting for Grant to resume his operations against Vicksburg. The idea particularly appealed to Major General John A. McClernand, who quietly planned his expedition without notifying either General-in-Chief Henry W. Halleck in Washington or Grant, the department commander.

Grant disliked the middle-aged McClernand, whose only military experience had come in the Black Hawk War. When the Civil War began McClernand was commissioned a brigadier general, but as the West Pointers knew, his appointment resulted from his prominence in the Democratic Party in Illinois and not his ability. He served under Grant at Forts Henry and Donelson, where he claimed his own troops should have received credit for capturing the Confederate posts.[7]

McClernand had conceived an idea to recruit a special expedition of midwestern troops to open the Mississippi River. When Halleck did not appear interested, he turned to Lincoln, who not only liked the plan but admired McClernand's enthusiasm and energy. As McClernand raised troops for the expedition down the river, however, Halleck forwarded them to Memphis within Grant's department.

Grant did all he could to obstruct McClernand's control of the river expedition, although he began to favor the idea of a river approach to Vicksburg. To assure that McClernand did not lead such an operation, Grant placed Major General William T. Sherman over the troops. McClernand angrily complained to Edwin M. Stanton, "Either through the intention of the General-in-chief or a strange occurrence of accidents, the authority of the President and yourself, as evidenced by your acts, has been set at naught, and I have been deprived of the command that had been committed to me."[8]

Exasperated, McClernand decided to push his operation in spite of all opposition; he knew he had the support of the president and did not need any other approval. After the successful Confederate raid on Grant's base at Holly Springs and Sherman's withdrawal from Chickasaw Bluffs, McClernand decided the time had come to reclaim his troops and headed immediately for Sherman's camp at Milliken's Bend. As soon as he arrived at the headquarters, he assumed command and created the "Army of the Mississippi," which he divided into corps under Sherman and George W. Morgan. The action he planned for these men, if he could prevail upon Rear Admiral David D. Porter to commit his fleet to the scheme, would be a coordinated land and naval attack up the Arkansas River to destroy the Confederate fort at Arkansas Post.[9] First, however, he had to coax Sherman to take part in the campaign. Then Sherman had to persuade Porter, who thought McClernand a braggart with little military ability, to agree.

As soon as McClernand convinced the commanders to join his operation, planning and implementation took scarcely over a week. McClernand's strategy was to deceive the Confederates at the post as to the destination of Porter's fleet. He ordered the admiral to steam by the mouth of the Arkansas as if heading toward Helena or Memphis. But after bypassing the Arkansas, Porter turned his vessels up the White River and headed toward a little-used cutoff that led back to the Arkansas below Fort Hindman. On January 9 the navy docked three miles below the fort and, to the astonishment of the Confederate scouts, began to debark thousands of men. No one, especially Churchill and Holmes, had expected what appeared to be Grant's entire army.[10]

By the next morning McClernand's forces were ready for an assault on the Confederate bastion. One division lost its way in the swampy countryside while trying to locate a road suitable for flanking the enemy position; the soldiers had to retrace their steps and rejoin the main column, wasting precious hours. The force advancing directly toward the fort drove Confederate defenders from the outlying earthworks, but because McClernand could not position his army to the satisfaction of all the commanders, the offensive stalled. By evening McClernand decided to postpone the attack until the following day.[11]

Churchill, whose orders were "to hold out till help arrived or until all dead," immediately applied to Holmes for reinforcements.[12] This anxious request caught Holmes off guard; he had few troops available to augment those at the beleaguered fortress. Churchill therefore had to face the initial onslaught with only those under his command. Outnumbered and bombarded by Porter's gunboats, whose artillery found the Confederate line within easy range, Churchill ordered his defenders to pull back to the rifle pits near the fort.

The Texas cavalry under Samuel Richardson played a crucial part in this retreat. Captain Richardson, operating with the Louisiana cavalry, covered the infantry's withdrawal toward the new position. Shot and shell raked the Texans. W. W. Heartsill, a member of Richardson's company, recalled, "every tree concealed a blue coat. . . . and I for one [was] dangerously scared."[13] This was the first time under fire for many of the Texas horsemen. When Captain Richardson ordered a halt, he asked twenty-three-year-old Private Witt, "Luther wher's your hat?" Luther, who normally served as bugler and was by occupation a painter, answered, "in the brush," and, he sheepishly continued, "Captain I've lost my Pistol too." Richardson, pulling himself up to his full six feet, narrowed his gray eyes and sharply chided: "Uh, you MUST have been in a hurry." To the amusement of all, Witt answered: "Yes, I was trying to KEEP UP with my Captain."[14]

Reinforcements arrived during the night. About 10:00 Alf Johnson and a part of his spy company skillfully eluded the pickets stationed along the Federal line and rode safely into the fort. Churchill quickly placed Johnson in command of all the cavalry, although both men realized that without more help the less than fifty men Johnson brought would be of little use. Heartsill thought Churchill made a grave mistake; Richardson, ranking officer by over six months, should command the cavalry. But Heartsill's devotion to his own captain made him forget that

Johnson had months of experience fighting in Arkansas; Richardson had none.[15]

Believing reinforcements could arrive in time, Holmes ordered nearly all the troops in Arkansas to head toward Fort Hindman. The Texas cavalrymen greeted the news with marked excitement. When Carter's men heard the order, they cheered wildly and began to clean their arms and accoutrements. Parsons's Twelfth Texas, after cooking two days' rations, left for the post by sunset on Saturday evening, and the rest of the brigade followed at daylight the next morning. Captain Martin M. Kenney of Company K, Twenty-first Texas, observed that the troops marched in a line two by two that strung out across the prairie for miles. "A song would be started at the head of the column," he recalled, "generally some old camp meeting hymn which would be taken up all along the line to the rear."[16]

General Holmes, unfortunately, did not share this optimism. Thomas B. Smith, a Texan on his way to Pine Bluff who breakfasted with Holmes early Sunday, recorded in his diary: "The General looks rather more savage this morning than usual."[17] By this time Holmes probably suspected that he could not save the post, but he had no idea that at that moment the Federal army occupied a position in front of Churchill's lines or that McClernand was making final preparations for his assault.

Early Sunday afternoon, as Parsons's cavalrymen rode toward the post, McClernand opened his attack. Porter's gunboats commenced shelling while the infantry launched an assault. On the extreme right of the Federal line was a brigade under the command of Charles E. Hovey, a brigadier general since his promotion after the battle of Cotton Plant. In front of him were three regiments he had faced in that July skirmish, although those Texans no longer had horses.

Two regiments that had once been part of Carter's Lancers were positioned near the fort, manning the right of a line that ran from the fort toward the bayou. The men had never received the promised lances, and their weapons did not compare to those of their Federal counterparts. Troops in the Twenty-fourth relied on the Model 1841 or Mississippi

Rifle, and many in the Twenty-fifth had old flintlocks that the government had hastily converted to percussion fire. Shotguns were still the staple of many Texas troops. Because these weapons would be useless at any distance, Churchill instructed the troops not to fire until the enemy was well within range.[18] F. C. Wilkes, the former Methodist minister who was the colonel of the Twenty-fourth Texas, ordered his men to wait and "shoot at their knees."[19]

The attack began on the Confederate left, so the Twenty-fourth and Twenty-fifth Texas did not feel the initial shock. When called upon to reinforce the line nearest the bayou, half of the companies from each of these two regiments headed for the new position. But the firing had become so fierce that the Texans had to crawl through the trenches on their hands and knees.[20]

The bombardment from Porter's gunboat devastated the Confederate position. Samuel T. Foster of the Twenty-fourth Texas watched the big square logs of the fort fly "about like they were fence rails." Iron flew in every direction.[21] As the cannonade efficiently reduced the fort, fires erupted in the wooden buildings and smoke choked soldiers trying to repel the Federal advance. By midafternoon shells had so damaged the three big guns defending the post that artillerists could not return fire or prevent the gunboats from moving on their flank. Once Porter positioned his boats behind the defenders, the Confederates were caught between the infantry and artillery in their front and the navy in their rear.

To many troops the situation seemed hopeless, and further punishment only delayed the inevitable. Samuel Foster heard someone on his left cry out: "*Hoist the white flag on the fort,—pass the word down the line.*" No one asked "whether it was a legitimate order or not," and no one knew where it had started. Reports said the flag first appeared in Wilkes's Twenty-fourth Texas, and Foster observed: "In a few minutes the Confederate flag is pulled down and a white flag run up on the flag staff in the fort, and white handkerchiefs or shirt tails are hoisted on ramrods and on guns all along the line as far as we can see . . . in a minute everything is as quite as a meeting-house."[22] Someone in the Confederate right occupied by Garland's First Brigade—consisting of the Sixth Texas Infantry, Twenty-fourth and Twenty-fifth Texas (dismounted cavalries), William Hart's battery, and Denson's cavalry—had signaled surrender.

All of the commanders expressed surprise and anger. Furious that the deed had occurred in his brigade, Garland blamed the men in Twenty-fourth Texas. He believed that the "white flag which thus treacherously deceived the rest of the command was raised" by Wilkes's regiment of dismounted cavalry. His own regiment, the Sixth Texas, had "refused to raise the white flag or to pass the word up the line."[23] Colonel James Deshler, commanding the Second Brigade, reported, "knowing that it was General Churchill's determination to fight to desperation, I did not think it possible that a surrender could be intended."[24] Churchill added that after watching the flags appear in the midst of the Twenty-fourth Texas, "I was forced to the humiliating necessity of surrendering the balance of the command."[25]

Churchill had hoped to hold out until help arrived, but the hierarchy had waited too long. By the time Parsons's cavalry reached the Arkansas River on Tuesday, news arrived that the post had surrendered Sunday evening. Henry Orr, whose two brothers were among those captured, bitterly admonished: "The infantry censure Gen. Holmes for not getting [John G.] Walker's Division at the Post before Churchill was compelled to surrender."[26] John Truss firmly believed: "If we could have got there we could have held the post in spite of all their efforts. Our forces was too much scattered."[27]

Though Holmes failed to aid Churchill's troops, not all the Confederates were captured. Many defenders fled from the post before the enemy soldiers cut off all lines of retreat. When Marshall Pierson heard, "We are surrounded!" he immediately shouldered his double-barrel shotgun and began walking toward the bayou on the west side of the fort. Without having a shot fired at him, he continued on until he reached the Confederate lines.[28]

Surrender was such an ignominious end. W. W. Heartsill moaned: "If the Cavalry had been with their horses when the white flag was run up, we could all have escaped; but by the time that our boys reached their horses from the ditches, the Yankee Cavalry was around in our rear."[29] Henry Orr, who later inspected the fortifications where his brothers had fought, concluded: "I have no doubt but half of them could have escaped after the fort was surrendered, but perhaps thought they would be paroled or shortly exchanged."[30]

For those who remained, relinquishing their possessions proved a gloomy task. To cavalrymen, surrender of their cherished mounts was distressing. Many Confederates refused to surrender their sidearms; instead they threw them into the muddy waters of the stagnant bayou as their captors approached.[31]

Upriver, chaos followed the fall of the post. When Thomas Smith arrived near Pine Bluff, he heard that Churchill had surrendered and the army expected Federal cavalry in the city by sundown.[32] Rumors multiplied; travelers just as often swore the fort still held out. Confirmation of the capitulation came from enemy soldiers, prisoners captured by Charles Morgan's men as the hungry Federals foraged the countryside near Porter's fleet.[33]

Confusion gave way to despair, anxious anticipation to uneasiness. The Texas cavalry, camped on the banks of the Arkansas River, waited for Holmes's next order. Martin Kenney remarked: "There were no more songs in our camp after these dismal tidings reached us, the sky was overcast with dark and threatening clouds, and the men prowled gloomily about the glaring camp fires." But they had no time to rest; at midnight orders came for the brigade to move south of the river. Scarcely had one company crossed on the ferry before a storm extinguished all the torches and made further movement impossible. With no shelter near, the men huddled on their horses and waited for daylight. The rain poured in ice-cold torrents, filling their boots and soaking their blankets. The Texans tried to shout and joke, but the rain outlasted even the most resolute; long before daylight all stood freezing and silent. Kenney looked at his men, "the little band of wet and shivering soldiers hovered on the bank, with most of their ammunition wet and their trembling horses standing humped up," and pondered. They seemed a forlorn defense, he mused, "against the countless host of the foe in warm and waterproof clothing and comfortably housed on their iron boats."[34]

Daylight proved no better. The command finally crossed the river, but it rained steadily all day with no chance for anything to dry. Kenney finally found an abandoned house where he took his company for relief from the bitter cold. The men had scarcely built a fire before the bugle sounded "to horse" and then "forward." He recalled: "I do not know when I hated to leave anything as bad as I did that fire, but there was no help for it, the men took it cheerfully enough, they were eating their dinner, but in five minutes we were in ranks again." They moved only a short distance before camping again and finishing their meals. Yet the rain never ceased, and when someone found a cache of whiskey the captains decided to issue it to the freezing men. As Kenney soon realized, however, "there was either a little too much of it, or long abstinence made them susceptible to its influence for when we started you would have thought that we were driving a herd of wild cattle."[35]

The weather frustrated their movement and seemed to taunt the miserable troops. As the whiskey died out it left the men colder than before. The brigade camped on a plantation where the horsemen took shelter in vacant slave dwellings with one company quartered in each cabin. Kenney, with forty men, decided to allow ten inside at once. But, he recalled, "the thirty outside froze faster than the ten inside could thaw and so we passed a miserable night; after dark it turned to a snow and snowed all night and all next day, being near a foot deep."[36] John Truss grumbled as he sat astride his horse: "It was even in my boot tops."[37]

Both infantry and cavalry suffered. When Kenney's men left their little hut at daylight, they passed the infantry and artillery struggling with "a helpless situation in mud knee deep."[38] In the camp of Walker's Texans, known to the infantrymen as "Camp Freeze Out," the soldiers built fortifications of mud, snow, and ice.[39] "There we lay for six or seven days without tents and with but little food," lamented John Simmons of the Twenty-second Texas Infantry, "amid snow eight inches deep, with but one blanket apiece, shivering around our campfires."[40] When the cavalry arrived at Walker's camp, the troops relieved the tired infantry pickets from duty just in time to suffer another downpour which began in the evening and continued all night, turning the snow to slush.

Fortunately, and much to the surprise of everyone, the Army of the

Mississippi retreated. Although the expedition had proved successful, it had angered Grant, who complained to Halleck, "Genl. McClernand has fallen back to White River and gone on a wild goose chase."[41] To McClernand, Grant protested: "I do not approve of your move on the 'Post of Arkansas.' . . . Unless you are acting under authority not derived from me, keep your command where it can soonest be assembled for the renewal of the attack on Vicksburg."[42]

The Federal commanders bitterly attacked each other. McClernand lamented to Lincoln just a fews days after the operation: "My success here is gall and wormwood to the clique of West Pointers who have been persecuting me for months."[43] To Grant, McClernand pointedly penned: "I take the responsibility of the expedition against Post Arkansas, and had anticipated your approval of the complete and signal success which crowned it, rather than your condemnation."[44] But as Admiral Porter pointed out, McClernand "actually had nothing to do with the management of the Army, and was down four miles below the forts during all the operations. Sherman was virtually the military commander."[45]

Ironically, the weather proved an advantage to the Confederate defenders waiting at Pine Bluff for the Federal attack. Although St. Charles, Clarendon, Devall's Bluff, and Des Arc fell to Brigadier General Willis A. Gorman, he could not pursue his advantage. He found the railroad from Devall's Bluff to Little Rock in good running condition, but the low marshy country between the two points was "one vast sheet of water."[46] The snow, melting rapidly, made any advance impossible. And Grant pointedly instructed McClernand, "unless there is some object not visible at this distance your forces should return to Millikin's Bend or some point convenient for operating on Vicksburg."[47]

The race for Arkansas Post had ended. It was, as McClernand insisted, a singular success for the Federal army. United States forces had captured almost five thousand Confederates; around seventy Southerners had died in the fighting and nearly two hundred suffered wounds. Many more rebels would succumb on the vessels transporting them to Northern prison camps as intense cold aggravated their illnesses and injuries.[48]

Although Parsons's brigade had not taken part in the fighting, Charles Morgan eventually gained three companies for his battalion as a result of the post's capitulation. Those men of Johnson's Spy Company and Richardson's Rifles not captured became companies E and I of Morgan's cavalry before the war ended. According to the service records, which are sometimes misleading, forty-seven members of Richardson's company surrendered, but sixty had been operating safely outside the fortification. Heartsill counted over forty men with him on the transport, but the Federals, he believed, did not recognize them as regular soldiers and he feared they would "be treated as Guerrillas" because they were an independent company. Service records for Johnson's Spy Company indicate some forty-seven captured and nearly seventy on detached service. Finally, Company H of the Eighteenth Texas Dismounted Cavalry was not at the post; after the authorities remounted these troops they became Company D of Morgan's cavalry.[49]

Most Confederates in Richardson's Rifles and Johnson's Spy Company captured at the post never returned to the Trans-Mississippi Department. After a brief confinement in Northern prison camps, they were exchanged and assigned to Braxton Bragg's Army of Tennessee as dismounted cavalry. A few fortunate officers returned to Holmes's department, including Captain Richardson. Others, members of the rank and file like W. W. Heartsill, eventually left Bragg's army and headed west without permission. Henry Orr wrote to his sister in June, "A few of Johnson's Spy Company have passed here enroute for their company east of White River; say they were in the battle on Big Black near Vicksburg."[50]

Yet these troops would not rejoin Alf Johnson. This perspicacious Texas scout died within a month of the surrender after becoming ill on the ship transporting the Confederate prisoners upriver. He was among those taken off at St. Louis and died at the City General Hospital of "chronic diarrhea" on February 7.[51] Heartsill, who learned of this in May, recorded in his diary, "by his death the Confederacy has lost one of her best officers—A BRAVE MAN HAS FALLEN."[52] The loss of Johnson and his spy company, which had operated so effectively with

Parsons's men, was a severe blow to the cavalry and would be keenly felt when the spring campaigns opened.

After the capitulation of Arkansas Post, the Texas cavalry remained in the area scouting along the lower Arkansas River. W. P. Zuber noted that Texans were the most important force near the Mississippi River; his regiment, the Twenty-first Texas, occupied a plantation belonging to a man named Jordan. Colonel Carter and his staff made their headquarters on the upper floor of a fine two-story frame mansion while the troops found enough vacant slave cabins for each mess to occupy one. Jordan had sufficient corn in the cribs to feed the entire regiment, including the animals, for several months. "So," observed Zuber, "we were well-housed and cared for."[53]

The Texas cavalry continued to serve as scouts and pickets for the army at Little Rock. Holmes stationed detachments along the state's eastern boundary, but a few scattered units rode into western Arkansas. Although the brigade's headquarters generally remained on the lower Arkansas River, the troops often operated many miles apart.[54]

As Grant siphoned off soldiers from Helena to join his Vicksburg expedition, the Federal cavalry stationed in eastern Arkansas contracted its lines, and the skirmishing so common in late 1862 decreased in frequency. Henry Orr wrote from Judge Thomas H. Fletcher's plantation on the Arkansas River in February: "Our command 'infests' this River for many miles." Yet picket duty proved boring without the challenge of outwitting Federal cavalry, and it became difficult to procure supplies for men away from headquarters. Henry Orr lamented to his sister: "I tell you, I would give a dollar for as many good biscuits as I could devour. I have not seen one in a coon's age."[55]

A major change occurred in the brigade early in 1863. Hawes, who had led the troops for less than two months, resigned; by spring he took command of an infantry brigade in Major General John G. Walker's division.[56] Since Parsons was still in Texas, Carter, by virtue of his seniority, assumed command. Fortunately the three regiments were so scattered the men had little time to contemplate Holmes's decision to place them under the ex-preacher.

As the winter season of rain and mud set in, Grant began various schemes to capture Vicksburg. Although he was preoccupied with this campaign, Arkansas was more vulnerable than ever after the loss of five thousand troops. A more serious problem also plagued the Trans-Mississippi Department: the ease with which the Federal army had swept down on Arkansas Post had potent psychological impact on the Confederates. Hindman's evacuation of northwest Arkansas had spread panic throughout the state, and many demoralized soldiers had deserted on the retreat.[57] Yet the ineffectual Holmes did little to improve the worsening conditions across the state. Moreover, as Grant pressed his bid to capture Vicksburg, the hierarchy at Little Rock tried to concoct schemes to aid the beleaguered Mississippi port.

THE CAPE GIRARDEAU RAID

April 17–May 2, 1863

MISSOURI

Rolla

Ironton

Fredericktown

Old Jackson

Springfield

Patterson

Cape Girardeau

Current River

Black River

Greenville

White

Scale in Miles

0   50

Van Buren

Swamps

Bloomfield

Eleven

Doniphan

Water

Chalk Bluff

Pea Ridge

White

Points

River

River

ARKANSAS

Batesville

St. Francis River

Jacksonport

Arkansas

Fort Smith

River

Mississippi

Little Rock

8.
Off to Missouri

As the situation in Arkansas worsened with Hindman's retreat from Prairie Grove in December 1862 and the surrender of Arkansas Post in January 1863, Confederates felt disheartened. Secretary of War James A. Seddon observed in March that "the most deplorable accounts reach the department of the disorder, confusion, and demoralization everywhere prevalent, both with the armies and people of that State." Holmes, he believed, had "lost the confidence and attachment of all," and the result was "fearful."[1] To improve conditions, Seddon relieved the general and placed Edmund Kirby Smith over the Trans-Mississippi Department; Holmes retained control of the district of Arkansas, including the Indian Territory and Missouri. Both Kirby Smith and Holmes refused to abandon Missouri and in the spring authorized a raid which they hoped would rally support among the Missourians and also feed an army threatened with starvation in Arkansas. Richard Taylor, who oversaw the district of Louisiana, bitterly asserted that Kirby Smith worried too much about "the recovery of his lost empire, to the detriment of the portion yet in his possession." He firmly believed this strategy was a mistake and pointed out that "the substance of Louisiana and Texas was staked against the shadow of Missouri and Northern Arkansas."[2]

Yet in the spring of 1863 the Union Department of the Missouri under Samuel R. Curtis appeared vulnerable. The general-in-chief, Henry W. Halleck, had ordered Curtis to send all available troops to join Grant's Vicksburg expedition and to retain only enough men "sufficient to hold a few important points" against "guerrillas and small detached forces." Curtis had dispatched several regiments and the marine brigade by March,[3] and the time seemed propitious for a Confederate raid. This prospect particularly pleased John S. Marmaduke, who commanded a division of cavalry in northern Arkansas and who frequently expressed concern about the apathy prevailing in the Confederate Congress since the Federal occupation of his native Missouri.

Marmaduke possessed impressive credentials not easily ignored by Richmond. His father, a former governor, had sent him to Yale and Harvard, and the young man had graduated from the United States Military Academy in 1857, thirtieth in a class of thirty-eight. As a member of the regular army he served under Albert Sidney Johnston in Utah; at the beginning of the war he resigned and joined Johnston in the service of the Confederacy. Following Shiloh he returned to the Trans-Mississippi region where he sedulously promoted Confederate support for Missouri.[4]

Marmaduke firmly believed that as long as the Confederacy demonstrated its concern for Missouri, its citizens with Southern sympathies would remain supportive. Convinced of the loyalty of his fellow Missourians, Marmaduke had led a raid into southwest Missouri after Christmas. While Federal gunboats steamed toward Arkansas Post early in January, his column of over two thousand cavalrymen rode across the Missouri border. The day the Federals assaulted Fort Hindman, Marmaduke attacked Springfield. His small raiding party could not hope to hold any territory, however, and he quickly retreated to Arkansas. Still, he judged his foray a success because "the heart of the people revived again at the presence of Confederate troops."[5]

Marmaduke's reception in Missouri encouraged him to outline a proposal for another invasion. His correspondence revealing his plan to Holmes has been lost, but Holmes's reply suggests much about Marmaduke's idea. "Your plan is a bold one," pronounced Holmes, "though I think you miscalculated the status of the Missouri people. I fear and believe they are thoroughly cowed, and now occupy that unenviable position that nothing short of an overwhelming force would induce them to raise a hand against their oppressors."[6]

Undiscouraged, Marmaduke continued to push for support. By late February Holmes wrote: "I have considered your proposition relative to Missouri very carefully, and with an earnest desire to foster the plan." But he correctly cautioned Marmaduke that without infantry to sustain him, Marmaduke could do nothing more than raid and return, leaving

Southern sympathizers to the wrath of the Union army. "It is expecting too much of weak human nature to suppose that they will sacrifice all, unless we can give them at least a reasonable show of permanent protection," warned Holmes. "Without this, though they would sympathize with us in their hearts, they would raise no hand to help us. . . . Consider this, and tell me what you think."[7]

Marmaduke nevertheless insisted the raid had every chance of success. In March Holmes told him that it was "certainly very tempting" and much to Marmaduke's pleasure invited the Missourian to "come down for a few days, in order that we may have a full conference."[8] At the same time Holmes obliquely suggested to Jefferson Davis that a move into Missouri might be necessary to provision his army.[9] Holmes also used this argument when proposing the raid to Kirby Smith, who arrived at Shreveport early in the month, and added that the scheme might relieve Vicksburg by forcing Grant to withdraw troops from his river expedition.

Marmaduke was elated when he finally received permission to implement his plan. The first step was to decide which troops Holmes could spare without endangering his district. Naturally Marmaduke desired as many men as possible, for he planned to sweep across the southeastern corner of the state destroying everything vital to the Union. There was no question that the major part of the force would consist of the Missouri brigades under Joseph Shelby, John Burbridge, and Colton Greene. But since Grant, concentrating on means to subdue Vicksburg, did not pose an immediate threat to lower Arkansas, Holmes decided he could release part of the Texas cavalry. All of Parsons's troops would accompany Marmaduke except those in the Twelfth Texas, which continued to scout along the Mississippi River.[10]

Since the surrender of Arkansas Post, the Texans had monitored movements up and down the river. But scouting had become monotonous; only Pratt's battery did any damage by occasionally firing on transports and gunboats. Henry Orr noted in February that two gunboats and four transports had landed troops in an attempt to capture Pratt as he was "playing along the River"; rumors credited him with sinking one Union vessel and crippling another.[11] In fact, when Pratt and his men left to join Marmaduke, Henry Orr recalled: "The ladies, feeling that Capt. Pratt ought to be remunerated for his valiant services, presented him with an embroidered night cap done up in style." The women, Orr continued, "put it in a large envelope and addressed it to Col. Parsons. Wonder if he sleeps with it on."[12]

Colonel Parsons again commanded the Texas brigade. After returning to Arkansas early in February he had superceded Carter, who took a detachment on special service. Parsons "is in fine spirits," observed Henry Orr, and "boasts of Magruder's exploit" of recapturing Galveston on New Year's Day.[13] The Pine Bluff *Southern*, commenting on Parsons's arrival, erroneously reported his elevation to the rank of brigadier general, "a promotion which he has so thoroughly merited for months past, having 'won his spurs' often and repeatedly, Arkansas owes him a deep debt of gratitude, and we are proud to acknowledge it."[14] Yet once more this proved a rumor, and a Texan bitterly charged: "The Dynasty here, while it holds our gallant and energetic Col. under law, and gives his acts no credit, and his reports no credence, has placed him in command of the outposts of Lower Arkansas, to protect single-handed and alone, the richest and of course the most productive valley of the South."[15]

The seniority dispute between Parsons and Carter probably influenced Holmes not to recommend either for promotion, and it may have prompted the general to order Carter—with the Nineteenth and Twenty-first Texas, Morgan's men, and a section of Pratt's artillery—to join Marmaduke. The command became known as Carter's brigade, an unforeseen development that probably irritated Parsons.[16]

The actual number of Texans with Carter is difficult to determine. A member of the Twenty-first Texas, who wrote to the editor of the Galveston paper soon after his arrival at Marmaduke's camp, claimed that his regiment alone numbered 719 healthy men. Although records do not indicate how many men Carter commanded at the beginning of the raid, a few days after it ended he reported 1,703 on paper. But he indicated only 79 officers and 866 men actually present for duty.[17]

Carter's proficiency as a brigade commander had not significantly improved since his inauguration as colonel of the troublesome Texas Lancers. In late March Thomas B. Smith recorded in his diary that he had seen the force at Pine Bluff en route to rendezvous with Marmaduke: "Col. Carter's Cav. cross the river today. I never saw men more lively than they are today. Hundreds of them drunk."[18]

This negligent control Carter demonstrated over his Texas troops would cause serious problems soon after the march north began. Colton Greene, commanding a Missouri brigade, later complained: "I regret to be compelled to report that the Texas troops have taken 800 bushels of corn and 2,000 bundles of fodder brought for my command. This practice must be stopped," he snapped, "or it will result in bad feelings and conflict between the troops." Greene quite judiciously exonerated Colonel Carter, a politic move since he would be placed under the Texan's command. "I have taken no notice of this offense," he equivocated, "believing that Colonel Carter was ignorant of the matter, and would not tolerate the practice."[19] It is unlikely that Morgan or Pratt allowed pilfering. It is even doubtful that the Nineteenth Texas had taken part, as Colonel Burford was in Dallas on furlough and the regiment was under the capable command of Lieutenant Colonel Benjamin Watson.[20]

A member of Parsons's Twelfth Texas succinctly diagnosed Carter's deficiencies in a letter addressed to the Houston *Telegraph*. Quoting a correspondent of the St. Louis *Republican*, the writer named the three brigades of Missourians and Arkansans, then added, "and *one of Texans, commanded by no one, but going it loose*." To clarify this he mockingly explained: "That means 'sloushing about.' That I will add was Carter's and Burford's Regiment, Col. Carter is the ranking Colonel."[21]

The troops that gathered in Arkansas under Marmaduke were an assorted lot. Although numbering over five thousand men, only a few more than four thousand carried arms, and many had no horses. Marmaduke reasoned that to leave behind the dismounted or unarmed would demoralize them and they might simply desert. Also, if the raid proceeded as planned, the Confederacy would mount and arm the men at the expense of Lincoln's government. Private William Zuber of the Twenty-first Texas recalled that he almost had to remain in Arkansas because his mount had given out, but an enterprising officer unhitched a "splendid" mule from one of the regimental supply wagons and presented Zuber the somewhat unmanageable animal to ride. "So," reflected Zuber, "I was to go to Missouri."[22]

When the force rendezvoused south of the Missouri border on Eleven Points River, William Zuber first viewed the man who would lead the expedition. Marmaduke, he observed, possessed a "singular appearance." He knew of Marmaduke's reputation as an "excellent raider" and was taken aback by the man he saw riding through the camps: a drab figure with yellow hair and a yellow complexion who "wore a yellow cap, a yellow coat, and a yellow vest and pants; he rode a yellowish bay or sorrel horse."[23] Yet in spite of his lackluster appearance, stories circulated through the camps about Marmaduke's gallant escape from Missouri in January, and few questioned his skill.

Marmaduke's plan was simple. After deciding that his initial proposal to move toward Rolla was impractical because forage was scarce, he settled upon an alternate route. He would march toward Patterson, capture the outpost of about six hundred militia, then head toward Bloomfield, east of the Mingo Swamps above Chalk Bluff, and strike John McNeil, who commanded some two thousand regulars.[24]

From the beginning Marmaduke faced serious problems. The Federals had destroyed all available forage and supplies north of Arkansas to prevent such a raid. Marmaduke had to divide his army into two columns and send them in different directions in order to find sufficient provisions. One under Shelby marched via Van Buren, the other under Carter traveled through Doniphan; both were to converge on Patterson the same day. From there one route to Bloomfield lay through the Mingo Swamps, which after heavy rains became almost impassable for the supply wagons and artillery. Marmaduke's failure to allow for the weather or to reconnoiter the swamps was a grave miscalculation.[25] Holmes, fearing the consequences if the raid miscarried, had cautioned Marmaduke in February to "please remember that you are intrusted with the entire defense of the northern frontier, and any disaster to you would be ruinous to us."[26]

As the two columns left for Missouri, however, none of these concerns troubled the troops. Shelby led his brigade and Burbridge's toward Van Buren while Carter, with his Texans and Colton Greene's Missourians, followed the shorter route toward Patterson through Doniphan. The Southerners' first objective was to destroy the garrison at Patterson before assaulting the one at Bloomfield.

In their first meeting with the enemy outposts stationed near Patterson, the Texans demonstrated their lack of adequate training and preparation. About midnight on Sunday, April 19, some thirty miles from the town, Carter detached Lieutenant Colonel D. C. Giddings with the Twenty-first Texas, Timothy Reves's company, and two pieces of Pratt's artillery to surprise the Federals at daybreak. About twelve miles from his destination Giddings successfully captured the pickets (one lieutenant and twenty-four men), but with little experience in combat he did not know how to attack correctly. He ordered Pratt to commence firing too soon, alarming Colonel Edwin Smart in the town and allowing him to order the Union stores set aflame while he and his men escaped.[27]

Giddings's impetuosity raised sharp criticism. John N. Edwards, adjutant of the Fifth Missouri Cavalry who wrote most of Shelby's battle reports, caustically observed: "Giddings, with a singularity of conduct not often developed in officers during active service, met Smart's pickets advantageously posted and full of fight. Not being as *smart* as Smart, he formed an elaborate line of battle, threw forward skirmishers, and actually *opened a vigorous fire with his artillery upon a dozen or so outlying videttes.*" Blaming the Texan for allowing Smart to flee, Edwards further reported that Charley Rainwater, a member of Marmaduke's staff who accompanied Giddings, had "remarked to him quietly, after all this absurdity: 'This is not the way *we* fight.'"[28] Marmaduke, however, simply commented that Giddings had "moved too slowly; did not take sufficient risk for the nature of his expedition, and allowed his artillery to open when within 2 miles of the fort," giving Smart enough warning to abandon his position and retreat toward Pilot Knob.[29]

In Patterson, chaos followed the Federals' evacuation. Many of the houses caught fire, and the Texans riding into the town added to the confusion and disorder. "The grocery stores—dry goods stores and all other places of business were raided," recalled Lieutenant Buck Walton. Nevertheless, Walton proudly emphasized, "the discipline I had given my men was apparent—not one had dismounted—had none of the spoil but sit their horses like soldiers." When ordered to pursue the fleeing Federals, the Confederates could not locate their companies and "all started on, pell mell, a veritable mob." [30]

Yet somehow the unruly force headed after Smart's cavalry. "I pushed to the front with my men," bragged Walton, while Colonel Giddings "rode every where through the men trying to restore order." [31] Marmaduke, who had criticized Giddings's approach to the town, now praised the Texan: "Colonel Giddings pursued them vigorously for 7 miles, killing, wounding, and capturing a number." [32]

When Carter's column united with Shelby's—which had been demonstrating around Thomasville and Houston—Marmaduke paused to reconsider his strategy. He ordered the two divisions to separate again, Carter to march southeast against McNeil at Bloomfield and Shelby to move north on Fredericktown to cut off any withdrawal McNeil might try to make in that direction. McNeil did indeed head down the road toward Fredericktown, but after encountering enemy videttes he halted and resolved to concentrate his force at Cape Girardeau, the important supply depot on the Mississippi River. [33]

Colonel Carter, who was supposed to prevent such a consolidation, instead experienced serious difficulties in moving his column. As the Twenty-first Texas, joined by the Nineteenth Texas and Greene's Missouri brigade, headed toward Bloomfield, heavy rains impeded their movement. Flooding on the St. Francis River, which they had to cross, had swept away boats normally used for ferries. After finally fording the river, Carter faced the boggy lowlands of the Mingo Swamps. Some thirty miles from Bloomfield, Carter decided to detach his supply train rather than burden the column with wagons. Simply moving Pratt's four artillery pieces kept the colonel constantly concerned, and the horses, worn down by the long march from Arkansas and a lack of forage, made any prospect of a forced march impractical. With the high water, marshes, and bad roads, Carter was unable to stop McNeil's retreat into Cape Girardeau.

Only a small detachment of Confederates skirmished with McNeil's forces. Near the bridge over the White Water, some Texans charged a Federal party of about forty under Captain S. V. Shipman of Company E, First Wisconsin Cavalry. After spirited firing, the Confederates counted six Federals killed, six wounded, and ten prisoners (who were immediately paroled).[34]

Subsequent movements were confused and unclear. Some Missourians along on the raid claimed that the invasion miscarried because Colonel Carter disregarded Marmaduke's orders, though neither Marmaduke nor Carter mention these non-extant orders in their official reports. Shelby's adjutant, John N. Edwards, insisted that they read: "Under no circumstances was Colonel Carter to pursue McNeil" if he moved toward New Madrid or Cape Girardeau, but should "return at once to Fredericktown if such intention was developed by McNeil."[35] But other participants thought Marmaduke had a different strategy. William Zuber of the Twenty-first Texas believed that Carter's and Greene's brigades (along with Timothy Reves's company) had orders from the general to move "immediately" toward Cape Girardeau. There, he asserted, Shelby would join the column for a combined assault on McNeil's position.[36]

Nevertheless, Carter followed McNeil to Cape Girardeau, and outside the town he tried some bold if unusual tactics. About ten o'clock Saturday night, Federal pickets reported that an odd-looking group of men bearing a flag of truce had arrived at their post. Lieutenant Colonel Benjamin Watson, along with three majors, two captains, and a small escort party, had brought a letter to the Federal commander. Zuber provided an amusing description of this entourage. He insisted that Colonel Carter, who had lived in Texas for scarcely a year, had become "fanciful." Zuber wrote: "He caused his ten messengers to go wrapped in striped Texas homemade blankets and to wear broad-brimmed hats." This dress, observed Zuber, "gave them the appearance of West Texas cowboys and was probably aimed to inspire the Federals with awe."[37]

But McNeil never had the opportunity to become intimidated; his pickets did not allow the Texans within three miles of town.[38] Carter's letter, however, was delivered to McNeil. Since it subsequently caused problems for the Confederate prisoners-of-war, the correspondence deserves attention. It read in part:

> Sir: By order of Maj. Gen. Sterling Price, commanding, I formally demand of you the immediate surrender, unconditionally, of the troops in Cape Girardeau and the adjoining forts, together with all the ammunition, stores, and other property belonging to the United States in the same. If the surrender is made, I pledge myself to treat the troops as prisoners of war, and to parole and exchange them as soon as practicable. I shall scrupulously protect private property. No difference will be made in this particular between parties, whether Union or Southern sentiment. One-half hour is allowed for your decision.[39]

Colonel William R. Strachan, acting for McNeil, requested Watson to tell Carter he must credit General McNeil with twenty-nine minutes, as one was sufficient for reply," and he wrote that the general declined to surrender Cape Girardeau as McNeil believed "himself able to maintain its possession."[40]

Yet the cocky Southerners had nothing to lose by trying to bluff McNeil. As soon as Marmaduke learned that Carter had pursued McNeil into Cape Girardeau he headed Shelby's column toward the river port. Upon arriving from Fredericktown, Marmaduke attempted to cajole McNeil into surrendering by the same means Carter had employed. Sending a party to the town bearing another flag of truce, Marmaduke reiterated Carter's demand then added an empty warning, "I deem it an easy task to storm and capture the town. . . . In case the demand is not immediately complied with, I request that you will inform all non-combatants in the town to provide for their safety, as I will immediately proceed to attack your position and storm the works." McNeil, however, angered with the brazen Confederates, refused to order a cease-fire as the party bearing the white flag approached. Major Henry Ewing, who led the Confederates, complained, but McNeil retorted "he was not engaged just then in exchanging compliments or cultivating the amenities of war." Moreover, he bellowed: "The rebels had his answer last night, and further discussion was superfluous." Although incensed with his reception, Ewing could not change McNeil's mind and quickly retired "amid the thunder of artillery and the sharp rattle of musketry." After this final demand, McNeil observed of Marmaduke, "he never saw such impudence in a white man."[41]

With this abrupt refusal Marmaduke ordered a demonstration by Shelby's brigade, whose troops knew and hated McNeil for his alleged atrocities against Southern sympathizers. They became so excited that Marmaduke reported the "demonstration amounted almost to an attack."[42] Adjutant Edwards claimed that Shelby was only to feint an assault on Cape Girardeau in order for Carter to withdraw his men from their "perilous position."[43] But William Zuber insisted that Shelby disobeyed instructions. Marmaduke, according to Zuber, was surprised at the intensity of the action and inquired, "Colonel Shelby! What are you doing?" Shelby answered: "Making a slight demonstration, sir."[44]

Marmaduke realized his situation was rapidly becoming untenable. McNeil had received reinforcements by water; at the same time artillery and infantry under Frank Vandever marched toward the port from Fredericktown. Sandwiched between the two forces which could attack him simultaneously, Marmaduke began to retire toward Jackson where he would turn south for Arkansas.[45]

The retreating Confederates were angry and frustrated, especially Missouri troops whose hatred for McNeil made withdrawal particularly abrasive. Someone had to take the blame; for many the finger pointed at the inexperienced Carter. Even Marmaduke may have privately subscribed to this belief, and he possibly shared his feelings with close staff members who later recorded their recollections. Marmaduke's official report did not mention Carter's actions, although a hint of disapproval might be construed from a letter Carter wrote to Henry Ewing. He reported that as the force began its retreat toward Jackson, Marmaduke had removed him from command over the column and returned him to his own brigade.[46]

John C. Moore, who served as chief of staff for both Marmaduke and Shelby, blamed the ultimate failure of the expedition upon the Texas colonel who he said "solicited and obtained command of the force." Further, he added: "Colonel Carter was a new man—an accomplished gentleman, but an untrained soldier—and was anxious for an opportunity to distinguish himself, and Marmaduke was disposed to oblige him." Rather unfairly he placed all the responsibility upon Carter and judged: "Carter blundered and the expedition miscarried."[47] But Carter's troops, considered unseasoned by the Missouri and Arkansas veterans, proved an asset. "The men of this brigade were not experienced, but they had grit, endurance and courage," penned Bennett H. Young in his version of the raid, "and they were not long in measuring up to the standard of veterans."[48]

Both Moore and Young later wrote detailed accounts of the affair. Moore in an article for *Confederate Military History* insisted Marmaduke had instructed Carter to join him near Fredericktown, but instead the Texan had pursued McNeil, "becoming excited in the chase." This move placed McNeil "inside the fortifications with a largely increased force, and Carter outside and unable to get away." Moore further insisted that this mistake compelled Marmaduke to change his strategy in order to "extricate Carter from his dangerous position," and the raiding party "lost four days by Carter's escapade."[49] Young, author of *Confederate Wizards of the Saddle*, drew a similar conclusion but added that this unfortunate predicament forced Marmaduke to send Shelby to rescue Carter from his "embarrassing situation." In a highly biased account Young claimed: "These four days lost meant much to General Marmaduke." He believed that the "exuberant zeal of one of Carter's colonels, coupled with his courage, had changed the Confederate plan and destroyed its successful accomplishment, and seriously affected the ultimate safety of Marmaduke's whole division."[50]

Yet historian Stephen Oates in *Confederate Cavalry West of the River* placed the responsibility on Marmaduke, whom he insisted had planned to attack Cape Girardeau all along. Oates found fault with Marmaduke rather than Carter. Poor planning prior to the raid, coupled with rain and poor road conditions, could not be blamed on Colonel Carter's lack of military experience. Marmaduke should have known that he could never take Cape Girardeau by siege; if his hit-and-run raid could not reach Cape Girardeau before McNeil, then his mission had failed.[51]

Nevertheless, many wounded Confederates who remained behind believed Carter had mismanaged the affair. "In those days of intense bitterness and malignity," wrote Bennett Young, being left in Missouri "was barely preferable to death."[52] Assistant Surgeon S. S. Harris volunteered to stay to succor the injured. He requested McNeil allow him to establish a hospital near Cape Girardeau where he could take the wounded. But McNeil refused; instead he ordered the captives moved along with the column following the retreating Southerners. McNeil promised that he would send Harris and his charges through the lines to Marmaduke as soon as possible, but he changed his mind. Irritated when the Confederate force escaped, McNeil appeared to vent his frustration on the sick and wounded. He returned all to Cape Girardeau and held them pending negotiations. According to Surgeon Harris, McNeil's reasoning was that Carter had demanded surrender in the name of General Price and therefore the men McNeil held belonged to that army. Believing Price to be at Little Rock, he decided to convey the prisoners to Helena for exchange. Harris did not reach the Confederate lines until over two weeks after the raid had ended.[53]

If Carter himself was under fire, at least his Texas troops distinguished themselves. By Marmaduke's orders, Carter's brigade and Shelby's shared rear-guard duty as the column moved from Jackson toward Bloomfield. Charles Morgan, recalled William Zuber, had requested to occupy the extreme rear in order "that he might be first to meet the enemy."[54] Skirmishing erupted as the Texans neared the White Water bridge; the troops charged a detachment of Vandever's force pursuing them. Carter reported that his men captured eighteen Yankees, including one captain.[55] A Federal account verified that Vandever had engaged the Confederates "and that part of one company of the third Iowa had been gobbled up by them."[56] Following this encounter Carter ordered the bridge demolished. When the Federals arrived in force they captured two Texans who had volunteered to remain behind and complete the destruction.[57]

The Confederate loss at the White Water bridge was light, although the Texas troops had several horses killed and at least four men captured. Perhaps it was Sergeant Atlas C. Norwood of Morgan's squadron, captured on that day, who confided to the Yankees, "if they had come up ten minutes sooner they could have had the rear-guard of some of fifty men, who destroyed the bridge, and had just disappeared."[58] McNeil ordered his men to rebuild the structure, and the column pressed on.

"They followed us," recalled Lieutenant Walton, "at a rapid rate. . . . Their horses were fresh—and ours weary."[59] A lame Missourian standing in his front yard yelled to the passing column: "We're glad to see you. You're the first Confederate soldiers we've seen in two years." But Private Zuber had sadly answered, "the Feds are driving us out. Every time we halt, their front fires upon our rear. They'll fire in five minutes."[60] Lieutenant Charles Dow of the First Iowa Cavalry wrote that the Confederates "would make a stand on the crest of every hill, (and it was a very rough country on either side of the road, which was on a ridge,) but our carbines and little bulldog [howitzer] always drove them [off]."[61]

Confusion prevailed on both sides. At one point McNeil ordered the Third Missouri Cavalry to silence the Confederate batteries which constantly annoyed the Federal position. As the enemy approached, Pratt's artillerymen opened a destructive fire with grape, driving the Federals back in disorder. Taking advantage of the temporary chaos, detachments of Texans under John B. Williams, Charles Morgan, and Martin M. Kenney charged. McNeil made a vain effort to hurry reinforcements and bring up his artillery, but he was unsuccessful.[62]

Lieutenant Dow of the First Iowa related one interesting story that may have referred to a Texan in Carter's command. "One cuss rode out of the rebel lines with a white flag or rag on his ramrod," wrote Dow, "but in the other [he held] a double-barreled shot-gun at an advance; the firing did not cease on their side." But, Dow observed, "you can't catch the First Iowa on a flag of truce more than once, especially with the bearer carrying a shot-gun and the enemy continuing to fire." His men recognized the ploy, "which was to gain time and so escape with their guns." As soon as the audacious Confederate left his cover "the bullets whistled round him like hail. He wheeled, fired both barrels of his gun at us, and vamosed."[63]

For the invaders a swift retreat became essential. "In those days it was easy enough to get into Missouri," wrote Bennett Young, "but sometimes it was extremely difficult to get out."[64] The floodwaters of the St. Francis posed a real obstacle to the Confederate army. Marmaduke ordered details of unarmed and noneffective troops in advance of the main column to construct a temporary bridge over the river. The water was turbulent because of the heavy rains, and the hastily constructed structure of huge logs was more like a raft that rose up and down in the swift water. In spite of the bridge's ominous appearance, however, it held until Carter's Texans, still the rear guard, crossed to the Arkansas bank. The cavalry dismounted and walked while the animals, pushed into the river, had to swim. As soon as Marmaduke believed the command safely on the Arkansas side, he ordered the bridge cut loose.[65]

But in his haste to escape, Marmaduke had failed to account for all of his troops; many Texans were still in Missouri. Lieutenant Walton, with about two hundred fifty men, had been guarding a road to prevent the Federals from flanking the retreating column. At daylight he and his men returned to join the main force; Walton recalled: "what was our surprise not to see a Confederate any where. The army had disappeared as completely as if it had been swallowed up by the earth—but there was a great activity to the north." Shot and shell quickly broke the oppressive silence as Walton discerned: "The enemy was getting ready to advance." Then astonishment turned to anger. "That was a pretty to do," snapped Walton. "We had been forgotten. . . . I was mad and mortified . . . but it was no time to waste in regrets or madness."[66]

Remaining on the Missouri bank meant certain capture or death, so the Texans raced for the makeshift log crossing. "Just as we got in sight of the bridge," recalled Walton, "we saw it swinging from the North bank slowly but surely to midstream, and thence to the southern bank." Walton's heart sunk as the structure broke loose and floated downstream. Incredulous, Walton exploded with anger: "We looked with astonishment, with fear and regret, as we saw the bridge settle down." As the Federals came into view, Walton yelled, "follow me—I am going to swim the river." With that he spurred his horse into the swirling current, swung from the saddle, grasped his animal's mane, and prayed. Other Texans grabbed their frightened horses by the tails, but all miraculously crossed even though bullets peppered the water. "We were safe," sighed Walton, though "wet as drowned rats" and "mighty badly scared."[67]

Furious, Walton headed straight for Marmaduke's headquarters. Yet the commander only laughed, "actually laughed—it was amusing" complained Walton, "but I felt that laugh for a long time." Instead of allowing Walton's weary men to rest, Marmaduke ordered them to dry their clothes, eat, and return to duty at the river to prevent McNeil from crossing.[68]

McNeil, however, had no intention of pursuing Marmaduke into Arkansas. Many critics charged he purposely avoided catching up with the cornered Confederates and intentionally allowed them to escape. Whatever his motives, the chase ended at the St. Francis, where the exhausted Federals camped on the Missouri side. On the riverbank Union pickets played cards and dice, unaware that any Southerners remained in the area.[69]

Marmaduke still feared McNeil might pursue his fleeing army, so he ordered some of his men to return to the riverbank and fire on the soldiers relaxing on the other side. As the quiet and tranquillity along the St. Francis burst into gunfire, Federal pickets scattered behind trees, stumps, or logs. In retaliation, McNeil ordered the artillery to open up on the concealed sharpshooters. The cannonade lasted two hours, until McNeil believed the enemy had retired.[70]

Feeling more secure in their position, the Southerners began to play with the enemy across the river. After the firing ceased, Walton returned to the top of the ridge to observe the damage and saw several Federal officers riding on the opposite side doing the same thing. Because they provided an easy mark, Walton motioned for about six men to hurry up the bank before his targets rode away. Walton had no idea who they were when he ordered his Texans to fire. But a St. Louis newspaper reported: "a sharp engagement ensued between McNeil on this side and the rebels on the other side, in which General McNeil and his aide Lieutenant Ankony, volunteer, both had their horses shot from under them. A terrific artillery fire served as a *de joie* for the final safety of the rebel force."[71] Back in camp Marmaduke continued to chide Walton: "Why Lieutenant, you kicked up a mighty fuss back at the river . . . if I had known you were going to have that much *fun*, I would have gone with you." Walton sarcastically added: "I forgot to say, that my men were so greatly worn, tired and sleepy, that many of them went sound to sleep, and slept all the time of the cannonade."[72]

One interesting anecdote came out of the foray into Missouri. Unfortunately, because of the completely disorganized nature of the raid, it is impossible to ascertain if this incident actually occurred. William H. Getzendaner, a member of the Twelfth Texas and after the war chairman of the executive committee of Parsons' Brigade Association, claimed that Watson successfully fought a duel, "using side-arms against a Union colonel in front of the troops of their opposed cavalry regiments. The Northern forces retired from the field when their commander fell."[73] Although this could have occurred, there is no record other than Getzendaner's word; as a member of the Twelfth Texas he had not participated in the raid.

Several Texans earned recognition. General Marmaduke "has taken a great fancy to the 'Texas boys,'" reported a member of the Twenty-first Texas, and Carter "has proven himself a General, wherever the battle rages hotest there he is directing and encouraging his men." Both Giddings and Watson drew compliments for their "coolness and skill" in combat. But John B. Williams, when praised for the manner his squadron had received and repulsed an enemy charge, said, "why sir I done less than any man I had."[74]

Not all Texans had performed this courageously. Soon after the expedition returned to Arkansas, Watson threatened to prefer charges of incompetence and cowardice against Frank G. Lemmon, a captain in Morgan's squadron. Fortunately Lemmon tendered his resignation, claiming that he was overage, needed at home, and wounded in the hand. Watson quipped: "the service will be greatly benefitted by its acceptance." James N. Scott replaced the dishonored Lemmon as captain of the company.[75]

Major B. D. Chenoweth of the Twenty-first Texas proudly wrote his sister that the raid had been a great success and "equal to anything that Marmaduke or Forrest have ever done."[76] Other evaluations, however, have been less enthusiastic. "In terms of strategic objectives, concluded Stephen Oates, "Marmaduke's second Missouri raid was a complete failure."[77] Marmaduke had hoped Missourians would rise and join him, but only about one hundred fifty new recruits took the place of the thirty killed, sixty wounded, and one hundred twenty reported missing. The Confederates had not destroyed the Federal supply depot nor had Marmaduke remained in the state long enough to draw troops from Grant's expedition. Instead of a hit-and-run raid, as he should have done with cavalry, Marmaduke had bogged down with supply wagons and had attempted a siege, a fundamental mistake for mounted troops. Kirby Smith reported that the objective of the expedition had been to relieve Arkansas from the necessity of supplying forage for the army. Even this failed, for the men and animals returned to Arkansas tired, jaded, and as hungry as when they left two weeks before.

Worse yet, Marmaduke's raid was overshadowed by a Union effort. On April 17 Federal Colonel Benjamin H. Grierson had left Memphis with seventeen hundred men and cut a sweeping path six hundred miles long that ended in Baton Rouge sixteen days later, on May 2. While Marmaduke's ill-fated raid ended in near-disaster, Grierson's was "the first long-range expedition by the Union cavalry into enemy territory."[78] Suddenly the Confederate cavalry no longer held a monopoly in the west and, as Grant observed, Grierson "has spread excitement throughout the State, destroying railroads, trestleworks, bridges, burning locomotives and railway stock, taking prisoners, and destroying stores of all kinds. To use the expression of my informant, 'Grierson has nocked the heart out of the State.'" It was quite a feat for a raid whose main objective had been to divert Confederate attention from Grant crossing the Mississippi south of Vicksburg.[79]

Events west of the river began to move at a rapid rate. Kirby Smith, the department commander, faced serious problems in northern Louisiana and could not dwell long on the failure of the expedition into Missouri. In fact, as Southerners began to plant their spring crops, news about the campaign against Vicksburg took priority over events in the East. If that city fell to Grant, the people across the Mississippi would be cut off from the rest of the Confederacy.

LOUISIANA

9.
"To Strike a Blow for Vicksburg"

I n June 1863 Theophilus H. Holmes in Arkansas received instructions from Edmund Kirby Smith, commander of the Trans-Mississippi Department, to operate "a cavalry force, at least a brigade, on the Mississippi River, as low down as Lake Providence." Kirby Smith believed the situation in Louisiana required immediate action by all his district commanders. "There are many plantations on the river being cultivated by the negroes for the Federals," he added. "All such should be destroyed and the negroes captured."[1] Although this meant Holmes's troops would go into Richard Taylor's district, cooperation was vital if the Confederacy hoped to alleviate the situation at Vicksburg. Holmes immediately dispatched Colonel Parsons; for the next few months the Texans would scout in the bayous of northern Louisiana.[2]

Soon after Kirby Smith had assumed command of the department he began concentrating available troops to reinforce Taylor. John Bankhead Magruder, in command of the District of Texas, reported he had forwarded 4,694 men toward Alexandria, where the Confederates had retreated in May.[3] From Arkansas Holmes sent John G. Walker's Texas Infantry Division to support Taylor.[4] Neither, however, arrived in time to prevent a Federal movement toward the city. Fortunately, after occupying Alexandria, Nathaniel P. Banks, commander of the Federal Department of the Gulf, halted his army. Urged by Ulysses S. Grant to take part in a joint campaign against Vicksburg and Port Hudson, Banks began to concentrate his army outside the Confederate stronghold on the lower Mississippi River.

With Banks outside Port Hudson and Grant threatening Vicksburg, Taylor had reason to worry. In an attempt to aid the Confederates opposing Grant, Walker's division attacked Milliken's Bend and Young's Point, both Federal supply depots on the Mississippi early in June. But these actions failed to bring any relief to the besieged city. Taylor considered transferring Walker's infantry south of the Red River to assist the Confederates around Port Hudson, but he decided instead to hold the force in northeastern Louisiana until the events at Vicksburg were "more fully developed." Walker's command was to raid plantations operated by the Federal government, destroy their crops, and capture former slaves.[5]

Holmes detailed Parsons's brigade to join Walker. Colonel Parsons had instructions to march his Twelfth Texas to Louisiana at once, while the remainder of the force would follow as soon as possible. In reality there was no such organization as Parsons's brigade, for the colonel had not seen most of his men since Carter left for Missouri with them several weeks before. Carter, operating near Helena, now believed he had permanent command of those troops under him and even suggested to Holmes that he could cross the Mississippi at Memphis and operate in Tennessee.[6] Holmes probably decided to explain the serious situation in person; he directed Carter to proceed to Pine Bluff, where the colonel would receive "special instructions."[7]

Carter's command had not been idle since returning from Missouri. Camped on Crowley's Ridge in northeast Arkansas, the force had repulsed a Union advance between the White and St. Francis rivers in early May. During the engagement at Taylor's Creek, a tributary of the L'Anguille River, on May 11 and 12, Carter performed ineptly and handled the troops poorly. According to W. P. Zuber, the colonel realized his blunder and later admitted, "through my error, we have let them escape."[8] Lieutenant Buck Walton agreed: "Our men had whipped the fight, and I was at a loss to know why they did not follow the enemy to & across the Languille River—and even farther, but I never got a satisfactory explanation, save the very unsatisfactory one—that our men were so cut up—they were not in condition to pursue."[9]

The men under Carter were rapidly becoming frustrated with their commander. Carter informed headquarters: "A good deal of dissatisfaction, verging on mutiny, has manifested itself in the brigade. . . . From what I can learn, it is avowedly caused by my personal interferences with the men and companies." Yet he added: "I believe other causes are operating, but will not state them till better informed."[10] Lieutenant

Walton elucidated: "The men, being rested got mischievious, and a great many complaints were brought in of hogs disappearing. Chickens & turkeys came up missing—wagons robbed—potatoe fields invaded—& other depredations." When Carter ordered public flogging of the perpetrators, the "men refused to drill—or to do duty of any kind. It got to be a serious matter," recalled Walton, "and threatened dissolution of the Regiment." Carter had to apologize to the troops before they agreed to remain under his command.[11]

Texans serving with Parsons along the Arkansas River south of Little Rock heard rumors of the strife. Lieutenant George W. Ingram of the Twelfth Texas informed his wife that Carter's men seemed "very much dissatisfied" with him and "petitioned Gen. Holmes to send Col. Parsons over there to take command of them."[12] Henry Orr penned an almost identical statement to his parents. The troops, he observed, were "greatly dissatisfied with Col. Carter and have petitioned for his removal . . . they are asking for Parsons as their commander."[13]

Yet frustration was not limited to Carter's troops. Parsons's Twelfth Texas suffered serious morale problems while stationed in southeast Arkansas between Pine Bluff and the Mississippi River. The men often watched Union vessels heading downstream to join Grant's Vicksburg expedition, but the Texans had received orders to remain out of sight and not to fire on them. If feeling ineffectual was not enough to discourage any member of the rank and file, Henry Orr also complained to his parents in late April that "the captains of this command are larger than a colonel ought to be, and the lieutenants generally as large as captains. Brass buttons are all the go; oh!"[14]

There were, however, some improvements in store for Parsons's men. In May D. N. Shropshire reported to his sister that the government had furnished the troops with six hundred sabers and two hundred Belgian rifles.[15] Orr told his family that there were enough sabers for all, and Parsons appointed Harper Goodloe, an "exceedingly active and sprightly soldier," as drillmaster for the regiment. "He performs admirably," observed Orr, "Parsons having drilled him for the above purpose; the boys are all learning fast," and many believed "the time is coming when it will be necessary for us to be proficient in sabre exercises."[16] By June there were even greater improvements; two companies received new arms (described as Sharp Shooting guns in the order). There were not enough, however, for the men in the other eight companies, who still carried shotguns.[17]

The decision to transfer the Texans to Louisiana came as a surprise. The men under Parsons thought they might be ordered closer to Carter's troops stationed near Helena.[18] At the same time Carter and Giddings had plans for the Twenty-first Texas to scout toward the Mississippi River with the objective "to ambush the Fifth Kansas."[19] A member of Burford's Nineteenth Texas noted his bewilderment when he wrote the command had "very suddenly received marching orders for Pine Bluff."[20]

Yet Holmes had a second surprise for the Texans; he had decided not to reunite the brigade. He ordered only the Nineteenth Texas under Benjamin Watson and one section of Pratt's battery under Isaac A. Clare to join Parsons's Twelfth Texas. Much to Colonel Carter's delight, his "special instructions" detached him from Colonel Parsons. The Twenty-first Texas, along with Charles Morgan, the rest of the gunners under Joseph Pratt, and all the squadrons and companies normally operating under Carter, received orders to join a division forming under newly arrived Brigadier General Lucius M. Walker. Holmes ordered this division to southeast Arkansas; the troops were to scout between the lower White River and the St. Francis and Mississippi rivers.[21]

Without the obstreperous Carter and his troublesome troops to annoy him, Parsons headed for Louisiana to join John G. Walker's Texas infantry. "The object of the expedition," a member of the Nineteenth Texas reported to the *Dallas Herald*, "proved to be to break up a nest of Federals who were cultivating cotton and corn in the valley of Bayou Mason and on the Miss. on the free labor system that is to say with hired negroes."[22] The two regiments arrived west of Lake Providence the last week of June, but Colonel Parsons was not with his men. Instead, a member of the Twelfth Texas wrote to the Houston *Telegraph* that Parsons was "scouting single-handed and alone, on his own hook, thro' the swamps, keeping his own counsel and learning the whereabouts of the

Federals, and finding the best point for striking a telling blow; which self-imposed task, as the sequel proved, he accomplished most successfully."[23]

The bond between Parsons and his men was clearly demonstrated when they reunited on June 27. As soon as the troops learned Parsons was near, they headed for the deserted slave quarters where he had stopped to spend the night. Taking him completely by surprise, the men surrounded the little cabin and shouted his name. Although "tired and worn," he promptly came outside at the call and addressed his command.[24] His speech and his manner of delivery strengthened the men's determination to follow him in the planned campaign. Henry Orr recalled that he addressed the troops "in an eloquent and patriotic strain, gave the soldiers great encouragement, and said he was glad that we are privileged to strike a blow for Vicksburg."[25] Another member of the Twelfth who listened to the "stirring, eloquent speech" observed, "it forcibly struck me, much as a father would talk to his boys, of whom he was proud." Parsons told "them of the brave garrison at Vicksburg . . . that he could not take them there, but that he would take them where they would hear the sullen boom of the Vicksburg cannon." The men, he observed, "resolved to follow where he would lead, and nobly do or die for Vicksburg."[26]

Just after sunrise the next morning, the troops left on the scout toward Lake Providence in the "highest spirits."[27] A member of the Nineteenth pointed out: "Under the leadership of our deservedly popular and able commander (for he's nothing less) we proceeded so cautiously and securely."[28] The troops stopped to rest in the camps of Walker's division and J. P. Blessington of the Sixteenth Texas Infantry commented: "As they passed by us, I could not but admire their horsemanship; they all appeared to be excellent horsemen, and at a distance their general appearance was decidedly showy and gallant." He noticed their uniforms "contained as many colors as the rainbow" and "their arms consisted mostly of Enfield rifles, slung to their saddles, while around the waist of each was buckled a heavy cavalry sword, which clattered at every movement of their horses. A pair of holster pistols attached to the pommels of their saddles completed their equipment."[29]

Parsons joined Walker on an expedition between Milliken's Bend and Lake Providence. The purpose was to destroy cotton crops under Federal leases and to capture the released slaves working for the Yankees. Walker had left on this march June 22 and had since broken up numerous plantations, burning the picked cotton and had returned numerous slaves to their owners.[30]

After leaving Walker's camp, Parsons's two regiments overtook Brigadier General James C. Tappan's Arkansas brigade and Colonel Horace Randal's Texas brigade, both infantry, accompanied by their scouts, Colonel Isaac F. Harrison's Louisiana cavalry. The latter was temporarily placed under Parsons's command along with a battery from Mississippi and another from Louisiana, for use in an attack on a Federal garrison near Lake Providence.[31]

Parsons divided his force. Harrison's cavalry and one battery took a road leading toward Goodrich's Landing on the Mississippi between Milliken's Bend and Lake Providence. Parsons headed his two regiments and the other battery toward a fortified position the Federals had constructed on an old Indian mound. The two infantry brigades followed behind to reinforce if needed.[32]

The fort, about ten miles below Lake Providence and one and one-half miles from the Mississippi, protected the plantations operated by the United States government. The garrison was made up of black troops under white officers. Along the fertile regions of the Mississippi this arrangement served a dual purpose. Black troops not only protected the former slaves working on the plantations, but they released white regiments from this duty, thus allowing more men at the front where the presence of blacks still caused dissension.[33]

To the Texans filing out of the dense undergrowth of bushes and briers, the mound presented an impressive appearance, rising about eighty to one hundred feet from an extensive open field. George Ingram called it "the most peculiar looking mound I ever saw."[34] The main fort was on the summit, which measured thirty or forty feet square and was only accessible by a single pathway on the south side. To discourage anyone from trying to scale the sides, the Federals had loosened the dirt for a distance of fifteen to twenty feet from the top so that anyone attempting to climb would lose his footing.[35]

The soldiers at the garrison had made other preparations for an assault. Surrounding the entire position was a trench some two and one-half to three feet deep, with the dirt thrown up in front to provide a light breastwork. Waiting in the ditch were troops of the First Arkansas Volunteers (African descent), adequately armed with Enfield rifles. On top of the mound were other blacks poised behind heavy timbers which they could roll down on anyone rash enough to try to scale the precipitous sides.[36] But there was no artillery. As the Confederate troops approached the fortification they realized that what had appeared to be a formidable eight-pounder was only a wooden log with a "vicious looking hole, some three inches in diameter, bored in one end of it."[37]

As the cavalry emerged from the woods, Parsons formed his men into a line of battle. The Twelfth Texas under Lieutenant Colonel Bell Burleson took the right, the Nineteenth Texas under Lieutenant Colonel Benjamin Watson the left, and the battery the center. Eight hundred yards from the Federal position, Parsons ordered a halt and instructed the battery to open fire.[38] George Ingram informed his wife that the blast from the four Confederate guns "caused the rascals in the fort to hide their heads."[39] As the Texans cautiously neared the garrison, Parsons ordered the Twelfth to form at right angles to the Nineteenth.[40]

Parsons detailed some of his men as sharpshooters in order to pick off the enemy exchanging rifle fire with his men. The troops of Company D, Nineteenth Texas, from Hill County, deployed on top of a smaller mound about one hundred fifty yards from the main location. As the two sides traded fire, Federal riflemen killed one member of the company and wounded several.[41]

The colonel judged he could not storm the fort without a great loss of life. The timely arrival of Tappan's Arkansas infantry, however, offered him a second option. He knew, and the officers atop the mound quickly realized, that resistance against such a large force was futile. Just as Parsons ordered the infantry to form a line of battle, he directed a flag of truce toward the fort and demanded unconditional surrender.[42]

The fort capitulated without further bloodshed. The white officers asked for a promise that their captors would treat them as prisoners-of-war, but they surrendered the armed blacks unconditionally. Parsons, after consulting with Brigadier General Tappan, accepted. Since the troops of Burford's regiment and the battery had been the only men actually engaged, Parsons allowed them to occupy the post of honor as one hundred thirteen blacks and three white officers grounded their arms.[43]

The black prisoners were a problem for both sides. Major General John G. Walker reported, "I consider it an unfortunate circumstance that any armed negroes were captured."[44] Grant had already issued a warning to Richard Taylor after rumors spread of blacks murdered in the fighting around Milliken's Bend. "It may be you propose a different line of policy toward black troops and officers commanding them, to that practiced toward white troops," observed Grant. "If so, I can assure you that these colored troops are regularly mustered into the service of the United States. The Government and all officers serving under the Government are bound to give the same protection to these troops that they do to any other troops."[45] Yet John Simmons of the Twenty-Second Texas Infantry wrote that as Walker's soldiers marched the captured blacks from the mound to camp, about "12 or 15" died before they arrived.[46]

Fighting former slaves was a new experience for the Texans. As historian Bell Wiley noted: "Most of the Rebs felt as the Mississippian who wrote his mother: 'I hope I may never see a Negro soldier . . . or I cannot be . . . a Christian soldier.'"[47] Colonel Parsons disliked engaging black troops and declared during the raid, "I would not give one of my brave men for the whole of them."[48] But another participant observed: "These negroes were *well drilled*, and used their guns with a precision equal with any troops, and here were killed three of the four men we lost."[49]

Colonel Parsons had no desire to remain at the mound any longer than necessary. After firing the buildings and turning the prisoners over to the infantry, Parsons's cavalrymen resumed their raid. The Confederates had orders to destroy everything useful to the United States government, and as they rode toward Lake Providence, they burned houses, gins, cotton, and captured all the blacks they came upon. But the troops failed to follow their orders implicitly; they left two mansions, both occupied by women, standing. At one of them the soldiers had commenced following their instructions when a lady moved her rocking chair prominently upon the levee. Just as the men prepared to torch her house, Colonel Parsons arrived and ordered them to spare it. The Texans, disliking their task and hesitant to turn a Southern lady out, surrounded their colonel and began cheering.[50]

However, the Texans demonstrated no compassion for plantations under Federal leases. Brigadier General Alfred W. Ellet, commanding the Mississippi Marine Brigade (an army unit despite its name), observed the destruction the next morning. "In passing by the negro quarters on three of the burning plantations," he reported, "we were shocked by the sight of the charred remains of human beings who had been burned in the general conflagration. No doubt they were the sick negroes. . . . I witnessed five such spectacles myself in passing the remains of three plantations that lay in our line of march."[51]

Some of the Confederates also plundered homes of Union sympathizers. Ellet further noted he had "found the road strewn with abandoned booty," but the stolen items seem to preclude any possibility that Parsons's mounted men had taken part. Rear Admiral David Porter claimed the plunder included "furniture, pianos, pictures," and Ellet described the piano as "a very fine" one. Since the cavalry had left their wagons behind, it would have been difficult for them to transport such pieces.[52]

Colonel Parsons, upon leaving the mound, ordered his troops to move rapidly toward Lake Providence. The men in the Nineteenth Texas, whose mounts had not yet recovered from their trip to Missouri, could not keep the pace and remained behind. When the regiment neared the village, Parsons's Twelfth Texas was well in advance of the rest of the force.[53]

Since news of the raid preceded the Confederates, the Federals had prepared for them. As the Texans emerged from a skirt of timber interspersed with heavy undergrowth, they rode into an ambush. Parsons promptly formed his regiment into a line of battle, and a man who was by the colonel's side recalled: "I don't know whether I was scared or not, but I do know that I was not too *badly* scared to observe him closely. I *know* that *he* was not scared. He watched every movement and gave his orders as deliberately as though he was in no danger." In the midst of the firing Colonel Parsons was everywhere, "and though the balls rattled all around him, he gave his orders and directions as coolly as if he was on a drill."[54]

The battle, although fierce, proved short. Parsons, in front of his men, shouted orders to dismount all but one squadron. Armed with their new rifles, the Texans rushed toward the enemy on foot, fighting "Indian or Texas fashion."[55] As the dismounted cavalrymen drove the troops of the First Kansas Mounted Regiment back about two to three hundred yards in a "pretty hot fight," Parsons ordered the Fifth Squadron to charge on horseback. Captain J. Em. Hawkins, at the head of his men, was severely wounded by the accurate fire of the retreating Kansans.[56]

For a second time in the day the fortuitous arrival of reinforcements saved further destruction. As the Nineteenth Texas under Lieutenant Colonel Benjamin Watson rode up, Parsons ordered them to charge. A participant recalled with pride, to "have heard the real Texan yell they sent forth and seen those brave determined men, as they dashed off, urging on their jaded horses, you would have cried with me, the 'Lone Star' is in hands of which she may well be proud." The race, he added, "continued for five miles. . . . But the Federal horses, being fresh, outran our horses and the jaded condition of both man and beast" forced Parsons to call a halt.[57]

The cavalry headed back to join Walker's main force. But a gunboat, the *Romeo*, along with the *John Raine*, a transport mounting two guns on the hurricane deck, shelled the Confederate column as it marched down the levee.[58] One observer noted "their shells burst harmlessly above and around us, doing no other damage than killing three negroes."[59] Admiral Porter reported the gunboat pursued the Confeder-

ate column for fifteen miles but was unable to prevent further destruction of houses and property.[60]

The Confederates left the fertile land in ruin. All around them columns of black smoke rose from burning houses, the red flames casting a
sullen glow on the horizon. As the boom of signal guns bore the news of
the fighting, one of Parsons's men proudly noted that the cannon informed the Confederates at Vicksburg "that a blow had been struck *for*
[them]" and, to "the besiegers, that a blow had been struck *against*
them." As twilight fell, the writer observed, the strange scene, enhanced
by the sobs of hundreds of blacks, was "grand, gloomy and peculiar."[61]

Federal pursuit came immediately. By two the following morning
General Ellet had debarked his entire force—infantry, artillery, and cavalry—at Goodrich's Landing, and at sunrise he started in search of the
raiders. The cavalry, travelling in advance of the main force, found the
Confederates resting on the west bank of Tensas Bayou and began a spirited skirmish.[62] Colonel Parsons, directing the fire in person, attempted
to cross the bayou and turn Ellet's right flank, but an advance line of
Union skirmishers repulsed the assault. One Texan believed the Federals
were "afraid to come out into an open space and give us a fair fight."[63]
Ellet, however, insisted that the arrival of his artillery, which opened up
on the Confederate position, convinced the Southerners to "precipitately"
retreat.[64] Parsons nevertheless ordered the bridge burned; then, following General Walker's orders, the Texas cavalry began to fall back, covering the infantry's rear.

Admiral Porter's reaction to the raid was matter-of-fact. "I am
much surprised that this has never been attempted before," he observed,
as "the temptation to plunder is very great, and there is nothing but the
black regiments to protect the coast." Porter criticized the Federal plantation system: not only did it mean excessive cost to the government, but
unobstructed navigation of the Mississippi under this arrangement required a large army of white soldiers and gunboats to safeguard the
blacks, whom he believed had proved unable to protect themselves.[65]

This raid was one of the most successful of its kind on the west bank
of the Mississippi, though the price had not been cheap. The Texans cap-

tured between thirteen and fifteen hundred blacks, over four hundred horses and mules, cattle, camp equipage and, important to the department, the infantry's wagons now held over two hundred Federal arms.[66] Yet several of Parsons's men were killed and a number wounded. Captain Hawkins of the Twelfth Texas suffered a minor wound in his left elbow and a dangerous one in his left side. Captain Allen Beard, the former Dallas County sheriff in whose company Colonel Burford had originally joined, had an injured right arm and returned to Dallas to recuperate.[67]

In spite of their efforts, the Confederates in Louisiana could do little to aid their comrades across the river. Major General John G. Walker informed Kirby Smith on July 3: "If there was the slightest hope that my small command could relieve Vicksburg, the mere probability of its capture or destruction ought not, and should not, as far as I am concerned, weigh a feather against making the attempt, but I consider it absolutely certain, unless the enemy are blind and stupid, that no part of my command would escape capture or destruction if such an attempt should be made."[68] When Confederate Lieutenant General John Pemberton, besieged by Grant's army at Vicksburg, ceased fighting the next day, Henry Orr wrote his sister: "The news of the surrender [of] Vicksburg was received with regret."[69]

After the capitulation of the city, there was a lull in the fighting. The Texas cavalry rested in the marshy bottoms of northern Louisiana, scouting occasionally in the direction of Lake Providence, while Walker's infantry division moved to the vicinity of Alexandria on the Red River. The unhealthy location of Parsons's troops caused George Ingram to write his wife that sickness had decimated the ranks. "We would," he complained, "like to get out of this swamp."[70] In mid-July Henry Orr prophetically observed: "If Louisiana is invaded, I fear we will be driven west."[71]

This prediction came true in late August. A Federal force under the command of Brigadier General John D. Stevenson—including the Third Division of the XVII Army Corps; the Third Brigade, Sixth Division, XVII Army Corps; two batteries; the howitzer section of the Eighth

Michigan Battery; and a battalion of cavalry—had organized for the purpose of breaking up rebel camps between the Mississippi River and Monroe, Louisiana, the terminus of the Vicksburg and Shreveport Railroad. When Stevenson's command arrived at Goodrich's Landing August 21, the Texas cavalry could do nothing to stop the superior force but retreat in the best order possible.[72] Lieutenant George Ingram informed his wife that Colonel Parsons had tried to skirmish with the Federal cavalry, but the enemy refused until supported by infantry. He believed that fighting on their terms would have proved foolish, as "we would have to retire or be surrounded."[73] There was, therefore, little skirmishing on the retreat.

Two miles east of Monroe, Parsons again decided to give battle, but Stevenson's force did not take the bait. Anxious citizens, fearing the destruction of their property, visited the Federal camp under a flag of truce offering to surrender the town without a fight. General Paul O. Hébert, in command of the subdistrict of northern Louisiana, reluctantly consented. According to Henry Orr, Colonel Parsons was "much displeased with this" but, following orders, fell back to Vienna.[74] Lieutenant Ingram, however, praised Parsons: "The Col. has conducted our retreat with as much Skill as any other man possibly could. We never lost any waggons or other property and but few of our sick fell into enemies hands."[75]

Fortunately for the Confederates, Stevenson's orders did not direct him to remain in northern Louisiana. He stayed at Monroe only overnight, then began his return march toward the Mississippi. "The military results of the expedition," he informed Major General J. B. McPherson, "were the breaking up of the several camps at Floyd, Delhi, Monticello, Oak Ridge, and Monroe, and the precipitate flight of the enemy beyond the Washita River, in the direction of Shreveport."[76]

As soon as Stevenson left, the Texas cavalry returned to its former position, but the success of the raid sent chills through the Confederate defenders. Henry Orr wrote his father, "it gives me no pleasure to go west the way we have been doing lately."[77] Perhaps George Ingram made the most prophetic statement when he wrote his wife: "The Yankees have gone back to the Mississippi River but I suppose that they come out in force to reconnoiter and that before a great while a larger force will try to go to Sh[re]veport, but if they do go there we will have one of the biggest fights that ever occurred on this side of the father of waters."[78] If Arkansas and Louisiana fell, Ingram feared, "Texas will be the battle ground."[79]

Indeed, once Vicksburg capitulated and the navy had opened the Mississippi River to Union shipping, political, economic, and diplomatic motives favored a Union offensive into Texas. In August Henry W. Halleck pointed out to Nathaniel Banks, commander of the Department of the Gulf, that there were "important reasons why our flag should be restored" upon the soil of Texas.[80] Banks tried an assault on the Texas coast at Sabine Pass in September and was decisively defeated. In October he moved overland toward Alexandria, stalled beyond Opelousas, then retreated, but the next month Banks established a base at the mouth of the Rio Grande.

Meanwhile, both Louisiana and Texas suffered from a plague of stragglers, deserters, and paroled prisoners who roamed the country preying upon citizens. Even some of the regular soldiers among Parsons's disciplined Twelfth Texas, grown weary of the swamps, began to vandalize the neighborhood. By late July there were frequent complaints that the cavalrymen were tearing down fences and letting out the cattle on plantations adjoining the camps in order to pasture their horses.[81]

Reports of men breaking military regulations escalated as the humid summer heat intensified the sickness and boredom in the camps. Colonel Parsons issued orders to prohibit soldiers from keeping or selling mules or blacks taken when raiding. When twenty-year-old James A. Callahan of Company A, Twelfth Texas, was found guilty of stealing a mule, he was "dishonorably dismounted as no longer worthy to be a member of the cavalry arm of the Confederate Army." His punishment, humiliating for any Texan, was transfer to the infantry. The colonel, the order read, was "pained to take this course," but in order to stay the "demoralizing results" and "save the honor of the honest men," he had to take drastic measures.[82]

In spite of the colonel's efforts, the situation continued to deteriorate.

In early September Parsons ordered Major L. J. Farrar to bring in all stragglers, deserters, and absent without leave from the command. The Third Louisiana Partisan Rangers and the Thirteenth Battalion Louisiana Cavalry joined him at Monroe to assist. In early October the colonel sent Sergeant Thomas Patterson of Company F, Twelfth Texas, and eight men into the swamps to arrest all of the men belonging to the brigade. It is difficult to assess how successful Patterson was at this task, however, because he was captured several weeks later.[83]

This lack of discipline was not characteristic of Parsons's Twelfth Texas, but sickness, shortages, and a sense of futility plagued the men all the time they stayed in Louisiana. The war had taken its toll, and by September of 1863 the colonel even had to request money from headquarters at Shreveport to buy horses for the artillery. He had "no funds on hand," and horses were "necessary to move the guns."[84]

While Parsons and his troops endured discouragement, boredom and disease in Louisiana, the situation in Arkansas became critical. With the United States Navy now in control of the Mississippi River, Lincoln's government could concentrate on bringing Arkansas back into the Union, and planning began for a movement to reclaim the capital at Little Rock. When the Federal columns began to move out from Helena, Confederates, including the men of Parsons's brigade under Colonel Carter, knew they had to halt the Federal drive south. Failure might mean the Union occupation of northern Texas.

10.

The Loss of Arkansas

"The capture of Vicksburg and Port Hudson by the forces under Generals Grant and Banks on the 4th and 8th of July, respectively," wrote Major General John M. Schofield, commanding the Department of the Missouri, "opened the way for active operations in Arkansas, and enabled General Grant to return to me the troops I had sent him."[1] This turn of events was a setback to the Confederates in Arkansas. As Schofield's command increased, the prospect of the Southerners maintaining their tenuous hold on the state faded. While Colonel Parsons and his two regiments went off to fight the Federals in Louisiana, Colonel Carter and his unit remained southeast of Little Rock—their duty to monitor enemy movement and report any unusual activity.

The Texas Brigade, as Carter's command was called, consisted of the Twenty-first Texas, Charles Morgan's men, part of Joseph Pratt's battery, and several independent companies, including troops of Johnson's Spy Company not captured at Arkansas Post. Carter's brigade and one composed of Archibald S. Dobbin's First Arkansas Cavalry and Robert C. Newton's Fifth Arkansas Cavalry formed a division under Brigadier General Lucius Marsh Walker.[2]

General Walker, born in Tennessee in 1829, had graduated in 1850 from the United States Military Academy, fifteenth in a class of forty-four. He had resigned from the army in 1852, but when the war broke out he received a colonel's commission and took command of the post at Memphis. The advantage of being a West Pointer was augmented by his family's prestige—ex-President James K. Polk was his uncle. By November 1862, however, Walker appeared in trouble with his superiors. After Braxton Bragg informed Adjutant and Inspector General Samuel Cooper that he believed Walker was not safe "to be entrusted with any command," Walker's application for transfer was approved, and he reported to the Trans-Mississippi Department in the spring of 1863.[3]

Not long after Walker arrived at General Holmes's Little Rock head-quarters, the action began to escalate. On July 4 Holmes attempted to capture Helena, the important Federal depot on the Mississippi. Walker took part in this action and led the Arkansas regiments of Dobbin and Newton in the unsuccessful assault. Although Carter's cavalry was part of Walker's division and some of the independent companies may have participated, Carter and most of his men remained in the southeast part of the state scouting in the direction of the Mississippi River.[4] By late August the brigade, headquartered at Pine Bluff, was temporarily under Major Charles Morgan with Captain L. J. Wilson of Company I commanding the Twenty-first Texas.[5] It is impossible to determine why Carter was not with his men, but records indicate he was in Texas on furlough a few weeks later and possibly he had already left his command.[6]

Nevertheless, with the Mississippi securely in the hands of the United States Navy after the fall of Vicksburg and Port Hudson and Grant returning the troops he had borrowed, the time seemed propitious for the Federals to take the offensive. Frederick Steele, in command of the force ordered to occupy Little Rock, began moving early in August and by the end of the month was ready to approach the state capital. Confederate cavalry, including parts of Walker's division, stubbornly contested every mile of the enemy's advance. The Southerners, unable to stop Steele, continually had to retreat. By the last week of August Sterling Price, who commanded the District of Arkansas while Holmes was on sick furlough, ordered the cavalry divisions of Marsh Walker and John Marmaduke to make a stand at Bayou Metoe.

When Steele's army attacked the Confederate position on the bayou, the smaller Southern force again fell back. As a result of the heated battle that lasted all day, a dispute developed between Walker, who by virtue of seniority had commanded, and Marmaduke. As soon as the fighting ended, Marmaduke criticized Walker's handling of the affair and promptly applied for a transfer.[7] According to John M. Harrell, a major in the Arkansas cavalry, Walker only laughed after learning Marmaduke objected to his troop placement. But when his friends persuaded him the charge might prove injurious, he grew angry, demanded an apology, then issued a challenge.[8]

Lieutenant Buck Walton of the Texas cavalry attended the duel that followed. He later recorded in his reminiscences that Marmaduke personally invited him, not as a second but as an observer to insure fairness in the meeting. (Walton had apparently recovered from his anger that Marmaduke left him on the Missouri side of the river in the retreat from Cape Girardeau.) Marmaduke, Walton recalled, requested the duel at dawn, believing the hazy early light might offset the fact he was nearsighted. "The distance," Walton later penned, "was ten paces." When the men fired, Walker fell, mortally wounded.[9]

John N. Edwards, adjutant for Joseph Shelby, whose brigade served under Marmaduke, also described the duel. According to Edwards, Walker believed Marmaduke had "cast imputations upon his courage." Marmaduke stubbornly insisted "he had never accused Walker of cowardice, but that his conduct had been such upon several occasions that he would no longer serve under him." The challenge followed instantly. Both generals carried fully loaded Colt navy revolvers, and although each missed his first shot, in the second round Marmaduke hit Walker, who died the next day.[10]

Repercussions from this affair were far-reaching. Sterling Price placed Marmaduke and both seconds under arrest but soon released his cavalry commander because of the pending engagement. As the troops retreated toward Little Rock, Price unfortunately placed Marmaduke as senior officer over all the cavalry. When Marmaduke arrived to assume command of Walker's old division, Archibald Dobbin, who had replaced the dead brigadier, refused to obey his commander's assailant. Although this occurred in the midst of battle, Marmaduke had Dobbin arrested and preferred charges against him for disobeying orders.[11] Thus, at a time when the Confederates needed unity, the defenders of Little Rock were torn by dissension.

While the Southern commanders quarreled, Steele steadily moved toward the capital. Price hoped the enemy would attack the fortifications he had prepared outside Little Rock, but Steele refused to fall for such an obvious ploy. Instead he ordered his cavalry to cross the river downstream from the town, flank Price's right, and move on the capital from below. The only resistance Federal troops met while executing this plan was the cavalry Price had ordered southeast of Little Rock.[12]

The final battle of the Little Rock campaign began at daylight on September 10. The Confederates discovered the enemy in force about eight miles below the town and made a determined stand at a crossing on the Arkansas River. Although the mounted troops could do little except delay the advance until Sterling Price could evacuate the capital, the batteries of C. B. Etter and Joseph Pratt hotly engaged the advancing columns.[13]

Joseph Pratt, anticipating the assault, had readied his Texas battery the evening before, ordering cotton hauled from a nearby farm to build a defensive structure around his guns. This makeshift fort not only protected his men, but it also resisted the enemy's shot. When Steele's cavalry arrived in his front, Pratt ordered his men to open fire and drove the enemy back from the riverbank. Federal artillerymen nevertheless quickly positioned two six-gun batteries and returned the rounds.[14]

This exchange of shot and shell proved destructive. Thirty-seven-year old Michael Gorman, a gunner from East Texas, harassed the Federal position with his accurate aim. One well-placed strike killed all the men on two of the enemy cannons and convinced the Federals to retreat some two hundred yards upriver. Pratt reported that the enemy did not harm him until one of his shells failed to explode; the Federals retrieved it, examined the fuse, then cut theirs the same way. "After this," recalled Pratt, "their shelling was very accurate."[15]

The Confederate defenders could not hold the position. As Federal troops crossed the river below the Southern lines, Pratt had to evacuate his fort and move to Bayou Fourche, a tributary of the Arkansas, where he positioned his cannon on the west side of the stream. There Colonel Newton, directing the brigade after Dobbin's arrest, ordered Major Samuel Corley to dismount his Arkansans and stay the advance while Morgan's Texans and W. B. Denson's Louisiana troops supported Pratt's battery on the right and left.[16] Corley, who had fought with the Texans since their first battle at Searcy, was killed as the Federals advanced.[17]

Colonel Newton watched Pratt throughout the fighting. When the engagement commenced he had ordered Pratt to reserve his fire until the infantry moved in force and "came within easy range, when he was to ply them vigorously with grape and canister." As soon as Pratt opened on them, reported Newton, he "quickly drove them back"; his "trusty guns" had "continued to rake them with canister and grape until Fletcher's field, which was immediately in my front, was entirely cleared of them." Pratt, he wrote, merited commendation "for the skill and bravery displayed here, as he has displayed them on every field where I have had occasion to observe him." Major Charles Morgan, commanding a squadron of Texans, also acted with promptness and zeal.[18]

Nevertheless, the Confederates could not save Little Rock. As soon as he realized that the enemy had forded the river south of town, Price ordered Marmaduke's cavalry to hold them in check while he withdrew the infantry and artillery. Pratt's gunners sustained considerable fire during the retreat but remained in position until ordered to retire. Unable to stop Steele's advance, the Southerners marched slowly through Little Rock, conceding the capital to the Federal army late in the day. Price continued an orderly retreat until he reached Arkadelphia.[19]

The loss of Little Rock had a demoralizing effect on all the Confederate troops, but the Twenty-first Texas came under increasing censure. In early October Holmes, again in command of the District of Arkansas, placed this regiment under Marmaduke.[20] Captain William M. Rust, a senior officer in the field, felt obligated to explain the men's problems to the new commander. Accusations from headquarters, he wrote, insinuated that the Twenty-first was "shirking service and trying to get away to Texas; that we were committing extraordinary depredations on private property, &c." This, he angrily claimed, was simply not true.[21]

This criticism had come about because the men of the Twenty-first did not take part in the attempt to hold Little Rock. When the capital fell, the regiment was on picket duty along the Arkansas River some twenty miles below the town. Rust complained that as the army retreated no one apprised him of the need to evacuate and no orders emanated from headquarters. He therefore impressed wagons to carry the sick and moved his base, without authorization, to a new position at Arkadelphia.[22]

Problems increased when the Twenty-first Texas, camped near Washington, received requests for troops from all directions. Price called for men to establish a courier line to Shreveport, Lieutenant Buck Walton requested cavalrymen to accompany him on a scout, and Holmes asked for fifteen men. When Captain Rust, in charge of the convalescent camp, was unable to fill all these requests, Holmes complained.[23] The captain protested to Marmaduke that he could not possibly meet all the requisitions. When Holmes pressed for his detail, Rust replied he had only thirty-three in camp well enough to ride and over two hundred sick from his own command as well as one hundred ailing infantry to care for. "Now, general," wrote Rust, "I should like to know who I am to obey. My instructions place me under orders of the medical director and inspector of hospitals. He directs me to go to a certain place; the general wants to know why I went there." Further, pointed out Rust: "You are placed in command of us, and direct us to use diligence in collecting all our men together as quickly as possible. The next day General Holmes sends an order to scatter them." Finally, observed Rust, everyone seemed to forget that this regiment was cavalry and had five hundred horses to provide for with only a few healthy men to gather and haul corn. "They seem to have an idea at headquarters that we are not as sick as we represent." This, he bitterly advised Marmaduke, was a misrepresentation of the truth.[24]

Rust also answered charges of depredations by the Twenty-first Texas. No one seemed to care that the regiment was without supplies. "Our brigade has been broken up, and the brigade quartermaster ordered away, and our regimental quartermaster ordered to furnish all the troops in the convalescent camp," admonished Rust. The citizens refused to sell, saying "they had more Confederate money than they wanted." Although Rust tried to stop the plunder, he admitted it was not easy. While in Missouri and northeastern Arkansas, the Texans had developed "very confused notions about the rights of property, and it is difficult to set them right."[25]

About this time Lieutenant Walton played a practical joke on Sarah Rust, wife of the just-mentioned Captain Rust. To entertain themselves in camp, the men used the prolific and numerous body lice for sport. "It is true that the grown bug," wrote Walton, "when taken from the bodies of different men—and placed close together, will rush at one another like bull dogs, and fight to the death—or until one, being whipped and wounded, will scramble out of reach of his adversary." Betting on the vermin flourished. After one particularly bloody match Walton recalled: "I called on two boys for two of their champion 'gladiators'—for a special purpose." After carefully securing the critters in an envelope, he mailed them to Sarah Rust. The two, continued Walton, "proved of the right gender—& before she was aware of it, she was in possession of a large & flourishing colony, which caused much washing and disenfectants before she could get rid of it."[26]

Although this amused the men, Walton had more serious duties; he was in charge of watching the Federal camp outside Pine Bluff. In mid-October he decided to make a dash at the headquarters of Powell Clayton, colonel of the notorious Fifth Kansas, which along with the First Indiana held the town. The Texans captured Clayton's headquarters, but Clayton was in Pine Bluff some distance away. "We got his papers—and some valuables—but Col. Clayton was safe. It was him we wanted."[27]

By late October Marmaduke also had developed plans to assault Clayton's position at Pine Bluff. The Federal commander had less than six hundred men, and Marmaduke believed he could muster over three times as many for an attack. All the troops under Marmaduke took part in this action, including the Texas Brigade under Major Benjamin D. Chenoweth. This brigade, which now included the Twenty-first Texas, Pratt's battery, and the squadrons of B. D. McKie and Charles Morgan, formed part of Newton's division, which also included D. A. Nunn's company of Texans fighting with John P. Bull's brigade.[28]

Marmaduke tried a ploy reminiscent of Cape Girardeau, with the same amount of success. Instead of charging and overpowering the small garrison, which he outnumbered over three to one, he stopped as he approached the town and under a flag of truce demanded Clayton's surrender. The colonel delayed his reply so he could fortify the town. He ordered blacks to roll cotton bales into the streets, throw up breastworks, then haul water from the river in preparation for a possible siege. Artillerymen positioned their guns to defend the courthouse, and sharpshooters concealed themselves upon nearby roofs. Scarcely an hour later, Federal Lieutenant F. M. Clark returned to the Confederate party waiting for Clayton's answer and abruptly advised them: "Colonel Clayton never surrenders, but is always anxious for you to come and take him, and you must get back to your command immediately, or I will order my men to fire on you." With this, skirmishing began in earnest.[29]

Marmaduke now had no choice but to attack. Chenoweth's Texans and Robert C. Wood's battalion of Missouri cavalry advanced from the southeast as Pratt's battery unleashed their guns upon the courthouse. When Federal sharpshooters began firing from their concealed positions, Newton ordered Pratt to turn his guns on the houses. The Confederates drove the enemy all the way to within a block of the courthouse, where they encountered the cotton fortifications surrounding the square. Within a hundred yards of the courthouse, the Federals opened a brisk fire on the attackers, who were instructed to lie down. Barricaded behind bales of cotton in a nearby shed, the Confederates remained facing the square until ordered to withdraw.[30]

Pratt's battery heatedly engaged the enemy. Clayton reported that Confederate artillery opened on the square with "12-pounder rifle guns, throwing both the Hotchkiss and the James projectiles."[31] Although Pratt's gunners silenced the Federal sharpshooters in the courthouse cupola and nearby storehouse, their cannon caused little other damage. Marmaduke therefore ordered Pratt to move around the lake and join Colton Greene's artillery near the Methodist church.[32] R. C. Newton observed: "Pratt, as usual, did good work that day, and his men behaved with their accustomed bravery and steadiness."[33]

As with the attack on Cape Girardeau, Marmaduke could only take the Federal position by a frontal assault. This, he reported, "would have cost me the loss of at least 500 men." In his own defense he continued, "I did not think it would pay."[34] Colton Greene, whose brigade had formed part of Carter's column on the Missouri raid, maintained that after five hours of constant action little damage had been done, "and it became evident that they could only be carried by a *coup de main*."[35] The Confederates therefore withdrew. Historian Edwin C. Bearss observed: "Though Marmaduke refused to take Pine Bluff by assault, he understood thoroughly that the failure of the expedition would be used by his enemies to attack him. But considering that he had in the first placed failed to capture the town by a miscalculation on his part, he declined to retrieve the error he had made by sacrificing the blood of his men without any compensating advantages."[36]

Maramduke's offensive indeed netted little. He reported the capture of over two hundred mules and horses, three hundred blacks, between six hundred and one thousand bales of cotton, and about forty men killed and wounded.[37] Clayton believed the greatest damage resulted from fires set by Southerners, which burned much of the Federal quarters, and Confederate artillery damaged many private homes in the town.[38] Lieutenant Buck Walton offered a sarcastic observation: "The result was that eight hundred men whipped at least 2500 of as good men as we had—losing about four hundred men, killed and wounded. We took our defeat 'manfully' and marched back to camp at Camden—and went into idleness again."[39]

In early November, Parsons and some of his troops returned from Louisiana to Arkansas, where the brigade reunited at Camden, only days after the Confederate repulse at Pine Bluff. That defeat had demoralized the troops, who now held only a small strip of southern Arkansas. Since the men from Louisiana were almost as discouraged and disheartened as those who had just retreated with Marmaduke, it was fortunate that Parsons and Carter did not have to dispute over command. Carter was still in Texas, and his regiment was under the capable command of Lieutenant Colonel Giddings. Some acrimony still remained, however: Parsons's and Burford's troops, along with Morgan's, camped on the south side of the Washita River near the Confederate headquarters at Camden, while the Twenty-first camped alone on the north bank.[40]

Inactivity bred discontent. Sometime after the battle at Pine Bluff, one company of the Twenty-first Texas left camp and headed home when they learned from their families of Mexican and Indian raids along the Texas frontier. When the commanding general asked Lieutenant Walton to stop them, Walton told him "it was useless—that I knew the men—and knew they would continue until they [heard] contrary news to what they had received." Further, Walton believed, "they would come back—whenever they found their families were in safety."[41]

Walton was correct. Ordered to overtake and escort the defiant troops back to Arkansas, he finally caught up with them several hundred miles from Camden. The company captain, whom Walton did not name, politely refused to retrace his steps but promised he would return and bring every man with him after he had ascertained why local authorities could not handle problems along the Texas frontier. True to his word, when the Texans discovered they had acted on exaggerated rumors, the entire command halted and returned to Arkansas.[42] Apparently no disciplinary action resulted from this desertion en masse. But W. C. Schaumburg of the inspector general's office critically reported in October 1863: "As far as I know, no officer has as yet been held accountable for the desertions of his men." Although he believed the rank and file might be excused, the officers, he insisted, could not.[43]

Lethargy prevailed everywhere. The only source of some pride for the Texas Brigade was Pratt's battery. The inspector general's report stated the artillerymen were "in very fine order, and a model command. Their discipline is very good. The men are well drilled, and care is taken of the horses and everything about the battery." By contrast, E. J. Gurley's Thirtieth Texas Cavalry, stationed in the Indian Territory but eventually to replace Carter's Twenty-first Texas in the brigade, "presented a very poor appearance." Major Schaumburg remarked: "I called on the three senior captains to drill the regiment in battalion drill, and each of them in turn admitted his incompetency to do so; finally the senior captain made the attempt, and failed most signally."[44]

Poorly drilled troops vexed Holmes, who needed disciplined men not only to fight Federals in the vast territory west of Arkansas but also to control the Indians. When Brigadier General William Steele, commander of the Indian Territory, applied to Holmes for more cavalry early in December 1863, Kirby Smith decided to send Parsons's veterans.[45] Steele apparently planned to attach the new force to R. M. Gano's brigade of Texans.[46]

Parsons's men, however, were too scattered. Some members of the brigade had been sent to Texas in October, before Parsons and the main force transferred to Camden. The companies of the Twelfth Texas under captains Tom Haley, J. Em. Hawkins, H. W. Kyser, A. M. Maddux, and William G. Veal, as well as Captain Allen Beard's company from the Nineteenth Texas, were detailed under Lieutenant Colonel Bell Burleson to the Bureau of Conscription to hunt for draft evaders and deserters. Ostensibly this provided a chance for the troops to visit their families, and on November 1 James J. Frazier informed his mother that he was in the city of Jefferson in eastern Texas with Burleson and headed for the interior.[47] But in December Agnes Frazier learned that James had died. Her other two sons served in different cavalry regiments—one in Burford's Nineteenth Texas with Colonel Parsons at Camden, Arkansas, the other in the Thirtieth Texas Cavalry at Camp Garland in the Indian Territory. James died before their three regiments could join to form a brigade. From Camden Robert Frazier wrote his mother that he could "hardly beleave" his older brother James was dead. "It may bee so . . . he was with Col Burleson in Texas."[48] Philip with the Thirtieth Texas confided: "I was not prepared to hear such bad news I was jus thinking that I would get to see him in a few days as we are to get with Parsons and Buffords Regts. . . . We are to start in the morning on a Scout and Parsons and Buffords Regts are to be with us and I hope to see Robert."[49]

This scout never took place. As 1864 opened, Confederate commanders in the Trans-Mississippi hesitated to weaken their defensive lines in Arkansas and Louisiana; thus Parsons's Texans never joined Steele north of the Red River. Moreover, Steele did not remain in command. Frustrated over conditions in the Indian Territory and concerned that his Northern origins hampered his discharge of duties, Steele applied for a transfer and was replaced by Brigadier General Samuel Maxey, an ex-lawyer from Texas who was more acceptable than the New York-born Steele. Early in January, Richard Taylor informed Maxey that "Colonel Parsons' brigade, to which you refer as Carter's, has not been ordered to you, but has gone up upon the Arkansas River."[50]

As this correspondence indicates, the Confederate hierarchy recognized that both Carter and Parsons had claims to commanding the brigade, and the bureaucracy tried for a second time to solve this vexing problem. Brigadier General Thomas J. Churchill, the unfortunate officer who surrendered Fort Hindman at Arkansas Post, was sent to the Trans-Mississippi shortly before Christmas, and placed over the Texans. The troops reacted even more promptly and heatedly than they had when Hawes superseded Parsons in 1862. George Ingram of the Twelfth Texas moaned: "I could weep like a child if it [would] do any good. Our Brigade is *ruined, ruined, ruined.*"[51] Robert Frazier censured General Holmes, who he believed "has taiken Col. Parsons away from us as Brg. Gen & put & Arkansawer over us." The men, he insisted, were "dissatisfyed with it & say wee wont surve unde him."[52]

Threats turned to action. When they heard the news, most of the men stayed up all night protesting. By morning they had saddled their horses, and only the pleading of the officers convinced them to remain in camp while a delegation petitioned Holmes to return Parsons. Lieutenant Ingram, believing the general would refuse, wrote home: "I fear the consequences to night." Private Frazier, who heard men planning to leave that evening, informed his mother that the troops would not desert but would report to Kirby Smith at Shreveport. Yet, he noted, it looked "mytey Bad" to have mutiny in the command. Archie Parks added that "the Texians all hate General Holms so bad that they want to kill him and some of them will do it if they get a chance at him. he dont like us ether he says that we are good fighters but he says we are a pack of damd theaves he givs us a bad name worse than we are."[53]

The situation in the camps would have proved even more serious if some companies of the Twelfth and Nineteenth Texas had not been in Texas on conscription detail. As it was, the men in camp made up for the shortage by angrily demonstrating against Churchill. The Texans kept up a constant chant: "Hurrah for Parsons, dam the Arkansaw General," and yelled they would have Parsons or no one. Only the colonel was able to cool the men's anger, although his arrival in the camp created further stir. The men ran toward his horse, throwing their hats into the air and shouting, "Col. Parsons has come." As they circled him they yelled, "here is the Champion of the West," and "we have him surrounded and we will never let him go away from us." Others loudly protested: "*He* is our commander, we want no other." George Ingram astutely observed: "I never saw a man so much beloved as a commander as he."[54]

Parsons delivered a speech intended to touch the hearts of his men. He relived their past achievements in defending Arkansas and Louisiana, told them to be proud of the reputation they had gained, and implored them to follow orders from the commanding general. He asked them not to do anything to disgrace their homes or their state. After about thirty minutes he rode out of the ring amid "deafening shouts and hurrah for Col. Parsons."[55]

The men of the Twenty-first Texas, camped across the river, had a different reaction. Private William P. Zuber later wrote that the troops of Parsons's and Burford's regiments "were strangely attached to Colonel Parsons, and they treated General Churchill with scorn. Seeing that his assumption of command would cause a general mutiny of those two regiments, the General abandoned the command and did not visit our regiment." The officers of the Twenty-first sent a letter to Churchill criticizing the conduct of the other two regiments and assuring him they would welcome his presence. Nevertheless, Churchill wisely advised Holmes to reinstate Parsons.[56] Lieutenant Ingram observed: "Consequently our command have cooled down and evrything glides on as quietly as usual except that it is Christmas times and some . . . have taken a little too much whiskey and are rather jolly."[57]

Holmes consistently refused to request a promotion for Colonel Parsons and this slight did not go unnoticed by the rank and file. Lieutenant Ingram aptly stated: "Old Holmes does all he can against Parsons." The attempt to change commanders was, in his opinion, intended "to gratify his evil nature and agravate Parsons."[58] Many officers also believed Parsons merited a promotion, and early in December several letters to that effect arrived in Richmond. Nathaniel Burford, commander of the Nineteenth Texas, and Brigadier General James F. Fagan, under whom Parsons served at Camden, wrote to influential friends in the Confederate Congress. Referring to the situation with Holmes, Burford pointedly stated: "Men and officers have expressed great astonishment at his not having been promoted."[59] Everyone knew of Parsons's "intrepid daring," Fagan added and his reputation "as a dashing Cavalry Officer." Further, Colonel Parsons had "won his spurs" repeatedly and often. Realizing the futility of assisting Parsons without Holmes's endorsement, Fagan sagaciously observed, "To treat Col Parsons much longer with indifference or neglect argues a poor return for the service he has done our State & South."[60]

Although these efforts proved unproductive, Parsons's supporters did not give up hope. In February 1864 a petition addressed directly to Secretary of War James A. Seddon requested that he and President Jefferson Davis take the matter of Parsons's promotion under consideration.[61] But the situation in Virginia overshadowed the war west of the Mississippi, and neither Seddon nor Davis appeared concerned about military events in Arkansas.

Both citizens and soldiers in the Trans-Mississippi recognized Richmond's lack of interest in an area cut off from the rest of the Confederacy since the fall of Vicksburg. Shortages prevailed and apathy had become widespread, but Kirby Smith nevertheless set about planning his spring strategy. He instructed Holmes to place his command in winter quarters in order to "discipline and improve their *morale*" for the coming campaigns. "The Texas Brigade," he wrote Taylor, "goes directly to Texas."[62]

There were numerous reasons to send the men there. Not only could they perform a service for the South by arresting anyone evading the conscript law, but their removal would lighten the burden of providing for their horses, since forage in Arkansas was almost nonexistent. Moreover, given their threats of mutiny and desertion just before Christmas, a trip to Texas would raise spirits.

But the strategy changed again. As 1864 opened the brigade, instead of heading for Texas as the men hoped, left Camden to join an attack on Pine Bluff. Although nothing came of the campaign, it delayed the march south for over a month. By the time the troops reached Shreveport, Lieutenant George Ingram observed: "The boys are very impatient and in great suspense. They have their heads set homewards and many are determined to go orders or no orders. I hope that we may be ordered to go very soon and that no one will disgrace themselves."[63]

By mid-February twenty-five of the companies under Parsons had returned to Texas, yet their respite would not last long. Henry W. Halleck had finally persuaded his western generals that an operation on the Red River was necessary, and definite plans for a movement in the west started to take form. As Parsons's Texans headed home, the Federal commanders conceived the largest invasion yet amassed against Confederates in the Trans-Mississippi.

THE RED RIVER CAMPAIGN

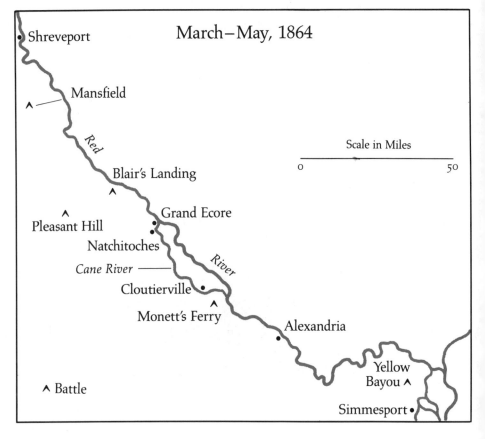

March–May, 1864

Shreveport

Mansfield

Red

Blair's Landing

Scale in Miles

0   50

Grand Ecore

Pleasant Hill

Natchitoches

Cane River ——

River

Cloutierville

Monett's Ferry

Alexandria

Yellow
Bayou ^

^ Battle

Simmesport •

11.

Whiskey and Gunpowder Aren't "Necessary to Enable a Southron to Make a Charge"

As 1864 opened, Henry W. Halleck in Washington watched the genesis of one of his long-cherished ideas—an invasion of Texas by way of the Red River. He believed a combined army and navy expedition to Alexandria, then Shreveport, would open the fertile regions of North Texas. Although Major General Nathaniel P. Banks, who oversaw the Department of the Gulf, had been operating off the Texas coast, by January he agreed to the change. Two important reasons influenced this decision. First, Banks harbored grand political ambitions and wanted to please the president. Abraham Lincoln's concern about the state's reconstructed government meant Banks needed to spend more time in Louisiana. Second, Banks recognized that along the proposed route he would find abundant cotton, which would pacify the wealthy mill owners in his home state of Massachusetts. To plan the largest-ever Federal invasion of the Trans-Mississippi, he exchanged correspondence with Frederick Steele, who would march south from Little Rock to join the expedition at Shreveport; Admiral David D. Porter, whose fleet would play an essential role; and William T. Sherman, who must commit soldiers if the movement was to succeed. The movement became known as the Red River expedition.[1]

Problems for the Federal high command began at once. The campaign would use troops from three different military departments, but Halleck refused to assign any one officer as general commander. Sherman, who agreed to send ten thousand veterans to Alexandria by March 17, was anxious to move up the Red River, but Steele did not share this enthusiasm. He cited numerous problems: bad roads, a shortage of troops, and the need for men to monitor the civil elections scheduled in his department in March. Rather than pledge his army to the campaign, he offered to feign an offensive and turn the Confederate flank.[2] This would not do, Sherman complained to Banks; the elections were "nothing compared with the fruits of military success."[3] Ulysses S. Grant, who had become a lieutenant general on March 12 and general-in-chief in Halleck's place, finally settled the matter. Three days after his promotion he instructed Steele to move his force toward Shreveport. "A mere demonstration," he pointed out, "would not be sufficient."[4]

The operation still had no overall commander. Sherman, who had been superintendent of the Seminary of Learning near Alexandria, clearly hoped for the position. "I wanted to go up Red River," he told his wife, "but as Banks was in command in person I thought it best not to go."[5] Banks, who had received his commission as major general of volunteers in May 1861, ranked Sherman, whose commission dated from May of 1862. During the initial planning of the expedition, Banks outranked every other Federal general except Benjamin Butler, another example of an inept political appointment.[6] Superseding the politician-turned-general was almost impossible; even Grant realized that, because Banks had influential friends, replacing him would almost certainly have serious political repercussions. Grant's elevation to general-in-chief did not occur in time for him to exert decisive influence. He had hoped to utilize Banks's army against Mobile and later wrote that he had "opposed the movement [up the Red River] strenuously, but acquiesced because it was the order of my superior at the time."[7]

A force of more than forty thousand, the most impressive Federal army ever amassed in the Trans-Mississippi, began to move toward Shreveport in March. Sherman sent ten thousand infantry and artillery taken from the XVI and XVII corps. Brigadier Generals Joseph A. Mower and Thomas Kilby Smith each led divisions, and A. W. Ellet contributed around one thousand of his Marine Brigade—all under the command of hardened veteran Brigadier General Andrew J. Smith. Admiral Porter brought thirteen ironclads, four tinclads, and five other armed vessels. In addition to the army transport and quartermaster boats, around sixty Federal ships mounting over two hundred guns headed upriver. Both Smith and Porter were to join almost twenty thousand soldiers from the

Department of the Gulf at Alexandria and then head for Shreveport, where they would unite with Frederick Steele's over eleven thousand troops.[8] The most serious drawback to the plan was that Sherman's men had to return to the Army of the Tennessee thirty days after their arrival on the Red River.

To meet the advance, Richard Taylor amassed all the Louisiana and Texas troops he could quickly pull together—some 5,800 infantry and artillery and 3,000 cavalry. Although Sterling Price (who had replaced Holmes as commander in Arkansas) sent 4,400 reinforcements, these soldiers did not join Taylor before the first battle opened.[9]

Banks, who separated his column from Porter's fleet at Grand Ecore, offered the Confederates an inviting advantage. Taylor recognized that his best chance at success depended upon stopping the army before it reunited with the navy below Shreveport. Banks had stretched his column out for miles on a narrow road scarcely wide enough for a wagon to pass and almost too narrow for one to turn around. The cavalry rode two to three miles in advance of the infantry because A. L. Lee refused William B. Franklin's request to place his cavalry train of some three hundred wagons at the rear with the infantry. Lee reasoned "that it was the cavalry's business to look after its own train."[10]

The Confederates, falling back in the face of Banks's advance, formed a line at Sabine Crossroads near the little town of Mansfield, and late on April 8 Taylor attacked. Historian Ludwell Johnson astutely points out that the Southerners won primarily because, "as a result of the faulty order of march, the Union army was strung out over twenty miles of road." As the battle opened, "Banks was outnumbered by the Confederates at every point of contact" although the Federals possessed a numerical superiority of almost 2.5 to 1. There is "no doubt," concluded Johnson, "that Taylor won a stunning victory at Sabine Crossroads."[11]

Taylor pursued the retreating army to the little village of Pleasant Hill, where he struck the following day. Had his plan worked out as conceived, he would have won a second brilliant victory. But success depended on Thomas J. Churchill flanking the Federal left. Churchill did not move far enough south and instead of rolling up the enemy, he crossed in front of the Federal position. When A. J. Smith realized this, he lashed into the Confederate line and Churchill had to fall back to save himself. "A worthy, gallant gentleman, General Churchill," Taylor reported, "but not fortunate in war."[12] Taylor later admitted: "Instead of intrusting the important attack by my right to a subordinate, I should have conducted it myself."[13]

Banks failed to take advantage of his victory, however, and after a council of war decided to withdraw his forces. Ludwell Johnson concluded: "Tactically, the battle of Pleasant Hill was distinctly a Northern victory, although the retreat to Grand Ecore turned it into a strategic defeat."[14] Banks's about-face proved fortunate for the Southerners, because Kirby Smith had pulled much of Taylor's army and sent it north to meet Frederick Steele's advance from Little Rock.

Parsons's brigade did not take part in either of these engagements. In February Kirby Smith, fearing a movement from the Rio Grande, had ordered Parsons's force to John B. Magruder, commanding the District of Texas.[15] Instead of trying to maintain the troops in one location, Magruder returned each company to its home county to hunt conscripts and deserters for the Bureau of Conscription.[16] Kirby Smith believed the enemy invasion would come up the Red and Washita rivers and not through Texas, but he had assured Richard Taylor that if troops were drawn from his district for the defense of Arkansas, Parsons's brigade would be sent to Louisiana.[17]

Thus, as the Federal plans for the march up the Red River began to unfold, Kirby Smith took steps to reform Parsons's force. On March 12 the anxious general urged Elkanah Greer, in charge of conscripts at Marshall, to "communicate immediately with Colonel Parsons, and direct him to hurry up as fast as possible the assembling of his brigade."[18] Over a week later Smith again stressed the need for speed: "Push forward as rapidly as possible the concentration of Parsons' brigade," he instructed Greer, for the rested horses and troops might soon be needed to defend Shreveport.[19]

Reorganizing and deploying the scattered men took time. The troops began to rendezvous at Marshall, but Kirby Smith held them in reserve until he decided which theater needed reinforcements the most.[20] Finally on April 8 he ordered Parsons's cavalry to join Taylor's army on the retreat up the Red River.[21] The brigade, however, was not complete. About seven hundred men stayed behind in Texas with orders to meet their wagon train carrying arms before joining the colonel. Then, observed Lieutenant George Ingram of the Twelfth Texas, we will "retrace our steps as quickly as possible to assist in the great battle that is now going on."[22] But in a personal directive to Parsons at 5 A.M. on the morning of April 9, Kirby Smith decided he could not wait; he instructed Parsons to proceed toward Mansfield as rapidly as possible with the troops at hand.[23]

Meanwhile, Admiral Porter, unaware of the engagement at Mansfield, struggled to direct his fleet upriver. About one mile above Loggy Bayou (located a little over halfway between Natchitoches and Shreveport), Porter found the river blocked. Taylor, attempting to delay the passage of the Federal fleet, had ordered the *New Falls City* sunk in the channel.[24] "It was," quipped Porter, "the smartest thing I ever knew the rebels to do. . . . An invitation in large letters to attend a ball in Shreveport was kindly left stuck up by the rebels, which," he sadly recalled, "we were never able to accept."[25]

While trying different methods to clear the obstruction from the river, Porter and Kilby Smith, whose division of 1,600 men from Sherman's XVII corps was along as guard, reconnoitered the countryside. After sighting Southern cavalry, Porter observed: "Banks has been defeated, or we wouldn't see those men here." The admiral felt that if Banks still advanced, the outposts would be on the road to Shreveport; if he had been defeated, the Confederates would wait for the arrival of his fleet, then attack the vessels.[26]

Indeed news soon arrived of Banks's retreat, along with a directive for Porter to save himself.[27] Withdrawing the fleet was difficult, however. The narrow channel of the Red River made turning around almost impossible; the larger vessels had to back downstream several miles before locating a place to reverse directions. Because of shallow water and frequent turns, several vessels sustained damage when they ran aground.[28]

Porter realized he provided an easy mark for the Confederates, and his haste to conduct the vessels toward Grand Ecore precipitated numerous accidents. On the morning of April 12 the wooden gunboat *Lexington* collided with the transport *Rob Roy*, forcing a delay for repairs. By afternoon most of the fleet had passed Blair's Landing, about forty-five miles above Grand Ecore, but five transports and two gunboats had to stop. The *Hastings* tied up at the landing to repair her wheel; the *Alice Vivian*, which carried four hundred horses, was aground in midstream, and Kilby Smith ordered the transports *Emerald* and *Clara Bell* to her assistance. Upstream the powerful monitor *Osage*, one of the two most effective boats afloat on inland water, was grounded even though the transport *Black Hawk* had tried, without success, to tow her around a bend. The gunboat *Lexington* lingered near the landing waiting for Commodore Thomas O. Selfridge to float the *Osage*, for Confederate snipers had begun to appear in increasing numbers.[29]

Taylor's hastily prepared plan was to destroy the fleet, but to execute this strategy he was forced to use only mounted troops. Kirby Smith had ordered most of the infantry to Arkansas, a move Taylor had protested, but Smith insisted that if Sterling Price did not receive reinforcements, he might be unable to halt Frederick Steele's advance toward Shreveport. Taylor disagreed. He believed that Steele, "who had less than ten thousand men, and was more than a hundred miles distant from Shreveport, would hear of Banks's disaster and retreat." Nevertheless, he critically observed, "General Kirby Smith's views differed from mine." Indeed, by the time the Confederate infantry reached Arkansas, the Federals were no longer moving south. Steele had positioned his army at Camden in order to shorten his communication line and hurry provisions to his hungry soldiers.[30]

But immediately following the battles near Mansfield and at Pleasant Hill, when Taylor needed the soldiers to attack Porter's fleet, they were gone. Taylor attempted to intercept the vessels with Arthur P. Bagby's cavalry, but the force failed to reach the river before the ships escaped. Taylor then dispatched Tom Green, along with his brother-in-

law James Major, at the head of a second column. Green's troops included all of Parsons's brigade except the seven hundred men who had
not arrived from Texas, the Twenty-third Texas Cavalry under Colonel
Nicholas C. Gould, and the Thirty-sixth Texas Cavalry commanded by
Colonel Peter C. Woods. Two small howitzers from a Louisiana battery
accompanied the Confederates as they headed toward the Red River.[31]

Colonel Parsons, detained at headquarters, was not with his men.
One Texan recalled that the troops "had great faith in Gen. Green" but
nevertheless "wanted Parsons too." Knowing this, Green "waited later
for his coming than he would have done."[32] Parsons, who raced on one
of his fleetest horses to join his command, overtook it in the vicinity of
Blair's plantation on the Red River. "Never shall I forget the low mur-
mur of greeting by my old veterans who had never gone into action
without my leadership, as I swiftly passed and moved up to the head of
the column," he recalled.[33] The troops shouted a greeting, and "you
would have known," noted an observer, "as I did, they were right glad to
see him, and felt greatly relieved."[34]

Green and Parsons hastily discussed the situation. Green quizzed
Parsons about his men, and the colonel replied that their illustrious reputation was not mere rumor. Green then asked him to suggest a plan.
Parsons replied that a night assault might prove successful since the
moon would be full enough for the Confederates to see the boats yet
dark enough to hide the attackers. But the two men decided a delay until
dark might permit their prey to elude the Southern cavalry a second
time. After pondering the possibilities, Green instructed Parsons to take
command of the troops on the field and lead them in the advance. Others
reported that Green confided, "he had heard a good deal about Col.
Parson's brigade, and now he was going to try it and see if it would
fight."[35]

After loading and capping their guns, the Confederates headed
for the river, toward Blair's Landing. A pilot on the *Black Hawk*, the
ship lashed to the *Osage*, informed the commanders he could see a large
force coming from the woods about two miles distant. "I ascended to the

pilot-house," later recalled Commodore Thomas O. Selfridge aboard the *Osage*, "and from their being dressed in Federal overcoats thought they were our troops; but soon their movements—dismounting and picketing their horses—convinced me they were enemies."[36]

Parsons, under the watchful eye of General Green, took command as ordered. Dismounting all but four hundred of the troops, the colonel gave the order: "On, Head of Regiments, Right into Line," and the Texans "swept with a true rebel yell across the fence and through the field to the river bank in front of the enemy's vessels."[37] Commodore Selfridge recalled: "Then commenced one of the most curious fights of the war, 2,500 infantry against a gunboat aground."[38] Parsons ordered his own dismounted troops to take the left, covered by half the mounted Texans under Colonel Carter. Woods's and Gould's untested regiments took the right, protected by Lieutenant Colonel Bell Burleson's horsemen. Colonel Parsons led the center.

As the Confederates reached the river, they saw the gunboats in motion and assumed this meant the Federals planned to retreat. David M. Fentress, assistant surgeon in Morgan's cavalry, noted the Texans "gave a hearty cheer" as they waved their arms in victory.[39] But their mistake was soon apparent. Instead of withdrawing, the enemy opened the ports on their vessels and began bombarding the river's edge with their guns. The bank, which was forty feet high, gave way as the shells enfiladed the Confederate line. Lieutenant George M. Bache, commanding the *Lexington*, observed that "one of the rebels tumbled down within a few feet of the vessel."[40]

Although the firing was heavy, Parsons's troops sustained few casualties. One observer described "shells bursting around, solid shot ploughing the ground, grape, cannister and minnie balls whistling through the ranks."[41] But Parsons's veterans, accustomed to fighting gunboats along the Mississippi and Arkansas rivers, proved hard to hit. The men laid upon their backs while loading their weapons and afforded a target for the enemy only when rising to fire. Troops in the other two regiments, failing to adopt this precaution, sustained more casualties.[42]

A recent experiment aboard the *Osage* proved valuable during the

Confederate attack on Porter's fleet (*Harper's New Monthly Magazine*,
April 1865).

Admiral Porter's fleet on the Red River

engagement. Chief engineer William Doughty earlier had suggested placing sights on top of the turret and using mirrors to train the guns on distant objects. Selfridge had not believed that what ultimately became known as the periscope would be useful, but during the afternoon he found that the invention, well protected by the turret, allowed him to survey the bank and accurately direct the fire.[43]

At the height of the action Parsons received an order to retreat, which he thought came from Green. But as the men began to pull back a brother of Green exclaimed: "Great God, Colonel! what does this mean?" Parsons replied, "I am ordered by General Green to withdraw my men." Green's brother exclaimed, "Sir, this cannot be, for my brother lies yonder dead."[44] Parsons immediately put the spurs to his

Porter's fleet passing the dam at Alexandria (*Harper's New Monthly*, April 1865).

horse and ordered: "About face; the post of safety is the post of duty; forward!" He turned the line back toward the riverbank.[45]

Indeed, the Confederates had lost their commander. Selfridge claimed that he had noticed an officer on a white horse about two hundred yards below the main line and, after aiming one of the guns at him, "saw him no longer. I learned after that the officer killed was their General Green."[46] As soon as Parsons learned of Green's death he believed the "entire responsibility of any further movement" fell on him.[47] Brigadier General James Major, sitting on his horse at the left of the line, apparently decided not to interfere, since he knew that Green had wished Colonel Parsons to direct the attack.

The fighting lasted until darkness compelled a Confederate retreat. Major, as the ranking officer on the field, finally issued an order for Parsons to withdraw, and the colonel began to pull back. The safety of

the timber was over a mile from the river, and the Texans, on foot, provided a tempting target for the defenders on the gunboats. Moreover, the
Federals had landed some infantry on the opposite bank; their fire raked
the Confederate line. Nevertheless, Colonel Parsons retired the troops in
perfect order.[48]

Dead and wounded covered the riverbank—even Tom Green remained on the field. As the fighting abated, Parsons instructed Captain
E. B. Millett of the Thirty-second Texas Cavalry to retrieve the general's
body before the Confederates surrendered the ground. Millett wrote in
1916 that enemy soldiers watched as he led a small group toward where
their commander lay, "but as we were unarmed and showed no hostile
intention, they evidently regarded us as on a peaceful mission and made
no attempt to fire upon us or to interfere with us."[49] Since it was almost
dark when the troops fell back, Colonel Carter and Captain William G.

Veal of the Twelfth Texas, both Methodist preachers, returned to the
river and buried the dead by moonlight.[50]

The Federals declined to renew the action because some of their vessels had sustained serious damage. During the battle, the pilot of the
transport *Black Hawk* could not escape from the iron pilot-house because
the gunfire was too intense. When the contest ended, no fewer than
sixty bullet marks dented the shield behind which he hid. "One regiment
would come up, deliver its fire, then fall back under cover, and another
advance," Selfridge later recalled.[51] In his official report he noted: "The
rebels fought with unusual pertinacity for over an hour, delivering the
heaviest and most concentrated fire of musketry that I have ever witnessed."[52] Parsons quoted Porter as saying the Texans' "desperate courage baffled description."[53]

Porter, who did not take part in the battle, reported that the rebels'
tenacity resulted from too much Louisiana rum. He claimed: "Every
man we picked up had his canteen half full of whiskey. [They were] well
set up with it or they wouldn't have attacked."[54] Colonel Parsons later
wrote that this was an "ignoble and unworthy intimation" on Texas
valor.[55] Assistant surgeon David Fentress insisted there was not even
enough liquor available to ease the pain of the wounded, much less allow
healthy men to avail themselves of it. Moreover, "the practice of ad-
ministering whisky and gunpowder" was not "necessary to enable the
Southron to make a charge."[56]

As the Confederates withdrew, Porter's fleet steamed south and a
few days later joined Banks at Grand Ecore. The Texans had not destroyed the squadron, but they had compelled Porter to flee in order to
avert further damage. A Union soldier who saw the vessels recorded in
his diary, "the sides of some of the transports are half shot away, and
their smoke-stacks look like huge pepper boxes."[57]

Yet Tom Green's death subdued any feeling of elation. Replacing the
popular Texan would be difficult, but Major General John A. Wharton, on
leave of absence from the Army of Tennessee, arrived at Shreveport soon
after the skirmish at Blair's Landing and at once received the position.
A Texan by birth, Wharton had fought with Terry's Texas Rangers in

Kentucky, then commanded the regiment at Shiloh. He led a brigade at Stones River and Chickamauga and had been promoted to major general for valiant service. Although Texans believed no one could supplant Green, Wharton proved acceptable as a corps commander.[58]

But the fighting was far from over. "At daybreak 'boots and saddles' were sounded by our bugles," later wrote Colonel Parsons, "and the brigade was on march to the lines around Natchitoches." From then until the battle at Yellow Bayou on May 18, "not a day or night elapsed that the sound of our guns were not heard in ceaseless attack, either upon Banks' retreating army and lines or Porter's equally demoralized gunboat fleet, upon which," Parsons proudly noted, "the first paralyzing blow was administered at Blair's Landing in the gunboat fight."[59]

12.

The Road to Yellow Bayou

Facing "ten and often twenty times their number," wrote Colonel William Parsons in his official report of the campaign down the Red River, "the world never witnessed such fights as those [of the] rebel troops who hung with such dogged valor" upon the rear of the Federal army and navy. From the time David Porter joined Nathaniel Banks at Grand Ecore until their forces reached the safety of the Mississippi River, the Confederate army pursued them without rest. For Parsons's troops this meant "long and continued privations, the oft recurring night watch, the incessant, never ending days fight, and the cool and unflinching courage which . . . bore them up against every apparent reverse."[1]

Just four days after the fleet arrived at Grand Ecore, Banks, with twenty-five thousand besieged by a mere five thousand, decided the time had come to move to Alexandria. Two important reasons forced this decision. The river was falling rapidly, threatening the safety of Porter's vessels and making advance virtually impossible. Equally critical was the need for Banks to return the men borrowed from William Sherman. Banks therefore ordered A. J. Smith's veteran western troops to occupy Natchitoches and cover the army's retreat.[2]

Before Parsons's troops headed after Banks's army, Taylor made an important change in command. Brigadier General William Steele, who oversaw the Indian Territory until his assignment to the defenses at Galveston, arrived from his post in Texas.[3] Steele, a native of New York, had graduated from the United States Military Academy in 1840, thirty-first in a class of forty-two. He served in the Seminole and Mexican wars before frontier service with the Second U.S. Dragoons. Resigning from the army in 1861, he joined the Seventh Texas Cavalry and participated in Henry H. Sibley's ill-fated New Mexico campaign. Under Taylor he took command of a division, but since the Louisiana cavalry assigned to him never reported, his command included only Colonel Parsons's brigade.[4]

Steele took over just as skirmishing began in earnest. Taylor's army followed Banks down the Cane River, once the route of the Red River until the Red cut a new course (the two channels split at Grand Ecore and ran a mile apart, reuniting some ten miles above Alexandria). Immediately west of the Red was an impassable marsh "in which," recalled William Zuber of the Twenty-first Texas, "a man's whole body would sink."[5] Thus Banks kept his army close to the Cane River while Taylor's cavalry raced for Monett's Ferry—the only practical place for the Federals to cross.

Taylor's troops harassed the enemy's every step. On the evening of April 19, the Union advance ran into hostile pickets near the Confederate camps outside Natchitoches. Henry Orr of the Twelfth Texas recalled that his squadron was thrown out in front to delay the advance and both sides exchanged shots until darkness fell. Early the next morning the firing resumed and continued all day, again with little damage to either side.[6]

The skirmishing became more intense as Banks neared Monett's Ferry. "Since daylight on the 22d, when we attacked the enemy at Natchitoches," reported Richard Taylor, "the fighting has never ceased one moment during light, [John A.] Wharton even anticipating the dawn and continuing after nightfall."[7] The heaviest fighting occurred near Cloutierville, a small town in a bend of the Cane River where the stream changed directions from south to almost due east.

Here Parsons's Texans hotly engaged the enemy. Wharton ordered nine companies of the Twenty-first and former Methodist preacher Captain William Veal's company of the Twelfth Texas to attack Lecompte's plantation near Cloutierville, where the Federals had stopped. Veal's veterans, nicknamed the "Methodist Bulls" and armed with long-range Enfields, led the advance on foot. Veal moved to the front where he could stand up, observe the dust as the bullets hit the ground, and instruct his men where to aim and how much to elevate their guns. "No man," observed William Zuber, "was more cool and thoughtful in battle than he."[8] Henry Orr of Veal's company insisted: "Captain Veal is one of the bravest men I ever saw."[9] Nevertheless, when the Federals unleashed their artillery on the Confederate position, the Texans retreated. "When the enemy had turned our left," reported Parsons, "the 12th under command of Lieut. Col. [Bell] Burleson, aided by Barnes' artillery, checked the enemy's advance, and the fight terminated."[10]

The fleeing Federals left a path of destruction for Taylor's little army to follow. Bitter about retreating, the Union soldiers burned or pillaged everything of value, and the devastation (blamed on Sherman's western troops) exceeded anything Taylor had ever seen. A. J. Smith's angry veterans started fires in both Natchitoches and Cloutierville, and although Wharton's cavalry arrived in time to put them out, hundreds of people lost their homes and possessions.

At Monett's Ferry Taylor had a chance to encircle the army while it was isolated from the protection of Porter's gunboats. He planned to place Hamilton Bee in front of the enemy on the south side of the Cane River, while Camille Polignac's men covered the road from Cloutierville, Brigadier General St. John R. Liddell held the crossing at the mouth of the river, and Wharton's cavalry harassed Banks's rear. The entire strategy, however, depended upon the inexperienced Bee holding the ford—a weakness Taylor recognized. He would have preferred to send the seasoned Wharton to this location and reported: "The importance of holding the position to the last extremity had been impressed upon General Bee both by Major-General Wharton and myself."[11]

The battle at Monett's Ferry began on April 23 and continued into the night. At three the next morning Wharton ordered William Veal's "Methodist Bulls," serving as advance guards, forward. As they approached the enemy camp, "bang! bang! went a dozen guns and the minnie came whistling amongst us," recalled Henry Orr. "We fronted into line in open order as skirmishers and halted. Directly we saw the lights spring up below and a little later, jewhillikins what a noise!" The batteries began to blaze and bombs burst in the enemy's camp. "I guess," observed Orr, Banks's men were "soon wide awake."[12] The bombardment of the sleeping camp, Parsons noted, produced "visible confusion and consternation."[13]

But the Federals refused to fight that early in the morning. Around nine Wharton ordered a charge; the troops put the spurs to their horses and with the loud Texas yell "bounded away as fast as" the animals could carry them. The first squadron of the Twenty-first Texas and Captain Veal's company of sharpshooters followed Lieutenant Colonel Dewitt Clinton Giddings's lead. After driving the Federals from their position, the Texans held it about an hour, until they were overpowered. Henry Orr boasted: "Gen. Wharton said of our charge (though on a small scale) that he never saw it equaled on the other side of the River."[14] Parsons agreed it was "one of the most brilliant and daring of the war."[15]

Yet Taylor's plan failed. Wharton's cavalry had vigorously attacked Banks's rear, but the untrained Bee fell back as the Federals advanced. Taylor severely criticized Bee while at the same time praising the veterans following Banks. Taylor reported: "It is difficult to estimate the importance of the service rendered by Wharton, Steele, and Parsons. The gallantry and pluck they exhibited in fighting such odds for three days is beyond praise." Parsons deserved special attention because he "displayed great courage and has the entire confidence of his brigade." Taylor recommended: "he should be promoted at once, as Steele commands a division. The service would be benefited."[16] (Since General Steele's division only contained the one brigade under Parsons, the colonel once again was not promoted.)

Intense skirmishing continued as the Confederates pushed the Federal army into Alexandria, where it halted. Several vessels from Porter's fleet, Banks discovered, could not pass the rapids. Parts of the river had fallen to scarcely over three feet deep, and the gunboats required seven feet to carry them over the falls. The important gunboats from Porter's Mississippi squadron were stranded, and without a rise in the river they seemed doomed. Although Lieutenant Colonel Joseph Bailey had offered a suggestion to dam the river, as was common in his Wisconsin logging country, Porter was not interested. He did not agree to the scheme until he secretly began to believe Banks might pull the army out of Alexandria. He feared waking up one morning and finding that Banks, whom he disliked, "had deserted him."[17]

While the problem of the fleet plagued Banks and Porter, the Confederate cavalry skirmished daily with the enemy outposts north of the city. Parsons's men served as pickets—two regiments on each side of Bayou Rapides—within sight of the Federals' main camp. But Parsons fell ill, and part of the time Carter commanded. The skirmishing, maintained Parsons, "was almost incessant," lasting from daylight until dark.[18] On May 10 Captain Veal took a squadron out, routing the pickets and driving them back to the safety of their lines. The Southerners then returned to the deserted Federal camps, where they enjoyed the coffee and breakfast the troops had prepared before fleeing. Captain Veal, unfortunately, was wounded in the fight.[19]

In Alexandria, Banks had become extremely anxious to retreat. "We have exhausted the country," he warned Porter, "and with the march that is before us it will be perilous to remain more than another day."[20] It took all of Porter's patience and persuasion to convince Banks to stay. "I hope, sir," he fervently pleaded, "you will not let anything divert you from the attempt to get these vessels all through safely, even if we have to stay here and eat mule meat."[21] But several uneasy days followed before the stranded part of the fleet safely passed the falls—thanks to Bailey's dam and perhaps a slight natural rise in the water.

Banks's retreat toward the Mississippi River began on May 13, with the cavalry in hot pursuit. "I at once commenced the attack on the enemy's flank in [an] open field," recalled Parsons. "Major [John B.] Williams, commanding skirmishers, distinguished himself by one of the most brilliant and successful charges . . . supported by the 19th, under the command of Col. Burford." Lieutenant Colonel Giddings, with the Twenty-first Texas, pressed the enemy through Alexandria and down the riverbank. But Williams's advance soon discovered that the retreating enemy had taken a strong position, and the engagement "became one of the hottest" of the chase. Reinforced by the Nineteenth Texas under Burford, one squadron of the Twelfth Texas under Captain Tom Haley, and Captain Edward Vontress's squadron from Morgan's command, the Confederates drove the enemy back.[22] Skirmishing continued all day, ending when Wharton withdrew the brigade. At Marksville, Captain Milton Boggess of Morgan's cavalry captured a wagon and thirty prisoners and left several Federals dead on the field.[23]

Although the veteran Texas troops distinguished themselves throughout this campaign, they occasionally refused to carry out instructions they considered injudicious. Lieutenant Buck Walton of the Twenty-first later related an instance of this hard-headed and practical outlook on war. During one of the skirmishes his detachment ran out of ammunition, and he ordered his men to take cover in a drainage ditch to wait for the supply wagon. When Brigadier General Steele rode up, he saw a line over a mile long waiting idly and angrily asked Walton why he had taken such a position. Although Walton explained, Steele ordered him, in a still "rougher and harsher voice," to charge. "We rode out of the ditch & charged," recalled Walton, "without a loaded gun in the ranks." Fortunately the Federals had begun retreating, but "being no educated soldier," Walton sarcastically observed, "I'll take to the ditch. . . . We were not cowards—we did not run—stood our ground—but were for the time invisible to the enemy. Irregular! may be so—but I had rather be a little irregular than to be shot to pieces being regular."[24]

Regular or not, the Confederates were driving Banks out of Louisiana. On May 17, 1864, Taylor's cavalry, including Parsons's, harassed the Union rear guard until almost dark. But Federal artillery, positioned near the deserted village of Simmesport on the Atchafalaya, opened a heavy fire upon the Confederates, who pulled back. The cannon's position, near Norwood's Plantation on Yellow Bayou or Bayou de Glaize, would become the battlefield the next day.[25]

The fight at Yellow Bayou on May 18 was the final engagement of Banks's Red River campaign, as well as the last major battle for Parsons's cavalrymen. Brigadier General Joseph Mower, ordered by A. J. Smith to clear out the rebels, took Sylvester Hill's brigade of the Thirty-third Missouri and the Thirty-fifth Iowa, along with the brigades of William F. Lynch and William T. Shaw, back to Yellow Bayou. These were, unfortunately for the Confederate attackers, hardened veterans of the XVI corps on loan from Sherman's army. Moreover, Mower also had the rifled guns of the Third Indiana Battery and four smooth-bore guns of the Ninth Indiana Battery.[26]

The Federal column headed toward Yellow Bayou to engage the advancing Confederates. As Mower emerged from a dense thicket, Confederate artillery opened on his line. He saw Southerners heading toward him in columns on his left and in line of battle along his front. He immediately sent for the reserves and ordered the battery to be "double-shotted with canister."[27]

Wharton personally directed the action. During the morning the Nineteenth and Twenty-first Texas received orders to charge and "feel the enemy" while the Twelfth Texas, dismounted, provided support from behind hastily constructed breastworks. But when the enemy advanced, the Texans had to fall back to a drain ditch in the center of the field, and the Federals occupied their defenses. After watching the fighting all morning, Parsons sent word to his superior that an attack would result in great loss of life on their side. When Harper Goodloe, Parsons's aide-de-camp, related this to Wharton, the major general let out an oath, then instructed the aide: "Tell Parsons to charge the enemy at once, or I will prefer charges for disobeying orders."[28] Henry Orr related that Parsons refused until directed a second time, when he sadly said, "If I must, I must."[29]

Parsons ordered the line of dismounted cavalry forward. The Federals had strengthened their right and the Twelfth Texas, positioned on the extreme left, moved straight into a "storm of grape and minnie balls" that decimated the ranks. Yet the colonel reported, "the line advanced as steadily as infantry veteran[s] over an open field," took position, and "held it until ordered to retire."[30]

At a critical moment they got support from M. V. McMahan's battery as the gunners' well-directed fire began to check the enemy advance. A shower of shot and shell surrounded Parsons as the Confederate line moved forward—his horse was wounded, his clothing riddled with bullet holes, and projectiles scraped his skin. Robert Frazier of the Nineteenth Texas told his mother that grape shot and artillery shells fell at times as "thick as hale."[31] When the troops were ordered to fall back to a better position, the men became disorganized. The colonel, in a booming voice yelled: "Halt! What! the gallant 12th behave this way with Federal cavalry on their heels? Halt! and if they charge you wheel and empty their saddles, G—— d—— them." B. F. Marchbanks recalled, "The line was right dressed, and moved out beautifully."[32]

When Parsons's men finally withdrew, other Confederates rushed into the charge. At one point they engaged four lines of the XVI corps at a distance of less than thirty paces. Federal soldiers yelled "surrender you damned Rebels or we'l Kill you all." As the Texans fell back they opened on the Union advance and drove it to the cover of the bushes. But when dusk came the Confederates retreated.[33]

Many Southerners believed the battle resulted in a needless loss of life, and Henry Orr observed that Wharton was "considerably censured for the manner in which he managed the fight."[34] Even Colonel Xavier Debray insisted it was an "unfortunate and unnecessary affair, the only result of which was to delay the enemy in reaching the eastern side of the Atchafalaya, where we wanted him to go, [and it] cost us over two hundred men killed and wounded."[35] Parsons, who felt Banks was already retreating as rapidly as possible, had hoped to save his men.[36] Lieutenant Buck Walton astutely concluded: "This was one of the bloodiest battles fought West of the Mississippi River—in which we got decently licked. The battle continued about six hours and was fiercely fought on both sides and there was great slaughter to both—I did not think" that the "battle ought to have been fought."[37]

The intense fighting brought unexpected praise for Taylor's troops. A Federal soldier recalled that the attackers had returned again and again "with a stubbornness and impetuosity" that reminded him "of the sort of assault Nathan Bedford Forrest was accustomed to make." This, concludes historian Ludwell Johnson, was "high praise indeed."[38] Union Colonel Thomas J. Kinney believed this was "one of the most severe battles of the war."[39] But perhaps the best compliment came from young Kate Stone in Tyler, who observed, after hearing of the Confederate victories along the Red River: "We will never laugh at our soldiers on this side of the Mississippi again."[40]

The price for the Confederates at Yellow Bayou was high. As usual with an attack, Taylor sustained more casualties than the entrenched defenders. He claimed around 452 killed and wounded and 156 taken prisoner, while the Federals reported losing only about 350 men. Colonel Parsons lost more men in this one battle than in any other encounter during the war. An incomplete list from Parsons's brigade reported 12 killed, 67 wounded, and 2 missing. Of this number, the Twelfth Texas suffered the most—10 killed, 61 wounded, and 2 missing. This is a striking figure when compared with the rest of the brigade—the Nineteenth Texas reported only 1 wounded, the Twenty-first counted 4 wounded, and Morgan's battalion reported 2 killed and 1 wounded.[41] It is important to note, however, that many casualties went unreported.

Two of the deaths in the Twelfth Texas were significant. Captain Joseph Wier of Company A, who led a charge while substituting for Lieutenant Colonel Bell Burleson, died instantly when shot through the head. Captain Thomas Haley of Company C, also mortally wounded in this battle, died after returning home; his son John, a lieutenant in the company, had been severely wounded in the skirmishing around Alexandria.[42]

One Texan of the Twelfth who succumbed during the night of May 18 had predicted his death. J. Sanford Turner, a corporal from Company D, confided to his friend Joseph Lafayette Estes as the two rode toward Yellow Bayou that he would not live another day. Estes asked him why he spoke such nonsense, and Turner replied: "I dreamed a dog bit me on the thigh." Private Estes laughed and replied he did not believe in premonitions. Yet both men were seriously wounded in the charge, Turner in the abdomen and Estes in the foot. Both were conveyed to the same hastily prepared hospital ward where Turner, as he had prophesied, died during the night.[43]

The Twelfth Texas reported two missing, Samuel A. Higgins and John W. Shropshire. Unknown to their friends and relatives, however, both were alive and prisoners of the Union army. When the war broke out, the two—young, idealistic, single, and anxious to fight—joined Captain Jeff Neal's "Johnson County Slashers." Surrounded by enemy soldiers at the height of the fighting, both Higgins and Shropshire had surrendered. Twenty-two-year old Higgins never returned home; he died in prison several months later, following numerous trips to the hospital, and was buried in New Orleans.[44]

A better fate awaited John Shropshire, the youngest of three brothers who along with their father had joined Captain Neal in 1861. The elder Shropshire, a middle-aged farrier, had been discharged early in the war and died at his home in 1862. Brothers James and David served as purchasing agents for the commissary department, where David's experience as a barkeeper came in handy. But young John, a farrier in the rank and file, had followed Captain Haley's charge and was wounded and captured.[45]

His fate, however, was unknown, and after his two brothers carefully searched the battlefield for his body, they wrote to their mother that John must have been among those hastily buried. While his family mourned his loss, John was in a hospital. After the fight he had been transported to Helena, Arkansas, where he made friends with N. V. McDowell of the Fifteenth Illinois Cavalry. He did not inform his family, probably because records indicate he took the oath of allegiance. Instead his new friend conveyed him to his home in Odell, Illinois. John was a handsome young man, not quite six feet tall with light hair and hazel eyes; while recuperating he stole the heart of his benefactor's sister Susan. In 1866 he finally told his family he was alive but did not return home until 1871 with, as Major A. J. Byrd noted, "his Yankee wife." The story Shropshire told to explain his lengthy absence was considerably different. According to John's version, he had never abandoned the Confederacy but had "escaped" to Illinois with the help of his Union accomplice.[46]

One recurring problem plagued the brigade during the campaign—the conflict between Carter and Parsons. The force had arrived in Louisiana under Parsons, but when he became ill on the first of May, he turned the troops over to Carter. On May 5 Parsons resumed command, only to suffer a relapse of fever the night of the sixth that again compelled a change of commanders. This second indisposition kept Parsons out of action until May 13. Nevertheless, while recuperating at McNutt's Hill, Parsons had ordered the Twenty-first Texas to move to another location without informing Carter first. Carter believed he officially headed the brigade during Parsons's absence, and he complained to Brigadier General Steele. Although the confusion over this "disputed precedence" annoyed Steele, it did not stop him from commending Parsons for his "uniform steadiness" in the rear of the retreating enemy.[47]

Actually, the actions of both men during the campaign had impressed their superiors. General Taylor informed headquarters on April 24 that Parsons "should be promoted at once," but he also believed Carter deserved recognition. He asked the chief of staff to locate two more regiments to assign to Wharton so he could create a brigade for Colonel Carter.[48] Steele wholeheartedly concurred. Carter, he wrote, "conducted himself in a manner worthy of commendation."[49] Numerous promotions followed the campaign, but neither Carter nor Parsons received one.

The arduous combat also pointed out weaknesses the brigade had as a fighting unit, and after Yellow Bayou Nathaniel Burford, colonel of the Nineteenth Texas, tendered his resignation. Burford realized he did not have the training necessary to lead a regiment into battle; Banks's Red River expedition only verified what he already recognized. He honestly admitted, "I have not the genius, nor talent requisite to make a successful military commander." Both Steele and Wharton agreed. Steele praised Major John Williams, who commanded the regiment during Lieutenant Colonel Benjamin Watson's absence, and observed that placing Williams in command would make an "efficient" regiment out of one "not so under the command of Col. Burford." Wharton concluded that Burford was a dedicated patriot, but that was not enough; Williams possessed true military talent.[50]

Congratulatory orders followed the successful campaign to rid the river valley of the invaders. The Confederate Congress issued a joint resolution thanking Taylor and the Southerners under his command.[51] Taylor, in turn, complimented his army. George Ingram of the Twelfth Texas informed his wife that the praise was in the "highest terms" for "the cavalry especially."[52] Wharton, quite naturally, commended his division but warned "the campaign is not over, nor will be until Louisiana and Arkansas are entirely rid of the enemy."[53]

The fighting along the Red River had ended, but the Texans had paid a high price for victory. According to historian Alwyn Barr, Texas losses for the entire campaign were an estimated 365 dead, 1,677 wounded, and 810 missing—a total of 2,852. As Barr noted, however, some casualties did not appear in the newspaper accounts of the campaign. The Houston *Daily Telegraph*, for instance, reported smaller losses for Parsons's brigade than the colonel did—20 killed and 124 wounded. Parsons reported 29 killed and 189 wounded (this last figure is probably a mistake since he accounted for only 159.) According to Parsons, the Twelfth Texas sustained 93 wounded and 14 killed, the Nineteenth Texas had 21 wounded and 7 killed, the Twenty-first counted 23 wounded and 3 killed, and Morgan's battalion had 5 killed and 22 wounded.[54]

But what had the Confederates accomplished with their victory? The men involved in the campaign, of course, bragged that they had prevented an invasion of Texas. But on a broader scale the Southerners had neither destroyed Porter's fleet nor stopped Banks's escape. Richard Taylor observed that the "19th corps reached Chesapeake Bay in time to save Washington from General [Jubal A.] Early's attack; while the 13th, 16th, and 17th corps reinforced Sherman in Georgia."[55]

The Union decision to send Banks up the Red River instead of against Mobile, as originally intended, probably altered overall Confederate strategy. Historian Richard McMurry points out: "Had Banks' forces been moving eastward against Mobile rather than westward toward Texas, it seems highly unlikely that the Confederate Government would have dared to send [Leonidus] Polk's Army of Mississippi and some of the garrison troops from Mobile and Florida to reinforce [Joseph E.] Johnston's army in Georgia."[56] If the twenty thousand men under Polk had not joined Johnston, and had Sherman never loaned ten thousand troops to Banks, the Union army could have pressed the Confederates back toward Atlanta much more rapidly. Grant, who had supported a campaign against Mobile, complained in his *Memoirs* that he "had tried for more than two years to have an expedition sent against Mobile when its possession by us would have been of great importance." When the town surrendered in May 1865, "its possession was of no importance."[57]

The consequences of the Red River campaign upon military operations in other areas escaped most men in Parsons's brigade—their interests were closer to home. They had accomplished what they set out to do, clearing the river valley of the enemy. But victory brought little relief. "Our horses are starving to death," wrote George Ingram in early June. "We have been fed upon promises untill our horses are skin and bone."[58] Yet the Texas cavalry remained in Louisiana several weeks. Finally, and much to the delight of the men, Parsons received instructions to report with his command to John Bankhead Magruder in Texas. It appeared that the cavalry's next duty was to be on the Rio Grande. Wharton assured Magruder, commander of the district, that this was the largest brigade he had, "equal to any to be found here or elsewhere in gallantry and soldierly qualities."[59] But the Texans had barely crossed the Sabine River when the order was countermanded, and they returned to the Piney Woods and interminable swamps along the banks of the Red River.[60]

While in Louisiana the brigade increased by one company. In January 1864 Kirby Smith had attached Samuel Richardson's company to Charles Morgan's command (bringing his battalion up to nine companies—Morgan needed ten to request designation as a regiment). At the time, however, Richardson's men were at Tyler in East Texas guarding Federal prisoners at Camp Ford and when Smith began to fear a Federal move up the Red River he had delayed sending replacements for the camp guards. It was July before Smith relieved them and early August before they actually joined the battalion below Natchitoches.[61]

The brigade remained between the Red and Mississippi rivers while the authorities tried to decide which region needed reinforcements.[62] The men were anxious to leave Louisiana. Henry Orr observed in June that everyone was "tired of Red River."[63] George W. Ingram, a captain since the death of Joseph Wier at Yellow Bayou, noted he would prefer anywhere "to this Swampy country."[64] And W. W. Heartsill, who had just arrived with Captain Richardson, quickly came to dislike the marshy lowlands. On September 1 he noted: "We are certainly off for Arkansas, or perhaps Missouri; we hope to the latter, at any rate we will take Arkansas in preference to Louisiana."[65]

During the summer, while uncertainty plagued the Trans-Mississippi Department, rumors kept the men tense and anxious. Sometimes the news that arrived bolstered morale, but most often it did not. Word came that Sherman had advanced into Georgia, Mobile appeared threatened, and Grant had initiated his siege of Petersburg. Thus when the Confederate hierarchy petitioned Kirby Smith to send reinforcements east, Texans feared they might be ordered to cross the Mississippi. This, coupled with food shortages, infrequent furloughs, no pay, and talk that the cavalry might be dismounted, only increased discontent. Heartsill bitterly observed, "It is reported, and I believe it is true; that this Army is ordered over the Mississippi, and I am sorry to say that a great many will desert before they will go."[66] When Parsons's men heard they might be sent across the river to guard cattle, George Ingram assured his wife he did not think they would go.[67] His prediction proved correct. Authorities in Richmond finally recognized the difficulties involved—even if the troops successfully avoided the river blockade, an uprising among disgruntled Confederates seemed a real possibility. In early August Jefferson Davis abandoned the idea.[68] But Kirby Smith had already launched a new campaign—his next venture would be a cavalry raid into Missouri.

13.
The Last Year

"From the action at Yellow Bayou, on the 18th of May 1864, to the close of the war in the following year," wrote Richard Taylor, "not a shot was fired in the 'Trans-Mississippi Department.'"[1] Although this statement is incorrect, it reflects the prevailing attitude in the last year of the war as well as current opinion among many historians. Events west of the Mississippi had little bearing on the ultimate outcome; operations in Virginia and Tennessee far outweighed affairs in the Trans-Mississippi.

West of the Mississippi, Southerners still refused to concede defeat although Confederate successes in the spring campaigns of 1864 had not brought relief to the department. As summer drew to a close, Robert E. Lee was on the defensive in Virginia and William T. Sherman's Federal army was advancing toward Atlanta. Southerners hoped, however, that when Northern voters visited the polls in November, Abraham Lincoln would not win reelection.

In an effort to rally Confederate sympathizers in Federal Missouri, the department commander Edmund Kirby Smith authorized yet another raid. The primary purpose of the expedition was to enlist recruits, collect weapons, and gather needed supplies, but Major General Sterling Price, who headed his columns north early in September, had higher aspirations. He hoped to take the state's capital and install a Confederate government. If all followed according to plan, he expected to disrupt the Northern presidential election.[2]

Southerners had confidence in Price. Captain George Ingram of the Twelfth Texas wrote his wife on October 20 that he had heard welcome news of Price's victories. "The Citizens hail him as a deliverer at almost evry step he advances," noted Ingram. "The ladies meet him, hug and kiss him, and shout for joy. . . . It is thought by some that Price's operations in Missouri will cause the Yankees to leave Little Rock and Pine Bluff and even now it is believed that they are getting away."[3] But John B.

Magruder, the new district commander who reached Arkansas just as Price left with twelve thousand cavalrymen, feared the enemy might try to take advantage of his state's weakened condition and petitioned Kirby Smith for reinforcements.[4]

Kirby Smith ordered Major General John Wharton to place his cavalry where Price's had been. Significantly, Wharton distinguished between Carter's and Parsons's commands when he wrote Smith from Alexandria in August: "Parsons' brigade (with Carter's regiment now in Texas, which can reach Arkansas almost as soon as troops from here) is very full, and having operated in Arkansas would be more efficient there than any other troops of my command."[5] These Texans recognized the adversaries they would meet in Arkansas, like their old antagonist Powell Clayton, who commanded the Federal garrison at Pine Bluff. As soon as the Texans arrived in the state, part of the brigade was promptly sent to watch Clayton's movements.[6]

Trans-Mississippi Confederates counted on Price's raid being a success, however, and their hopes fell as his army began retreating. John S. Marmaduke, who led a division under Price, was captured on October 25 while fighting a rear-guard action along the Kansas-Missouri border. On the next day Joseph H. Pratt, now a major commanding a battalion of artillery assigned to Marmaduke, was seriously wounded.[7] Of the other Texas artillerymen, William Hewitt was captured at Mound City, Kansas, on October 24 (while manning the guns of Captain S. S. Harris's Missouri battery), and John Coffey was shot at Mine Creek, Kansas, on October 28.[8]

For the members of Parsons's Twelfth Texas October 28 was more than just a date for a battle somewhere in Kansas. On that day, a Monday in 1861, with bright hopes and anxious anticipation, many of these same men had sworn their allegiance to the Confederacy. But now, three years later, they were tired and disillusioned—the troops longed to return to Texas. "Nearly all of the men in some of the companies say the[y] are going home after the 28th of this month," Captain Ingram reported to his wife. The discontent resulted partly from a shortage of forage for the horses and food for the men. But Ingram's company, which was on scout at the time of the letter, had plenty of provisions. "I think," he predicted, "the boys in this company will behave themselves as becometh good soldiers."[9]

Discontent was not limited to the Twelfth Texas. J. C. Morriss of the Twenty-first Texas wrote his wife in early November, "I think I will get to be of no account as a soldier for when a soldier sets his head to go home, I have noticed, that they are no account until they do get to go, and I have got my head set homeward and I will never be satisfied until I get there."[10]

Certainly the men missed their families; many even began to question why they were fighting and often headed for Texas without permission. Because the cavalry kept poor records, however, it is difficult to estimate the percentage of deserters in this brigade—the service records simply do not reflect an accurate count. But extant correspondence reveals that it was a problem in this command just as it is possible to conclude that desertions increased after the troops reached Louisiana in 1863, and again became a serious problem after the Red River campaign of 1864. There were those who chose to leave without permission or decided not to return at the end of a furlough. In Company G, Twelfth Texas, there were eight men with the last name Daugherty, seven of whom deserted on the same day in June 1864.[11] Certainly by late 1864 this was a serious problem in all the Southern armies, and to their credit, the majority of Texans stayed with Parsons until he officially dismissed them in May 1865.

In fact, not everyone who left the brigade was gone for good. Some of the citizen-soldiers simply needed a break from the war. Dave Nance, the private who had been wounded three times in the battle at Cotton Plant in July 1862, left for home, without authorization, after he received two more wounds during the Red River campaign. War, he had discovered, was not the romantic adventure he had expected when he had enlisted in Parsons's Twelfth Texas in 1861. As he headed for Texas in May 1864, he was still young, only twenty-one, but he had matured beyond his years. Disillusioned and discouraged with the fighting, he soon resolved to "never again fire another gun in battle." Nevertheless, by August he had returned to his command, and the men of his company elected him orderly. He later wrote: "[Perhaps] because of my numerous and unusual misfortunes, Company E made me their first sergeant. . . . It was considered, and rightly, too, the most difficult position to fill because the orderly had to look after the welfare of every man in the company as to both food and clothes for them and food for his horse."[12]

As Nance quickly learned, by late 1864 the Trans-Mississippi units were struggling with chronic shortages. When Price brought his defeated and disheartened army back from Missouri to Arkansas early in November, he had to head much of the cavalry directly through Indian Territory to Texas in order to procure needed supplies. Similarly William Steele, who arrived in October to replace Parsons in command of the brigade, needed not only provisions for men and horses, but also weapons.[13] When informed that two thousand arms had crossed the Mississippi River but he must send wagons for them, he replied, "I believe that this Brigade has less transportation than any other Brig in the Trans-Miss. Department, Having no Quartermaster Comissary or Ordnance Train, Company Bagage wagons being used for these purposes."[14]

Food and arms were certainly necessary, but to many soldiers— from privates to generals—the tobacco that had crossed the river was equally essential. Wharton realized this and instructed that the tobacco could "be hauled from the river, provided it can be done without interfering with more important interests." For escorting the supply wagons, Colonel Parsons received permission to retain one-fifteenth of the tobacco for his brigade.[15]

Just to feed men and animals, Steele had to keep them constantly on the move. From his headquarters at Warren, he informed Magruder: "There is no forage that I can hear of between this place and Camden. . . . Col. [Benjamin] Watson wrote yesterday that he was entirely out of corn. . . . He will be obliged to move about the country and scatter his command still more."[16] Fortunately, on the following day Steele learned that Watson had located enough provisions to provide half rations. Still, Steele complained, "Some of the Animals here have no corn today, part less than half rations."[17]

Although conditions were critical, Steele hoped to camouflage the real situation. Realizing he had to shift Watson's command, which included the Nineteenth Texas and Morgan's men, to a better location, he ordered Watson to withdraw but instructed him: "it would be advisable to say nothing to any of your officers of the destination of your command but make the impression that it is a scout."[18]

Considering the plight of Confederate Arkansas, it came as little surprise to anyone when the Texans threatened to take matters into their own hands. Lieutenant Colonel Bell Burleson, along with some of the officers, presented a petition, first to Wharton and then to Magruder, requesting that members of the Twelfth Texas be allowed to go home on October 28. According to Henry Orr, the request stated "that if the 12th was not furloughed at the expiration of their term that they believed they would go home in spite of all the officers could do." Parsons, noted Orr, neither approved nor disapproved it; Wharton disapproved it and so did Magruder. Many noncommissioned officers and privates became angry that Burleson had taken the step without their knowledge or approval and drew up their own document, which they sent to Magruder, saying "they had been misrepresented." Magruder apparently considered Burleson's action insubordinate because a few days later he ordered the lieutenant colonel's arrest.[19]

By November something had to be done. Knowing that they might soon be ordered to dismount, some companies began to drill in infantry tactics.[20] By midmonth Kirby Smith had decided to move Wharton's cavalry to Nacogdoches in East Texas as soon as Price's cavalry could replace it in southeast Arkansas.[21] Henry Orr of the Twelfth Texas sarcastically observed on November 28: "We Landed in Louisiana day before yesterday. . . . It is supposed we will go over on the Mississippi, if Gen. Magruder in his intoxication does not order us in some other direction. We can't keep pace with his orders of late."[22]

Foraging meant survival for both man and horse, but it increased the time required to move an entire command. As the Twelfth and Nineteenth Texas and Morgan's cavalry progressed slowly toward Louisiana, Steele complained: "The transportation of my Brigade which was inadequate to its necessities under the most favorable circumstances, is now much more so from the bad state of the roads and the conditions of the mules, broken down as they are by constant marching and scarcity of forage." Additionally, he had with him a number of troops without horses, and he felt they were "an incumbrance."[23]

To their delight, most of the horsemen finally turned west toward Texas. Colonel Carter's Twenty-first Texas remained in Arkansas, waiting for Price's cavalry to recover sufficiently from the Missouri raid, but once Price could take over, Carter's regiment was to join Wharton at Nacogdoches.[24] Kirby Smith had two important reasons for the move to Nacogdoches. The obvious one was that forage could be found there. But he also believed that Federals were concentrating at New Orleans, and he feared an attack on Mobile or along the Texas coast. By placing Wharton in a central position, he could quickly move the cavalrymen to support John G. Walker in Texas or Simon B. Buckner in western Louisiana. If the Federals attacked the coast at Galveston, Walker had instructions to fall back and defend Houston. To increase Confederate strength for such a possibility, Richard M. Gano's cavalry left the Indian Territory and joined the growing number of Confederates in their home state.[25]

As the concentration of mounted soldiers in Texas increased, their horses became a burden on the resources. By January 1865 Kirby Smith believed it was necessary "to reduce their number by at least one-half."[26] He instructed Wharton to dismount part of his command—six regiments from Samuel B. Maxey's division, two from Wharton's division, and one escort company. He left the final choice to Wharton but noted, "it would be most just and recommend to you that the regiments longest in the service be continued mounted." Smith suggested giving Steele a cavalry brigade consisting of the Twelfth, Twenty-first, and Thirty-third Texas (James Duff's Partisan Rangers, Fourteenth Battalion) along with the Thirteenth Battalion of Edward Waller, Jr. William P. Hardeman would command another mounted brigade consisting of his own Fourth regiment, the Nineteenth Texas, Edward J. Gurley's Thirtieth Texas, and Charles Morgan's command.[27]

This arrangement, which would have totally dissolved Parsons's old brigade, never became official. Instead Wharton gave Steele a cavalry corps of two brigades. Parsons commanded one—the Twelfth and Nineteenth Texas plus Morgan's regiment, with the Thirtieth Texas replacing the Twenty-first—and the Twenty-first was reassigned to Steele's second brigade under Walter P. Lane.[28]

While Confederate commanders worked out details of the reorganization, rumors spread that Kirby Smith planned to dismount additional regiments. Early in March Philip Frazier of the Thirtieth Texas wrote his mother that when the regiment had received orders to dismount, "I reckon you nevver [heard] such an uproar."[29] W. W. Heartsill observed late in the month that he believed the brigade would be dismounted and there were "a great many who will desert rather than walk."[30]

Although the men never had to surrender their mounts, they did lose their division commander. Major General Wharton died April 6 at Houston after Colonel George W. Baylor shot him at Magruder's headquarters in the Fannin Hotel. Baylor wrote in 1898 that Wharton had come "into Gen. Magruder's private room after we had had a difficulty on the street, and struck me in the face and called me a liar. He ought to have known I would resent it at once, for he had seen me in battle. The whole thing has been a lifelong sorrow to me."[31] Captain George Ingram wrote his wife, "A report has just reached here that Col. Baylor Killed Genl. Wharton this morning at daylight but I dont believe a word of it though it *may* by true."[32] Henry Orr informed his mother, "I am very sorry to hear . . . of Gen. Wharton."[33]

The day of Wharton's death, however, the troops in Parsons's command had reason to celebrate because Parsons returned as brigade commander. Although their enthusiasm for war may have waned, their loyalty to Colonel Parsons had not. George Ingram recalled the men "determined to have a speech from him." Since he was "quite hoarse," Parsons had tried to avoid a public appearance. Nevertheless, the Texans soon learned his location and sent runners to the different regiments revealing it. "They raised a yell," wrote Ingram, "and about twelve or fifteen hundred went out to the house and called for him. He came out, got up into a buggy and made the best speech I have heard from him."[34]

Parsons's return significantly improved the Southerners' sinking morale, although it did not ease their fear that they might lose their horses. "The health of the army is very good," noted George Ingram on the day after the colonel's return, "and in fine spirits generally." If the Federals attacked the coast of Texas, "we are prepared to give them fits."[35] Nonetheless, a few days earlier W. W. Heartsill had recorded in his diary that he had "heard of several Regiments being dismounted, and we are all looking for our turn next. . . . a great many of the dismounted men are deserting."[36]

When rumors of Robert E. Lee's surrender in Virginia began to reach Texas, the men realized the war was almost over. In preparation for the end, brigade members met at Camp Walker in Robertson County on May 2. The Texans listened to Colonel Parsons speak, then a committee drafted resolutions pledging the Confederates' support for their "fellow-soldiers everywhere" and vowing they would not lay down their weapons "as long as the breath of a Yankee miscreant pollutes the pure air of our own Sunny South."[37] But disheartening confirmation of Lee's surrender soon followed, and just two weeks after their resolutions passed, brigade officers met with Steele. Heartsill recorded, "some said their Companies would not fight any more, others said that they believed one half their men would stand in any extremity; a FEW of the Company commanders believed ALL their men would stand true, to the bitter end. Capt [Milton M.] Boggess (who is in Command) stated to Genl Steele that nearly every man of Morgan's Regiment would stand by their colors; the same was said by the Commanders of the 19th. While the Cod'g officers of the 12th and 30th believed that seven tenths of their men would never go into another fight." On May 19 about twelve men from Morgan's regiment, around thirty of the Twelfth Texas, and over seventy-five of the Nineteenth headed home.[38]

The end came late in May. On the twentieth, the regiments assembled at the little village of Sterling, not far from where the brigade members had met early in the month. "All is excitement and confusion," recalled Heartsill. Parsons called the impatient Texans to order, then proclaimed what the men already knew: "THAT WE AS AN

ARMY DISBAND." He gave the company members permission to take their wagons home and instructed the men to retain their organization in order to protect their counties from "roving bands of theives and robbers." He then "bade his Brigade an affectionate farewell, and requested all who were willing to emigrate with him to Sonora to meet him at the 'Falls of ths[e] little Brazos,' within 60 days; his closing sentence was; 'Soldiers of the First Texas Cavalry Brigade, YOU ARE ONCE MORE CITIZENS OF TEXAS, FAREWELL." A sorrowful Heartsill repined: "So our bright dream is or'e, our country is subjugated, our armies are scattered to the 'Four winds of the Heavens,' our cause is lost,! Lost,!! LOST.!!!"[39] For many men, sadness over the Confederate defeat was tempered with happiness and relief to be heading home.

The Confederacy had not won its independence, but the Texans who fought with Parsons could be proud of their record. From May 1862, when the first companies had arrived at Little Rock, until early 1865 when they returned to Texas, the troops were constantly in the field. Except for the few weeks home prior to the Red River campaign, they had served as scouts and skirmishers with little rest, less pay, and few rewards except for the knowledge they had successfully protected their families. Indeed, Henry Orr had spoken for many members of the brigade when he wrote his sister Mollie in 1862: "It does me good to know that we will be placed between the enemy and Texas."[40]

Epilogue

The war was not won or lost in the Trans-Mississippi, but the region's importance should not be ignored. Fighting west of the Mississippi was different from the other theaters, but the men who served on the "other side" of the river shared a common heritage with other Confederate soldiers: they were typical Southerners who fought with a reckless bravery that again and again impressed their Yankee opponents. Southerners were emotional—often quick to anger and always anxious to fight. These hardheaded and individualistic men had learned to ride and shoot at an early age and understood a culture that respected and honored the martial skills.

The traditions of the Old South that shaped their values, habits, and manners also determined their strengths and weaknesses as soldiers. Early in the war Southerners gained a reputation for their aggressive charges coupled with the characteristic rebel yell. The peculiar scream used by the Texans sent fear through Union cavalrymen and caused the Yankees to dub Parsons's men the "Hell Yelpers."[1] From the first successful battle at Searcy, Arkansas, until the last disastrous charge at Yellow Bayou, Louisiana, the Texans almost always charged—usually on horseback but sometimes on foot—even when a frontal assault proved suicidal; as Grady McWhiney has pointed out, this devotion to the charge indicates that Southerners "valued tradition more than success."[2]

Southerners particularly treasured their independence. Texans had a tendency to disregard orders they disagreed with, and Richard Taylor observed that discipline among the Texas cavalrymen was "shining by its utter absence."[3] There are numerous instances where the men who belonged to Parsons's brigade refused to allow military regulations to interfere with their liberties; as Buck Walton of the Twenty-first Texas explained, the Texans "were free men" who only happened to be soldiers.[4]

Many of the nonprofessional citizen-soldiers who served in the Southern armies exhibited a strong allegiance to their leaders. The Texans under Parsons and Carter displayed a mystifying loyalty to one or the other of these two men, and the conflict over command of the brigade that developed between Colonel Parsons and Colonel Carter at times hampered the unit's effectiveness. This was manifest during the Red River campaign when the two men issued conflicting orders.

Nevertheless, the majority of the Texans in the brigade, those belonging to the Twelfth and Nineteenth Texas and many under Morgan, displayed a clannish attachment to Parsons. The men's devotion and admiration for him and his corresponding respect for their lives and well-being turned the hardheaded, individualistic Texans into fine soldiers, and Parsons's brigade became one of the finest units in the Trans-Mississippi.

After the Civil War ended, the three colonels—Parsons, Carter, and Burford—had long, active lives awaiting them, beginning with prominent roles in Reconstruction politics.[5] Colonel Parsons left for South America but soon returned and served in the state senate from 1869 until 1871.[6] In May 1865 Colonel Carter, who had claimed a disability from field duty, announced his intention to run for governor of Texas.[7] Colonel Burford, after resigning from the service, helped establish a Soldier's Home in Dallas, then was elected speaker of the Texas House in 1866.[8]

Two of the three eventually left Texas. In 1871, after President Ulysses S. Grant appointed him a United States Centennial Commissioner, Parsons moved to New York. He held various positions in the United States government and lived in Virginia and Washington, D.C. In the 1880s he visited his brother Albert in Chicago, where the younger Parsons was on trial and was later executed for his involvement in the Haymarket Square riot. At the age of eighty-one, on October 2, 1907, the colonel died at the home of his son Edgar in Chicago. He was buried next to his second wife Myra in the Mount Hope Cemetery, Hastings-on-Hudson, New York.[9]

Colonel Carter also relocated. By 1870 he was involved in the heated politics of Louisiana, served in the Louisiana legislature, and became speaker of the house. In 1881 he was appointed the United States ambassador to Venezuela. Although he did not return to preaching after the war, Carter's name reappeared in the Methodist records of Virginia in 1892 when he was admitted on trial and appointed to Bedford City in the Lynchburg District. Three years later, however, he discontinued active service. In November 1900 Carter requested admittance into the Maryland Line Confederate Soldiers' Home at Pikesville, giving his occupation as lecturer. He died there on May 11, 1901, and was buried at Loudon Park in Baltimore. In an ironic turn of fate, the records at Loudon Park identify Carter as a private in the Twenty-first cavalry.[10]

Of the three regimental commanders, only Colonel Burford remained in Texas. No one had ever questioned his loyalty to the South, so his inability to command a regiment in battle had not seriously damaged his reputation. His election as speaker of the House in the Eleventh Legislature proved that the people of Texas respected his judgment. Following his term in Austin he returned to Dallas, where in the 1870s he served as a county and district judge, then a United States commissioner. He died there on May 10, 1898, and was buried at Greenwood Cemetery.[11]

Appendix

The ideal composition of a Confederate brigade such as Parsons's was three or four regiments, with ten companies constituting a regiment. The command structure at brigade level consisted of a brigadier general and his staff, but as noted with this brigade, a colonel in that position was not uncommon. Parsons's brigade staff included J. H. Brandon as the assistant adjutant general and A. J. Byrd as commissary of supplies, as well as aides-de-camp and a chief of ordnance. At the regimental level each headquarters also had its own staff while each company designated by one of the letters A through K with J omitted, had elected officers under the control of a captain.

A captain was instrumental in motivating his men's performance in the field. At the beginning of the war, prominent citizens with influence and sufficient capital competed for the position of captain by offering their services to a colonel on the condition that they could raise a full company. Recruiting took money and often required travelling through several counties to fill the quota, and occasionally a hopeful captain had to provide for the needs of the enlistees out of his own pocket. Necessarily a captain also had to possess a horse and equipment of value equal, if not superior, to those of his men. Obviously the average man could not often afford to raise a company.

Since companies were strictly volunteer in 1861, the men had to be induced to join by the wit of the recruiter or promises of a better deal than from another officer. A good orator would fill his quota much quicker than a poor speaker. Military background did not necessarily guarantee a man would be successful in raising a command; personal popularity generally proved a much greater factor in the selection of officers.

This did not necessarily mean a man would remain a captain throughout the war. The office was prestigious and frequently used as a stepping stone to higher rank. Significantly, since officers were elected, the men had the option of selecting their company commander. After the troops had engaged in combat, citizen soldiers generally replaced an incompetent officer—even if he had originally raised the company—with a man who exhibited outstanding qualities under fire.

The captains could make a great deal of difference in the performance of individual commands. As the war progressed, casualties and resignations meant changes in officers, and actual performance in battle began to count for more in the elections. It was not unusual that the best men died leading troops in battle, since bravery was expected and death was the best testimony of one's courage. Experience counted, of course, but other factors also made some captains much more effective than others. A leader who displayed gallantry and daring could inspire his troops to follow with prideful zeal, but they would shrink away from one who failed to live up to their expectations. A captain often reflected the best qualities of the men he led, and the man elected to that position might indicate the type of personality respected and admired by the rank and file. The Texans who held this position in Parsons's brigade were a varied lot; some seemed born leaders, while others relied on power and money to obtain an office for which they had no background and very little natural ability.

TWELFTH TEXAS CAVALRY REGIMENT[1]

Field and Staff
William H. Parsons—colonel
John W. Mullen—lieutenant colonel
A. Bell Burleson—lieutenant colonel
Emory W. Rogers—major
Lochlin J. Farrar—major
William G. Vardell—adjutant
A. Bell Burleson—adjutant
William M. Daviess—adjutant
T. G. A. Willis—quartermaster & commissary
Henry L. Rankin—quartermaster & commissary
R. A. Terrell—quartermaster

F. H. Ayres—commissary
J. R. Grover—quartermaster
John D. Hogan—surgeon
Thomas M. Matthews—surgeon
W. H. B. Goodwin—surgeon
Thomas D. Lorance—assistant surgeon
A. J. Embree—assistant surgeon
William Bethell—detailed surgeon
W. F. Compton—chaplain
J. Fred Cox—chaplain
Elisha Terry—chaplain

COMPANY CAPTAINS:

The Twelfth Texas was the cadre of Parsons's brigade. By the time the Nineteenth and Twenty-first Texas arrived in Arkansas in 1862, Parsons's regiment had turned back the Federal advance toward Little Rock, and earned a reputation for daring fighting that endured throughout the war.

Three captains from Parsons's brigade gave their lives in combat, and all three led companies in the Twelfth Texas (Table 1). One of these was Joseph Wier, captain of the "Hill County Volunteers," who was widely known for his "integrity, sobriety and intelligence." A comrade believed Wier was "as brave a man as ever lived." By profession he was an attorney. Although he owned only two slaves, the citizens of Hill and Navarro counties had chosen him to represent them at Austin during the secession controversy early in 1861. After returning home he raised a company from the area around Hillsboro. Wier often served as the regiment's senior captain, and while substituting for Lieutenant Colonel Bell Burleson during the charge at Yellow Bayou, he was fatally wounded. His men buried him on the battlefield, but the next year his family returned his remains to Texas.[2]

Upon Wier's death, George W. Ingram, a farmer and horse raiser from near Hillsboro, inherited the office. Since Wier's position in the

TWELFTH TEXAS CAVALRY REGIMENT

Company	Captain	Age (1861)	County of Residence
A	Joseph Wier	30	Hill
	George W. Ingram	31	Hill
B	Appleton M. Maddux	28	Freestone
C	William Jeff Neal	26	Johnson
	Thomas F. Haley	44	Johnson
	Benjamin Barnes	28	Johnson
D	M. B. Highsmith	33	Bastrop
E	John C. Brown	32	Ellis
F	William G. Veal	32	Parker
G	H. W. Kyser	38	Kaufman
H	W. J. Stokes	36	Ellis
	J. Em. Hawkins	31	Ellis
	William M. Campbell	21	Ellis
I	J. W. Mullen	50	Williamson
	Wiley Peace	43	Williamson
	James C. S. Morrow	22	Travis
K	A. F. Moss	46	Limestone
	James P. Brown	32	Limestone

regiment forced him to spend much time away from the "Volunteers," Ingram, as first lieutenant, gained valuable experience leading the company even before his formal promotion. His letters to his wife indicate a strong personal loyalty to Colonel Parsons and a dedication to the South that endured throughout the war. He named a son born in 1864 after Robert E. Lee.[3]

Table 1. These figures are based upon microfilm of the Compiled Service Records of Confederate Soldiers Who Served in Organizations from the State of Texas, National Archives Records Service, Washington, D.C. and the Eighth Census of the United States, Schedule 1: Free Inhabitants, United States Bureau of the Census, National Archives, Washington, D.C.

State Born	Occupation	Real Estate	Personal Estate
Virginia	Attorney	$ 4,000	$ 4,500
N. Carolina	Stock Raiser	1,000	2,000
Alabama	Farmer	2,600	15,709
Tennessee	Lawyer	40	0
Alabama	Farmer	3,150	15,205
Georgia	Stock Raiser	0	4,000
Missouri	Farmer	1,000	1,000
Tennessee	Farmer	0	1,450
Tennessee	Methodist Minister	8,000	1,500
Tennessee	County Surveyor	800	200
Tennessee	Stock Raiser	725	5,300
Indiana	Lawyer	4,575	7,000
Tennessee	Clerk	0	0
Delaware	Farmer	1,000	500
N. Carolina	Stock Raiser	8,000	6,000
Kentucky	Clerk	0	100
N. Carolina	Farmer	27,000	14,000
Georgia	Farmer	1,500	7,500

Equally dedicated to the South was William J. Stokes, captain of the "Ellis Blues." The men who belonged to this company, however, delighted in the sobriquet "Hell Roaring Blues." Stokes, who had come to Texas in the late 1830s with his mother and her brother, a veteran of San Jacinto, raised sheep on his farm near Tellico. After an outbreak of violence near his home in the autumn of 1860, he organized a body of minutemen, and a newspaperman reported that Stokes was "the very man to lead such a company." He left no question as to his political beliefs; the motto of the minutemen was, "Equality in the Union, or independence out of it!"[4]

When Stokes resigned, the troops selected J. Em. Hawkins as his replacement. Hawkins, a prominent Ellis County lawyer who owned thirteen slaves, had emigrated to Texas with the entire family clan soon after Texas acquired statehood. The census indicated that he lived in the Waxahachie Hotel with his Cherokee wife, although he owned land where he raised cattle, sheep, pigs, a few horses, and mules. A. J. Byrd, who served as commissary for Parsons's brigade as well as being the colonel's brother-in-law, recalled Hawkins as a man of "infinite good humor" who "never lost an opportunity to perpetrate an innocent joke." But in one case, the joke was on him. When crossing a river one dark night, Hawkins's companion told him the water was very deep and swift. Without taking time necessary to investigate the truth of the statement, Hawkins climbed off his horse, stripped, then remounted. When he rode to the riverbank his friend waited on the opposite side "rolling on the grass and boisterous with laughter at his victim's expense," for the river was "as dry as a bone." Hawkins led the "Blues" until the wounds he received at Lake Providence in June 1863 forced him to resign the following year; his replacement was William M. Campbell, a young clerk who lived alone at the Waxahachie Hotel.[5]

Thirty-two-year old John C. Brown raised a second company from the county, the "Ellis Grays." Brown lived with his father, J. J. Brown, a farmer originally from North Carolina. Although Captain Brown possessed no slaves, his father, who was worth almost twenty thousand dollars, owned seven.[6]

A third group raised in Ellis County did not represent all local boys, nor was the captain a resident of the county. The "Texas Mounted Guards" from Ellis County joined with the "Texas Mounted Rangers" from Parker County, since neither unit had the minimum required to constitute a full company, and the new body became the "Ellis Rangers." To avoid dissension, the troops elected officers alternately from each county; William G. Veal, a prominent Methodist minister from near Weatherford, became captain.[7] Veal proved an extraordinary motivator of men although somewhat unconventional in his private life. Initially the contingent from Ellis County distrusted him. One of the sergeants wrote soon after meeting him: "He has got the swellhead or likes to go to Houston and Galveston too well and associate with the big bugs. He is unpopular both in the regiment and his own company." But before the war ended, this same man reported, "Capt. Veal is one of the bravest men I ever saw."[8] Known far and wide as the "Texas Bull" for his bull-dog tenacity as a fighter, Veal gained a reputation for his mad, impetuous charges, and by 1864 his men were called the "Methodist Bulls." His numerous liaisons with women over the years had caused newspapers to dub him the "Passionate Parson" and forced him to leave the ministry. Following the war he served as president of the Parsons' Brigade Association for eleven consecutive years. While serving as master of ceremonies at a statewide Confederate Convention in 1892 at Dallas, Veal was murdered by an angry husband.[9]

One officer, William Jeff Neal, the twenty-six-year-old captain of the "Johnson County Slashers," deserves special attention. In addition to being the youngest of the original ten captains, he was a self-made man with a strong commitment to the South and a rare ability to stimulate others. In June 1861 he wrote Adjutant General William Byrd that his men were ready for service, assuring him "my Company is composed of picked men from every section of the County—men who have engaged in the Indian Warfare of the last few years on our border, and who are inured to danger & hardship." Feeling this might not be enough to convince the hierarchy of his men's ability, Neal continued: "We organized as Cavalry because we are accustomed to such service, and we are anxious that our county shall have a company in the field that will shed luster upon her name. We have been very particular in enlisting trained men who we know to be true." Neal added: "We want no more fame than to know that we have done our duty; and we want no more honored graves, than those prepared for us on the battle field." He achieved this goal. In July 1862 he was wounded while leading a charging column in the battle at Cotton Plant. Neal died several weeks later, and his final resting place was an unmarked spot in northern Arkansas.[10]

Jeff Neal did not appear in the 1860 census of Johnson County. It may be that he was the W. J. Neal listed in Hopkins County—a twenty-five-year-old farm laborer born in Tennessee. In 1861, however, Johnson County tax rolls showed that he owned a forty-dollar lot in the town of Buchanan. Although little is known about Neal other than that he claimed to be a lawyer, Colonel Parsons wrote in the young man's obituary that he had come to Texas from northeast Arkansas where he had grown up as an orphan.[11]

Neal's death elevated well-respected but much more mature Thomas Haley to the office. Alabama-born Haley had emigrated to Texas during the period of the Republic. In the 1850s he had moved to Johnson County, where owning fifteen blacks made him one of the largest slaveholders in the county. Haley bred fine horses and owned a well-known race track. When the war began he and his sons joined Parsons, and he led the "Johnson County Slashers" until seriously wounded in the charge at Yellow Bayou. He returned home to recuperate but died from complications in February 1865.[12]

After Haley's injury, the office devolved on Lieutenant Benjamin Barnes, who had moved to Texas in the 1850s and whose wealthy father owned saw, flour, woolen, and rice mills in Georgia. Since the troops probably believed that Haley would eventually return, Barnes never received an official promotion, although he commanded the "Slashers" until the war ended.[13]

Appleton M. Maddux, a prosperous farmer who owned thirteen slaves, raised a company from the area around Fairfield in Central Texas. This group, known as the "Freestone Boys," included enough men from neighboring Navarro County to prompt a resident to offer the captain five hundred dollars to claim Navarro rather than Freestone. Maddux rejected this proposition and declared he would "prove true to his county." Although it was fairly common for local residents to vie in supporting various companies, Maddux supplied the troops at his own expense rather than allow citizens from a rival county to equip them.[14]

While these two counties argued, adjoining Limestone County provided a company under Anson F. Moss. Since many of the men came from the little town of Eutaw, the troops appropriately called themselves the "Eutaw Blues." Moss, who owned nine slaves, had settled in the area in the 1840s and was by far one of the wealthiest men in the county. The 1860 agricultural census listed him as owning three different farms. He grew no cotton, but he tried raising tobacco, and one farm produced twenty-five pounds. When the war began, Moss was nearly fifty years old; he resigned and James P. Brown replaced him.[15]

Malcijah B. Highsmith, known to his friends as "Kige," brought the "Bastrop Cavalry Company" from south of Austin to join Parsons's regiment. As the son of noted Texas Ranger Samuel Highsmith, Kige had military experience of the frontier sort. He had accompanied his father on various Indian campaigns while in his teens and learned how to fight from a horse as a young man. This skill proved valuable when he scouted along the west bank of the Mississippi River.[16]

John W. Mullen raised a second company from around Austin. The men who joined the "Williamson Bowies" rode all the way from Georgetown to join Parsons. Mullen's election to lieutenant colonel forced him to pass the captaincy on to Wiley Peace, a middle-aged stock raiser who did not last long. After the first engagement, Joseph Clay Stiles Morrow, a twenty-two-year-old bookkeeper from Austin, replaced Peace.[17]

Morrow proved an excellent choice. He was a dedicated Confederate in spite of the fact that his father was a prominent Kentucky Unionist. The young man, who had little money of his own, seldom spoke of this, and his troops did not hold him accountable for his father's loyalist proclivities. Perhaps he felt a need to atone for his family's political convictions by fighting harder than other soldiers; he missed only one of thirty-seven battles. But after the war the fact that his father had sided with the Union proved beneficial; the elder Morrow could assist his son financially. Soon after the war ended, Morrow married Nancy Elizabeth Houston, one of Sam Houston's daughters.[18]

One company that arrived at Parsons's camp of instruction failed to appreciate the regimen that accompanied army life. Lochlin J. Farrar raised a sixty-two-man contingent known as the "Limestone County Volunteers." The recruits arrived in camp anxious to leave for the war, and they resented the endless hours spent drilling with no fighting in the foreseeable future. After only about three weeks they disbanded and returned home, although Farrar remained.

The loss of the "Volunteers" depleted Parsons's command to nine companies instead of the required ten,[19] but the "Kaufman Guards" quickly filled the vacancy. The captain, H. W. Kyser, had emigrated to Texas the year the state joined the Union and settled near Rockwall in 1856 where he was a county surveyor when the war began. Since Kyser had not expected to enlist under Parsons and indeed could not have joined without the unexpected departure of Farrar's men, the "Guards" provided the final addition to the regiment.[20]

TWENTY-FIRST TEXAS CAVALRY REGIMENT[21]

Field and Staff
George W. Carter—colonel
DeWitt Clinton Giddings—lieutenant colonel
B. D. Chenoweth—major
S. G. Ward—adjutant
W. J. Coroles (or Cowles)—adjutant
B. F. Cockson—adjutant
Robert Graham—quartermaster
Wellington Triplett—quartermaster
P. W. Connell—quartermaster
J. J. Lyons—commissary
A. H. McCleish—commissary
J. T. Norris—surgeon
Thomas Norris—surgeon
T. J. Petty—assistant surgeon
D. C. Hewson—assistant surgeon

COMPANY CAPTAINS:

Democratic methods of choosing officers did not mean that capable men always won. Usually elections insured the selection of wealthy or influential citizens, and Carter's Twenty-first Texas was no exception. Several of the captains were professionals—lawyers, a doctor, even a senator—and fairly wealthy (Table 2). These men had spent their own money, recruiting with little return except personal satisfaction and the prestige accorded a commissioned officer. Even Martin M. Kenney, a young lawyer in Goliad who reported only three hundred dollars worth of personal possessions and owned no slaves, could boast of family wealth—his father was a Methodist minister in Austin County who was worth almost fifty thousand dollars and owned six slaves.[22]

The instructions given to Kenney are typical of what Colonel Carter expected from his volunteers:

1) Each man must furnish his own arms to consist of one gun and Bowie Knife, and if practicable one or more pistols.

2) Each man must furnish his own horse which must be between five and twelve years of age and not less than thirteen and a half hands high for which the government would pay twelve dollars for month hire, and full value if the horse should be killed in the service. Also each man must furnish his own saddle, bridle, and blanket, and one pair spurs.

3) Each man must provide himself with 2 new pants, 2 drawers, 2 shirts, 2 pair socks, one double breasted blanket, one canteen, and one tin cup.[23]

Illinois-born Kenney proved an excellent recruiter. He raised a company for Carter's Lancers from the area around the historic La Bahia mission and quickly filled his seventy-two man minimum with well over one hundred recruits. Kenney's company would be the largest in the Twenty-first regiment throughout the war.

William M. Rust, on the other hand, led the smallest regular company. His recruits called themselves the "Austin City Light Infantry" and came from the frontier west of the state's capital. By 1864 his command had dwindled to half of its original strength, and Rust resigned to build a Confederate powder mill near his home. He invested $25,000 of his own money in the venture, and its success was vital to his financial well-being.[24]

TWENTY-FIRST TEXAS CAVALRY REGIMENT

Company	Captain	Age (1862)	County of Residence
A	Anthony Martin Branch	38	Walker
	G. W. Farris	36	Walker
B	William M. Rust	37	Burnet
	William M. Walton	30	Travis
C	Thomas B. Shannon	30	Montgomery
	R. Sample Howard	27	Anderson
D	G. R. Freeman	31	Travis
E	W. Hess Jones	38	Gonzales
	William M. Harper	37	Lavaca
F	D. C. Giddings	34	Washington
	John C. Lusk	30	Washington
G	J. H. Hannah	38	Orange
H	John R. S. Alston	27	
I	L. J. Wilson	48	
K	Martin M. Kenney	30	Goliad
L	J. B. Rocke	29	McLennan

Rust was replaced by William M. (Buck) Walton, a stern and impressive man who lived only a few doors from Sam Houston's Austin home and owned two slaves. Walton had served as Governor Francis Lubbock's private secretary before the war and claimed he had given the first secession speech on the Capitol grounds in Austin. He kept his men under close control and believed his company the best drilled and most obedient of any in the regiment. His opinionated, delightful reminiscences provide one of the few extant accounts of the regiment.[25]

Table 2. These figures are based upon microfilm of the Compiled Service Records of Confederate Soldiers Who Served in Organizations from the State of Texas, National Archives Records Service, Washington, D.C. and the Eighth Census of the United States, Schedule 1: Free Inhabitants, United States Bureau of the Census, National Archives, Washington, D.C.

State Born	Occupation	Real Estate	Personal Estate
Virginia	Lawyer	$ 5,960	$ 5,350
Tennessee	Farmer	3,690	8,815
Virginia	Farmer	4,000	6,000
Mississippi	Lawyer	12,000	6,250
Alabama	Miller	14,000	5,600
Mississippi	Farmer	0	500
Kentucky	Lawyer	20,000	5,000
Tennessee	Farmer	3,000	300
Tennessee	Farmer	3,000	10,000
Pennsylvania	Lawyer	10,000	5,000
Alabama	Stable Keeper	4,000	1,700
Dist. of Col.	Merchant	0	3,000
Illinois	Lawyer	0	300
Virginia	M.D.	0	3,500

Another lieutenant to replace his busy captain was George Washington Farris. Known as "Black Wash" for his dark complexion and black hair, he had fought in the Mexican War under General Winfield Scott. He commanded the company in the absence of Captain Anthony (Tony) Branch, a noted politician who eventually resigned after his election to the Confederate Congress at Richmond.[26]

Little is known of Lorenzo J. Wilson, who raised a company from Brazos County. He does not appear in the 1860 population census, although he apparently lived in Bryan City at that time. The 1862 tax rolls indicate that he owned a town lot, three slaves, and a few cattle for a net worth of $2,360. In 1867 Bryan's two thousand citizens elected Wilson mayor, but there is no evidence that he ever served. His Confederate record probably induced the Republican administration to refuse confirmation of the election.[27]

Thomas Brandon Shannon, who owned seven slaves, was captain of a company organized after the recruits reached camps Hébert and Carter in the spring of 1862. Many of the men came from Montgomery and Grimes counties—the area settled by the influential and wealthy Shannon family. He resigned after barely a year, claiming medical reasons, and R. Sample (Sam) Howard replaced him.[28]

George R. Freeman, who lived in Austin, raised his company primarily from Bell County. Census records indicate that he was the wealthiest man to hold the office. He owned twenty thousand unimproved acres where he ran almost three hundred sheep and fifty horses. In spite of his vast holdings, he did not own any slaves.[29]

W. Hess Jones, captain of Company E from South Texas, only served a few months. By the summer of 1862 doctors had diagnosed tuberculosis; they also operated on a fistula, making it impossible for him to ride comfortably. He returned to his farm, where he raised a few cattle and pigs and cultivated only enough corn for his personal needs.[30]

His replacement was William M. Harper, a farmer from Halletsville. Harper, who owned nine slaves, appeared prosperous. In 1860 he reported that his land had produced over one thousand bushels of corn and thirty-eight bales of cotton as well as Irish and sweet potatoes.[31]

J. H. Hannah, a merchant from the District of Columbia who owned no slaves nor land, led an assortment of Texas and Louisiana troops. Other than the information in the 1860 census which indicated he lived alone with two daughters, Hannah remains a mystery.[32]

J. B. Rocke, captain of the small contingent from McLennan County, had been elected in September 1861 by only two votes over his nearest opponent. But the company he led in 1861 was not the same he headed under Carter. The men of Company L were the overflow from Company C, Twenty-fourth Texas Cavalry, and had been enlisted not by Rocke but by the captain from the Twenty-fourth Texas. Rocke, a struggling young doctor when the war began, assumed command of the recruits from the frontier towns of Gatesville and Lampasas. He owned no land (although he reported fifty horses) nor slaves and lived with the R. F. Logan family in Waco. Rocke resigned in the spring of 1863 after a lengthy illness. Since there is no record indicating who replaced him, his small group might have been consolidated with another company.[33]

Finally, nothing is known of John Rutledge Smith (J. R. S.) Alston other than that he led a company of men from Grimes County and the surrounding area. William Zuber, author of the enjoyable *My Eighty Years in Texas*, recalled that when he visited the Prairie Plains post office in March 1862 and saw Alston recruiting for Carter's Lancers, he joined the company. Although Zuber mentioned his captain frequently in his reminiscences, he never indicated where Alston lived. Alston does not appear in the 1860 population census, but his service record indicates he rode only eight miles to join Carter at Hempstead.[34]

NINETEENTH TEXAS CAVALRY REGIMENT[35]

Field and Staff
Nathaniel M. Burford—colonel
Benjamin Watson—lieutenant colonel
Joel T. Daves—major
John B. Williams—major
James E. Terrell—adjutant
Scott Whitfield—adjutant
Alex Harwood—quartermaster
Jefferson J. Mallord—commissary
William H. Pyle—surgeon
John W. Knight—assistant surgeon
W. B. Dashiell—assistant surgeon
William H. Hughs—chaplain
Fountain P. Ray—chaplain

NINETEENTH TEXAS CAVALRY REGIMENT

Company	Captain	Age (1862)	County of Residence
A	William W. Parks	42	Ellis
	William W. Peevy	38	Ellis
B	Allen Beard	42	Dallas
	James T. Hasbrook	31	
C	Benjamin Watson	32	Ellis
	Car Forrest	33	Ellis
D	John B. Williams	28	Hill
	James B. Doak	29	Hill
E	Reuben E. Sanders	40	
F	Patrick H. Saunders	28	
	Fauntleroy R. Ball	27	Parker
G	Dubart Murphy	56	Kaufman
	William O. Michaux	28	Kaufman
H	John M. Stone	26	McLennan
I	Samuel Wright	46	Navarro
	Nicholas T. Sneed	36	Navarro
K	James Thomas	39	Dallas

COMPANY CAPTAINS:
Burford's regiment clearly demonstrated the problems inherent in
electing officers, for popularity and prestige could override military capa-

---

Table 3. These figures are based upon microfilm of the Compiled Service
Records of Confederate Soldiers Who Served in Organizations from the State of
Texas, National Archives Records Service, Washington, D.C. and the Eighth
Census of the United States, Schedule 1: Free Inhabitants, United States Bureau
of the Census, National Archives, Washington, D.C.

State Born	Occupation	Real Estate	Personal Estate
Tennessee	Court Clerk	$2,500	$ 6,200
Alabama	Farmer	1,950	2,550
Tennessee	Sheriff	1,200	1,500
Virginia	Farmer	7,000	26,000
Tennessee	Merchant	4,000	7,000
Georgia	Merchant		
Tennessee	Stock Raiser	0	2,000
Kentucky	Grocer	75	1,360
Missouri	Farmer	1,720	6,832
Florida	Merchant	500	8,000
Alabama	Farmer	759	1,900
Tennessee	Farmer	1,800	1,440
Tennessee	Farmer	1,200	4,000
Tennessee	Farmer	3,000	4,000

bility. Many of the men who raised troops for this regiment decided for various reasons that they did not want to fight in a war. Resignations (including Burford's own) plagued the command, and the Nineteenth Texas suffered the highest rate of any under Parsons. Of seventeen men elected as captain, five resigned. Four, however, were over the age of forty when the war began (Table 3).

All of the company captains appeared in the 1860 population census except Reuben E. Sanders of Company E and Patrick H. Saunders of Company F. Both of these men led companies raised near Weatherford in Parker County.

Captain Samuel J. Richardson (W. W. Heartsill, *Fourteen Hundred and 91 Days in the Confederate Army*, 1876, reprinted 1954, Bell Irvin Wiley, ed.).

MORGAN'S REGIMENT[36]

Field and Staff
Charles L. Morgan—lieutenant colonel
Benjamin D. McKie—major
W. H. Carl—adjutant
D. Fentress—assistant surgeon

COMPANY CAPTAINS:

Morgan's command was an interesting hodgepodge of independent companies thrown together to form a regiment (Table 4). Each company had its own unique history, which makes it impossible to draw any conclusions about the command as a whole. Military records provide only a skeleton account of this group, but there is information in reminiscences written long after the war or in applications for Confederate pensions (both tend to be biased) and in county histories (although errors frequently appear in these accounts).

Charles Morgan's pending promotion to colonel in 1865 meant that Samuel J. Richardson would become lieutenant colonel, but the war ended before either man received official confirmation of this change from Richmond. Richardson, a radical secessionist, had not joined the brigade until 1864 although he had raised his company, the W. P. Lane Rangers, soon after the fighting started. The company had adopted this name because Lane, a leading citizen of Marshall where the unit originated, had ceremoniously sent the troops off to join the Confederate army in April 1861. The commander was the popular if somewhat eccentric Captain Richardson. In his midthirties when the war began, Richardson stood six feet tall and had piercing gray eyes hidden behind a tiny pair of spectacles.[37]

His mother, a wealthy widow, had raised her son alone and taught him early to take responsibility. A story which circulated in Marshall told that when Richardson's mother had objected to the railroad laying a track in front of her home, Sam waited for the builders to reach her prop-

MORGAN'S REGIMENT

Company	Captain	Age (1860)	County of Residence
A	Edward H. Vontress	33	Williamson
	John W. Posey	19	Williamson
B	Milton M. Boggess	30	Rusk
C	David Alexander Nunn	23	Houston
D	Franklin L. Farrar	38	Ellis
	William Ivy Coggins	26	Ellis
E	Alf Johnson	45	Collin
	Thomas James	44	Hopkins
	R. B. Carr	28	Collin
F	Benjamin D. McKie	34	Navarro
	A. G. Hervey	34	Navarro
G	F. G. Lemmon	43	Cass
	James N. Scott	23	Marion
H	Drury Field	32	Panola
I	Samuel Richardson	35	Harrison
K	William Herbert Beazley	22	Harris

erty, then "took his stand there with a shotgun and said he would kill the first man who stuck a pick or shovel on that line."[38] The track passed further to the north.

He was equally dedicated to the South. In fact, he belonged to the radical Knights of the Golden Circle, a secret, prewar, pro-Southern organization. Early in 1860 he had visited New Orleans to discuss the status of the KGC in Texas and possibly finalize plans for an invasion of

Table 4. These figures are based upon microfilm of the Compiled Service Records of Confederate Soldiers Who Served in Organizations from the State of Texas, National Archives Records Service, Washington, D.C. and the Eighth Census of the United States, Schedule 1: Free Inhabitants, United States Bureau of the Census, National Archives, Washington, D.C.

State Born	Occupation	Real Estate	Personal Estate
Kentucky	Judge 17th District	$22,150	$ 2,400
S. Carolina	School Student	0	0
Georgia	Clerk	0	300
Mississippi	Lawyer	0	2,000
S. Carolina	Farmer Bricklayer	0	9,500
Alabama	Farmer	18,000	4,200
Tennessee	Farmer	1,000	2,300
Tennessee	Farmer	11,160	6,000
Tennessee	Doctor	8,000	7,000
Tennessee	Farmer	3,000	12,000
Kentucky	Farmer	3,000	7,705
Mississippi	Farmer	2,800	15,500
Tennessee	Lawyer	2,000	13,000
Virginia			
Mississippi	Trader (later M.D.)	0	650

Mexico. But their hopes for establishing a protectorate over Mexico ended as the problems within the Union intensified. Richardson therefore turned his attention to the preservation of states' rights.[39]

Richardson does not appear in the 1860 Federal census. Possibly he was at the KGC meeting in New Orleans when the census taker visited his house. The tax records for 1861 indicate that he and his mother jointly held nine slaves and some cattle for a net worth of $17,000.[40]

A member of the Rangers, William W. Heartsill, recorded his exploits in *Fourteen Hundred and 91 Days in the Confederate Army*, his journal for four years, one month and one day. Heartsill missed little in the men's daily lives. He recalled how in 1861 the Rangers had joined the Second Texas Cavalry, commanded by Colonel John S. Ford. Serving on the Texas frontier the first year of the war, Richardson made several pleas and at least two trips to Richmond before obtaining permission for his company to become an independent command. At the reorganization of the Confederate armies in the spring of 1862, Heartsill counted ninety out of one hundred who heeded Captain Richardson's appeal to rejoin, then "the boys all went to town to pledge their fidelity to each other and their country; by getting on a big spree." [41]

Richardson finally obtained permission to march his company north to join other Confederates defending Fort Hindman at Arkansas Post. About half of Richardson's men, including the captain, were among those captured when the post surrendered in January 1863. Although exchanged after a brief confinement in Northern prison camps, most of the troops never recrossed the Mississippi River but instead received orders to report to General Braxton Bragg in the Army of Tennessee. Although Captain Richardson joined the remnants of his command still west of the river, the enlisted men, including Heartsill, remained on the east side of the Mississippi.

Service in Tennessee was not what these Texans had bargained for. Heartsill, as did many others, criticized his "detainment" in Bragg's army although the general assured the men they would return to their proper commands as soon as he could possibly spare them. Heartsill resented, as every Texan did, fighting as infantry when he had enlisted as cavalry. In addition, his company, consolidated with others, was under the command of an officer who was not his choice, nor even from his own state. Determined to suffer no longer at the hand of strangers, Heartsill and three companions, armed with only a dozen biscuits each and a few other essentials, left for Louisiana. Travelling over seven hundred miles under assumed names, faked orders, and good luck, the men returned to Captain Richardson's command by Christmas 1863. Upon his arrival at Shreveport, Heartsill learned that his company had spent the past months scouting and was presently stationed at Camp Ford in East Texas guarding Federal prisoners. In 1864 the company officially joined Morgan's Texas cavalry. [42]

Along with Richardson's men, the members of Alf Johnson's Spy

Company captured at Arkansas Post and later exchanged also were ordered to the Army of Tennessee. Many of these Texans likewise disliked service east of the Mississippi River. Soon after joining Bragg's army, three who headed west were arrested in Mississippi. One of these, Philip H. Yelton, had permission to leave camp; the official report recorded: "Sent across the Tenn. River by orders of Genl. Cleburne in Aug. on a scout. Not yet returned." But all three escaped punishment when Patrick R. Cleburne, their commanding officer, stated: "THAT IT IS EVIDENT THAT THESE MEN WERE ON THEIR WAY BACK TO THEIR COMMAND PROPER, AND THE SOLDIER WHO WILL NOT GO TO HIS COMMAND IS THE ONE TO BE PUNISHED."[43] Heartsill, emphasizing this statement with capitals, had sympathized with the deserters. The official rolls do not indicate if Yelton stayed in Tennessee, but of the other two who had tried to escape with him, one, Drury Connelly, left again with Heartsill in November. Heartsill does not give the fate of the third member of the spy company, W. A. Thompson, but his service record indicates that he deserted at the same time, November 1863.[44] Captain Johnson died at St. Louis (see Chapter 3), but the men who escaped capture continued to use his name and eventually became Company E in Morgan's cavalry.

The other companies under Morgan could not claim such an unusual history. Milton M. Boggess of Rusk County, who would have replaced McKie as major had the regiment obtained recognition from Richmond, entered the Confederate army soon after Fort Sumter. His company, formed in April 1861, had joined the First Texas Mounted Riflemen under Henry E. McCulloch in San Antonio and had remained in frontier service until the spring of 1862, when their one-year enlistment ended. Reorganized, they eventually joined McKie's squadron, and after consolidation they became part of Morgan's command.[45]

The Crockett Boys of Houston County elected a handsome twenty-six-year-old lawyer, David Alexander Nunn, a native of Tennessee, as their captain. Nunn, a newcomer to Texas, had arrived in Crockett in 1858, served as the town's first mayor, and organized a law-abiding administration in the rural East Texas village. The Crockett Boys originally joined the Twenty-eighth Texas Cavalry but eventually became an independent command. This was the second company called the Crockett Boys that Nunn had led; the first had joined the Fourth Texas Cavalry serving under Henry H. Sibley in New Mexico. Nunn, however, had returned home after the battle at Glorieta Pass.[46]

Several other unattached companies eventually joined Morgan. One of these, raised by Edward H. Vontress, came from Williamson County. Vontress, a district judge and legislator, owned four slaves and a farm that produced wheat, corn, and some oats. In 1862 the state senate granted him a three-month leave of absence, but two years later he still led troops in the field. Shortly after the Red River campaign, Vontress was among a group of officers who disliked their orders to remain in the war-ravaged river valley where food and forage were scarce. Selected to carry a petition to Richard Taylor requesting that he move the regiments to a more favorable location, Vontress was struck and killed by lightning en route. John W. Posey, a prosperous farmer, replaced him.[47]

The third captain from Morgan's cavalry to die in the service was Franklin Lewis Farrar from Ellis County. As a young man he had served as a captain in the Regulator and Moderator War in East Texas. After moving to Ellis County he reported owning three slaves, and the agricultural census indicated he farmed twenty acres. His company had belonged to the Eighteenth Texas Cavalry but was not with the regiment in January 1863 when it was captured at Arkansas Post. Farrar died at Austin, Arkansas, from a wound he suffered in 1862, and according to family history, from a lack of food.[48]

William Ivy Coggins, who replaced Farrar, does not appear in the 1860 census, although on his Confederate Pension he indicated he moved to Ellis County around 1863. He gave his occupation as a bricklayer, but this probably referred to the years following the war.[49]

Only one man resigned from the office of captain because of incompetence—F. G. Lemmon of Company G. Both Lemmon and his replacement, James N. Scott, are difficult to verify because of a large number of possibilities among family members. Based on numerous sources, including the population, slave, and agricultural schedules of the Federal census, the two listed in Table 4 are probably correct. Lemmon, who was a prosperous farmer, owned seven slaves. Scott, who raised primarily cotton and corn, possessed nineteen.[50]

There is virtually no information on Company H raised by Drury Field, a wealthy lawyer who owned twelve slaves. Only a few names appear on the muster rolls. The unit appears to have been organized in 1864 from former members of 1 Battalion Cavalry Texas State Troops.[51]

One unusual company was attached to Morgan's assortment of troops simply to give it enough companies to reach regimental strength. According to its captain, W. Herbert Beazley, the company was attached to Morgan's unit only two days before the end of the war.[52] Members of this command consisted of pardoned deserters from other Texas organizations along with Indians from the Alabama and Coushatta tribes living in Polk County as well as one or two from the Muscogee tribe. Beazley's company was about equally divided; sixty-four Indians appear on the roll and sixty-nine white men. Sixty of the men seem to have been deserters, of whom fifty-two were still on the roll at the end of the war. Beazley, as commander of the boat yards on the Trinity River near Liberty, engaged in transporting supplies to the army and never used his company as he had originally intended. His initial suggestion involved utilizing the Indians as scouts in the swamps and canebrakes of Louisiana, since a branch of the tribe lived near Opelousas.[53]

But Beazley never had the opportunity. Instead, while recruiting Indians, he had talked with many deserters who were hiding among the tribes. Writing to Captain E. P. Turner, Beazley confided, "Most of them [the deserters] I found to be ignorant and misguided young men, anxious to escape from the position in which they had rashly placed themselves." Since he knew many of them personally he pleaded, "They are in a position in which a slight degree of clemency will make of them good citizens and soldiers, and premature severity may plunge them into irreclaimable hostility, and lead to much bloodshed among them, and those whose duty it will be to arrest them; [this would] alienate from our cause, their wide circle of friends and relatives." Beazley displayed unusual compassion when he requested: "If without injury to the service I could be allowed the privilege of bringing into my own company all who voluntarily surrender, I think I could save all who are worth saving, and thus raise a force which would dispose of those who are irreclaimable, without further trouble." [54]

Naturally the Texas authorities hesitated in granting this unusual request. But in a curt reply Beazley received permission for his humanitarian gesture: "Full pardon will be granted to the deserters if they will come in but no conditions will be made with them as to what companies they shall join." However, the authorities granted Beazley permission to attach them to his company until notified otherwise. [55] Ironically, at the time of this decision, part of Parsons's command was in Texas arresting Confederate deserters.

THIRTIETH TEXAS CAVALRY REGIMENT [56]

Field and Staff
Edward J. Gurley—colonel
Nicholas W. Battle—lieutenant colonel
John H. Davenport—major
Oscar H. Leland—adjutant
M. W. Jones—adjutant
John Abney—quartermaster
W. W. Slaughter—commissary
J. H. Sears—surgeon
John W. Maddin—assistant surgeon
J. F. Shelton—assistant surgeon
William H. Pierce—assistant surgeon
J. J. Riddle—chaplain

THIRTIETH TEXAS CAVALRY REGIMENT

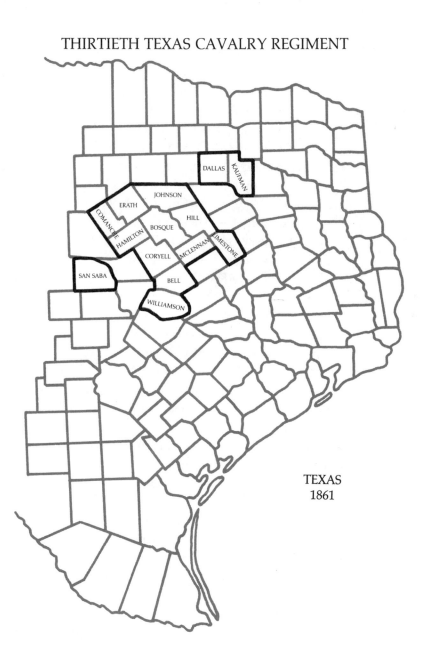

TEXAS
1861

Figure 5. E. J. Gurley raised his regiment from the counties around his home at Waco. Many of the men in this organization had belonged to local defense units until the conscription law forced them to join the Confederate army.

Company Captains
Company A—James M. Wright
Company B—J. P. Morris
Company C—Oscar J. Downs
Company D—Samuel M. Strayhorn
Company E—Samuel Caruthers
Company F—C. C. McCurry, L. R. Love
Company G—Thomas C. Frost
Company H—Jackson Puckett
Company I—J. L. Smith
Company K—C. Murry Lea

The Thirtieth Texas joined Parsons's brigade just before the war ended. The regiment, raised by wealthy Waco lawyer Edward J. Gurley, was similar in makeup to the Nineteenth Texas. Most of the men lived in one region of Central Texas (Figure 5). They were family men, often older than those of the Twelfth Texas, and they did not join the Confederate army until after the passage of the conscription law in 1862. Authorized by Major General Thomas C. Hindman June 2, the regiment officially mustered in on August 18, 1862.[57]

After organization this regiment remained in Texas. In December 1862 the men received orders to make ready to move to Vicksburg, but Major General J. Bankhead Magruder, commander of the District of Texas, requested that the regiment remain near Columbus in South Texas to protect the frontier and supply lines. Moreover, Magruder offered to arm Gurley's men (who possessed few weapons) if he could retain the regiment in Texas.[58]

Almost one year passed before the troops headed out of the state. In the summer of 1863 Gurley received instructions to report to Brigadier General William Steele, who commanded the Indian Territory.[59] For the next two years the Texans fought in various engagements there and in southern Arkansas. Most of the time, however, the men engaged in the tedious and boring duty of scouting near the Union stronghold of Fort Smith.

These troops displayed the same inadequacies found in many Texas regiments and very similar to those of the Nineteenth and Twenty-first Texas. In October 1863, W. C. Schaumburg from the Inspector General's office submitted a critical evaluation of the men's military abilities. He noted that Smith P. Bankhead's command (which the Thirtieth Texas joined) was in "poor condition as a brigade" and in discipline of the regiments. Gurley's cavalry, in particular, "presented a very poor appearance." Schaumburg requested the senior captains in charge of the men to drill them, "and each of them in turn admitted his incompetency to do so; finally the senior captain made the attempt, and failed most signally."[60]

It is quite possible, however, that the men refused to drill as an expression of their displeasure with the Confederate government. Their clothing had been left at Bonham in North Texas, and the authorities, unable to provide transportation to the command, had done little to relieve the conditions. Steele reported the Texans, "suffering for want of proper clothing for the season, were commencing to desert."[61]

A poignant letter written by First Lieutenant John W. Berry of Company E verified the hardships. In January 1864 he informed a friend that all the men were "living very hard and have suffered much from cold. My health is tolerably good. I had fine health for sometime untill the last scout the weather was so bad and I had to take it out of door with one blanket." Berry confided: "I am suffering some with cold taken on our last trap."[62]

Frustration plagued the command. Not only were the men suffering, but, Berry noted, "The officers have rather a hard time of it as several of them have been suspended and others under arrest so that duty comes pretty often. . . . I have [been] in command of Regiment the greater portion of the time since 25 December."[63]

Discontent swept all the way to the top of the regimental structure. Colonel Gurley, who disliked being placed under Smith Bankhead, protested to E. Kirby Smith. Bankhead, on the other hand, complained to his relative J. B. Magruder that Gurley's actions "had a bad effect on the regiment." Further, he added sarcastically, it was "insubordinate, and in keeping with the general conduct of Texas officers and men."[64]

But changes occurred in late 1864. A troop return in December indicated the Thirtieth Texas belonged to Richard M. Gano's brigade in Samuel Bell Maxey's division.[65] The change to William Steele's corps, Parsons's brigade, did not occur until March 1865.[66] Colonel Parsons reported the regiment arrived at his camp in April 1865.[67]

Although the men were pleased to return to Texas, they did not like what awaited them there. Philip Frazier wrote his family early in March that the command had arrived at Columbus in South Texas. But Colonel Gurley, he informed them, had received instructions to dismount the men. According to Frazier, the troops were furious. "I reckin you nevver [heard] such an uproar," he related. To prevent mutiny Lieutenant Colonel Battle immediately left for Houston and persuaded General John Magruder to countermand the order.[68] Soon after this the troops joined Parsons at Wallace Prairie. They were with him when news of the surrender arrived in Texas.

Notes

INTRODUCTION

1. W. H. Parsons to W. H. Getzendaner, June 24, 1878, *A Brief and Condensed History of Parsons' Texas Cavalry Brigade Composed of Twelfth, Nineteenth, Twenty-First, Morgan's Battalion, and Pratt's Battery of Artillery of the Confederate States: Together with Roster of the several Commands as far as obtainable—Some Historical Sketches—General Orders and a Memoranda of Parson's Brigade Association* (Waxahachie, Texas: J. M. Flemister, Printer, 1892), 19.

2 George H. Hogan, "Parsons's Brigade of Texas Cavalry," *Confederate Veteran*, 33 (January 1925), 17.

3. Norman D. Brown, ed., *Journey to Pleasant Hill: The Civil War Letters of Captain Elijah P. Petty, Walker's Texas Division, C.S.A.* (San Antonio: Institute of Texan Cultures, 1982), xiii.

4. W. H. Parsons to W. H. Getzendaner, June 24, 1878, *Brief History of Parsons' Brigade*, 18–19.

5. For an extensive analysis of the Southern characteristics of Texans in 1860 see Terry G. Jordan, "The Imprint of the Upper and Lower South in Mid-Nineteenth Century Texas," *Annals of the Association of American Geographers* 57 (December 1967): 667–690. For the distinctive characteristics of Southerners see Grady McWhiney, *Cracker Culture: Celtic Ways in the Old South* (Tuscaloosa and London: The University of Alabama Press, 1988).

6. For a discussion of loyalty to leaders see Grady McWhiney and Perry D. Jamieson, *Attack and Die: Civil War Military Tactics and the Southern Heritage* (University, Alabama: The University of Alabama Press, 1982), 187.

7. J. C. Morriss to Amanda Morriss, September 20, 1862, in Jakie L. Pruett and Scott Black, eds., *Civil War Letters: 1861–1865. A Glimpse of the War Between the States* (Austin: Eakin Press, 1985), 33–34.

8. Ibid., 34.

9. Cavalry tactics changed during the Civil War. For more on the use of the cavalry see McWhiney and Jamieson, *Attack and Die*, 126–139.

10. Letter of James F. Fagan to C. B. Mitchel, November 27, 1863, photocopy in the collection of Joe and Ann Cerney, Wichita Falls, Texas. Mrs. Cerney to Anne Bailey, February 18, 1985. Joe's wife Ann Cerney is a descendent of William Parsons's son, Harry Dennard Parsons. *Civil War Letters*, 35–38.

12. McWhiney, *Cracker Culture*, 271.

13. Robert L. Kerby, *Kirby Smith's Confederacy: The Trans-Mississippi South, 1863–1865* (New York: Columbia University Press, 1972), 431.

CHAPTER ONE

1. W. H. Parsons to W. H. Getzendaner, June 24, 1878, *A Brief and Condensed History of Parsons' Texas Cavalry Brigade Composed of Twelfth, Nineteenth, Twenty-First, Morgan's Battalion, and Pratt's Battery of Artillery of the Confederate States: Together with Roster of the several Commands as far as obtainable—Some Historical Sketches—General Orders and a Memoranda of Parsons' Brigade Association* (Waxahachie, Texas: J. M. Flemister, Printer, 1892), 21.

2. Ibid., 17, 18.

3. George H. Hogan, "Parsons's Brigade of Texas Cavalry," *Confederate Veteran*, 33 (January 1925): 17. Hogan served in Company E, Twelfth Texas Cavalry and as adjutant of Parsons' Brigade Association of veterans after the war.

4. The quote is from a sketch of Frank M. Files. *Itasca* [Texas] *Item*, April 25, 1924. He belonged to Company C, Nineteenth Texas Cavalry. Fifteen-year-old Albert Parsons, who joined his brother's regiment in Arkansas, recorded in his autobiography that the soldiers "invested" the colonel with the sobriquet "Wild Bill." Lucy E. Parsons, ed., *Life of Albert R. Parsons* (1889; reprint, Chicago: Lucy E. Parsons, 1903), 14.

5. In 1866 Nathaniel M. Burford was Speaker of the House of Representatives in the Eleventh Legislature of the State of Texas. During the war he had tried to secure Parsons's promotion to brigadier general but was unsuccessful. He probably used his influence to obtain this recognition after the war ended. Joe Cerney to Anne Bailey, February 18, 1985.

6. *Condensed History of Parsons Texas Cavalry Brigade 1861–1865: Together with Inside History and Heretofore Unwritten Chapters of the Red River Campaign of 1864* (Corsicana, Texas: 1903), 4.

7. Samuel Parsons married into the Tompkins-Broadwell family of New Jersey. There is a great deal of information concerning Parsons's ancestors. His younger brother Albert moved north following the war and was among those

executed for the killings at Chicago's Haymarket Square Riot in May 1886. Parsons, *Life of Albert R. Parsons*, 12–15; Philip S. Foner, ed., *The Autobiographies of the Haymarket Martyrs* (New York: Humanities Press, 1969), 27–29; Paul Avrich, *The Haymarket Tragedy* (Princeton: Princeton University Press, 1984), 3–5; "The New England and Southern Stock from Whom A. R. Parsons Sprang—Revolutionary Soldiers, Scholars and Honorable Men," *Knights of Labor* (November 1886), 31–32; Carolyn Ashbaugh, *Lucy Parsons, American Revolutionary* (Chicago: Charles H. Kerr Publishing Co., 1976), 13–14.

8. Foner, *The Autobiographies of the Haymarket Martyrs*, 27–29; Parsons, *Life of Albert R. Parsons*, 12–15; United States Bureau of the Census, Seventh Census of the United States, Montgomery County, Alabama, 1850.

9. William H. Parsons, "Personal Reminiscences," in *Condensed History of Parsons Brigade*, 105–106; Dolores J. Hall, Emory University, to Anne Bailey, January 2, 1985. Oxford College of Emory University still exists as the junior college near Covington. But since Parsons did not graduate, there is no record of his attendance. His mother, a devout Methodist, probably influenced his decision to attend this school.

10. William H. Parsons, "Personal Reminiscences," in *Condensed History of Parsons Brigade*, 105–106.

11. William Parsons married Louisa Dennard in February 1851; they had four sons and one daughter; Sid S. Johnson, *Some Biographies of Old Settlers: Historical, Personal, and Reminiscent* (Tyler, Texas: Sid S. Johnson, Publisher, 1900), 109.

12. According to Sid Johnson, Parsons accepted the challenge and selected rifles as the weapon to settle the difference; ibid., 109–110, 175. But Frederick Law Olmsted, *A Journey Through Texas; or, A Saddle-trip on the Southwestern Frontier* (New York: Dix, Edwards & Co., 1857), 498, printed an excerpt from the *Jefferson Herald* reporting the matter had gone to a Board of Honor. Grinsted selected W. B. Ochiltree, lawyer and judge, while Parsons chose Colonel M. D. Ector, and the referees added Colonel J. C. Robertson. The Board agreed upon the following terms of settlement: "That all remarks and relections emanating from either gentleman, tending in any manner to impugn the character for courage, honesty, or integrity of the other, and every remark of a personal character, which has fallen from either of the parties with regard to the other, be withdrawn." The paper reported: "We are truly glad that this precedent for the settling of difficulties between editors has been established. We are decidedly op-

posed to the shooting mode of settling such disputes. It is very apt to derange the nervous system and destroy the appetite." According to Marilyn McAdams Sibley, *Lone Stars and State Gazettes; Texas Newspapers before the Civil War* (College Station: Texas A & M Press, 1983), 371, contemporary newspaper accounts identified Parsons's assailant as John Morgan.

13. W. H. Parsons, "Southern Emigration to Arizona and Sonora," *Dallas Herald*, March 30, 1859.

14. According to an old resident there is "no doubt that this was the most brilliantly edited sheet that Waco ever had, and, is admitted to be even by those who thought Parsons extravagant and picturesque in his proposals." The *South West* was purely a war paper and died after it served its purpose. *A Memorial and Biographical History of McLennan, Falls, Bell and Coryell counties, Texas* (Chicago: Lewis Publishing Company, 1893), 118; Sibley, *Lone Stars and State Gazettes*, 374.

15. *South West*, October 17, 1860.

16. Eighth Census of the United States, McLennan County, Texas, Schedule 1: Free Inhabitants and Schedule 2: Slave Inhabitants, 1860; Foner, *Autobiographies of the Haymarket Martyrs*, 29. Albert Parsons recalled that Aunt Esther, who was fifty years old in 1860, had raised him when an orphan "with great kindness and a mother's love."

17. *South West*, October 17, 1860.

18. Parsons and Nathaniel Burford were nominated as delegates for the convention at Montgomery, Alabama, but both withdrew their names before the third ballot. George Carter, a Methodist minister known for his eloquence, addressed the audience at recess. Ernest William Winkler, ed., *Journal of the Secession Convention of Texas, 1861* (Austin: Austin Printing Co., 1912), 19, 78–79.

19. Parsons received instructions to raise a regiment of mounted troops from the ninth military district, composed of the counties of Ellis, Hill, Navarro, McLennan, Limestone, Freestone, Bell, Falls, Johnson, and Williamson. Special Orders No. 18, July 25, 1861, U. S. War Department, *The War of the Rebellion: A Compilation of the Official Records of the Union and Confederate Armies* (128 vols., Washington, D. C., 1880–1901), Series I, 4:95 (hereafter cited as *OR*; unless otherwise indicated, all references are to Series I).

20. *Governor's Message, November 1, 1861*, 10; Texas Adjutant General, *Report, November, 1861*, 1–2.

21. James A. L. Fremantle, *Three Months in the Southern States April-June 1863* (1863; reprint, Alexandria, Virginia: Time-Life Books Inc., 1984), 72.

22. Stephen B. Oates, *Confederate Cavalry West of the River* (Austin: University of Texas Press, 1961), 26–27.

23. W. O. Wynn, *Biographical Sketch of the Life of an Old Confederate Soldier* (Greenville, Texas: Greenville Printing Co., Inc., 1916), 36. In 1861 Wynn was still too young to join the Confederate army, but his employer left with Captain Jeff Neal. Five companies, including Neal's, formed a battalion under Lieutenant Colonel A. C. Hoyle, Major John W. Berry, and Silas A. Carpenter, acting adjutant. Initially they became part of the Twentieth Brigade, Texas State Troops. *Dallas Herald*, July 10, 1861. At the time of enlistment Neal mustered in forty-three men. S. A. Carpenter to William Byrd, June 24, 1861, Johnson County Volunteers, Texas State Archives, Austin, Texas.

24. *Dallas Herald*, July 10, 1861.

25. Compiled Service Records of Confederate Soldiers who Served in Organizations from the State of Texas, Twelfth Texas Cavalry, Microfilm Rolls 323 : 71–74 (hereafter cited as Compiled Service Records), National Archives, Washington, D. C.

26. George W. Ingram to Martha Ingram, July 27, 1861, in Henry L. Ingram, comp., *Civil War Letters of George W. and Martha F. Ingram 1861–1865* (College Station: Texas A & M Press, 1973), 4.

27. The letter originally designated for five of the companies did not stay the same: Company E became H, Company F became E, Company G became F, Company H became I, and Company I became G. For this reason there were often errors when transcribing members. Wiley Peace, for example, was erroneously listed under Company H; he was captain of Company I. The chart in the Appendix lists the companies as they were recorded in the Compiled Service Records.

28. Little Rock *Arkansas True Democrat*, June 5, 1862; Houston *Tri-Weekly Telegraph*, June 20, 1862; Eighth Census of the United States, Williamson County, Texas.

29. Andrew Bell Burleson, son of John Shipman Burleson and his wife Rebecca Bell, was named for his grandfather Andrew Bell. In October 1864 he started a petition "stating that if the 12th was not furloughed at the expiration of their term that they believed they would go home in spite of all the officers could do." Soon after this he was arrested. Henry Orr to "Sister," November 12,

1864, in John Q. Anderson, ed., *Campaigning with Parsons' Texas Cavalry Brigade, CSA: The War Journals and Letters of the Four Orr Brothers, 12th Texas Cavalry Regiment* (Hillsboro, Texas: Hill Junior College Press, 1967), 149–150; Henry Orr to "Father," November 24, 1864, ibid., 151. After the war ended Burleson began to drink heavily, and a family historian, Rita Bryan, related that before his death he wandered the streets muttering to himself. He apparently died alone; his wife had divorced him, probably as a result of his alcoholism.

30. Little Rock *Arkansas True Democrat*, May 29, 1862; Houston *Tri-Weekly Telegraph*, June 20, 1862; *Ellis County History: The Basic 1892 book (With the Presidents Selection deleted) with Additional Biographies compiled by The Ellis County Historical Museum and Art Gallery, Inc. in Memory of the Courageous Pioneers and Builders of Ellis, County* (Fort Worth & Arlington: Historical Publishers, 1972), 726–729; Eighth Census of the United States, Ellis County, Texas.

31. *A Memorial and Biographical History of Navarro, Henderson, Anderson, Limestone, Freestone and Leon Counties, Texas* (Chicago: The Lewis Publishing Co., 1892), 368; Roy A. Walter, *A History of Limestone County* (Austin: Von Boeckmann-Jones, 1959), 50–51; Eighth Census of the United States, Limestone County, Texas.

32. The committee that reported the event September 11 consisted of W. H. Getzendaner, J. Fred Cox, who served as chaplain for the regiment, and A. M. Dechman, acting assistant adjutant general of the brigade. *Condensed History of Parsons Brigade*, 7–9.

33. Most companies in the regiment had been stationed at Camp Hébert in Collin County. They left North Texas the last of October, stayed briefly at Camp Moss near Eutaw, then moved on to a camp on Clear Creek two miles from Hempstead, in the neighborhood of Colonels Groce, Kirby, and Woodward; Houston *Tri-Weekly Telegraph*, November 15, 1861; Journal entry of Henry Orr, dated October 20, 1861, in Anderson, *Campaigning with Parsons' Brigade*, 6; Corsicana *Navarro Express*, November 21, 1861.

34. James J. Frazier to Agnes Frazier, November 2, 1861, Frazier Family Papers, Barker Texas History Center, Austin, Texas.

35. Journal entry of Henry Orr, dated October 1861, in Anderson, *Campaigning with Parsons' Brigade*, 8; Henry Orr to Mary Orr, October 31, 1861, ibid., 9–11.

36. James J. Frazier to R. F. Frazier, December 5, 1861, Frazier Family

Papers; Journal entry of Henry Orr, dated October 1861, in Anderson, *Campaigning with Parsons' Brigade*, 8; Henry Orr to Mary Orr, October 31, 1861, ibid., 9–11; G. W. Ingram to Martha Ingram, November 6, 1861, *Civil War Letters*, 8–9.

37. P. H. Goodloe, "Service in the Trans-Mississippi," *Confederate Veteran*, 33 (January 1915): 31–32. Although Goodloe's reminiscences are very inaccurate, his anecdote may reflect the truth since Colonel Parsons generally overlooked minor infractions of regulations.

38. Houston *Tri-Weekly Telegraph*, November 12, 1861.

39. *Dallas Herald*, January 8, 1862; Robert Orr to Sam Orr, January 10, 1862, in Anderson, *Campaigning With Parsons' Brigade*, 20–21.

40. James J. Frazier to "Mother, Brothers & Sisters," January 7, 1862, Frazier Family Papers.

41. Parsons, "Personal Reminiscences," *Condensed History of Parsons Brigade*, 106.

42. Corsicana *Navarro Express*, November 21, 1861.

43. Henry Orr to "Brother and Family," February 25, 1862, in Anderson, *Campaigning with Parsons' Brigade*, 31.

44. Journal entry of Henry Orr, dated February 27, 1862, ibid., 32.

45. Ibid.

46. Richard Taylor, *Destruction and Reconstruction: Experiences of the Late War* (Edinburgh and London: William Blackwood and Sons, 1879), 162.

47. Although mustangs abounded in West Texas, no self-respecting cavalryman wanted to ride one. Bloodlines meant a great deal to cavalrymen all across the South, and Texas was no exception. When Nathaniel Banks occupied Texas along the Rio Grande in November 1863 he "arranged to buy locally 'about 600 horses (mustang)' but then discovered that to improve the condition of the animals, he had to have oats shipped to him from New Orleans." Stephen Z. Starr, *The Union Cavalry in the Civil War*, vol. 3: *The War in the West 1861–1865* (Baton Rouge: Louisiana State University Press, 1985), 483.

48. Little Rock *Arkansas True Democrat*, June 5, 1862.

49. L. T. Wheeler, "Introduction," *Condensed History of Parsons Brigade*, 4.

50. Byrd had been describing the previously mentioned Harper Goodloe, who became a member of Parsons's staff. Goodloe, asserted Byrd, was remembered for "his pride at times bordering on vanity," but "it was excusable in him,

for he came by it innocently, in fact, by absorption or friction, being always near to the person of Col. Parsons." A. J. Byrd, *History and Description of Johnson County, and its Principal Towns* (Marshall, Texas: Jennings Brothers, 1879), 86–87.

CHAPTER TWO

1. Susan Anna Good to John Jay Good, April 20, 1862, in Lester Newton Fitzhugh, ed., *Cannon Smoke: The Letters of Captain John J. Good, Good-Douglas Texas Battery, CSA* (Hillsboro, Texas: Hill Junior College Press, 1971), 182–184.

2. Henry Clay Warmoth, *War, Politics and Reconstruction: Stormy Days in Louisiana* (1930; reprint, New York: Negro Universities Press, 1970), 109–112.

3. J. C. Morriss to Amanda Morriss, October 1, 1862, in Jakie L. Pruett and Scott Black, eds., *Civil War Letters: 1861–1865. A Glimpse of the War Between the States* (Austin: Eakin Press, 1985), 35–38.

4. Application of George W. Carter for admission to the Maryland Line Confederate Soldiers' Home at Pikesville, Maryland, dated November 6, 1900; typescript of article on George W. Carter for the forthcoming *Handbook of Louisiana*; obituary in the *Washington Post*, May 13, 1901; Macum Phelan, *A History of Early Methodism in Texas 1817–1866* (Dallas: Cokesbury Press, 1924), 424. Also see the *Minutes of the Annual Conferences of the Methodist Episcopal Church, South, for the years 1847 through 1865* (Nashville: Southern Methodist Publishing House, 1848–1870).

5. Phelan, *Early Methodism in Texas*, 402–405, 464; John H. McLean, "Our Early Schools," *Texas Methodist Historical Quarterly* 2 (July 1910): 64.

6. Phelan, *Early Methodism in Texas*, 405, 464–465.

7. Ernest William Winkler, ed., *Journal of the Secession Convention of Texas, 1861* (Austin: Austin Printing Co., 1912), 19; Frank Brown, "Annals of Travis County and the City of Austin," typescript in the Texas State Archives, Austin, 21 : 14. Both of these report a speech favoring resistance and secession which Carter gave in the Representative Hall on January 28, 1861.

8. Tax Rolls for Washington County, 1861, Texas State Archives, Austin, Texas.

9. Phelan, *Early Methodism in Texas*, 465–468.

10. Extract from a letter of an unnamed faculty member at Soule Univer-

sity, March 26, 1862, ibid., 465–466. Soule University resumed operation in 1867 on a more or less regular basis, but in 1888 the school closed permanently.

11. Houston *Tri-Weekly Telegraph*, November 1, 1861; *Dallas Herald*, November 27, 1861; R. H. Chilton to P. O. Hébert, October 4, 1861, in the service record of George W. Carter, Compiled Service Records of Confederate Soldiers Who Served in Organizations from the State of Texas, Twenty-first Texas Cavalry, Microfilm Rolls 323 : 110–112 (hereafter cited as Compiled Service Records), National Archives, Washington, D. C.

12. Warmoth, *War, Politics and Reconstruction*, 109.

13. New Orleans *Daily Picayune*, February 20, 1872.

14. Austin *Texas State Gazette*, November 16, 1861.

15. Joseph E. Johnston, *Narrative of Military Operations Directed During the Late War Between the States* (1874; reprint, Bloomington: Indiana University Press, 1959), 479.

16. Henry W. Halleck, *Elements of Military Art and Science; or, Course of Instructions in Strategy, Fortification, Tactics of Battles, &c.* (New York: D. Appleton & Co., 1846), 127–128.

17. Joseph Wheeler, *A Revised System of Cavalry Tactics for the Use of the Cavalry and Mounted Infantry, C.S.A.* (Mobile: S. H. Goetzel & Co., 1863), 63.

18. G. W. Carter to P. O. Hébert, December 4, 1861, Compiled Service Record of G. W. Carter. Colonel Carter, who apparently had trouble convincing Hébert to send a mustering officer, was not above resorting to coercion. He urged Hébert to listen to the statements of his representatives "before making your decision" but then warned, "If you can not meet my wishes in the matter" then the volunteers must be mustered in "under the special law referred to, when I first presented this subject for your consideration."

19. Francis R. Lubbock to J. P. Benjamin, February 25, 1862, U.S. War Department, *The War of the Rebellion: A Compilation of the Official Records of the Union and Confederate Armies* (128 vols., Washington, D. C., 1880–1901), Series I, 53 : 790 (hereafter cited as *OR*; unless otherwise indicated all references are to Series I).

20. Phelan, *Early Methodism in Texas*, 470. Phelan mentioned that in compiling the history of the church he had in his possession the original journal of Oscar M. Addison, who joined Joseph Bates's Thirteenth Texas Infantry as chaplain after leaving Carter's command.

21. *Bellville* [Texas] *Countryman*, March 1, 1862.

22. Expense report for travelling from Hempstead to Richmond and return, March 1 to April 6, 1862, $350.00, Compiled Service Record of George W. Carter; *Bellville Countryman*, May 3, 1863. According to church records, Clayton C. Gillespie had been transferred from Texas to New Orleans in 1858; *Minutes of the Methodist Episcopal Church, South, 1858*, 82. Also see account of William Physick Zuber, *My Eighty Years in Texas*, ed. by Janis Boyle Mayfield (Austin: University of Texas Press, 1971), 135. Born in 1820 in Georgia, Zuber moved with his parents to Texas in 1830. His amusing narrative covers his recollections of the Texas Revolution as well as the Civil War. He served in Company H, a unit he said "had very few religious men, but many gamblers and profane men, and I was not happy in my association with them" (143). Zuber died at his home in Grimes County in 1913.

23. Francis R. Lubbock to J. P. Benjamin, March 15, 1862, *OR*, Series IV, 1 : 1001–1002.

24. Company L became the eleventh company in the Twenty-first Texas Cavalry. It was composed principally of members from Company C, Twenty-fourth Texas Cavalry, who had been enlisted by the captain, William A. Taylor. Compiled Service Records of the members of that company; Zuber, *My Eighty Years*, 137. Company L was a small contingent of fifty-five men under Captain J. B. Rocke; they came from the far western frontier around Lampasas and Gatesville.

25. Compiled Service Records of troops in Company G commanded by J. H. Hannah.

26. Compiled Service Record of G. R. Freeman; Muster Roll of Freeman's company dated April 2, 1862, Confederate Muster Rolls, No. 278, Texas State Archives, Austin, Texas.

27. In a letter from the Adjutant and Inspector General's Office dated October 4, 1861, Robert H. Chilton informed P. O. Hébert that Carter had a cavalry regiment that had been accepted by the secretary of war. Compiled Service Record of G. W. Carter. In April 1862, however, George W. Randolph, who had become secretary of war in March, informed Governor Lubbock that Carter's regiment had not been "tendered to the department until already organized. Authority was then given to muster them into service." George Randolph to Francis Lubbock, April 8, 1862, Francis Lubbock Papers, Texas State Archives, Austin, Texas.

28. The troops, however, realized their unique status. J. C. Morriss pointed out that Brigadier General Henry McCulloch ordered the brigade to Little Rock

when McCulloch had no "authority to order us anywhere. I rather think he has no power to command over us." J. C. Morriss to Amanda Morriss, June 29, 1862, in Pruett and Black, *Civil War Letters*, 23–24; Zuber, *My Eighty Years*, 135.

29. George Flournoy to Samuel Boyer Davis, April 14, 1862, Compiled Service Record of George W. Carter. Since the communication is found in Carter's papers, it is safe to assume Davis forwarded a copy to him.

30. J. P. Blessington, *The Campaigns of Walker's Texas Division* (New York: Lange, Little & Co., 1875), 22–23. Blessington, an Irishman, arrived in Texas on the eve of the war. He joined Company H, Sixteenth Texas Infantry, and by 1864 had risen to corporal on the personal staff of William R. Scurry.

31. Zuber, *My Eighty Years*, 135–136.

32. Blessington, *Walker's Texas Division*, 22.

33. W. W. Frizzell to John H. Reagan, May 15, 1862, *OR* 15:823. Reagan made a note at the bottom of the letter that simply identified Frizzell as a "respected citizen."

34. Ibid.

35. Marshall *Texas Republican*, August 30, 1862, quoted both the *Tri-Weekly Telegraph* and the Goliad *Messenger*; Houston *Tri-Weekly Telegraph*, August 15, 1862.

36. Marshall *Texas Republican*, August 30, 1862.

37. The Houston *Tri-Weekly Telegraph*, August 15, 1862, printed a letter written by Carter from Minden, Louisiana, on August 4, 1862, denying the charges. This is also found in the *San Antonio Weekly Herald*, August 16, 1862.

38. G. W. Carter to P. O. Hébert, June 11, 1862, Compiled Service Record of G. W. Carter.

39. J. C. Morriss to Amanda Morriss, May 17, 1862, in Pruett and Black, *Civil War Letters*, 11.

40. This information comes from the Compiled Service Records of the Twenty-first Texas; also see Mrs. R. E. Pennington, *The History of Brenham and Washington County* (Houston: Standard Printing Lithographing Co., 1915), 64–81, for a biographical sketch of the Giddings family. In addition consult the Eighth Census of the United States for Washington County, where Giddings lived, and McLennan County, where Chenoweth resided with Dr. J. N. Mullins. See also appendix.

41. Elijah Sterling Clack Robertson to Mary Robertson, June 22, 1862, Robertson Colony Collection, Special Collections, University of Texas, Arling-

ton, Texas. Robertson was an aide-de-camp to General McCulloch. In a letter dated June 16, he also mentioned that Carter's regiments were much better armed than he expected to find them.

42. Marshall *Texas Republican*, August 30, 1862.

43. Thomas O. Moore to George W. Randolph, July 8, 1862, *OR* 15 : 773–774. The party Governor Moore alluded to was led by a Captain Taylor, probably William A. Taylor of Company C, Twenty-fourth Texas Cavalry. Moore believed that Thomas C. Hindman, commander of the Trans-Mississippi Department, did not know about the actions of Wilkes's troops. But, he asserted, "With Butler below and Hindman above, each by his officers committing the same outrages, I am forced to self-protection."

44. P. O. Hébert to George W. Randolph, October 8, 1862, ibid., 822.

45. General Orders No. 11, Trans-Mississippi District South of the Red River, July 11, 1862, ibid., 824–825. Hébert noted he had "learned that officers of the Confederate Army have, upon divers occasions, seized and appropriated the private property of good and loyal citizens. That officers in the service should perpetrate such outrageously illegal acts would seem incredible were it not for the irrefragable proofs furnished. Such conduct is in direct violation of all law, of the Regulations and Articles of War, and unbecoming an officer and a gentleman." He directed that any officer guilty of such conduct be promptly arrested, charged, and tried by court-martial. As a deterrent to future offenses he ordered the severest punishment possible inflicted upon those judged guilty.

46. J. C. Morriss to Amanda Morriss, June 29, 1862, in Pruett and Black, *Civil War Letters*, 23–24.

47. William M. (Buck) Walton, *An Epitome of My Life: Civil War Reminiscences* (Austin: The Waterloo Press, 1965), 23–25.

48. C. M. Mason to M. C. Manning, July 12, 1862, *OR* 15 : 824. Mason, in Texas, tried to assure Manning, in Louisiana, that those responsible for the outrages committed by Carter's command would be punished. In a letter the same day to Colonel Carter, Manning ordered immediate attention to the matter. C. M. Mason to G. W. Carter, July 12, 1862, ibid.

49. Zuber, *My Eighty Years*, 141; Walton, *Epitome of My Life*, 25–26; R. A. Cameron to Alvin P. Hovey, October 29, 1862, *OR* 13 : 768–771. Cameron, colonel of the Thirty-fourth Indiana Volunteers, informed General Hovey, commanding the United States forces at Helena, Arkansas, that the Twenty-fourth of Colonel Wilkes and the Twenty-fifth of Colonel Gillespie were among those units dismounted because of a lack of forage. These two dismounted cav-

alry regiments were among those captured when Fort Hindman at Arkansas Post surrendered January 11, 1863. They were transported to Northern prison camps and exchanged several months later. These men ended up under the command of Major General Patrick Ronayne Cleburne. His determination to make soldiers out of the Texans resulted in nothing short of a miracle and they became part of one of the finest divisions in the Army of Tennessee, eventually serving under another Texan, Hiram B. Granbury from Waco.

50. Zuber, *My Eighty Years*, 141–142. Zuber's narrative is the only extant account of the circumstances surrounding the formation of the brigade. Other accounts do not give the details of Giddings's actions.

51. J. C. Morriss to Amanda Morriss, June 29, 1862, in Pruett and Black, *Civil War Letters*, 23–24.

52. Zuber, *My Eighty Years*, 145–146. Zuber made a mistake when he called Parsons's command "six-months" men; they had enlisted for one year. The disagreement between Parsons and Carter was well-known in Texas and would cause serious problems. Carter finally received authorization to detach his command and joined the brigade of Walter P. Lane. Parsons and Lane, however, made up the two brigades in the cavalry corps of William Steele.

53. Walton, *Epitome of My Life*, 41.

54. Ibid., 54–55.

55. *Bellville* [Texas] *Countryman*, April 11, 1863.

56. Walton, *Epitome of My Life*, 54.

CHAPTER THREE

1. Bryan Marsh to Araminta Marsh, July 29, 1862, "The Confederate Letters of Bryan Marsh," *Chronicles of Smith County, Texas* 14 (Winter 1975): 14–15.

2. Sketch of Frank M. Files, *Itasca* [Texas] *Item*, April 25, 1924. Files was a private in Company C, Nineteenth Texas Cavalry Regiment.

3. Compiled Service Record of Nathaniel Macon Burford, Compiled Service Records of Confederate Soldiers Who Served in Organizations from the State of Texas, Nineteenth Texas Cavalry, Microfilm Rolls 323 : 104–106 (hereafter cited as Compiled Service Record), National Archives, Washington, D. C.; Muster Roll of Allen Beard's company dated March 21, 1862, Confederate Muster Rolls, No. 1184, Texas State Archives, Austin, Texas; William S. Speer, ed., *The Encyclopedia of the New West* (Marshall, Texas: The United States Bio-

graphical Publishing Co., 1881), 52–53. The revising editor of this book was John Henry Brown, historian, statesman, and personal friend of Burford. The quote comes from the last paragraph of Burford's biography and may reflect Brown's personal opinion.

4. Burford adjourned his court for two weeks in the spring of 1861 so farmers might harvest their wheat crop. He then irritated legislators in Austin by joining the army and not holding his court at all; they did not want to pay him for the missed days. *Dallas Herald*, May 22, 1861; James M. Day, ed., *Senate Journal of the Ninth Legislature of the State of Texas November 4, 1861–January 14, 1862* (Austin: Texas Library and Historical Commission, 1963), 186.

5. Philip Lindsley, *A History of Greater Dallas and Vicinity* (Chicago: The Lewis Publishing Co., 1909), 53; *Memorial and Biographical History of Dallas County, Texas* (Chicago: Lewis Publishing Co., 1892), 337–338. Burford married Mary Knight of Tennessee in 1854; they had eight children. Speer, *Encyclopedia of the New West*, 52–53.

6. John H. Reagan, *Memoirs, with Special References to Secession and the Civil War* (New York: The Neale Publishing Co., 1906; reprint, Austin: The Pemberton Press, 1968), 58, 61; United States Bureau of the Census, Seventh and Eighth Census of the United States, Dallas County, Schedule 1: Free Inhabitants and Schedule 4: Productions of Agriculture. In the 1850 census Burford reported $200 in personal estate; in 1860 this amount had increased to $4,675, and he owned $15,000 worth of real estate. Yet when he reported his possessions for taxing purposes in 1861 the total was $13,430.

7. A. J. Byrd, *History and Description of Johnson County, and its Principal Towns* (Marshall, Texas: Jennings Brothers, 1879), 17. Byrd does not date this incident, but Burford served as a district judge from 1856 until 1862 and again in 1876.

8. Lindsley, *A History of Greater Dallas and Vicinity*, 63; Eighth Census of the United States, Dallas County, Schedule 2: Slave Inhabitants.

9. Lester Newton Fitzhugh, ed., *Cannon Smoke: The Letters of Captain John J. Good, Good-Douglas Battery, CSA* (Hillsboro, Texas: Hill Junior College Press, 1971), 198.

10. John J. Good to Susan Anna Good, August 1861, ibid., 40–42; August 4, 1861, 37–40; October 29, 1861, 110–113; November 6, 1861, 113–115.

11. John J. Good to Susan Anna Good, December 6, 1861, ibid., 140–143; December 20, 1861, 148–151; Speer, *Encyclopedia of the New West*, 52–53.

There is no other reference to Reagan's assistance, but since John Henry Brown, revising editor of the encyclopedia, was Ben McCulloch's aide and personal friend at the time of this appointment, there is little reason to doubt that Reagan's influence was pivotal.

12. Francis R. Lubbock to Judah P. Benjamin, March 7, 1862, U. S. War Department, *The War of the Rebellion; A Compilation of the Official Records of the Union and Confederate Armies* (128 vols., Washington, D. C., 1880–1901), Series IV, 1 : 977–979 (hereafter cited as *OR*; unless otherwise indicated all references are to Series I).

13. N. M. Burford to E. H. Cushing, February 17, 1862, Houston *Tri-Weekly Telegraph*, April 23, 1862.

14. Susan Anna Good to John J. Good, April 20, 1862, in Fitzhugh, *Cannon Smoke*, 182–184. Hawpe, colonel of the Thirty-first Texas Cavalry, was stabbed to death in August 1863 on the Dallas courthouse square. Apparently Hawpe's hot temper was well-known and probably resulted in his death; the man who killed him was never prosecuted.

15. There was little doubt the men would select Burford as their colonel, but he followed a common custom of going through a formal election by the troops. Compiled Service Record of Nathaniel M. Burford; John Cochran, *Dallas County A Record of its Pioneers and Progress* (Dallas: A. S. Mathis Service Publishing Co., 1928), 97–101.

16. *Ellis County History: The Basic 1892 book (With the Presidents Selection deleted) with Additional Biographies compiled by the Ellis County Historical Museum and Art Gallery, Inc. in Memory of the Courageous Pioneers and Builders of Ellis County* (Fort Worth & Arlington: Historical Publishers, 1972), 462–463, 698–699. Watson had come to Texas in 1833. Although named for his father's six brothers, Benjamin William Abner Joseph John Frederick Watson, the future lieutenant colonel, usually went by the shortened Benjamin Watson.

17. *Minutes of the Annual Conferences of the Methodist Episcopal Church, South, for the Year 1861* (Nashville, Tennessee: Southern Methodist Publishing House, 1870), 351; Joel T. Daves to Samuel Cooper, March 22, 1863, Compiled Service Record of Joel T. Daves. The second major, John G. Williams, married Martha Ann McMullan (Matt) and returned to his home in Hillsboro following the war. But his brother-in-law Frank McMullan refused to live under Yankee rule, headed south, and established a Confederate colony in Brazil. See William Clark Griggs, *The Elusive Eden: Frank McMullan's Confederate*

Colony in Brazil (Austin: University of Texas Press, 1987), 11, 31, 49. Also consult *A Memorial and Biographical History of Johnson and Hill Counties, Texas* (Chicago: Lewis Publishing Company, 1892), 539–540.

18. William J. Simms to Rebecca Simms, June 28, 1862, typescript in the Confederate Research Center, Hillsboro, Texas.

19. N. M. Burford to P. O. Hébert, May 16, 1862, and May 29, 1862, Compiled Service Record of Nathaniel M. Burford.

20. Nathaniel M. Burford to P. O. Hébert, May 29, 1862, Compiled Service Record of Nathaniel M. Burford. On the outside of Burford's letter is a note recommending the regiment's transfer to infantry service. The *Dallas Herald* reported on June 7, 1862, that Colonel Burford had recently returned home from Richmond where "he had been on important business, connected with his regiment."

21. William J. Simms to Rebecca Simms, September 18, 1862, Confederate Research Center. Also see Special Orders, No. 84, October 16, 1862, Special Order Book of Parsons' Brigade, Collection of Parsons' Brigade Association Texas Cavalry, Sims Library, Waxahachie, Texas.

22. Henry Orr to "Father and Mother," October 6, 1862, in John Q. Anderson, ed., *Campaigning with Parsons' Texas Cavalry Brigade, CSA: The War Journals and Letters of the Four Orr Brothers, 12th Texas Cavalry Regiment* (Hillsboro, Texas: Hill Junior College Press, 1967), 72–74.

23. Henry Orr to Mollie Orr, November 10, 1862, ibid., 80–81.

24. Charles Morgan's father, Hiram S. Morgan, received a land grant in Texas dated 1839. Gifford White, *1840 Citizens of Texas*, vol. 1: *Land Grants* (Austin: 1983), 180. Hiram, who died while Charles was a child, left his widow with several children. Although Charles's service with Terry's Texas Rangers was brief, he came home something of a celebrity. L. B. Giles, *Terry's Texas Rangers* (privately printed, 1911), 13, 25.

25. Hiram Morgan "spent a good deal of his own money equipping his men, 'The Morgan Rangers.' They were outfitted in gray double-breasted coats and gray trousers with yellow cavalry stripes on the legs." James M. McCaffrey, *This Band of Heroes: Granbury's Texas Brigade, C.S.A.* (Austin: Eakin Press, 1985), 18. Charles Morgan's squadron, about 150 men, is mentioned in the "Abstract from Return of Troops in the District of Arkansas," September 17, 1862, *OR* 13:881.

26. William W. Heartsill, *Fourteen Hundred and 91 Days in the Confederate Army*, edited by Bell Irvin Wiley (1876; reprint, Jackson, Tenn.: McCowat-Mercer Press, 1954), 199.

27. Compiled Service Record of Morgan's Cavalry, Microfilm Rolls 323 : 207–209. Morgan's men often rode with companies attached to Captain L. M. Nutt's Louisiana Cavalry (Red River Rangers). William B. Denson commanded Company A, Sixth Louisiana Cavalry. Both of these Louisiana officers lost many of their men when Arkansas Post was captured in January 1863. Captain Nutt, however, escaped off the ship carrying the prisoners north.

28. Compiled Service Record of B. D. McKie; Corsicana *Navarro Express*, May 29, 1861; *A Memorial and Biographical History of Navarro, Anderson, Limestone, Freestone and Leon Counties, Texas* (Chicago: The Lewis Publishing Co., 1893), 547–549. McKie's squadron was composed of his own company and that of Milton M. Boggess from Rusk County. McKie's company originally joined the Twentieth Texas Cavalry Regiment but was detached about October 1, 1862, to become an independent mounted ranger company. Subsequently McKie's own company became Company F, Morgan's battalion. Also see Heartsill, *Fourteen Hundred and 91 Days*, 212; John W. Spencer, *The Confederate Guns of Navarro County* (Corsicana: The Texas Press, 1986), 52–61.

29. Houston *Tri-Weekly Telegraph*, June 27, 1862.

30. Sketch of A. S. Graves in Mamie Yeary, *Reminiscences of the Boys in Gray, 1861–1865* (Dallas: Press of the Wilkinson Printing Co., 1912), 280.

31. John J. Good to Susan Anna Good, October 24, 1861, and October 29, 1861, in Fitzhugh, *Cannon Smoke*, 102–103, 110–113. The incident occurred sometime between the two letters Good wrote to his wife because he mentioned it in both. The quote came from October 29th letter.

32. Sketch of A. S. Graves in Yeary, *Boys in Gray*, 280.

33. Compiled Service Records of Alf Johnson and B. D. McKie.

34. Compiled Service Record of Pratt's Battery, Microfilm Roll 323: 240; Sketch of R. J. Oliphant, Yeary, *Boys in Gray*, 575.

35. See the officer roster of Co. G, Captain F. G. Lemmon, Compiled Service Record of Morgan's Cavalry.

36. At various times H. C. Hynson or Isaac A. Clare commanded sections of the battery. Organization of the Army of the Trans-Mississippi Department, September 30, 1864, OR 41, pt. 2, 966–971. Compiled Service Records of J. H.

Pratt, H. C. Hynson, and Isaac A. Clare. Before the war, Hynson, who was eighteen years old when he joined, had been associated with the Jefferson Ice Manufacturing Company (although he gave his home as Marshall). Clare, who was twenty-six when he enlisted, had been appointed on April 4, 1861, to survey the boundary between Marion and Cass counties.

CHAPTER FOUR

1. W. H. Parsons to W. H. Getzendaner, June 24, 1878, *A Brief and Condensed History of Parsons' Texas Cavalry Brigade Composed of Twelfth, Nineteenth, Twenty-First, Morgan's Battalion, and Pratt's Battery of Artillery of the Confederate States: Together with Roster of the several Commands as far as obtainable—Some Historical Sketches—General Orders and a Memoranda of Parson's Brigade Association* (Waxahachie, Texas: J. M. Flemister, 1892), 21.

2. Ibid., 23.

3. "Saving the State," Little Rock *Arkansas True Democrat*, October 1, 1862.

4. John M. Harrell, "Arkansas," in Clement A. Evans, ed., *Confederate Military History*, 12 vols. (Atlanta: Confederate Publishing Co., 1899), 10: 98.

5. J.T.S., "Campaign in Arkansas: Battle of Cotton Plant," July 22, 1862, Houston *Tri-Weekly Telegraph*, August 6, 1862; Journal of Henry Orr, April 27, 1862, in John Q. Anderson, ed., *Campaigning with Parsons' Texas Cavalry Brigade, CSA: The War Journals and Letters of the Four Orr Brothers, 12th Texas Cavalry Regiment* (Hillsboro, Texas: Hill Junior College Press, 1967), 39; John W. Truss to Rebecca Truss, April 18, 1862, in Johnette Highsmith Ray, ed., "Civil War Letters From Parsons' Texas Cavalry Brigade," *Southwestern Historical Quarterly* 69 (October 1965): 212–213; George W. Ingram to Martha Ingram, May 14, 1862, in Henry L. Ingram, comp., *Civil War Letters of George W. and Martha F. Ingram, 1861–1865* (College Station: Texas A & M Press, 1973), 20–22.

6. J.T.S., "Battle of Cotton Plant"; "Texas Dragoons," Little Rock *Arkansas True Democrat*, June 5, 1862.

7. Henry Orr to James and Lafayette Orr, May 9, 1862, in Anderson, *Campaigning With Parsons' Brigade*, 40–42.

8. J.T.S., "Battle of Cotton Plant"; Henry Orr to Mollie Orr, May 16, 1862, in Anderson, *Campaigning With Parsons' Brigade*, 43–46; George W.

Ingram to Martha Ingram, May 14, 1862, *Civil War Letters*, 20–22; J. J. Frazier to "Mother and Brother," May 21, 1862, Frazier Family Papers, Barker Texas History Center, Austin, Texas.

9. George W. Ingram to Martha Ingram, May 14, 1862, *Civil War Letters*, 20–22.

10. J. J. Frazier to "Mother and Brother," May 21, 1862.

11. George W. Ingram to Martha Ingram, May 14, 1862, *Civil War Letters*, 20–22.

12. David N. Shropshire to "My Dear Brother," May 14, 1862, Shropshire Letters, Confederate Research Center, Hillsboro, Texas. Three brothers along with their father (who resigned and died at home in 1862) joined the Twelfth Texas; David and John Shropshire belonged to the brigade's commissary department. A. J. Byrd remarked that men in other commands often complained that Parsons's troops were better fed than any others and "it was due to such indefatigable workers as were the Shropshire boys." A. J. Byrd, *History and Description of Johnson County, and its Principal Towns* (Marshall, Texas: Jennings Brothers, 1879), 117.

13. Harrell, "Arkansas," 99.

14. The Little Red River empties into the White River below Searcy. It is impossible to tell which river was actually the one in question as Johnson scouted near both. Little Rock *Arkansas True Democrat*, May 15, 1862.

15. George W. Ingram to Martha Ingram, May 14, 1862, *Civil War Letters*, 20–22.

16. D. N. Shropshire to "My Dear Brother," May 14, 1862.

17. Little Rock *Arkansas True Democrat*, May 22, 1862.

18. Ibid.

19. There is no extant report of this scout, but the "official" reports of both Rogers and Chrisman appeared in Texas and Arkansas newspapers. E. W. Rogers to J. B. Roane, May 21, 1862, Little Rock *Arkansas True Democrat*, May 22, 1862; Report of F. M. Chrisman, May 19, 1862, ibid.; E. W. Rogers to J. S. Roane, May 24?, 1862, *San Antonio [Texas] Herald*, June 14, 1862.

20. Report of Samuel R. Curtis, May 24, 1862, U. S. War Department, *The War of the Rebellion; A Compilation of the Official Records of the Union and Confederate Armies* (128 vols., Washington, D. C., 1880–1901), Series I, 13 : 69–70 (hereafter cited as *OR*; unless otherwise indicated all references are to Series I); Report of George E. Waring, Jr., May 17, 1862, *OR* 13 : 68–69; Harrell, "Arkansas," 93.

21. The Federal account of the skirmish near Searcy, Arkansas, May 19, 1862, is well documented, *OR* 13 : 69–79. For the Confederate point of view see the reports of Rogers and Chrisman; for the enlisted man's version refer to Mamie Yeary, *Reminiscences of the Boys in Gray, 1861–1865* (Dallas: Press of Wilkinson Printing Co., 1912). Confederate recollections appear in the sketches by J. D. Beauchamp, George H. Denison, Joseph Lafayette Estes, John W. Morrison, and Finas A. Stone. George H. Hogan remembered that since Searcy was "our 'maiden' fight, it made an impression on my boyish mind which I have not forgotten" (ibid., 338–339). Hogan also wrote a much more exaggerated account which claimed 185 Yankees killed; "Parsons's Brigade of Texas Cavalry," *Confederate Veteran* 33 (January 1925), 17–20. For other information on the battle, see the published histories of White County, "The Battle of Whitney's Lane or The Battle of Searcy," *White County Heritage* 1 (1963): 7–10; Raymond Lee Muncy, *Searcy, Arkansas: A Frontier Town Grows Up With America* (Searcy: Harding Press, 1976), 46–48.

22. Report of Eugene Kielmansegge, May 20, 1862, *OR* 13 : 73–75.

23. Report of F. M. Chrisman, May 19, 1862, Little Rock *Arkansas True Democrat*, May 22, 1862; E. W. Rogers to J. S. Roane, May 24?, 1862, *San Antonio* [Texas] *Herald*, June 14, 1862.

24. *San Antonio Herald*, June 14, 1862.

25. Ibid.

26. Report of Henry Neun, May 20, 1862, *OR* 13 : 78–79; Report of August Fischer, May 20, 1862, ibid., 77–78.

27. Report of Eugene Kielmansegge, May 20, 1862, ibid., 73–75.

28. Report of Henry Neun, ibid., 78–79.

29. Golliger, "The Fight near Searcy," May 24, 1862, Houston *Tri-Weekly Telegraph*, June 9, 1862.

30. Henry Orr to "Parents, Sister and Brother," May 26, 1863, in Anderson, *Campaigning With Parsons' Brigade*, 101–104. This letter was erroneously identified by the book's editor as 1863. The contents clearly refer to events in May 1862.

31. E. W. Rogers to J. S. Roane, May 24?, 1862, *San Antonio Herald*, June 14, 1862; Report of F. M. Chrisman, May 19, 1862, Little Rock *Arkansas True Democrat*, May 22, 1862. The quote comes from M. L. Hickey, "Parsons' Brigade," *A Memorial and Biographical History of Johnson and Hill Counties, Texas* (Chicago: The Lewis Publishing Co., 1892), 259–261.

32. Houston *Tri-Weekly Telegraph*, June 20, June 29, 1862; Hickey,

"Parsons' Brigade," 259–261. George Hogan boasted, "The man killed was Lieut. McDonald, who threw his life away and when found had seventeen of the enemy around and near him dead"; Yeary, *Boys in Gray*, 338–339. Hogan again tended to magnify his comrades' exploits as the years passed.

33. Henry Orr to "Parents, Sister and Brothers," May 26, 1863 [1862], in Anderson, *Campaigning With Parsons' Brigade*, 101–104.

34. Report of Henry Neun, May 20, 1862, *OR* 13 : 78–79.

35. E. W. Rogers to J. B. Roane, May 24?, 1862, *San Antonio Herald*, June 14, 1862.

36. Casualties on both sides were extremely exaggerated by the participants and newspapers, ibid.; Report of F. M. Chrisman, May 19, 1862, Little Rock *Arkansas True Democrat*, May 22, 1862; E. W. Rogers to J. B. Roane, May 19, 1862, and May 22, 1862, ibid.; Report of Peter J. Osterhaus, May 19, 1862, *OR* 13 : 70–71; Report of John Kaegi, May 21, 1862, ibid., 77–78.

37. Little Rock *Arkansas True Democrat*, May 29, 1862.

38. *Brief History of Parsons' Brigade*, 19–20; Report of Samuel R. Curtis, May 24, 1862, *OR* 13 : 69–70.

39. *San Antonio Herald*, June 14, 1862.

40. Henry Orr to Mollie Orr, May 18, 1862, in Anderson, *Campaigning With Parsons' Brigade*, 43–46.

41. "McCulloch's Pistol," Houston *Tri-Weekly Telegraph*, July 28, 1862; Compiled Service Record of A. McCulloch, Compiled Service Records of Confederate Soldiers Who Served in Organizations from the State of Texas, Microfilm Rolls 323 : 71–74 (hereafter cited as Compiled Services Records), National Archives, Washington, D. C. Alexander, son of John S. McCulloch, served in Company H, Twelfth Texas. This company was raised in Ellis County, where several of the McCulloch family resided. John, Ben McCulloch's brother, was a captain in the quartermaster department. Alexander later served as acting assistant inspector general for another of his uncles, Brigadier General Henry E. McCulloch. William S. Speer, ed., *The Encyclopedia of the New West* (Marshall, Texas: The United States Biographical Publishing Co., 1881), 281.

42. Compiled Service Records of E. W. Rogers and John W. Mullen; Henry Orr to "Parents, Sister and Brothers," May 26, 1863 [1862], in Anderson, *Campaigning With Parsons' Brigade*, 101–104.

43. J.T.S., "Battle of Cotton Plant"; Reports of Thomas C. Hindman of Operations May 31–November 3, 1862, *OR* 13 : 26–46. Rust had represented the southern district of Arkansas in Congress at the time of secession. He raised

a regiment and fought in Virginia before returning to Arkansas to take command of the cavalry forces.

44. Letter of G. W. Sweet, June 11, 1862, *San Antonio Weekly Herald*, July 5, 1862.

45. George W. Ingram to Martha Ingram, June 17, 1862, *Civil War Letters*, 23–25.

46. Letter of G. W. Sweet, May 24, 1862, *San Antonio Herald*, June 14, 1862.

47. Report of Samuel R. Curtis, May 24, 1862, *OR* 13 : 69–70.

48. Golliger, "The Fight near Searcy."

49. *San Antonio Herald*, June 14, 1862.

50. T. C. Hindman's Report of Operations May 3–November 3, 1862, *OR* 13 : 28–46. Major General Thomas Carmichael Hindman, a small man of only five feet one inch tall, had fought in the Mexican War but had made politics his vocation. He was serving as a congressman from Arkansas when the war began.

51. George W. Ingram to Martha Ingram, June 17, 1862, *Civil War Letters*, 23–25. For another viewpoint see Henry Orr to James Orr, June 9, 1862, in Anderson, *Campaigning With Parsons' Brigade*, 52–53. Henry Orr thought the reduction in equipage was a "good thing, for we will not be bothered with the trouble of a heavy guard to protect our baggage. . . . So while in the timber we will fight as light cavalry."

52. George W. Ingram to Martha Ingram, June 11, 1862, *Civil War Letters*, 22–23.

53. Henry Orr to "Parents, Sister and Brothers," May 26, 1863 [1862], Anderson, *Campaigning With Parsons' Brigade*, 101–104; Henry Orr to James Orr, June 9, 1862, ibid., 52–53.

54. Gil McKay to R. W. Loughery, June 26, 1862, Marshall *Texas Republican*, July 19, 1862. McKay was captain of Company K, Seventeenth Texas Cavalry Regiment. R. W. Loughery was editor of the *Republican*; Loughery's son R. W. Jr. was a member of Samuel Richardson's company. The young Loughery, however, was captured at Arkansas Post and never actually served with Parsons's brigade.

55. Gil McKay to R. W. Loughery, June 13, 1862, ibid., June 28, 1862.

56. Letter of G. W. Sweet, June 11, 1862, *San Antonio Weekly Herald*, July 5, 1862.

57. Henry Orr to "Father and Mother," June 6, 1862, in Anderson, *Campaigning With Parsons' Brigade*, 47–49.

58. Gil McKay to R. W. Loughery, June 13, 1862, Marshall *Texas Republican*, June 28, 1862. Also see *Dallas Herald*, June 7, 1862.

59. Jakie L. Pruett and Scott Black, eds., *Civil War Letters: 1861–1865; A Glimpse of the War Between the States* (Austin: Eakin Press, 1985), 34.

60. Gil McKay to R. W. Loughery, June 26, 1862, Marshall *Texas Republican*, July 19, 1862.

61. R. M. Collins, *Chapters from the Unwritten History of the War Between the States or, The Incidents in the Life of a Confederate Soldier in Camp, on the March, in the Great Battles, and in Prison* (St. Louis: Nixon-Jones Printing Co., 1893), 34.

62. *Brief History of Parsons' Brigade*, 19. Only a few regiments of Texans had arrived in Arkansas by the time Curtis began his movement down the White River. These included Parsons's Twelfth Texas, Middleton T. Johnson's Fourteenth Texas, George W. Sweet's Fifteenth Texas, William Fitzhugh's Sixteenth Texas, James R. Taylor's Seventeenth Texas, and Nicholas Darnell's Eighteenth Texas. In addition to these cavalry, Allison Nelson's Tenth Texas Infantry took part in the campaign. In early June Taylor's Seventeenth Texas and Fitzhugh's Sixteenth Texas received orders to report to Colonel Parsons; Special Orders, No. 9 and 11, June 4, 1862, Special Order Book of Parsons' Brigade, Collection of Parsons' Brigade Association Texas Cavalry, Sims Library, Waxahachie, Texas. For a more detailed account see T. C. Hindman's Report of Operations May 31–November 3, 1862, *OR* 13 : 28–44, and Collins, *Unwritten History of the War*, 27. R. M. Collins belonged to Company B, Fifteenth Texas Cavalry Regiment.

CHAPTER FIVE

1. W. H. Parsons to W. H. Getzendaner, June 24, 1878, *A Brief and Condensed History of Parsons' Texas Cavalry Brigade Composed of Twelfth, Nineteenth, Twenty-First, Morgan's Battalion, and Pratt's Battery of Artillery of the Confederate States: Together with Roster of the several Commands as far as obtainable—Some Historical Sketches—General Orders and a Memoranda of Parson's Brigade Association* (Waxahachie, Texas: J. M. Flemister, Printer, 1892), 20.

2. T. C. Hindman's Report of Operations May 31-November 3, 1862, U. S. War Department, *The War of the Rebellion; A Compilation of the Official Records of the Union and Confederate Armies* (128 vols., Washington, D. C.,

1880–1901), Series I, 13 : 28–46 (hereafter cited as *OR;* unless otherwise indicated, all references are to Series I); quote on page 31.

3. *Brief History of Parsons' Brigade,* 21.

4. Hindman's Report of Operations May 31–November 3, 1862, *OR* 13 : 36.

5. D. N. Shropshire to "My Beloved Sister," July 4, 1862, Shropshire Letters, Confederate Research Center, Hillsboro, Texas.

6. Hindman's Report of Operations May 31–November 3, 1862, *OR* 13 : 35; S. R. Curtis to Henry W. Halleck, June 25, 1862, and Henry W. Halleck to S. R. Curtis, June 26, 1862, Little Rock *Arkansas State Gazette,* July 12, 1862; S. R. Curtis to Henry W. Halleck, July 10, 1862, *OR* 13 : 141; Thomas L. Snead, "The Conquest of Arkansas," in Robert Underwood Johnson and Clarence Clough Buel, eds., *Battles and Leaders of the Civil War,* 4 vols. (New York: The Century Company, 1887–1888), 3 : 441–461; James Russell Soley, "Naval Operations in the Vicksburg Campaign," ibid., 551–570. The DuValls family settled on the high bluffs along the White River sometime after 1838, and the town that grew up there was known as DuValls Bluff; Samuel H. Weems, "The Importance of DeValls Bluff, Arkansas During the Civil War (1861–1865)" typescript (copy in possession of the author). Although the spelling changed during the war, contemporary accounts generally refer to it as DeValls or Devall's Bluff.

7. George W. Ingram to Martha Ingram, July 9, 1862, in Henry L. Ingram, comp., *Civil War Letters of George W. and Martha F. Ingram, 1861–1865* (College Station: Texas A & M Press, 1973), 27–29.

8. Hindman's Report of Operations May 31-November 3, 1862, *OR* 13 : 36.

9. "More Skirmishing in Arkansas," Houston *Tri-Weekly Telegraph,* June 27, 1862.

10. Hindman's Report of Operations May 31–November 3, 1862, *OR* 13 : 35.

11. Ibid., 37.

12. Ibid.; also see the Federal reports of the action at Hill's Plantation, Cache River, July 7, 1862, ibid., 141–151; "St. Louis 'Democrat' Account" [of the battle near Bayou Cache] in Frank Moore, ed., *The Rebellion Record: A Diary of American Events,* 12 vols. (1861–1868; reprint, New York: Arno Press, 1977), 5 : 275–277 (hereafter cited as "Battle near Bayou Cache"); *Brief History of Parsons' Brigade,* 20. Private William Zuber, who visited the battle-

ground a few weeks later, observed it was a dense forest and thicket. Near the battlefield there were two knobs or hills shaped like an old-fashioned loaf of sugar. On one of these hills "the Yankees had buried all their dead except one man," who had died later at Hill's Plantation. Zuber talked with Hill's nephew, who told him that Mr. Hill had been away when the battle occurred. William Physick Zuber, *My Eighty Years in Texas*, ed. by Janis Boyle Mayfield (Austin: University of Texas Press, 1971), 149.

13. George W. Ingram to Martha Ingram, July 13, 1862, *Civil War Letters*, 29–30; also see Henry Orr to "Father, Mother, Sister, and Brother," July 15, 1862, in John Q. Anderson, ed., *Campaigning with Parsons' Texas Cavalry Brigade, CSA: The War Journals and Letters of the Four Orr Brothers, 12th Texas Cavalry Regiment* (Hillsboro, Texas: Hill Junior College Press, 1967), 55–58; S. B. Hendricks to R. W. Loughery, August 1, 1862, Marshall *Texas Republican*, August 30, 1862; Letter from Nelson's Regiment, September 16, 1862, by T.J.C., Houston *Tri-Weekly Telegraph*, October 13, 1862; J.T.S., "Campaign in Arkansas: Battle of Cotton Plant" (July 22, 1862), Houston *Tri-Weekly Telegraph*, August 6, 1862.

14. The historian of the Second Wisconsin Cavalry related that his regiment was in the extreme advance with Companies D, G, I, and H acting as skirmishers. Under orders they fell back, leaving the fighting to Hovey's force. William De Loss Love, *Wisconsin in the War* (Chicago: Church & Goodman, and New York: Sheldon & Co., 1866), 569. Quote is from C. E. Hovey to J. W. Paddock, July 7, 1862, *OR* 13 : 143–145.

15. Ibid.

16. Henry Orr to "Father, Mother, Sister, and Brother," July 15, 1862, in Anderson, *Campaigning with Parsons' Brigade*, 55–58.

17. Thomas Green to "Brother," September 3, 1862, *Chronicles of Smith County, Texas* 6 (Spring 1967): 38–39.

18. George W. Ingram to Martha Ingram, July 9, 1862, *Civil War Letters*, 27–29. All of the Confederate accounts agree that Parsons took temporary possession of the First Indiana's small cannon, but Hovey's report failed to mention this loss. A history of the Thirty-third Illinois Infantry stated "several companies participated in a battle with Texas rangers, in which Company A rescued and brought off a field piece belonging to our cavalry"; *Report of the Adjutant General of the State of Illinois* (Springfield: H. W. Rooker, State Printer & Binder, 1886), 2 : 651. The *Arkansas State Gazette*, July 12, 1862, reported that the Confederates captured "one 6 pounder rifle piece." See also S. B. Hendricks

to R. W. Loughery, August 1, 1862, Marshall *Texas Republican*, August 30, 1862; Thomas Green to brother, September 3, 1862, *Chronicles of Smith County, Texas*, 6 : 38–39; George W. Ingram to Martha Ingram, July 13, 1862, *Civil War Letters*, 29–30. At some point during the fighting the Twelfth Texas lost its regimental flag to the enemy, possibly as the men relinquished the cannon they had captured.

19. Henry Orr to "Father, Mother, Sister, and Brother," July 15, 1862, in Anderson, *Campaigning with Parsons' Brigade*, 55–58.

20. Moore, "Battle near Bayou Cache," 276.

21. Henry Orr to "Father, Mother, Sister, and Brother," July 15, 1862, in Anderson, *Campaigning with Parsons' Brigade*, 55–58.

22. Henry Orr to James and Lafayette Orr, August 21, 1862, in Anderson, *Campaigning with Parsons' Brigade*, 64–67. When Henry's younger brothers, James and Lafayette, arrived in Arkansas they were told they could not reach Parsons's regiment. Instead they joined Nicholas Darnell's Eighteenth Texas Cavalry. In this letter Henry brings them up to date on his activities. But this account appears to be combined with another letter or else parts are missing. Henry began to tell his brothers about the battle at the L'Anguille River on August 3, but abruptly shifted to the battle at Cotton Plant in the next paragraph. The rest of the letter refers to events immediately following the skirmish July 7, because Henry related the cavalry was dismounted on Saturday (July 12). Anderson, when editing these letters, did not realize that Henry was telling about Cotton Plant and not the battle at L'Anguille.

23. Bryan Marsh to Araminta Marsh, July 29, 1862, "The Confederate Letters of Bryan Marsh," *Chronicles of Smith County, Texas* 14 (Winter 1975): 14–15. Marsh was the captain of Company C, Seventeenth Texas Cavalry.

24. J.T.S., "Battle of Cotton Plant."

25. Henry Orr to "Father, Mother, Sister, and Brother," July 15, 1862, in Anderson, *Campaigning with Parsons' Brigade*, 55–58.

26. J.T.S., "Battle of Cotton Plant."

27. Bryan Marsh to Araminta Marsh, July 29, 1862, "Confederate Letters," 14–15.

28. Report of Frederick Steele, July 20, 1862, *OR* 13 : 141–142.

29. T.J.C., "Letter from Nelson's Regiment."

30. Henry Orr to "Brothers [James and Lafayette]" August 21, 1862, in Anderson, *Campaigning with Parsons' Brigade*, 64–67.

31. Thomas Green to "Brother," September 3, 1862, *Chronicles of Smith County, Texas*, 6 : 38–39.

32. Henry Orr to "Father, Mother, Sister, and Brother," July 15, 1862, in Anderson, *Campaigning with Parsons' Brigade*, 55–58.

33. George W. Ingram to Martha Ingram, July 13, 1862, *Civil War Letters*, 29–30. Henry Orr, however, in his letter of August 21 believed that Rust had accompanied Taylor's Seventeenth Texas Cavalry as it tried to outflank the Federals.

34. T.J.C., "Letter from Nelson's Regiment."

35. "Casualty Report of Parsons' Regiment, Texas Dragoons, in the Cotton Plant fight," July 22, 1862, Houston *Tri-Weekly Telegraph*, August 6, 1862.

36. B. P. Gallaway, "A Texas Farm Boy Enlists in the 12th Cavalry," *Texas Military History* 8 (1970): 87–95.

37. Obituary of John M. Sullivan, written by B. F. Marchbanks to U.D.C. Camp Winnie Davis: No. 108, July 1, 1923. United Confederate Veterans Scrapbook, Sims Library, Waxahachie, Texas. Marchbanks, who served with both Sullivan and Nance, devoted over half of an eight-page obituary to Nance: "So closely were the lives of John Sullivan and Dave Nance united," he wrote, "it is not amiss to speak of the life of Dave Nance."

38. Ibid.; Gallaway, "Texas Farm Boy Enlists," 91; B. P. Gallaway, *The Ragged Rebel: A Common Soldier in W. H. Parsons' Texas Cavalry, 1861–1865* (Austin: University of Texas Press, 1988), 55–56. Gallaway, as Nance's biographer, also told that the homespun shirt Nance wore during the battle was in the possession of his great-granddaughter, Mrs. W. D. Lawson of Abilene, Texas. This bullet-pierced shirt has a strip torn from it which Nance used to bind his head wound.

39. Report of Conrad Baker, July 20, 1862, *OR* 13 : 146. The report which Lieutenant Colonel William F. Wood sent to Colonel Conrad Baker, commanding the Fourth Brigade, was referred by Brigadier General Frederick Steele to Colonel Hovey, who made seven corrections before returning it to Wood to amend. Instead, Wood stood by his original account of the affair and challenged each of Hovey's seven corrections. The dispute seemed to center on whether the infantry or the cavalry should receive credit for the victory. Wood sincerely believed that Hovey misrepresented his contribution to the battle.

40. Indorsement No. 1 by Frederick Steele, July 18, 1862, ibid., 151.

41. Report of Frederick Steele, July 20, 1862, ibid., 141–142; Indorsement by H. W. Halleck, August 17, 1862, ibid., 142; Indorsement by Edwin M. Stanton, ibid.

42. Indorsement No. 2 by Samuel Curtis, July 24, 1862, ibid., 151.

43. Report of Samuel R. Curtis, July 10, 1862, ibid., 141. Also see *History*

of the Forty-Sixth Regiment Indiana Volunteer Infantry, September, 1861–
September, 1865 (Logansport, Indiana, 1888), 39–40; *Report of the Adjutant
General of the State of Indiana* (Indianapolis, 1865), 2 : 240, 342, 461.

44. E. S. C. Robertson, aide-de-camp to Brigadier General Henry Mc-
Culloch, wrote detailed accounts of his commander's daily activities. He reported
that the Texas cavalry in Arkansas included Parsons's Twelfth, Johnson's Fourteenth, Sweet's Fifteenth, Fitzhugh's Sixteenth, Taylor's Seventeenth, and Darnell's Eighteenth Texas as well as Alf Johnson's and Edward Vontress's companies for a total of 7,400. Robertson does not mention Allison Nelson's Tenth
Texas Infantry or B. D. McKie's company, which were also in Arkansas at
the time. Troops stationed near Tyler included Carter's three regiments and
Burford's Nineteenth Texas, also M. M. Boggess's company from Rusk. All of
these men would eventually join Parsons except Carter's Twenty-fourth and
Twenty-fifth regiments, which became dismounted cavalry. Although Robertson
estimated that over twenty thousand Texans would soon be in Arkansas, he
pointed out many men were sick and quite a few had died. E. S. C. Robertson to
Mary Robertson, June 2, 1862, Robertson Colony Collection, Special Collections, University of Texas at Arlington Library, Arlington, Texas.

45. *Brief History of Parsons' Brigade*, 20.

46. Henry Orr to James and Lafayette Orr, August 21, 1863, in Anderson,
Campaigning with Parsons' Brigade, 64–67.

47. J.T.S., "Battle of Cotton Plant." Hindman ordered the cavalry dis-
mounted on Saturday, July 12, and most were inspected on Sunday. Special
Orders, No. 2, July 1862, and Special Orders, No. 18, July 12, 1862, ordered the
Twelfth Texas to dismount all but 750 men; Special Order Book of Parsons' Brigade, Collection of Parsons' Brigade Association Texas Cavalry, Sims Library,
Waxahachie, Texas. For other comments on this decision see George W. Ingram
to Martha Ingram, July 18, 1862, *Civil War Letters,* 31; Henry Orr to W. T.
Payne, August 12, 1862, in Anderson, *Campaigning with Parsons' Brigade*,
61–62, and Henry Orr to James and Lafayette Orr, August 21, 1862, ibid.,
64–67; John W. Truss to Rebecca Truss, July 14, 1862, "Civil War Letters from
Parsons' Texas Cavalry Brigade," *Southwestern Historical Quarterly* 69 (October 1965): 214–215.

48. John W. Truss to Rebecca Truss, July 14, 1862; Special Orders, No.
19, July 12, 1862, ordered the horses belonging to the dismounted men returned
to Texas; Special Order Book of Parsons' Brigade.

49. Henry Orr to James and Lafayette Orr, August 21, 1862, in Anderson, *Campaigning with Parsons' Brigade*, 64–67.

50. Ibid.; J.T.S., "Battle of Cotton Plant."

51. This dispute over seniority, which was a serious problem in all Confederate armies, probably ended any thoughts that the authorities had of promoting Parsons to brigadier general, as Carter consistently insisted that he was senior colonel. Zuber, *My Eighty Years*, 141, 145–146; Henry Orr to [Mary & Sammie], July ?, 1862, in Anderson, *Campaigning with Parsons' Brigade*, 59–60; Special Orders, No. 2, July 31, 1862, ordered Parsons to assume command of Giddings's battalion, Major Johnson's battalion, Alf Johnson's Spy Company, Captain Anderson's company, and all other mounted men east of the White River; Special Order Book of Parsons' Brigade. Special Orders, No. 25, August 4, 1862, ordered Giddings to move to the west bank of Bayou de View near Cotton Plant, ibid.

52. Henry Orr to [Mary & Sammie], July ?, 1862, in Anderson, *Campaigning with Parsons' Brigade*, 59–60.

53. George W. Ingram to Martha Ingram, August 21, 1862, *Civil War Letters*, 32–35; "The L'Anguille Battle," *Brief History of Parsons' Brigade*, 29–33 (hereafter cited as "The L'Anguille Battle'). Although not stated, the author of this account is probably W. H. Getzendaner, who commanded the Fourth Squadron in the battle.

54. "The L'Anguille Battle"; Report of O. H. La Grange, August 4, 1862, *OR* 13 : 202; Report of Henry S. Eggleston, August 9, 1862, ibid., 202–205; "Battle of Anguille: A Wisconsin Regiments Experience in the Rebellion—Lost for Six Weeks in the Bayous of Arkansas," *Brief History of Parsons' Brigade*, 33–41 (hereafter cited as "Battle of Anguille.") The unnamed author of this account was a lieutenant in Company M, First Wisconsin Volunteer Cavalry. Getzendaner, who read this story in the Milwaukee *Sentinel*, July 31, 1881, reprinted it in the history of the brigade. The author was probably Second Lieutenant John A. Owen, First Wisconsin Cavalry, whose account, taken from the Chicago *Republican*, January 2, 1866, was chronicled in Love, *Wisconsin in the War*, 556–557.

55. "Battle of Anguille"; Report of O. H. La Grange, August 4, 1862, *OR* 13 : 202.

56. Henry Orr to "Parents," August 21, 1862, in Anderson, *Campaigning with Parsons' Brigade*, 62–64; George W. Ingram to Martha Ingram, August

21, 1862, *Civil War Letters*, 32–35; "The L'Anguille Battle," 29–33.

57. "The L'Anguille Battle"; Report of O. H. La Grange, August 4, 1862, *OR* 13 : 202.

58. Ibid.

59. "Battle of Anguille," 37.

60. Ibid.; "The L'Anguille Battle," 31.

61. George W. Ingram to Martha Ingram, August 21, 1862, *Civil War Letters*, 32–35. Unfortunately, following this quote two pages of the letter are missing; the letter ends with the conclusion of the battle.

62. "Battle of Anguille," 37–38.

63. Ibid., 38.

64. Ibid.; Report of Henry S. Eggleston, August 9, 1862, *OR* 13 : 202–205.

65. Henry Orr to "Parents," August 21, 1862, in Anderson, *Campaigning with Parsons' Brigade*, 62–64.

66. "Battle of Anguille," 38.

67. Love, *Wisconsin in the War*, 557.

68. There were several conflicting reports of casualties. Major Eggleston counted 14 of his men dead, 40 wounded, and 25 captured. The Federal lieutenant in Company M, First Wisconsin Volunteer Cavalry stated there were 13 killed, 35 wounded, and 47 captured. Eggleston believed about 25 Confederates had died, but Henry Orr claimed only 2 Texas cavalrymen had died and only 9 had received wounds. He thought the Texans had captured 63 Federal infantrymen, killed 40, and wounded 43. Orr also bragged that 40 blacks had been killed and 120 captured, as well as 150 horses, 200 mules, 13 wagons, and 200 guns. W. H. Getzendaner reported 2 Confederates killed and 2 mortally wounded but gave enemy casualties as 12 Federals wounded, 50 blacks killed, and 230 blacks captured. "The L'Anguille Battle," 32–33; "Battle of Anguille," 38; Report of T. C. Hindman's Operations May 31–November 3, 1862, *OR* 13 : 37–38; Report of Henry S. Eggleston, August 9, 1862, ibid., 202–205; Report of O. H. La Grange, August 4, 1862, ibid., 202; Little Rock *Arkansas True Democrat*, August 6, 1862; George W. Ingram to Martha Ingram, August 21, 1862, *Civil War Letters*, 32–35.

69. "The L'Anguille Battle," 33; Henry Orr to "Parents," August 21, 1862, in Anderson, *Campaigning with Parsons' Brigade*, 62–64.

70. Report of T. C. Hindman's Operations May 31–November 3, 1862, *OR* 13 : 37–38.

71. Henry Orr to W. T. Payne, August 12, 1862, in Anderson, *Campaigning with Parsons' Brigade*, 61–62.

72. "More Skirmishing in Arkansas," Houston *Tri-Weekly Telegraph,* June 27, 1862.

73. Henry Orr to "Parents," August 21, 1862, in Anderson, *Campaigning with Parsons' Brigade,* 62–64.

74. A. J. Embree, senior surgeon of the Twelfth Texas Dragoons, sent a report of conditions in his regiment to the Texas press dated July 22, 1862, Houston *Tri-Weekly Telegraph,* August 6, 1862.

75. *Brief History of Parsons' Brigade,* 16.

76. Report of T. C. Hindman's Operations May 31–November 3, 1862, *OR* 13 : 38.

CHAPTER SIX

1. Letter to E. H. Cushing, from Camp Hope, Arkansas, September 29, 1862, Houston *Tri-Weekly Telegraph,* October 22, 1862.

2. The Federals completed Fort Curtis at Helena in the autumn, and it became their main base in eastern Arkansas; *Dallas Herald,* December 6, 1862.

3. Letter to E. H. Cushing, September 29, 1862.

4. E. P. Petty to Ella Petty, October 26, 1862, in Norman Brown, ed., *Journey to Pleasant Hill: The Civil War Letters of Captain Elijah P. Petty, Walker's Texas Division, C.S.A.* (San Antonio: Institute of Texan Cultures, 1982), 96–97.

5. Chrisman's battalion subsequently became part of the First Arkansas Cavalry under Archibald S. Dobbin. Francis M. Chrisman was a thirty-two-year-old doctor from Searcy who became the lieutenant colonel of the First Arkansas. He resigned in August 1863 as a result of a gunshot wound he received in his right arm near Helena on May 25, 1862. Chrisman's battalion consisted of Company A, "Corley's Spies," from Helena under Samuel Corley, who died in combat September 10, 1863; Company B, "Anderson's Company Partisan Rangers," commanded by Rufus D. Anderson; Company C, an infantry company ordered mounted, which had previously been Company I, Thirtieth Arkansas Infantry under James H. McGeehee; and Company D under George W. Rutherford from Batesville. Special Orders, No. 39, September 28, 1862, U. S. War Department, *The War of the Rebellion; A Compilation of the Official Records of the Union and Confederate Armies* (128 vols., Washington, D. C. 1880–1901), Series I, 13 : 883–885 (hereafter cited as *OR;* unless otherwise indicated all references are to Series I); United States Bureau of the Census, Eighth Census of the United States, White County, Arkansas, 1860; Compiled Service

Records of Confederate Soldiers Who Served in Organizations from the State of Arkansas, 1st (Dobbin's) Arkansas Cavalry Regiment (formerly Chrisman's Battalion Arkansas Cavalry), Microfilm Rolls 317 : 2–3 (hereafter cited as Compiled Service Records), National Archives, Washington, D. C. When Holmes reorganized the army he also authorized Colonel Parsons to increase the number of men in each company to 110. This meant that the Twelfth Texas could recruit 360 additional troops and the Twenty-First Texas 315. Special Orders No. 56, September 26, 1862, Special Order Book of Parsons' Brigade, Collection of Parsons' Brigade Association Texas Cavalry, Sims Library, Waxahachie, Texas.

6. Compiled Service Records of Confederate Soldiers Who Served in Organizations from the State of Texas, Morgan's Cavalry, Microfilm Rolls 323 : 207–209 (hereafter cited as Compiled Service Records); Composition of Frost's Division (Defenses of Lower Arkansas), May 31, 1863, *OR* 22, pt. 2, 851.

7. When Holmes reorganized the army he ordered Burford's regiment to "move immediately, and take post at Elk Mills, reporting to Brigadier General J. S. Rains, at Elkhorn," Special Orders, No. 39, September 28, 1862, *OR* 13 : 883–885.

8. William Physick Zuber, *My Eighty Years in Texas*, ed. by Janis Boyle Mayfield (Austin: University of Texas Press, 1971), 155.

9. W. J. Simms owned one of four horses in Company C worth $250, which gave him a mark of distinction. He was also one of the few to possess a gun worth thirty dollars and one of only eight to own a pistol. W. J. Simms to Rebecca Simms, September 18, 1862, Simms Letters, Confederate Research Center, Hillsboro, Texas; Compiled Service Records, Nineteenth Texas Cavalry, Microfilm Rolls 323 : 104–106; Confederate Muster Rolls, No. 1267, Texas State Archives, Austin, Texas. Colonel Parsons, however, already had problems with his troops. In September local citizens reported that his men were committing depredations; this news prompted him to issue an order stating that he hoped "never to hear of similar complaints in the future." Special Orders No. 50, September 14, 1862, Special Order Book of Parsons' Brigade. Yet the problems continued, and in October Brigadier General Henry E. McCulloch preferred charges against Lieutenant (later captain) Nicholas Sneed of Company I, Nineteenth Texas as well as other officers of the regiment. The order, however, did not specify what charges had been preferred against the men. Special Orders No. 91, October 24, 1862, Special Order Book of Parsons' Brigade.

10. One of Burford's weaknesses was his compassion for other people; this failing would become his downfall as a commanding officer. It was not the first time he had refused to force unpleasant duties on his friends and neighbors. The Texas Senate had withheld some of his pay in the spring of 1861 because he closed his court while the farmers harvested their wheat crops. See John J. Good to Susan Anna Good, May 21, 1861, in Lester Newton Fitzhugh, ed., *Cannon Smoke: The Letters of Captain John J. Good, Good-Douglas Battery, CSA* (Hillsboro, Texas: Hill Junior College Press, 1971), 13–14; James M. Day, ed., *Senate Journal of the Ninth Legislature of the State of Texas: November 4, 1861–January 14, 1862* (Austin: Texas State Library and Historical Commission, 1963), 57. Quote from Henry Orr to "Father and Mother," October 6, 1862, in John Q. Anderson, ed., *Campaigning with Parsons' Cavalry Brigade, CSA: The War Journals and Letters of the Four Orr Brothers, 12th Texas Cavalry Regiment* (Hillsboro, Texas: Hill Junior College Press, 1967), 72–74. Also see E. S. C. Robertson to Mary Robertson, October 9 and 11, 1862, Robertson Colony Collection, Special Collections, University of Texas at Arlington Library, Arlington, Texas.

11. W. J. Simms to Rebecca Simms, September 18, 1862, Simms Letters.

12. T. H. Holmes to Samuel Cooper, October 26, 1862, *OR* 13 : 898–899.

13. If Orr was correct in his charge that Burford was under arrest, it might have proved embarrassing for Holmes to order the Nineteenth Texas to Elkhorn without its colonel. After all, Burford was a former law partner of the Confederate postmaster general and had just returned from one of his frequent trips to Richmond. He also had numerous friends in Texas who had influence with the government, and one cannot discount the fact that Colonel Parsons probably promoted the merger. Also see Special Orders No. 69, October 9, 1862, instructing Burford's officers to report to Colonel Parsons for duty, Special Order Book of Parsons' Brigade.

14. A good example of families with members serving in different regiments is that of Agnes Frazier of Hill County. Of her three sons still living at home, twenty-two-year-old James belonged to Company C, Twelfth Texas, twenty-year-old Robert to Company D, Nineteenth Texas, and eighteen-year-old Philip to Company H, Thirtieth Texas (which joined Parsons's brigade in 1865). In addition, there were several Frazier cousins scattered throughout the regiments. Frazier Papers, Barker Texas History Center; Eighth Census of the

United States, Hill County, 1860. For the quote, see Henry Orr to Mary Orr, November 10, 1862, in Anderson, *Campaigning with Parsons' Brigade*, 80–81.

15. The funeral of Jeff Neal is the only one recorded in the Order Book of the brigade. On October 16 Colonel Parsons detailed Captain J. C. S. Morrow's company from Devall's Bluff to serve as escort at Captain Neal's burial and to report to Lieutenant Colonel Bell Burleson at Des Arc with "the greatest possible dispatch." Special Orders No. 80, October 16, 1862, Special Order Book of Parsons' Brigade. Neal died October 15, 1862, Houston *Tri-Weekly Telegraph*, November 14, 1862; *Dallas Herald*, November 22, 1862; Compiled Service Record of William Jeff Neal reported his death on October 14, but Henry Orr wrote his family that Neal died September 28; Henry Orr to "Father and Mother," October 6, 1862, in Anderson, *Campaigning with Parsons' Brigade*, 72–74. Neal had probably been seriously ill for some time since medicine was scarce in Arkansas. Y. L. McNeil had visited Neal July 23 and had noted that although badly wounded in the groin, he was recovering in a private home; Houston *Tri-Weekly Telegraph*, August 6, 1862. Medical conditions were terrible, as W. J. Simms pointed out to his wife: "I had as soon be shot as to be sent to the hospital they die there for the want of attention, just imagine that yourself in a room with 50 sick men lying on the floor on their blankets, the dead and dying all in sight [of] each other, as soon as one is put in the coffin another takes his place on the floor. Dr. [R. P.] Sweat has left us [Burford's regiment] now & gone to Parsons Reg, we will remember him for it, he left us in the time we needed him most." W. J. Simms to Rebecca Simms, November 27, 1862, Simms Letters.

16. Compiled Service Records, Twenty-first Texas Cavalry Regiment, Microfilm Rolls 323 : 110–112.

17. William M. (Buck) Walton, *An Epitome of My Life: Civil War Reminiscences* (Austin: The Waterloo Press, 1965), 31.

18. W. P. Zuber to the *Telegraph*, February 14, 1863, Houston *Tri-Weekly Telegraph*, March 16, 1863 (hereafter cited as Zuber to the *Telegraph*); Zuber, *My Eighty Years*, 186. Stephen Starr, the undisputed historian of Union cavalry, chronicled the organization of the Fifth Kansas under James H. Lane. Many of the men under Lane, he asserted, "ostensibly organized as the 5th and 6th Kansas, insofar as they were organized at all, were simply Kansans who chose to join Lane on horseback instead of on foot." In September his men burned the town of Osceola "after looting it of everything worth hauling away."

Stephen Z. Starr, *The Union Cavalry in the Civil War*, vol. 3: *The War in the West 1861–1865* (Baton Rouge: Louisiana State University Press, 1985), 34–35. Yet a regimental history written after the war claimed that the men improved substantially when Lieutenant Colonel Powell Clayton assumed command in February 1862. "From the time of arrival at Helena until mid winter, the regiment was engaged weekly, and almost daily, in skirmishing with the rebel cavalry hovering around that post, and with invariable success. Major Walker became a terror to all guerilla bands, capturing from time to time many men and horses." *Official. Military History of Kansas Regiments During the War for the Suppression of the Great Rebellion* (Leavenworth: W. S. Burke, 1870), 108–111.

19. Walton, *Epitome of My Life*, 32.

20. This incident occurred October 4, 1862. James Townsend died eight weeks later at Des Arc; Jerome Alexander died while a prisoner at St. Louis. See the Confederate Service Records of Jerome H. Alexander, Clayton W. Carnes, Napoleon Kelly, Alfred P. Luckett, Dunk McClennan (McLennan), James Townsend, and Elijah (Jack) Wicker; E. S. C. Robertson to Mary Robertson, October 8, 1862, Robertson Colony Collection; Walton, *Epitome of My Life*, 32–33; Sketch of Napoleon Kelly, *A Memorial and Biographical History of McLennan, Falls, Bell and Coryell Counties* (Chicago: Lewis Publishing Co., 1893), 450–452. Kelley remembered the detachment under the command of Lieutenant Carnes of Company L; Walton recalled he had left Lieutenant Luckett of Company B in charge.

21. Walton, *Epitome of My Life*, 33.

22. J. D. Giddings arrived in Texas in 1838. George H. Giddings was a colonel in John S. Ford's regiment and commanded troops at Palmito Ranch in 1865. "The Giddings," in Mrs. R. E. Pennington, *The History of Brenham and Washington County* (Houston: Standard Printing & Lithographing Co., 1915), 64–81.

23. Walton, *Epitome of My Life*, 33.

24. William Forse Scott, *The Story of a Cavalry Regiment: The Career of the Fourth Iowa Veteran Volunteers from Kansas to Georgia 1861–1865* (New York: G. P. Putnam's Sons, 1893), 50–55.

25. Ibid.

26. The Federal account comes from an undated newspaper clipping belonging to Giddings, "Fight Near Helena, Arkansas" from our Special Correspondent, Helena, October 12, 1862, D. C. Giddings's Papers, Barker Texas

History Center, Austin, Texas. Claims that the Wisconsin cavalry captured Giddings came from Leon, "Texians Making a Raid into Missouri, under Gen. Marmaduke, and Col. G. W. Carter," *Galveston Weekly News*, June 3, 1863. Walton, however, attributed Giddings's capture to Major Walker; *Epitome of My Life*, 33. The Federals named this the battle of "Jones's Lane" or "Lick Creek," while William P. Zuber called it "Shell Creek" or "Shell Bridge." Zuber to the *Telegraph*; Zuber, *My Eighty Years*, 151–152; E. A. Carr to Samuel R. Curtis, October 12, 1862, *OR* 13 : 314–315; E. S. C. Robertson to Mary Robertson, October 20, 1862, Robertson Colony Collection. A. J. Bradberry took part in the charge on Major Rector's party, but Giddings had detailed him to escort the prisoners to camp; therefore, he escaped capture. Sketch of A. J. Bradberry in Mamie Yeary, *Reminiscences of the Boys in Gray, 1861–1865* (Dallas: Press of Wilkinson Printing Co., 1912), 74. Also see Henry Orr to Mary Orr, November 10, 1862, in Anderson, *Campaigning with Parsons' Brigade*, 80–81.

27. Henry Orr to Mary Orr, November 10, 1862, in Anderson, *Campaigning with Parsons' Brigade*, 80–81.

28. Zuber to the *Telegraph*.

29. The party was given by Molly Simpson of La Grange, whom Giddings privately believed was a Federal sympathizer. In spite of warnings that it might be a trap, he went anyway and died January 27, 1863. It was rumored that Miss Simpson left the area immediately, fearing retaliation by the Texans. Ibid. Also see Compiled Service Record of E. T. Giddings.

30. Giddings's report of his confinement appeared in the Houston *Tri-Weekly Telegraph*, January 21, 1863. Giddings's problems had resulted from the murder of Private Allen. W. P. Zuber, who recollected the incident, did not identify the culprit regiment; *My Eighty Years*, 151–153. However, Adjutant William F. Scott placed the blame on the Twenty-first Texas and devoted an entire paragraph to Allen's memory; Scott, *Story of a Regiment*, 51–53. Brigadier General E. A. Carr had written to General Holmes that he "was tempted to retaliate on Lieutenant-Colonel Giddings and his party, but concluded to wait for an opportunity to ask an explanation and redress of the above grievance, which I now request you to furnish"; E. A. Carr to T. H. Holmes, October 15, 1862, *OR*, Series IV, 4 : 628–629. This bitter correspondence continued through several letters, although Holmes denied knowledge of the murder. T. H. Holmes to E. A. Carr, October 21, 1862, ibid., 664–665; A. P. Hovey to T. H. Holmes, October 29, 1862, ibid., 665. Also see the Compiled Service Records of Jerome H. Alexander, Wilferd Brown, Jesse F. Burdett, Clayton W. Carnes, D. C.

Giddings, Thomas E. Giles, Napoleon L. Kelly, Alfred P. Luckett, William F. Kroschel (various spellings), W. M. Morris, Alfred Richards, Burgoyne H. Robertson, John W. Ross, Ed Rundell, Noah Taylor, and Elijah J. Wicker.

31. "Fight Near Helena, Arkansas," D. C. Giddings Papers.

32. D. C. Giddings to Colonel McConnell, November 1, 1862, letter in the Compiled Service Record of J. H. Alexander requesting permission from Federal authorities to move the young man to the hospital; D. C. Giddings to Samuel Curtis, October 29, 1862, *OR*, Series IV, 4 : 666–667; D. C. Giddings to Samuel Curtis, November 4, 1862, ibid., 688; D. C. Giddings to Samuel Curtis, November 7, 1862, ibid., 695.

33. John N. Noble to S. R. Curtis, September 5, 1862, ibid., 492–495; John N. Noble to T. H. Holmes, November 12, 1862, ibid., 704; John N. Noble to D. C. Giddings, October 25, 1862, D. C. Giddings Papers.

34. E. S. C. Robertson to Mary Robertson, December 1 and 2, 1862, Robertson Colony Collection; Zuber, *My Eighty Years*, 152. Major Rector died soon after his exchange. As Grant siphoned off troops for his Vicksburg expedition, the Federal lines were contracted from the hills west of Helena to the unhealthy region near the Mississippi River where Rector became ill. Scott, *Story of a Regiment*, 59–60.

35. Zuber to the *Telegraph*.

36. Scott, *Story of a Regiment*, 55.

37. Alf Johnson to T. H. Holmes, October 23, 1862, Little Rock *Arkansas True Democrat*, November 5, 1862; W. H. Parsons to T. H. Holmes, October 27, 1862, and S. Corley to W. H. Parsons, October 27, 1862, Houston *Tri-Weekly Telegraph*, November 21, 1862; Henry Orr to Mary Orr, November 4, 1862, in Anderson, *Campaigning with Parsons' Brigade*, 78–79; E. S. C. Robertson to Mary Robertson, October 28, and 29, 1862, Robertson Colony Collection; Scott, *Story of a Regiment*, 55; General Orders No. 33, October 28, 1862, *OR* 13 : 907. Holmes wrote: "Let the energy and enterprise of Captains Johnson and Corley be more frequently emulated." It is interesting there is no account of this in the history of the Fifth Kansas Cavalry Regiment, *Official History of Kansas Regiments*, 108–118.

38. E. S. C. Robertson to Mary Robertson, November 14, 1862, Robertson Colony Collection.

39. J. C. Morriss to Amanda Morriss, September 20, 1862, in Jakie L. Pruett and Scott Black, eds., *Civil War Letters: 1861–1865. A Glimpse of the War Between the States* (Austin: Eakin Press, 1985), 33–34. Morriss noted

there was "a peculiarity about the people of this country." The citizens would stand in the road and yell: "Huza for the brave Texas Rangers." J. C. Morriss to Amanda Morriss, October 26, 1862, ibid., 43–45.

40. Walton, *Epitome of My Life*, 35–36.

41. J. J. Frazier to Agnes Frazier, November 22, 1862, Frazier Family Papers, Dallas Historical Society, Dallas, Texas.

42. Compiled Service Record of Ed Rundell.

43. R. A. Cameron to A. P. Hovey, October 29, 1862, *OR* 13 : 768–771.

44. John Truss to Rebecca Truss, November 5, 1862, "Civil War Letters From Parsons' Texas Cavalry Brigade," ed. by Johnette Highsmith Ray, *Southwestern Historical Quarterly* 69 (October 1965): 217–219.

45. Samuel Cooper to T. H. Holmes, October 15, 1862, *OR* 13 : 888; T. H. Holmes to Samuel Cooper, November 2, 1862, ibid., 907; Herman Hattaway and Archer Jones, *How the North Won: A Military History of the Civil War* (Urbana: University of Illinois Press, 1983), 276–277.

46. Samuel Cooper to T. H. Holmes, November 19, 1862, ibid., 921.

47. Report of Alvin P. Hovey, November 22, 1862, ibid., 358–360; T. H. Holmes to Samuel Cooper, November 25, 1862, ibid., 927–928. An informative account of the Fourth Iowa Cavalry Regiment's participation in the attack on Arkansas Post is found in Scott, *Story of a Regiment*, 56–58.

48. T. H. Holmes to Samuel Cooper, November 25, 1862, *OR* 13 : 927–928.

49. T. H. Holmes to Samuel Cooper, November 22, 1862, ibid., 926; T. H. Holmes to Samuel Cooper, December 5, 1862, *OR* 17: pt 2, 783–784.

50. Samuel Cooper to T. H. Holmes, December 6, 1862, ibid., 786.

51. T. H. Holmes to Samuel Cooper, December 8, 1862, ibid., 787–788.

52. Samuel Cooper to J. M. Hawes, September 25, 1862, *OR* 13 : 883; T. H. Holmes to T. C. Hindman, October 26, 1862, ibid., 898; T. H. Holmes to Samuel Cooper, November 3, 1862, ibid., 908.

53. Hawes (1823–1889) graduated from the United States Military Academy in 1845, twenty-ninth in a class of forty-one. He fought in the Mexican War before taking an assignment to teach infantry and cavalry tactics and mathematics at West Point. In the 1850s he served in Kansas, resigning from the army in May 1861. Under Albert Sidney Johnston he commanded the cavalry at Shiloh but requested to be relieved to lead a brigade in Breckinridge's division. Mark M. Boatner III, *The Civil War Dictionary* (New York: David McKay Company, Inc., 1959), 386. Also see Ezra J. Warner, *Generals in Gray: Lives of*

the Confederate Commanders (Baton Rouge: Louisiana State University Press, 1959), 128–129.

54. Henry Orr to Mary Orr, November 24, 1862, in Anderson, *Campaigning with Parsons' Brigade* 84–85; Henry Orr to "Father," December 17, 1862, ibid., 85–86.

55. George W. Ingram to Martha Ingram, November 30, 1862, Henry L. Ingram, comp., *Civil War Letters of George W. and Martha F. Ingram 1861–1865* (College Station: Texas A & M Press, 1973), 39–40.

56. Zuber, *My Eighty Years*, 153–154.

57. Henry Orr had shot a hog. Although nothing came of the incident, Parsons sent him to Little Rock to explain. Orr blamed Parsons for not settling the matter in camp. The quote reads: "So Col. Parsons comes to his regiment," but is probably a mistake on the part of the editor. Henry Orr to "Mother and Father," November 4, 1862, in Anderson, *Campaigning with Parsons' Brigade*, 75–78.

58. Henry Orr to "Father," December 17, 1862, in Anderson, *Campaigning with Parsons' Brigade*, 85–86; Special Orders No. 17, December 9, 1862, Special Order Book of Parsons' Brigade.

59. John W. Truss to Rebecca Truss, November 5, 1862, "Letters From Parsons' Brigade," 217–219; George W. Ingram to Martha Ingram, December 22, 1862, *Civil War Letters*, 42–43.

60. Alf Johnson's men, scouting near Helena, reported large shipments of soldiers leaving there on December 20 and 21 headed down the river; Alf Johnson to T. H. Holmes, December 16 and December 24, 1862; Little Rock *Arkansas True Democrat*, December 31, 1862.

CHAPTER SEVEN

1. George W. Ingram to Martha Ingram, January 2, 1863, in Henry L. Ingram, *Civil War Letters of George W. and Martha F. Ingram 1861–1865* (College Station: Texas A & M Press, 1973), 46–47; also see John W. Truss to Rebecca Truss, January 9, 1863, "Civil War Letters From Parsons' Texas Cavalry Brigade," ed. by Johnette Highsmith Ray, *Southwestern Historical Quarterly* 69 (October 1965): 220–221.

2. George W. Ingram to Martha Ingram, January 2, 1863, *Civil War Letters*, 46–47.

3. For a more detailed account of the arrival of Samuel Richardson's com-

pany, see W. W. Heartsill, *Fourteen Hundred and 91 Days in the Confederate Army*, ed. by Bell Irvin Wiley, (1876; reprint, Jackson, Tennessee: McCowat-Mercer Press, 1954), 85–89.

4. McKay referred to the surrender of Fort Donelson in February 1862; Ibid., 85.

5. M. S. Pierson, "The Diary and Memoirs of Marshall Samuel Pierson, Company C, 17th Reg., Texas Cavalry 1862–1865," ed. by Norman C. Delaney, *Military History of Texas and the Southwest* 13 (1976): 27.

6. F. W. Perry to Eva Perry, December 21, 1862, in Joe R. Wise, ed., "The Letters of Lt. Flavius W. Perry, 17th Texas Cavalry, 1862–1863," ibid., 27–29.

7. Mark M. Boatner III, *The Civil War Dictionary* (New York: David McKay Company, Inc., 1959), 525. Also see Ezra J. Warner, *Generals in Blue: Lives of the Union Commanders* (Baton Rouge: Louisiana State University Press, 1964), 293–294.

8. J. A. McClernand to Edwin Stanton, January 3, 1863, U. S. War Department, *The War of the Rebellion; A Compilation of the Official Records of the Union and Confederate Armies* (128 vols., Washington, D. C., 1880–1901), Series I, 17, pt. 2, 528–530 (hereafter cited as *OR*; unless otherwise indicated all references are to Series I).

9. Both Confederate and Federal reports are in *OR* 17, pt. 1, 698–796. Federal navy reports are in U. S. Naval War Records Office, *Official Records of the Union and Confederate Navies in the War of the Rebellion* (30 vols., Washington, D. C., 1894–1922), Series I, 24 : 98–127 (hereafter cited as *ORN*; unless otherwise indicated all references are to Series I). There are a number of excellent studies on the battle at Arkansas Post as well as regimental histories detailing the participation of different units. For an interesting account written primarily from the official records, see Edwin C. Bearss, "The Battle of the Post of Arkansas," *Arkansas Historical Quarterly* 18 (Autumn 1959): 237–279. For a personal perspective, see David D. Porter, *The Naval History of the Civil War* (New York: The Sherman Publishing Co., 1886), 292. Also see Robert S. Huffstot, "The Battle of Arkansas Post," a souvenir booklet from the editors of *Civil War Times Illustrated* (Harrisburg, Pa.: Historical Times, Inc., 1969).

10. Huffstot, "The Battle of Arkansas Post."

11. Ibid.

12. Report of T. J. Churchill, May 6, 1863, *OR* 17, pt. 1, 780–782.

13. Heartsill, *Fourteen Hundred and 91 Days*, 92.

14. Ibid., 93–94.

15. Ibid.; Report of James Deshler, March 25, 1863, *OR* 17, pt. 1, 790–796; Report of T. J. Churchill, May 6, 1863, ibid., 780–782.

16. "Letter from Arkansas," M. M. Kenney to "Sister," January 27, 1863, *Bellville* [Texas] *Countryman*, March 21, 1863 (hereafter cited as Kenney, "Letter from Arkansas"); Log of events, January 10, 1863, in John Q. Anderson, ed., *Campaigning with Parsons' Texas Cavalry Brigade, CSA: The War Journals and Letters of the Four Orr Brothers, 12th Texas Cavalry Regiment* (Hillsboro, Texas: Hill Junior College Press, 1967), 89.

17. Entry dated January 11, 1863, Thomas B. Smith Diaries, Layland Museum, Cleburne, Texas.

18. S. W. Bishop, "The Battle of Arkansas Post," *Confederate Veteran* 5 (April 1897): 151–152.

19. L. V. Caraway, "The Battle of Arkansas Post," *Confederate Veteran* 14 (March 1906): 127–128.

20. Report of James Deshler, March 25, 1863, *OR* 17, pt. 1, 790–796.

21. Norman D. Brown, ed., *One of Cleburne's Command: The Civil War Reminiscences and Diary of Capt. Samuel T. Foster, Granbury's Texas Brigade, CSA* (Austin: University of Texas Press, 1980), 17–22.

22. Ibid.

23. Report of Robert R. Garland with application for a Court of Inquiry, July 14, 1863, *OR* 17, pt. 1, 783–786. Secretary of War James A. Seddon submitted to Jefferson Davis the following: "The strange circumstances causing the capture of the Arkansas Post demand investigation. I recommend a court of inquiry, and that meanwhile Colonels Garland and Wilkes, and I incline to think General Churchill likewise, should be relieved from their present commands over the men surrendered." J. A. Seddon to Jefferson Davis, May 9, 1863, ibid., 782. Although Garland's request was denied, he preferred charges against Colonel Wilkes. Wilkes was found not guilty, but their animosity lasted throughout the war.

24. Deshler reported that when he saw the flags he "could not believe them to be white flags, and supposed that they were small company flags, such as are frequently carried by volunteer companies. They did have a dingy white color, but I supposed that to be owing to the peculiar light in which they were with reference to the sun and to the fact that they were probably faded." Report of James Deshler, March 25, 1863, ibid., 790–796.

25. Report of T. J. Churchill, May 6, 1863, ibid., 780–782. Churchill was unable to live down the embarrassment of being the commander who had sur-

rendered Arkansas Post. In the summer after the troops had joined Braxton Bragg's army Churchill was replaced by James Deshler.

26. In December Major General John G. Walker arrived in Arkansas and assumed command of the division of Texas infantry under Brigadier General Henry E. McCulloch, who received orders to become a brigade commander. The quote is found in Henry Orr to "Father," January 21, 1863, in Anderson, *Campaigning with Parsons' Brigade*, 90.

27. John W. Truss to Rebecca Truss, January 3, 1863, "Letters from Parsons' Brigade," 219–220. Since Truss is telling his wife about the fall of Arkansas Post, the letter would have to be after January 11, probably January 13 or 23.

28. Pierson, "Diary and Memoirs," 28.

29. Heartsill, *Fourteen Hundred and 91 Days*, 97.

30. Henry Orr to "Father and Mother," February 18, 1863, in Anderson, *Campaigning with Parsons' Brigade*, 91–92.

31. Heartsill, *Fourteen Hundred and 91 Days*, 97.

32. Smith wrote in his diary on January 12, 1863, that he met a man about ten miles from Pine Bluff "who told us the post had fallen with all its forces in the hands of the Feds and that there was federal cavalry looked for this evening at Pine Bluff which really made some of us feel pale about the gills. Directly we would meet another who would tell us it was not taken . . . but just at dark we reached Pine Bluff and learned that it was really so." Thomas B. Smith Diaries. Captain Elijah Petty also described the threat to his wife: "The Post is the key to all Arkansas and they now have a bill of sale to it." E. P. Petty to Ella Petty, January 12, 1863, in Norman D. Brown, ed., *Journey to Pleasant Hill: The Civil War Letters of Captain Elijah P. Petty, Walker's Texas Division, C.S.A.* (San Antonio: Institute of Texan Cultures, 1982), 128–132.

33. Diary entry dated January 14, 1863, J. P. Blessington, *The Campaigns of Walker's Texas Division by a Private Soldier* (New York: Lange, Little & Co., 1875), 70–71.

34. Kenney, "Letter from Arkansas." Thomas B. Smith recorded in his diary that Carter's and Parsons's regiments crossed the river at Pine Bluff that morning. He also noted it had rained heavily all night and continued through the day. The town, he observed, was full of soldiers and the hotels crowded. "Negroes by droves," he noted, "pass through today running from the feds." Diary entry dated January 13, 1863, Thomas B. Smith Diaries.

35. Captain Kenney complained: "As daylight came the men crowded to-

ward the little ferry boat and we had great difficulty to make the men keep their ranks and wait their turn"; "Letter from Arkansas."

36. Ibid.

37. John W. Truss to Rebecca Truss, January 3 [13 or 23], 1863, "Letters from Parsons' Brigade," 219–220.

38. Kenney, "Letter from Arkansas."

39. Entry for January 13, 1863, Blessington, *Campaigns of Walker's Division*, 70.

40. John Simmons to Nancy Simmons, February 5, 1863, in Jon Harrison, ed., "Civil War Letters of John Simmons," *Chronicles of Smith County, Texas* 14 (Summer 1975): 31.

41. U. S. Grant to H. W. Halleck, January 11, 1863, *The Papers of Ulysses S. Grant*, ed. by John Y. Simon, (Carbondale: Southern Illinois University Press, 1967), 7 : 209.

42. U. S. Grant to John A. McClernand, January 11, 1863, ibid., 210.

43. John A. McClernand to Abraham Lincoln, January 16, 1863, OR 17, pt. 2, 566–567.

44. John A. McClernand to U. S. Grant, January 16, 1863, ibid., 567.

45. Porter, *Naval History of the Civil War*, 292. Also see W. T. Sherman, *Personal Memoirs of Gen. W. T. Sherman*, 4th ed. (New York: Charles L. Webster & Co., 1891), 293–331.

46. See Federal reports of the expedition from Helena up the White River, January 13–19, 1863, OR 22, pt. 1, 216–219.

47. U. S. Grant to John A. McClernand, January 13, 1863, *Papers of U. S. Grant*, 7 : 218–219.

48. McClernand reported 134 killed, 898 wounded, and 29 missing for a total of 1,061. The Confederates lost around 60 killed, less than 80 wounded, and 4,791 prisoners. *OR* 17, pt. 1, 708, 716–719.

49. Compiled Service Records of the men in Companies D, E, and I. Compiled Service Records of Confederate Soldiers Who Served in Organizations from the State of Texas, Morgan's Cavalry, Microfilm Rolls 323 : 207–209. Further information on Richardson's company is found in Heartsill, *Fourteen Hundred and 91 Days*, 98–99. The Compiled Service Record of Laban R. Bayless, April 26, 1863, counted forty-seven members of Richardson's company captured and sixty escaped.

50. Henry Orr to "Sister," June 11, 1863, in Anderson, *Campaigning with Parsons' Brigade*, 106–107.

51. Unfortunately there is no record to indicate whether Johnson had sustained a wound in the battle at Arkansas Post. Compiled Service Record of Alf Johnson.

52. This statement was certainly a change from Heartsill's initial evaluation that Captain Richardson should have been placed in command of the cavalry at Arkansas Post. Diary entry dated March 28, 1863, Heartsill, *Fourteen Hundred and 91 Days*, 116.

53. William Physick Zuber, *My Eighty Years in Texas* ed. by Janis Boyle Mayfield (Austin: University of Texas Press, 1971), 160–165.

54. Ibid.

55. Henry Orr to "Sister," February 22, 1863, in Anderson, *Campaigning with Parsons' Brigade* 92–93.

56. At Pine Bluff, Brigadier General James M. Hawes took command of the First Brigade of John G. Walker's division, which had been under Colonel Overton Young. Blessington, *Campaigns of Walker's Division*, 77–78.

57. Robert L. Kerby, *Kirby Smith's Confederacy: The Trans-Mississippi South, 1863–1865* (New York: Columbia University Press, 1972), 35–37; Joseph Howard Parks, *General Edmund Kirby Smith, C.S.A.* (Baton Rouge: Louisiana State University Press, 1954), 254.

CHAPTER EIGHT

1. James A. Seddon to E. Kirby Smith, March 18, 1863, U.S. War Department, *The War of the Rebellion; A Compilation of the Official Records of the Union and Confederate Armies* (128 vols., Washington, D.C., 1880–1901), Series I, 22, pt. 2, 802–803 (hereafter cited as *OR*; unless otherwise indicated, all references are to Series I).

2. Richard Taylor, *Destruction and Reconstruction: Personal Experiences of the Late War in the United States* (Edinburgh and London: William Blackwood and Sons, 1879), 163.

3. Henry W. Halleck to Samuel R. Curtis, February 17, 1863, *OR* 22, pt. 2, 113; Samuel R. Curtis to Henry W. Halleck, March 24, 1863, ibid., 176–177.

4. Mark M. Boatner III, *The Civil War Dictionary* (New York: David McKay, Inc., 1959), 513; Ezra J. Warner, *Generals in Gray: Lives of the Confederate Commanders* (Baton Rouge: Louisiana State University Press, 1959), 211–212.

5. Report of John S. Marmaduke, February 1, 1863, *OR* 22, pt. 1, 195–198.

6. T. H. Holmes to John S. Marmaduke, February 16, 1863, *OR* 22, pt. 2, 788.

7. T. H. Holmes to John S. Marmaduke, February 27, 1863, ibid., 790.

8. T. H. Holmes to John S. Marmaduke, March 5, 1863, ibid., 794.

9. T. H. Holmes to Jefferson Davis, March 6, 1863, ibid., 796–797.

10. Shelby's command consisted of the Missouri regiments of Beal G. Jeans, B. Frank Gordon, George W. Thompson, and the battalions of Benjamin Elliott and David Shanks. Greene's included the Missouri regiments of Leonidas C. Campbell and W. L. Jeffers as well as M. L. Young's battalion. John Burbridge's troops included those of his own regiment, R. C. Newton's Fifth Arkansas Cavalry, and S. G. Kitchen's Missouri battalion. Stephen B. Oates, *Confederate Cavalry West of the River* (Austin: University of Texas Press, 1961), 124.

11. Henry Orr to "Father and Mother," February 18, 1863, in John Q. Anderson, ed., *Campaigning with Parsons' Texas Cavalry Brigade, CSA: The War Journals and Letters of the Four Orr Brothers, 12th Texas Cavalry Regiment* (Hillsboro, Texas: Hill Junior College Press, 1967), 91–92. Also see Henry Orr to "Father," February 13, 1863, ibid., 90–91.

12. Henry Orr to Sam Orr, March 29, 1863, ibid., 93–95.

13. On January 1, 1863, John B. Magruder surprised the Federal garrison that had occupied Galveston since October 1862. After a brief battle the Federals surrendered. Henry Orr to "Father and Mother," February 18, 1863, ibid., 91–92.

14. *Dallas Herald,* March 25, 1863, quoting the Pine Bluff *Southern.*

15. "Letter from Arkansas" by Soldat (sometimes spelled Solidat), May 13, 1863, Houston *Tri-Weekly Telegraph,* June 3, 1863 (hereafter cited as Soldat, "Letter from Arkansas").

16. Morgan's squadron consisted of two companies: Company A under Frank G. Lemmon and Company B under Edward Vontress. In addition, part of Joseph Pratt's artillery accompanied the brigade. William Physick Zuber, *My Eighty Years in Texas,* ed. by Janis Boyle Mayfield (Austin: University of Texas Press, 1971), 167–168. Also see the Abstract from return of the District of Arkansas for April 1863, *OR* 22, pt. 2, 832–833.

17. Carter's brigade included his own men plus Timothy Reves's Missouri cavalry. Abstract from Field Return of Marmaduke's cavalry division, May 20, 1863, *OR* 22, pt. 2, 845. In July Carter's brigade was estimated at 1,800 with around 800 present for duty. Estimate of Troops in Trans-Mississippi Depart-

ment after battle at Helena [July 4, 1863], *OR* 22, pt. 1, 439. Also see "Letter from Missouri," dated April 15, 1863, in *Galveston Weekly News*, May 20, 1863.

18. Diary entry for Tuesday, March 24, 1863, Thomas B. Smith Diaries, Layland Museum, Cleburne, Texas.

19. Colton Greene to E. G. Williams, April 8, 1863, *OR* 22, pt. 2, 814–815. Considering the location of Greene's brigade, the date of this letter is probably April 18, not April 8.

20. Burford arrived home around the first of April; he did not rejoin his regiment until after it had returned from the Missouri raid; *Dallas Herald*, April 8, 1863.

21. Soldat, "Letter from Arkansas."

22. Zuber, *My Eighty Years*, 166.

23. Ibid.

24. Report of John S. Marmaduke, May 20, 1863, *OR* 22, pt. 1, 285–288.

25. Ibid.

26. T. H. Holmes to John S. Marmaduke, February 27, 1863, *OR* 22, pt. 2, 790.

27. Report of George W. Carter, May 5, 1863, *OR* 22, pt. 1, 300–301; Report of John S. Marmaduke, May 20, 1863, ibid., 285–288; William M. (Buck) Walton, *An Epitome of My Life: Civil War Reminiscences* (Austin, Texas: The Waterloo Press, 1965), 46–47.

28. John N. Edwards, *Shelby and His Men; or, The War in the West* (1867; reprint, Kansas City, Mo.: Hudson-Kimberly Publishing Co., 1897), 126.

29. Report of John S. Marmaduke, May 20, 1863, *OR* 22, pt. 1, 285–288.

30. Walton, *Epitome of My Life*, 46.

31. Ibid., 46–47.

32. Report of John S. Marmaduke, May 20, 1863, *OR* 22, pt. 1, 285–288.

33. For the entire Confederate version of the raid see ibid., 251–305. A most interesting Federal account is "The Marmaduke Raid into South-East Missouri," extracted from the *Missouri Democrat* in Frank Moore, ed., *The Rebellion Record: A Diary of American Events*, 12 vols. (1861–1868; reprint, New York: Arno Press, 1977), 6:561–564 (hereafter cited as "The Marmaduke Raid"). The surgeon in the First Iowa Cavalry, Charles Henry Lothrop, provided an informative observation in his *A History of the First regiment Iowa cavalry veteran volunteers . . .* (Lyons, Iowa: Beers & Eaton, 1890), 107–124. A pro-Southern version taken from a Little Rock newspaper appeared in "Gen. Marmaduke's Expedition," *Dallas Herald*, June 3, 1863.

34. The Confederates in the skirmish consisted of Timothy Reves's company under Lieutenant B. A. Johnson and the Texans under Captain John S. Carrington, assistant adjutant general of the Twenty-first Texas. Report of George W. Carter, April 22, 1863, *OR* 22, pt. 1, 299–300; Report of George W. Carter, May 5, 1863, ibid., 300–303; Report of John S. Marmaduke, May 20, 1863, ibid., 285–288. Also see William De Loss Love, *Wisconsin in the War* (Chicago: Church & Goodman, 1866), 562.

35. Edwards, *Shelby and His Men*, 127.

36. Zuber, *My Eighty Years*, 175.

37. Ibid.

38. "The Marmaduke Raid," 562.

39. G. W. Carter to Officer Commanding U. S. Forces in and around Cape Girardeau, April 25, 1863, *OR* 22, pt. 1, 305. This demand was also printed in "The Marmaduke Raid," 562.

40. "The Marmaduke Raid," 562; Love, *Wisconsin in the War*, 563.

41. "The Marmaduke Raid," 562; Love, *Wisconsin in the War*, 564.

42. Report of John S. Marmaduke, May 20, 1863, *OR* 22, pt. 1, 285–288.

43. Edwards, *Shelby and His Men*, 128.

44. Zuber, *My Eighty Years*, 176.

45. Ibid., 176–177; Bennett H. Young, *Confederate Wizards of the Saddle* (1914; reprint, Kennesaw, Ga.: Continental Book Co., 1958), 545–548; John C. Moore, "Missouri," in *Confederate Military History*, ed. by Clement A. Evans, 12 vols. (Atlanta: Confederate Publishing Co., 1899), 9 : 131–132; Edwards, *Shelby and his Men*, 129–131.

46. Report of G. W. Carter, May 5, 1863, *OR* 22, pt. 1, 300–301.

47. Moore, "Missouri," 132, 134.

48. Young, *Confederate Wizards*, 541.

49. Moore, "Missouri," 132.

50. Young, *Confederate Wizards*, 546–547.

51. Oates, *Confederate Cavalry West*, 130–131.

52. Young, *Confederate Wizards*, 546.

53. Harris had asked for and received a copy of Carter's demand for surrender, which he included with his letter. But it would have been an easy matter to obtain one since it had been printed in newspapers in Missouri. Report of S. S. Harris, May 27, 1863, *OR* 22, pt. 1, 304.

54. Zuber, *My Eighty Years*, 178.

55. Report of G. W. Carter, May 5, 1863, *OR* 22, pt. 1, 300–303; Report

of John S. Marmaduke, May 20, 1863, ibid., 285–288.

56. "The Marmaduke Raid," 563. Also see Charles W. W. Dow to his father and family, May 28, 1863, in Lothrop, *History of First Iowa cavalry*, 112–117. Dow was a lieutenant in Company F, First Iowa.

57. The skirmish at White Water successfully detained the Federals for three hours while they built another bridge. Part of the advance guard instrumental in constructing a temporary structure was the First Wisconsin Cavalry under the command of Oscar La Grange, the same officer who had lost part of his force and wagon train to Parsons's Twelfth Texas at the L'Anguille River in August; "The Marmaduke Raid," 563. In Carter's report he noted that Watson, Giddings, Morgan, and Pratt deserved special notice for their "gallantry and energy" in detaining the enemy. Report of G. W. Carter, May 5, 1863, OR 22, pt. 1, 302–303; Love, *Wisconsin in the War*, 564.

58. "The Marmaduke Raid," 563; Compiled Service Records of Atlas C. Norwood of Morgan's Cavalry, Hugh M. Powers and John Hudson of the Nineteenth Texas, and Lucius Olds and William M. Chase of the Twenty-first Texas. Powers died May 6 in the hospital at Cape Girardeau, Hudson was exchanged, Norwood escaped, and Olds had expressed that he did not wish to be exchanged although he was back in Mississippi in 1864. Unfortunately, since records can often be misleading it is difficult to ascertain the facts exactly; both sides not only exaggerated casualties but often failed to report them. Compiled Service Records of Confederate Soldiers Who Served in Organizations from the State of Texas, Nineteenth Texas Cavalry, Microfilm Rolls 323 : 104–106, Twenty-first Texas Cavalry, Microfilm Rolls 323 : 110–112, Morgan's Cavalry, Microfilm Rolls 323 : 207–209. In the Return of Casualties in Marmaduke's Cavalry Division, OR 22, pt. 1, 288, the Texans had seven men killed, thirty-seven wounded, and ten missing. A report of casualties was also carried in the press; Houston *Tri-Weekly Telegraph*, June 15, 1863. One Federal reported the rebel loss could not have been less than 1,500. Love, *Wisconsin in the War*, 565.

59. Walton, *Epitome of My Life*, 48.

60. Zuber, *My Eighty Years*, 179.

61. Charles W. W. Dow to his father and family, May 28, 1863, in Lothrop, *History of First Iowa cavalry*, 117.

62. "The Marmaduke Raid," 564; Report of G. W. Carter, May 5, 1863, OR 22, pt. 1, 302–303; Report of John Q. Burbridge, May 11, 1863, ibid., 296–298; Report of G. W. Thompson, May 15, 1863, ibid., 289–293; Report of John S. Marmaduke, May 20, 1863, ibid., 285–288; Zuber, *My Eighty Years*, 177–184; Walton, *Epitome of My Life*, 48–51.

63. Charles W. W. Dow to his father and family, May 28, 1863, in Lothrop, *History of First Iowa cavalry*, 117.

64. Young, *Confederate Wizards*, 549.

65. Ibid., 561; Moore, "Missouri," 133–134; Edwards, *Shelby and his Men*, 133; Report of John S. Marmaduke, May 20, 1863, OR 22, pt. 1, 285–288; Zuber, *My Eighty Years*, 183.

66. Walton, *Epitome of My Life*, 51–52.

67. Ibid.

68. Ibid.

69. Many Missourians at the time believed that McNeil allowed Marmaduke to escape, and this resulted in a newspaper controversy shortly after the raid ended. In fact, several times during the retreat McNeil apparently had the advantage but failed to press it sufficiently. Moore, "Missouri," 133; "The Marmaduke Raid," 563.

70. Walton, *Epitome of My Life*, 51–52.

71. Ibid.; "The Marmaduke Raid," 564.

72. Walton, *Epitome of My Life*, 53.

73. Since Getzendaner was not on the raid his information was second-hand. *Ellis County History: The Basic 1892 book (With the Presidents Selection deleted) with Additional Biographies compiled by the Ellis County Historical Museum and Art Gallery, Inc. in Memory of the Courageous Pioneers and Builders of Ellis, County* (Fort Worth and Arlington: Historical Publishers, 1972), 698–699.

74. Leon to editor, May 9, 1863, "Texians Making a Raid into Missouri, under Gen. Marmaduke, and Col. G. W. Carter," *Galveston Weekly News*, June 3, 1863. According to the newspaper, the author of this correspondence was an officer in the Twenty-first Texas.

75. Compiled Service Record of F. G. Lemmon.

76. B. D. Chenoweth to sister, May 10, 1863, Houston *Tri-Weekly Telegraph*, June 8, 1863. Stephen Oates, highly critical of Marmaduke's planning, asserted that the general "allowed himself to remain ignorant of road conditions, the forces available to the enemy, and the strength of the four forts at Cape Girardeau." Oates, *Confederate Cavalry West*, 130–131; Report of John S. Marmaduke, May 20, 1863, OR 22, pt. 1, 285–288. Lieutenant Walton accurately stated the results of the raid although he wrote his version much later. He noted, "at the time I thought and now I know, it was unwise, hardy—& foolish thing to do. . . . We did not lose many—that's true—because we just run up there—& run back a good deal faster than we went." Walton, *Epitome of My*

Life, 45. In addition, William Zuber wrote that Colonel Carter explained, "the purpose of our visit to Missouri was to provoke them [the Federals] to turn their attention to the defense of that state." Rather stretching a point, Carter had continued, "We had not only diverted their attention from their conquest of Arkansas, Texas, and Louisiana to the defense of Missouri, but, destroying bridges and telegraph lines and tearing up railroads, we had also crippled their communication between their garrisons in Missouri." Zuber, *My Eighty Years*, 184.

77. Oates, *Confederate Cavalry West*, 130.

78. Stephen Z. Starr, *The Union Cavalry in the Civil War*, vol. 3, *The War in the West 1861–1865* (Baton Rouge: Louisiana State University Press, 1985), 193.

79. U. S. Grant to H. W. Halleck, May 3, 1863, *OR* 24, pt. 1, 33–34.

CHAPTER NINE

1. S. S. Anderson to T. H. Holmes, June 4, 1863, U. S. War Department, *The War of the Rebellion; A Compilation of the Official Records of the Union and Confederate Armies* (128 vols., Washington, D. C., 1880–1901), Series I, 22, pt. 2, 856–857 (hereafter cited as *OR*; unless otherwise indicated, all references are to Series I).

2. T. H. Holmes to Sterling Price, June 13, 1863, ibid., 866; W. B. Blair to Sterling Price, June 9, 1863, ibid., 864; T. H. Holmes to Sterling Price, June 9, 1863, ibid.

3. Report of J. B. Magruder, June 8, 1863, *OR* 26, pt. 2, 58.

4. E. K. Smith to T. H. Holmes, April 14, 1863, *OR* 15, 1041; E. K. Smith to T. H. Holmes, April 15, 1863, ibid., 1042–1043; E. K. Smith to T. H. Holmes, April 19, 1863, *OR* 22, pt. 2, 828; Richard Taylor, *Destruction and Reconstruction: Personal Experiences of the Late War in the United States* (London and Edinburgh: William Blackwood and Sons, 1879), 178–179; John D. Winters, *The Civil War in Louisiana* (Baton Rouge: Louisiana State University Press, 1963), 198.

5. Jackson Beauregard Davis, "The Life of Richard Taylor" (Master's thesis, Louisiana State University, 1937), 75–76; Report of Richard Taylor, June 11, 1863 *OR* 24, pt. 2, 461–462: Report of J. G. Walker, July 10, 1863, ibid., 466.

6. G. W. Carter to Henry Ewing, June 5, 1863, *OR* 22, pt. 2, 857–859.

7. W. B. Blair to Sterling Price, June 9, 1863, ibid., 864; Carter's brigade was reported to have 1,170 total present at the time it left for Pine Bluff. Sterling Price to T. H. Holmes, June 9, 1863, ibid., 863.

8. William Physick Zuber, *My Eighty Years in Texas*, ed. by Janis Boyle Mayfield (Austin: University of Texas Press, 1971), 187.

9. William M. (Buck) Walton, *An Epitome of My Life: Civil War Reminiscences* (Austin: The Waterloo Press, 1965), 57. The most serious casualty in this skirmish was Captain Martin M. Kenney, who had related the delightful account of the trip to reinforce Arkansas Post. Kenney was shot through the windpipe, and "long after his wound had healed he could speak only in whispers"; Zuber, *My Eighty Years*, 187. Report of John S. Marmaduke, May 24, 1863, *OR* 22, pt. 1, 323–326; Report of George W. Carter, May 15, 1863, ibid., 327–328; George W. Carter to Henry Ewing, May 10, 1863, *OR* 22, pt. 2, 836–837; *Bellville* [Texas] *Countryman*, June 27, 1863.

10. G. W. Carter to Henry Ewing, May 20, 1863, *OR* 22, pt. 2, 845.

11. Walton, *Epitome of My Life*, 53–54.

12. George W. Ingram to Martha Ingram, June 17, 1863, in Henry L. Ingram, comp., *Civil War Letters of George W. and Martha F. Ingram 1861–1865* (College Station: Texas A & M Press, 1973), 52–53.

13. Henry Orr to "Father and Mother," May 30, 1863, in John Q. Anderson, ed., *Campaigning with Parsons' Texas Cavalry Brigade, CSA: The War Journals and Letters of the Four Orr Brothers, 12th Texas Cavalry Regiment* (Hillsboro, Texas: Hill Junior College Press, 1967), 105.

14. Henry Orr to "Father," April 4, 1863, ibid., 95–96; Henry Orr to "Sister," April 30, 1863, ibid., 96–97.

15. D. N. Shropshire to "Sister," May 10, 1863, Shropshire Letters, Confederate Research Center, Hillsboro, Texas.

16. Henry Orr to "Friends at Home," May 22, 1863, in Anderson, *Campaigning with Parsons' Brigade*, 99–100. The description of Harper Goodloe is that of A. J. Byrd, Colonel Parsons's brother-in-law and commissary of the brigade. Byrd elucidated: Harper, known as "Our Harper," "was proud in his person—his pride at times bordering on vanity—but never more so than when he had 'by hook or crook' obtained the possession of some flashing article with which to deck out, and as he thought to ornament his comely person. He was a good judge of a horse, and he never rode any other. During the war, he had one or more horses killed under him; and when Harper was mounted and spurred *cap-a-pie*; sashed, sabred and feathered—he always wore a feather or feathers in his slouched hat—he became at once a bright particular star, of no mean military magnitude, and the observed of all." A. J. Byrd, *History and Description of Johnson County, and its Principal Towns* (Marshall, Texas: Jennings Bros., Printers, 1879), 86–87.

17. Letter of Henry Orr, June 1863, in Anderson, *Campaigning with Parsons' Brigade*, 106; Special Orders, May 21, 1863, Special Order Book of Parsons' Brigade, Collection of Parsons' Brigade Association Texas Cavalry, Sims Library, Waxahachie, Texas.

18. John W. Truss to Rebecca Truss, June 7, 1863, "Civil War Letters From Parsons' Texas Cavalry Brigade," ed. by Johnette Highsmith Ray, *Southwestern Historical Quarterly* 69 (October 1965): 221–222.

19. Giddings had personal reasons for hoping to find and attack the Fifth Kansas Cavalry; this was the regiment responsible for the death of his nephew Edmund T. Giddings in January. G. W. Carter to Henry Ewing, June 5, 1863, *OR* 22, pt. 2, 857–859.

20. The Nineteenth Regiment left Colonel N. B. Burford in Pine Bluff. "Letter from Burford's Regiment," from J.E.T., July 18, 1863, *Dallas Herald*, August 5, 1863 (hereinafter cited as J.E.T., "Letter from Burford's Regiment"). J.E.T. was probably James E. Terrell, adjutant of the regiment, who died at Jackson, Mississippi, in November 1863 while on his way to Richmond.

21. When Brigadier General L. Marsh Walker reported for duty at Little Rock, General Holmes ordered him to organize a division consisting of Carter's command as well as the Arkansas regiments of Archibald S. Dobbin and Robert C. Newton. Special Orders, No. 71, June 2, 1863, *OR* 22, pt. 2, 851.

22. J.E.T., "Letter from Burford's Regiment."

23. "Col. Parsons' Cavalry Raid in the Valley of the Mississippi, nearly opposite Vicksburg," by Soldat, Houston *Weekly Telegraph*, August 4, 1863 (hereafter cited as Soldat, "Parsons' Cavalry Raid"). Soldat, sometimes spelled Solidat, was a member of the Twelfth Texas (probably on the colonel's staff) who wrote numerous articles for the Houston paper.

24. Ibid.

25. Henry Orr to "Father," June 27, 1863, in Anderson, *Campaigning with Parsons' Brigade* 110–111.

26. Soldat, "Parsons' Cavalry Raid."

27. Henry Orr to "Father," June 27, 1863, in Anderson, *Campaigning with Parsons' Brigade*, 110–111.

28. J.E.T., "Letter from Burford's Regiment."

29. J. P. Blessington, *The Campaigns of Walker's Texas Division by a Private Soldier* (New York: Lange, Little & Co., 1875), 113–114. Blessington mistakingly dated this account May instead of June. "Walker's Greyhounds" had

been ordered from Arkansas in April to assist General Richard Taylor; the division arrived in Louisiana early in May. On the morning of June 7 the Texans assaulted a Federal fortification manned by black troops at Milliken's Bend. Walker's division consisted of the brigades of Henry E. McCulloch, Horace Randal, and James M. Hawes, former commander of Parsons's cavalry. After the battle at Milliken's Bend, Brigadier General James Tappan and his Arkansas brigade joined the Texans in Louisiana. For a detailed account see Norman Brown, ed., *Journey to Pleasant Hill: The Civil War Letters of Captain Elijah P. Petty, Walker's Texas Division, C.S.A.* (San Antonio: Institute of Texan Cultures, 1982), 234–245.

30. Walker travelled through the region east of Bayou Maçon; his objective was the area around Goodrich's Landing on the Mississippi. Report of J. G. Walker, July 10, 1863, *OR* 24, pt. 2, 466.

31. Soldat, "Parsons' Cavalry Raid."

32. Ibid.

33. For a complete account of the decision to station troops along the Mississippi River, see Dudley Taylor Cornish, *The Sable Arm: Negro Troops in the Union Army, 1861–1865* (1956; reprint, New York: W. W. Norton & Co., Inc., 1966), 115–119, 163–169. A description of life on a Federal plantation is found in Thomas W. Knox, *Camp-fire and Cotton-field: Southern Adventure in Time of War. Life with the Union Armies, and Residence on a Louisiana Plantation* (New York: Blelock and Co., 1865), 305–390, 417–454.

34. George W. Ingram to Martha Ingram, July 18, 1863, *Civil War Letters*, 55–56.

35. J.E.T., "Letter from Burford's Regiment"; Soldat, "Parsons' Cavalry Raid."

36. Soldat, "Parsons' Cavalry Raid"; Winters, *Civil War in Louisiana*, 203–204. Winters mistakenly identified Parsons's command as two Arkansas regiments of Tappan's brigade.

37. Soldat, "Parsons' Cavalry Raid."

38. Ibid.

39. George W. Ingram to Martha Ingram, July 18, 1863, *Civil War Letters*, 55–56.

40. Ibid.

41. Ibid.; Soldat, "Parsons' Cavalry Raid"; James J. Frazier to "Mother, Brothers, & Sisters," July 7, [1863], Frazier Family Papers, Barker Texas History

Center, Austin, Texas.

42. J.E.T., "Letter from Burford's Regiment"; Soldat, "Parsons' Cavalry Raid."

43. Soldat credited the Louisiana battery, but J.E.T. claimed the Mississippi battery had accompanied Parsons. J.E.T., "Letter from Burford's Regiment"; Soldat, "Parsons' Cavalry Raid."

44. Report of J. G. Walker, July 10, 1863, *OR* 24, pt. 2, 466.

45. After hearing rumors that Walker's troops had hanged several black soldiers, a white captain, and a white sergeant, Grant told Taylor he hoped there was "some mistake in the evidence" or that "the act of hanging had no official sanction, and that the parties guilty of it" would be punished. U. S. Grant to Richard Taylor, June 22, 1863, *OR* 24, pt. 3, 425–426; Richard Taylor to U. S. Grant, June 27, 1863, ibid., 443–444; U. S. Grant to Richard Taylor, July 4, 1863, ibid., 469.

46. John Simmons to Nancy Simmons, July 2, 1863, "The Confederate Letters of John Simmons," ed. by Jon Harrison, *Chronicles of Smith County, Texas* 14 (Summer 1975): 33–34.

47. Bell Irvin Wiley, *Life of Johnny Reb: The Common Soldier of the Confederacy* 1943; reprint, Baton Rouge: Louisiana State University Press, 1978), 314. In 1864 the Thirtieth Texas, which would join Parsons in the spring of 1865, took part in the most publicized murder of former slaves recorded in the Trans-Mississippi Department. Six days after Nathan Bedford Forrest led the assault on black troops at Fort Pillow, Tennessee, the Texans, in an outburst of anger and personal hatred, murdered black soldiers at Poison Spring, Arkansas, on April 18, 1864. Historian Robert Kerby concluded: "The so-called battle of Poison Spring was a one-sided massacre: the Union escorts were torn to shreds" and the Confederates "deliberately drove captured wagons back and forth over the fallen Negro wounded, and execution squads went about the field shooting incapacitated prisoners"; *Kirby Smith's Confederacy: The Trans-Mississippi South, 1863–1865* (New York: Columbia University Press, 1972), 312. Kirby Smith confided to his wife that the Southerners had taken "some 200 prisoners and left 600 reported dead on the field principally negroes who neither gave or recd quarter. . . . I saw but two negro prisoners"; ibid. When Henry Orr of the Twelfth Texas visited the battle site some months later, he wrote his sister that "a great many Negroes were killed. The Yankees were invited to come and bury them after the battle; three days after they came and threw a little dirt over them, but the hogs rooted them up; I reckon I saw

half a wagonload of *bones*"; Henry Orr to "Sister," November 12, 1864, in Anderson, *Campaigning with Parsons' Brigade*, 149– 151. For the violence associated with Southerners fighting black soldiers, see Cornish, *The Sable Arm*, and Albert Castel, "The Fort Pillow Massacre," *Civil War History* 4 (March 1958): 37–50.

48. Soldat, "Parsons' Cavalry Raid."

49. Ibid.

50. Ibid.

51. Alfred W. Ellet to D. D. Porter, July 3, 1863, U. S. Naval War Records Office, *Official Records of the Union and Confederate Navies in the War of the Rebellion* (30 vols., Washington, D. C., 1894–1922), Series I, 25 : 215–216 (hereafter cited as *ORN*; unless otherwise indicated all references are to Series I). The Mississippi Marine Brigade, with Alfred W. Ellet commanding, at this time consisted of seven steamers and generally operated on the river near Vicksburg; ibid., 220. For information concerning marines on the Mississippi River, see James P. Jones and Edward F. Keuchel, eds., *Civil War Marine: A Diary of the Red River Expedition, 1864* (Washington, D. C.: U. S. Government Printing Office, 1975), 13–14.

52. Alfred W. Ellet to D. D. Porter, July 3, 1863, *ORN* 25 : 215–216; Report of David D. Porter, July 2, 1863, ibid., 212–214.

53. Soldat, "Parsons' Cavalry Raid."

54. J.E.T., "Letter from Burford's Regiment."

55. Ibid.; Soldat, "Parsons' Cavalry Raid"; George W. Ingram to Martha Ingram, July 18, 1863, *Civil War Letters*, 55–56.

56. George W. Ingram to Martha Ingram, July 18, 1863, *Civil War Letters*, 55–56; Henry Orr to "Sister," July 2, 1863, in Anderson, *Campaigning with Parsons' Brigade*, 111–113.

57. Brigadier General H. T. Reid, who had dispatched the First Kansas Mounted Regiment, reported it was Parsons's cavalry "which did the mischief in this vicinity." Report of H. T. Reid, July 6, 1863, *OR* 24, pt. 2, 450. Also see Soldat, "Parsons' Cavalry Raid."

58. Porter reported to the Secretary of the Navy that the *John Raine* had arrived "as the rebels were setting fire to the so-called Government plantations, and supposing her to be an ordinary transport they opened fire on her with fieldpieces, but were much surprised to have the fire returned with shrapnel, which fell among them, killing and wounding a number." The *Raine* was soon joined by the gunboat *Romeo*, which commenced shelling the enemy troops.

Report of David D. Porter, July 2, 1863, *ORN* 25 : 212–214.

59. Soldat, "Parsons' Cavalry Raid."

60. Report of David D. Porter, July 2, 1863, *ORN* 25 : 212–214.

61. A member of Parsons's regiment watching the scene described it as "the grandest sight I ever witnessed, and, were I to live threescore years and ten more, perhaps will never see again. Words are impotent well nigh, for 'twas almost beyond description. As that long and tortuous line of cavalry slowly wound its way through what was once the garden spot of the great Mississippi Valley, now reduced almost to a wilderness—as it marched leisurely along through the Yankee peon cotton farms, with the lurid shells from the gunboats bursting . . . in every direction might be seen the thick tall columns of black smoke of the burning houses . . . the red flame darting forth"; Soldat, "Parsons' Cavalry Raid."

62. Alfred W. Ellet to D. D. Porter, July 3, 1863, *ORN* 25 : 215–216.

63. Soldat, "Parsons' Cavalry Raid."

64. After Ellet crossed the bayou he followed Parsons's troops for nearly two miles as they fell back to join Walker. Alfred W. Ellet to D. D. Porter, July 3, 1863, *ORN* 25 : 215–216.

65. Porter's comments may be viewed as an example of Northern racial views not always being equalitarian. Report of David D. Porter, July 2, 1863, ibid., 212–214.

66. Report of J. G. Walker, July 10, 1863, *OR* 24, pt. 2, 466; Soldat, "Parsons' Cavalry Raid"; J.E.T., "Letter from Burford's Regiment."

67. G. W. Ingram to Martha Ingram, July 18, 1863; *Civil War Letters*, 55–56; Henry Orr to "Sister," July 2, 1863, in Anderson, *Campaigning with Parsons' Brigade*, 111–113; Soldat, "Parsons' Calvary Raid"; J.E.T., "Letter from Burford's Regiment."

68. Walker pointed out that at no time did his force amount to more than 4,700 men; with the bad weather and "deleterious effect of the climate" the number was reduced to barely 2,500 fit for duty. Although reinforced by Tappan's Arkansas Brigade, Taylor never had more than 4,200 men. J. G. Walker to E. Kirby Smith, July 3, 1863, *OR* 22, pt. 2, 915–916.

69. Henry Orr to "Sister," July 15, 1863, in Anderson, *Campaigning with Parsons' Brigade*, 113–114.

70. G. W. Ingram to Martha Ingram, July 18, 1863, *Civil War Letters*, 55–56. By late summer Ingram observed: "You never saw a worse looking set in your life. Two thirds of them have not courage enough to fight an army of old women. We have not more than 25 men in our company that I could depend upon in a close place in their present condition. This swamp fever seems to make

them indifferent to everything but eating and they have not life enough to cook that." G. W. Ingram to Martha Ingram, September 3, 1863, ibid., 62–63.

71. Henry Orr to "Sister," July 15, 1863, in Anderson, *Campaigning with Parsons' Brigade*, 113–114.

72. Report of John D. Stevenson, September 3, 1863, *OR* 26, pt. 1, 248–249.

73. G. W. Ingram to Martha Ingram, August 30, 1863, *Civil War Letters*, 60–61.

74. Henry Orr to "Father," August 30, 1863, in Anderson, *Campaigning with Parsons' Brigade*, 116–117. Kate Stone, a young refugee at Elysian Fields, Lamar County, Texas, wrote in her diary on October 8: "The Yankee cavalry came out to Monroe by invitation, and a number of citizens signed a petition asking them to come out and drive away our soldiers still there. This is too disgraceful to be true." John Q. Anderson, ed., *Brokenburn: The Journal of Kate Stone, 1861–1868* (Baton Rouge: Louisiana State University Press, 1955), 249.

75. G. W. Ingram to Martha Ingram, August 30, 1863, *Civil War Letters*, 60–61.

76. Report of John D. Stevenson, September 3, 1863, *OR* 26, pt. 1, 248–249.

77. Henry Orr to "Father," August 30, 1863, in Anderson, *Campaigning with Parsons' Brigade*, 116–117.

78. G. W. Ingram to Martha Ingram, September 3, 1863, *Civil War Letters*, 62–63.

79. G. W. Ingram to Martha Ingram, August 30, 1863, ibid., 60–61.

80. Henry W. Halleck to N. P. Banks, August 6, 1863, *OR* 26, pt. 1, 672.

81. Special Orders, July 27, 1862, Special Order Book of Parsons' Brigade.

82. Special Orders No. 3, August 16, 1863, ibid.

83. Special Orders No. 18, 19, 20, September 4, 1863, Special Orders No. 23, October 9, 1863, ibid. Compiled Service Record of Thomas Patterson, Compiled Service Records of Confederate Soldiers Who Served in Organizations from the State of Texas, Twelfth Texas Cavalry, Microfilm Rolls 323 : 71–74.

84. Special Orders, September 18, 1863, Special Order Book of Parsons' Brigade.

CHAPTER TEN

1. Report of John M. Schofield, December 10, 1863, U. S. War Department, *The War of the Rebellion: A Compilation of the Official Records of the*

Union and Confederate Armies (128 vols., Washington, D. C., 1880–1901), Series I, 22, pt. 1, 12–17 (hereafter cited as *OR*; unless otherwise indicated, all references are to Series I).

2. It is difficult to ascertain exactly what independent Texas companies became part of L. Marsh Walker's division because of frequent changes. In September Johnson's Spy Company (which retained this name even after Alf Johnson's death) and W. B. Denson's command (usually including D. A. Nunn's Texas company) belonged to the division. Sterling Price estimated that Carter's brigade had 1,170 present. Sterling Price to T. H. Holmes, June 9, 1863, *OR* 22, pt. 2, 863. Report of Archibald S. Dobbin, November 19, 1863, *OR* 22, pt. 1, 523–525; Special Orders, No. 71, June 2, 1863, *OR* 22, pt. 2, 851; Thomas L. Snead to L. M. Walker, August 31, 1863, ibid., 985–986.

3. Mark M. Boatner III, *The Civil War Dictionary* (New York: David McKay Co., Inc., 1959), 885. Also see Ezra J. Warner, *Generals in Gray: Lives of the Confederate Commanders* (Baton Rouge: Louisiana State University Press, 1959), 321–322.

4. An order in August directed Walker to "resume command of Carter's brigade, together with all the squadrons and companies which have been attached to that brigade or which may be near Pine Bluff, South Bend, or Gaines' Landing," indicating the Texans did not accompany him to Helena. Thomas L. Snead to L. M. Walker, August 31, 1863, *OR* 22, pt. 2, 985–986. Three detached cavalry companies under Captain W. B. Denson acted as vedettes during the attack on Helena. One of these was probably D. A. Nunn's company of Texans; the second could have been Johnson's company. Report of T. H. Holmes, August 14, 1863, *OR* 22, pt. 1, 408–411; Report of James F. Fagan, July 21, 1863, ibid., 423–427. Colonel W. H. Brooks of the Thirty-fourth Arkansas Infantry later reported: "Captain Denson, commanding cavalry detachment, rendered efficient service in counteracting his movements and protecting my right flank." Report of W. H. Brooks, July 10, 1863, ibid., 430–431; Edwin C. Bearss, "The Battle of Helena, July 4, 1863," *Arkansas Historical Quarterly* 20 (Autumn 1961), 256–297.

5. Thomas L. Snead to L. M. Walker, August 31, 1863, *OR* 22, pt. 2, 985–986.

6. Carter returned to Texas sometime late in the summer or early in the fall. The *Telegraph* reported him speaking in Brenham on September 24, Huntsville on October 3, and Anderson on October 5. Houston *Tri-Weekly Telegraph*, September 21 and September 30, 1863. *Galveston Tri-Weekly News* carried one

of his speeches on October 5, 1863, and mentioned his return to the army was near.

7. For the reports of the Union advance upon Little Rock (August 1 to September 14, 1863), see *OR* 22, pt. 1, 468–544; correspondence is found in *OR* 22, pt. 2. On the retreat Marmaduke criticized Walker's handling of the troops at Reed's Bridge on Bayou Metoe northeast of Little Rock, beginning a heated exchange between the two men. Also see Leo E. Huff, "The Union Expedition Against Little Rock, August-September, 1863," *Arkansas Historical Quarterly* 22 (Fall 1963), 224–237. Other accounts of the expedition are found in Thomas L. Snead, "The Conquest of Arkansas," in *Battles and Leaders of the Civil War*, ed. by Robert V. Johnson and Clarence C. Buel, 4 vols. (New York: The Century Company, 1887–1888), 3 : 456–461; Stephen Z. Starr, *The Union Cavalry in the Civil War*, vol. 3, *The War in the West* (Baton Rouge: Louisiana State University Press, 1985), 168–171; *Official. Military History of Kansas Regiments* (Leavenworth: W. S. Burke, 1870), 114.

8. John M. Harrell, "Arkansas," in *Confederate Military History*, ed. by Clement A. Evans, 12 vols. (Atlanta: Confederate Publishing Co., 1899), 10 : 220–221. On October 21 the *Washington Telegraph* published the exchange of notes leading to the duel as well as the terms agreed upon. Leo E. Huff, "The Last Duel in Arkansas: The Marmaduke-Walker Duel," *Arkansas Historical Quarterly* 23 (Spring 1964): 36–49. For a reprint of the 1838 Code of Honor of dueling, see Jack K. Williams, *Dueling in the Old South* (College Station: Texas A & M Press, 1980), 87–104.

9. William M. (Buck) Walton, *An Epitome of My Life: Civil War Reminiscences* (Austin: The Waterloo Press, 1965), 68–69.

10. Edwards reported that during the battle of Bayou Metoe, "General Walker made his appearance on the field, but after a stay of not more than fifteen minutes, retired again to the rear." As the battle intensified an aide of Marmaduke requested Walker's "temporary presence on the field" to direct the action. When Walker chose not to appear, Marmaduke sent a written summons; Edwards charged Walker "treated the note with contempt" and refused to reply. John N. Edwards, *Shelby and His Men; or, the War in the West* (1867; reprint, Kansas City, Mo.: Hudson-Kimberly Publishing Co., 1897), 145–151. Also see Huff, "Last Duel in Arkansas."

11. After Marmaduke arrested Dobbin, Sterling Price suspended the order and instructed Dobbin to return to his brigade. But when Holmes resumed command of the district, he ordered charges be preferred against Dobbin and ab-

solved Marmaduke in Walker's death. Although both seconds in the duel were also exonerated, Holmes insisted, despite Price's protests, that Dobbin still be charged for disobedience of orders. Sterling Price to Archibald S. Dobbin, November 25, 1863, *OR* 22, pt. 1, 525–526. On October 24 there was a court-martial stating Dobbin had refused to obey General Marmaduke in the "face of the enemy." He was dismissed on November 23, 1863, but on January 29, 1864, was reinstated to duty. Compiled Service Record of Archibald S. Dobbin, Compiled Services Records of Confederate Soldiers Who Served in Organizations from the State of Arkansas, 1st (Dobbin's) Arkansas Cavalry Regiment (formerly Chrisman's Battalion Arkansas Cavalry), Microfilm Rolls 317 : 2–3 (hereafter cited as Compiled Service Records), National Archives, Washington, D. C.

12. Report of Sterling Price, November 20, 1863, *OR* 22, pt. 1, 520–521; Report of Archibald S. Dobbin, November 19, 1863, ibid., 523–525; Report of John S. Marmaduke, December –, 1863, ibid., 526–528; Report of Robert C. Newton, December 3, 1863, ibid., 535–541; Frederick Steele to John Schofield, September 12, 1863; ibid., 474–477; "Battle near Little Rock, Arkansas: A National Account," in Frank Moore, ed., *The Rebellion Record: A Diary of American Events*, 12 vols. (1861–1868; reprint, New York: Arno Press, 1977), 7 : 417–423; Huff, "Union Expedition Against Little Rock."

13. Colonel Robert Newton noted that after Dobbin's arrest he had "assumed command of all of Dobbin's force, which included my own brigade, [W. B.] Denson's Louisiana cavalry company, [C. L.] Morgan's Texas squadron, and Pratt's and Etter's batteries"; Report of Robert C. Newton, December 3, 1863, *OR* 22, pt. 1, 535–541.

14. Report of Joseph Pratt, November 20, 1863, ibid., 542–543.

15. Ibid.

16. Report of Robert C. Newton, December 3, 1863, ibid., 535–541.

17. Compiled Service Record of Samuel Corley.

18. Report of Robert C. Newton, December 3, 1863, *OR* 22, pt. 1, 535–541.

19. A soldier in the Sixty-first Illinois Infantry wrote, "I have always thought that General Steele effected the capture of Little Rock with commendable skill and in a manner that displayed sound military judgment. . . . Gen. Price, seeing that his position was turned and that his line of retreat was in danger of being cut off, withdrew his troops from the east side and evacuated Little Rock about five o'clock in the afternoon, retreating southwest." Leander Stillwell, *The Story of a Common Soldier of Army Life in the Civil War 1861–1865*

(1920; reprint, Alexandria, Va.: Time-Life Books, Inc., 1983), 160–161; Report of Sterling Price, November 20, 1863, *OR* 22, pt. 1, 520–522.

20. Report of Robert C. Newton, December 3, 1863, ibid., 535–541.

21. Captain Rust, a native of Virginia, had recruited a company for Carter's brigade of Texas Lancers from Burnet and Milam counties along the frontier line. William M. Rust to J. S. Marmaduke, October [4], 1863, *OR* 22, pt. 2, 1031–1034.

22. On September 15 Price placed Rust in command of a convalescent camp comprised of the Twenty-first Regiment, B. D. McKie's squadron, and C. L. Morgan's squadron as well as two hundred infantry; ibid.

23. Ibid. Lieutenant Buck Walton had been on detached service for General Holmes for several months and not with the Twenty-first Regiment. When he returned and requested the Texans for a scout he wrote: "I was glad to have my old men with me." Walton, *Epitome of My Life*, 72.

24. William M. Rust to J. S. Marmaduke, October [4], 1863, *OR* 22, pt. 2, 1031–1034.

25. Ibid.

26. Upon discovering that he had body lice in the fall of 1863, Walton wrote: "I told nobody of it, but the first opportunity, I went off in the woods by myself and examined my clothing. Yes there they were—in every seam of my flannel shirt, they were embedded." Naturally, he believed that he had acquired them after staying in an old abandoned Federal camp. Walton, *Epitome of My Life*, 73–74.

27. Ibid., 74–75.

28. A comprehensive account of the Pine Bluff expedition is in Edwin C. Bearss, "Marmaduke Attacks Pine Bluff," *Arkansas Historical Quarterly* 23 (Winter 1964), 291–313; Reports of the Action at Pine Bluff, Arkansas, *OR* 22, pt. 1, 721–739; Charles Henry Lothrop, *A History of the First regiment Iowa cavalry veteran volunteers* . . . (Lyons, Iowa: Beers & Eaton, 1890), 141–142; *Official History of Kansas Regiments*, 115–116; Edwards, *Shelby and His Men*, 198–199; Harrell, "Arkansas," 228–230; Walton, *Epitome of My Life*, 75–76; William Physick Zuber, *My Eighty Years in Texas*, ed. by Janis Boyle Mayfield (Austin: University of Texas Press, 1971), 196; Account of the attack on Pine Bluff from the Chicago *Tribune*, in Moore, *The Rebellion Record*, 7 : 577–578.

29. Report of Powell Clayton, October 27, 1863, *OR* 22, pt. 1, 723–724. The account in the Chicago *Tribune* reported Lieutenant Clark's statement: "Colonel Clayton never surrenders, but is always anxious for General Marma-

duke to come and take him; and now, God damn you, get back to your place immediately, or I will order my men to fire on you." Moore, *The Rebellion Record*, 7 : 577. Also see *Official History of Kansas Regiments*, 115–116.

30. Report of Robert C. Newton, December 4, 1863, OR 22, pt. 1, 734–736; Report of John P. Bull, October 31, 1863, ibid., 737–738; Report of W. B. Denson, October 27, 1863, ibid., 738; Report of B. D. Chenoweth, October 27, 1863, ibid., 738–739.

31. Report of Powell Clayton, October 27, 1863, ibid., 723–724.

32. Report of Robert C. Newton, December 4, 1863, ibid., 734–736; Report of Colton Greene, October 28, 1863, ibid., 730–731.

33. Report of Robert C. Newton, December 4, 1863, ibid., 734–736.

34. Report of J. S. Marmaduke, October 26, 1863, ibid., 730.

35. Report of Colton Greene, October 28, 1863, ibid., 730–731.

36. Bearss, "Marmaduke Attacks Pine Bluff," 313.

37. Report of J. S. Marmaduke, October 26, 1863, OR 22, pt. 1, 730.

38. Report of Powell Clayton, October 27, 1863, ibid., 723–724.

39. Walton, *Epitome of My Life*, 76. After this victory over Marmaduke, Colonel Clayton's reputation soared. He was "highly complimented for his brave defense, and well he deserved it. Few Officers would have held out as he did." The Federals became known as the "gallant six hundred" and masters of the field. *Official History of Kansas Regiments*, 115. Moore in *The Rebellion Record*, 7 : 578, reported that the Chicago press printed the lines:

"Bravely they fought and well,
The gallant six hundred."

40. Zuber, *My Eighty Years*, 196.

41. Walton, *Epitome of My Life*, 77–78.

42. Although Walton does not name the company, only three originated along the border of the settled region of Texas. The company under William Rust was raised in Travis and Burnet counties, and Martin M. Kenney's company was from Goliad and Refugio counties. But quite possibly the one involved was Company L, originally raised by J. B. Rocke from the counties of Lampasas and Coryell. By 1864 Indians were raiding around the towns of Gatesville and Lampasas where most of these men lived; *Texas Almanac* (Galveston: D. Richardson & Co., 1865), 42–43. For a more detailed account of the Indian problem see J. W. Wilbarger, *Indian Depredations in Texas* 2d ed. (Austin: Hutchings Printing House, 1890). Indian raids are mentioned in James Bourland to Henry E. McCulloch, December 24, 1863, OR 26, pt. 2, 531–532.

43. W. C. Schaumburg to W. R. Boggs, Semi-annual Inspection by the Inspector General's Office, October 26, 1863, *OR* 22, pt. 2, 1049–1053.

44. Ibid.

45. William Steele to T. H. Holmes, December 2, 1863, *OR* 22, pt. 2, 1085; C. S. West to William Steele, December 10, 1863, ibid., 1093.

46. William Steele to R. M. Gano, December 19, 1863, ibid., 1102.

47. James J. Frazier to "Mother, Brother & Sister," November 1, 1863, Frazier Family Papers, Barker Texas History Center, Austin, Texas.

48. Robert F. Frazier to "Ma," December 23, 1863, ibid.

49. Philip Frazier to Agnes Frazier, December 22, 1863, ibid.

50. E. Cunningham to S. B. Maxey, January 4, 1864, *OR* 34, pt. 2, 819–820. For a more detailed account of affairs in the Indian Territory in 1863–1864, see Lary C. Rampp and Donald L. Rampp, *The Civil War in the Indian Territory* (Austin: Presidial Press, 1975), 101–121.

51. George W. Ingram to Martha Ingram, December 22, 1863, in Henry L. Ingram, comp., *Civil War Letters of George W. and Martha F. Ingram 1861–1865* (College Station: Texas A & M Press, 1973), 66–67.

52. Robert F. Frazier to "Ma," December 23, 1863, Frazier Family Papers.

53. Ibid.; George W. Ingram to Martha Ingram, December 22, 1863, *Civil War Letters*, 66–67; A. Parks to "Mother," January 22, 1864, photocopy in possession of the author.

54. George W. Ingram to Martha Ingram, December 22, 1863, *Civil War Letters*, 66–67.

55. Ibid.

56. Zuber, *My Eighty Years*, 197.

57. George W. Ingram to Martha Ingram, December 24, 1863, *Civil War Letters*, 67–68.

58. George W. Ingram to Martha Ingram, December 22, 1863, ibid., 66–67.

59. Letter of Nat M. Burford, November 27, 1863, photocopy in the collection of Joe and Ann Cerney, Wichita Falls, Texas.

60. Letter of James F. Fagan, November 27, 1863, photocopy in the collection of Joe and Ann Cerney.

61. Petition to James A. Seddon for Parsons's promotion, signed by a number of soldiers, February 1, 1864, photocopy in the collection of Joe and Ann Cerney.

62. E. Kirby Smith to Richard Taylor, December 23, 1863, *OR* 22, pt. 2, 1110–1111.

63. George W. Ingram to Martha Ingram, February 6, 1864, *Civil War Letters*, 68–69; J. S. Marmaduke to Henry Ewing, December 28, 1863, *OR* 22, pt. 2, 1113–1114; Zuber, *My Eighty Years*, 197; Edwards, *Shelby and His Men*, 202–204; Special Orders dated February 22, 1864, Special Order Book of Parsons' Brigade, Collection of Parsons' Brigade Association Texas Cavalry, Sims Library, Waxahachie, Texas.

CHAPTER ELEVEN

1. Correspondence and reports relating to the Red River Campaign are found in U. S. War Department, *The War of the Rebellion; A Compilation of the Official Records of the Union and Confederate Armies* (128 vols., Washington, D. C., 1880–1901), Series I, 34, pts. 1–4 (hereafter cited as *OR*; unless otherwise indicated, all references are to Series I).

2. W. T. Sherman to Frederick Steele, March 4, 1864, ibid., pt. 2, 496–497; Frederick Steele to N. P. Banks, March 7, 1864, ibid., 518–519; Frederick Steele to W. T. Sherman, March 7, 1864, ibid., 522–523; Frederick Steele to H. W. Halleck, March 12, 1863, ibid., 576.

3. Indorsement, W. T. Sherman to N. P. Banks, March 4, 1864, ibid., 448–449.

4. U. S. Grant to Frederick Steele, March 15, 1864, ibid., 616; U. S. Grant to Frederick Steele, March 14, 1864, ibid., 603.

5. William T. Sherman, *Home Letters of General Sherman*, ed. by M. A. De Wolfe (New York: Charles Scribner's Sons, 1909), 286–287.

6. Ludwell H. Johnson, *Red River Campaign: Politics and Cotton in the Civil War* (Baltimore: The Johns Hopkins Press, 1958), 84.

7. U. S. Grant, *Personal Memoirs of U. S. Grant*, 2 vols. (New York: Charles L. Webster & Co., 1885), 2 : 139.

8. Stephen Z. Starr, *The Union Cavalry in the Civil War*, vol. 3: *The War in the West, 1861–1865* (Baton Rouge: Louisiana State University Press, 1985), 488–489; Johnson, *Red River Campaign*, 99–100; Robert U. Johnson and Clarence C. Buel, eds., *Battles and Leaders of the Civil War*, 4 vols. (New York: The Century Company, 1887–1888), 4 : 367–370.

9. Lester N. Fitzhugh, "Texas Forces in the Red River Campaign, March-May, 1864," *Texas Military History* 3 (Spring 1963), 15–22; Johnson, *Red River Campaign*, 132; Starr, *Union Cavalry in the Civil War*, 3 : 494; Richard Taylor, *Destruction and Reconstruction: Personal Experiences of the Late War*

in the United States (Edinburgh and London: William Blackwood and Sons, 1879), 208, 212.

10. Starr, *Union Cavalry in the Civil War*, 3 : 495; Johnson, *Red River Campaign*, 125.

11. Johnson, *Red River Campaign*, 141, 145.

12. Taylor, *Destruction and Reconstruction*, 223.

13. Ibid., 224–225.

14. Johnson, *Red River Campaign*, 165–166. Also see Taylor, *Destruction and Reconstruction*, 215–216.

15. Kirby Smith feared a movement from Matagorda Bay toward San Antonio or Houston; E. Kirby Smith to Jefferson Davis, January 20, 1864, OR 34, pt. 2, 895–896.

16. Special Orders February 22, 1864, Special Order Book of Parsons' Brigade, Collection of Parsons' Brigade Association Texas Cavalry, Sims Library, Waxahachie, Texas.

17. Richard Taylor to E. Kirby Smith, January 4, 1864, U. S. Naval War Records Office, *Official Records of the Union and Confederate Navies in the War of the Rebellion* (30 vols., Washington, D. C., 1894–1922), Series I, 26 : 162–163 (hereafter cited as *ORN*; unless otherwise indicated all references are to Series I); John G. Meem, Jr., to W. H. Parsons, April 9, 1864, OR 34, pt. 3, 754.

18. S. S. Anderson to E. Greer, March 12, 1864, OR 34, pt. 2, 1038.

19. E. Cunningham to E. Greer, March 20, 1864, ibid., 1061; E. Cunningham to T. H. Holmes, March 7, 1864, ibid., 1026; E. Cunningham to E. Greer, March 24, 1864, ibid., 1077–1078.

20. Kirby Smith assured Samuel B. Maxey in the Indian Territory that Parsons's brigade was "within supporting distance of you in case of emergency." E. Cunningham to S. B. Maxey, March 8, 1864, ibid., 1030; W. H. Parsons, *Inside History and Heretofore Unwritten Chapters on the Red River Campaign of 1864 and the Participation therein of Parsons Texas Cavalry Brigade* in *Condensed History of Parsons Texas Cavalry Brigade 1861–1865* . . . (Corsicana, Texas: 1903), 83–84.

21. E. Kirby Smith to Richard Taylor, April 8, 1864, OR 34, pt. 1, 528.

22. George W. Ingram to Martha Ingram, April 9, 1864, in Henry L. Ingram, comp., *Civil War Letters of George W. and Martha F. Ingram 1861–1865* (College Station: Texas A & M Press, 1973), 71.

23. John G. Meem, Jr., to W. H. Parsons, April 9, 1864, OR 34, pt. 3, 754.

24. E. Surget to A. H. May, March 21, 1864, ibid., 503–504; Richard Taylor to W. R. Boggs, April 4, 1864, ibid., 522; Richard Taylor to W. R. Boggs, April 5, 1864, ibid., 523.

25. David D. Porter to W. T. Sherman, April 16, 1864, *ORN* 26 : 57–63; David D. Porter, *The Naval History of the Civil War* (New York: The Sherman Publishing Co., 1886), 502.

26. Ibid.

27. On board Porter's flagship *Cricket* was a twenty-seven-man Marine guard commanded by Lieutenant Frank L. Church (not to be confused with Alfred W. Ellet's Marine Brigade, an army unit, also along on the expedition). On April 10 Church entered in his diary that Porter had received "dispatches of very unfavorable character from General Banks." James P. Jones and Edward F. Keuchel, eds., *Civil War Marine: A Diary of the Red River Expedition, 1864* (Washington, D.C.: U.S. Government Printing Office, 1975), 46; Report of Thomas Kilby Smith, April 16, 1864, *OR* 34, pt. 1, 379–383.

28. David D. Porter to W. T. Sherman, April 16, 1864, *ORN* 26 : 57–63.

29. Frank Church wrote in his diary on April 11 that one of the vessels had been fired on by "200 or 300 guerillas with muskets." Jones and Keuchel, *Civil War Marine*, 46; Report of T. Kilby Smith, April 16, 1864, *OR* 34, pt. 1, 379–383; Thomas O. Selfridge to David D. Porter, April 16, 1863, *ORN* 26 : 49; George M. Bache to David D. Porter, April 13, 1864, ibid., 50; Abstract Log of the *Lexington*, ibid., 788–791; David D. Porter to W. T. Sherman, April 16, 1864, ibid., 57–63; Porter, *Naval History of the Civil War*, 512–513.

30. Taylor, *Destruction and Reconstruction*, 236–237; Johnson, *Red River Campaign*, 181–183; Robert L. Kerby, *Kirby Smith's Confederacy: The Trans-Mississippi South, 1863–1865* (New York: Columbia University Press, 1972), 311; John D. Winters, *The Civil War in Louisiana* (Baton Rouge: Louisiana State University Press, 1963), 361–362; Joseph Howard Parks, *General Edmund Kirby Smith, C.S.A.* (Baton Rouge: Louisiana State University Press, 1954), 275.

31. Alwyn Barr, "The Battle of Blair's Landing," *Louisiana Studies* 2 (Winter 1963): 204–212.

32. "The Battle with the Gunboats at Blair's Landing at Red River," by Soldat, Houston *Daily Telegraph*, Sarah Glenn Riddell Scrapbook, Texas State Archives, Austin, Texas. Also see J. H. McLeary, "History of Green's Brigade," in Dudley G. Wooten, ed., *A Comprehensive History of Texas, 1865–1897*, 2 vols. (Dallas: William G. Scarff, 1898), 2 : 730.

33. Parsons, *Inside History*, 87. Also see Barr, "Battle of Blair's Landing."

34. Solidat, "The Battle with Gunboats."

35. Ibid. Also see Parsons, *Inside History*, 87–88.

36. Thomas O. Selfridge to D. D. Porter, June 2, 1880, in Thomas O. Selfridge, *Memoirs of Thomas O. Selfridge . . .* (New York and London: G. P. Putnam's Sons, 1924), 102.

37. Parsons, *Inside History*, 88.

38. Thomas O. Selfridge to D. D. Porter, June 2, 1880, in Selfridge, *Memoirs*, 102.

39. David W. Fentress to Editor, May 17, 1864, Galveston *Tri-Weekly News*, June 3, 1864.

40. George M. Bache to David D. Porter, April 13, 1864, ORN 26 : 50.

41. Solidat, "The Battle with Gunboats."

42. Fentress to Editor, May 17, 1864.

43. Selfridge, *Memoirs*, 93.

44. Assistant Surgeon Fentress asserted that Parsons later learned this order had come from Brigadier General Major, Fentress to Editor, May 17, 1864.

45. Parsons, *Inside History*, 89.

46. Thomas O. Selfridge to D. D. Porter, June 2, 1880, in Selfridge, *Memoirs*, 103.

47. Parsons, *Inside History*, 89.

48. Fentress to Editor, May 17, 1864.

49. There seemed to be some disagreement over the events following Green's death. Captain Millett wrote his version in 1916 to answer an article by Harper Goodloe of the Twelfth Texas in 1915. Goodloe, who tended to exaggerate, wrote that he had retrieved Green's body amid heavy firing and had personally placed it on the general's horse. Millett's account, however, is probably closer to the truth. P. H. Goodloe, "Service in the Trans-Mississippi," *Confederate Veteran* 23 (January 1915): 31–32; E. B. Millett, "When General Green was Killed," ibid., 24 (September 1916): 408–409.

50. Fentress to Editor, May 17, 1864.

51. Thomas O. Selfridge to D. D. Porter, June 2, 1880, in Selfridge, *Memoirs*, 103; diary entry for April 12, 1864, in Jones and Keuchel, *Civil War Marine*, 46–47.

52. T. O. Selfridge to David D. Porter, April 16, 1864, ORN 26 : 49.

53. W. H. Parsons to W. Steele, June 3, 1864, Galveston *News Bulletin*, July 9, 1864.

54. Porter claimed: "It is not the intention of these rebels to fight." He believed that they had only done so because they were drunk. Report of

David D. Porter, April 14, 1864, *ORN* 26 : 52.

55. Parsons, *Inside History*, 95.

56. Fentress to Editor, May 17, 1864.

57. Johnson, *Red River Campaign*, 214.

58. Mark M. Boatner III, *The Civil War Dictionary* (New York: David McKay Company, Inc., 1959), 909; Francis R. Lubbock, *Six Decades in Texas or Memoirs of Francis Richard Lubbock: Governor of Texas in War-Time, 1861–63*, ed. by C. W. Raines (Austin: Ben C. Jones & Co., 1900), 538–539. Also see Ezra J. Warner, *Generals in Gray: Lives of the Confederate Commanders* (Baton Rouge: Louisiana State University Press, 1959), 331–332.

59. Parsons, *Inside History*, 95.

CHAPTER TWELVE

1. W. H. Parsons to W. Steele, June 3, 1864, Galveston *News Bulletin*, July 9, 1864 (hereafter cited as Parsons's Report).

2. N. P. Banks to U. S. Grant, April 30, 1864, U. S. War Department, *The War of the Rebellion; A Compilation of the Official Records of the Union and Confederate Armies* (128 vols., Washington, D. C. 1880–1901), Series I, 34, pt. 1, 189–192 (hereafter cited as *OR*; unless otherwise indicated all references are to Series I).

3. Special Orders, No. 34, February 11, 1864, *OR* 34, pt. 2, 961; Special Orders, No. 72, March 12, 1864, ibid., 1037; Special Orders, No. 78, March 18, 1864, ibid., 1058.

4. Mark M. Boatner III, *The Civil War Dictionary* (New York: David McKay Company, Inc., 1959), 795; Report of William Steele, June 5, 1864, *OR* 34, pt. 1, 625–628. Also see Ezra J. Warner, *Generals in Gray: Lives of the Confederate Commanders* (Baton Rouge: Louisiana State University Press, 1959), 289–290.

5. William Physick Zuber, *My Eighty Years in Texas*, ed. by Janis Boyle Mayfield (Austin: University of Texas Press, 1971), 215.

6. Henry Orr to "Father, Mother, and Family," April 27, 1864, in John Q. Anderson, ed., *Campaigning with Parsons' Texas Cavalry Brigade, CSA: The War Journals and Letters of the Four Orr Brothers, 12th Texas Cavalry Regiment* (Hillsboro, Texas: Hill Junior College Press, 1967), 131–134; Zuber, *My Eighty Years*, 202–214.

7. Report of Richard Taylor, April 24, 1864, *OR* 34, pt. 1, 579–580; Re-

port of Richard Taylor, April 27, 1864, ibid., 583–584; Zuber, *My Eighty Years,* 204–214.

8. The Texans attacked the plantation above Cloutierville and the next day skirmished below the town. Report of William Steele, June 5, 1864, *OR* 34, pt. 1, 625–628; Zuber, *My Eighty Years,* 209–212.

9. Henry Orr to "Father, Mother, and Family," April 27, 1864, in Anderson, *Campaigning with Parsons' Brigade,* 131–134.

10. Parsons's Report.

11. Richard Taylor, *Destruction and Reconstruction: Personal Experiences of the Late War in the United States* (Edinburgh and London: William Blackwood and Sons, 1879), 240–241; X. B. Debray, "A Sketch of Debray's Twenty-Sixth Regiment of Texas Cavalry: Paper No. 2, "*Southern Historical Society Papers* 13 (January-December 1885), 153–165; Report of Richard Taylor, April 24, 1864, *OR* 34, pt. 1, 580–581; Ludwell H. Johnson, *Red River Campaign: Politics and Cotton in the Civil War* (Baltimore: The Johns Hopkins Press, 1958), 226–234; Francis R. Lubbock, *Six Decades in Texas: The Memoirs of Francis Richard Lubbock, Governor of Texas in War-Time,* ed. by C. W. Raines (Austin: Ben C. Jones & Co., 1900), 539–540; John D. Winters, *The Civil War in Louisiana* (Baton Rouge: Louisiana State University Press, 1963), 362.

12. Henry Orr to "Father, Mother, and Family," April 27, 1864, in Anderson, *Campaigning with Parsons' Brigade,* 131–134; Johnson, *Red River Campaign,* 232; Report of N. P. Banks, April 30, 1864, *OR* 34, pt. 1, 189–192.

13. Parsons's Report.

14. Henry Orr to "Father, Mother, and Family," April 27, 1864, in Anderson, *Campaigning with Parsons' Brigade,* 131–134.

15. Parsons's Report.

16. Report of Richard Taylor, April 24, 1864, *OR* 34, pt. 1, 580–581.

17. David D. Porter, *The Naval History of the Civil War* (New York: The Sherman Publishing Co., 1886), 525–527; Johnson, *Red River Campaign,* 264–265.

18. Parsons's Report.

19. Report of William Steele, June 5, 1864, *OR* 34, pt. 1, 625–628.

20. N. P. Banks to David D. Porter, May 9, 1864, U. S. Naval War Records Office, *Official Records of the Union and Confederate Navies in the War of the Rebellion* (30 vols., Washington, D. C., 1894–1922), Series I, 26 : 136 (hereafter cited as *ORN;* unless otherwise indicated all references are to Series I).

21. David D. Porter to N. P. Banks, May 11, 1864, ibid., 140–141.

22. Parsons's Report.

23. Report of William Steele, June 5, 1864, *OR* 34, pt. 1, 625–628.

24. William M. [Buck] Walton, *An Epitome of My Life: Civil War Reminiscences* (Austin: The Waterloo Press, 1965), 82–83.

25. Johnson, *Red River Campaign*, 274–275.

26. Report of Joseph A. Mower, May 23, 1864, *OR* 34, pt. 1, 320–321; Report of Sylvester G. Hill, March [May] 25, 1864, ibid., 326–328; Report of S. G. Hill, May 28, 1864, ibid., 329–330; Report of George W. Van Beek, April 13, 1864, ibid., 335–337; Report of Thomas J. Kinney, May 20, 1864, ibid., 347–349; Report of William T. Shaw, May 26, 1864, ibid., 357–358; Report of William Steele, June 5, 1864, ibid., 625–628; Report of Richard Taylor, May 19, 1864, ibid., 594–595; Report of George Wythe Baylor, April 8, 1864 [includes operations through May 18], ibid., 616–625.

27. Report of Joseph A. Mower, May 23, 1864, ibid., 320–321.

28. Parsons's Report; P. H. Goodloe, "Service in the Trans-Mississippi," *Confederate Veteran* 23 (January 1915): 31–32.

29. Henry Orr to "Father," May 25, 1864, in Anderson, *Campaigning with Parsons' Brigade*, 139–140.

30. Parsons's Report.

31. Robert F. Frazier to "Mother," May 19, 1864, Frazier Family Papers, Barker Texas History Center, Austin, Texas.

32. Parsons, *Inside History*, 104.

33. Alwyn Barr, *Polignac's Texas Brigade*, a booklet published by the Texas Gulf Coast Historical Association (November 1964), 45–47.

34. Henry Orr to "Father," May 25, 1864, in Anderson, *Campaigning with Parsons' Brigade*, 139–140.

35. Debray, "Sketch of Debray's Twenty-Sixth Regiment," 163.

36. Goodloe, "Service in the Trans-Mississippi," 31–32; Parsons, *Inside History*, 104.

37. Walton, *Epitome of My Life*, 83.

38. Johnson, *Red River Campaign*, 275.

39. Report of Thomas J. Kinney, May 20, 1864, *OR* 34, pt. 1, 347–348.

40. Diary entry dated April 15, 1864, in John Q. Anderson, ed., *Brokenburn: The Journal of Kate Stone, 1861–1868* (Baton Rouge: Louisiana State University Press, 1955), 278–279.

41. For the total losses at Yellow Bayou see Johnson, *Red River Cam-*

paign, 275; Taylor, *Destruction and Reconstruction*, 254; Report of A. J. Smith, September 26, 1865, *OR* 34, pt. 1, 311. For Texas casualty count see the Houston *Daily Telegraph*, June 8, 1864, and Alwyn Barr, "Texas Losses in the Red River Campaign, 1864," *Texas Military History* 3 (Summer 1963): 103–110.

42. Compiled Service Records of Joseph Wier and Thomas Haley, Compiled Service Records of Confederate Soldiers who Served in Organizations from the State of Texas, Twelfth Texas Cavalry, Microfilm Rolls 323 : 71–74 (hereafter cited as Compiled Service Records), National Archives, Washington, D. C.; *A Memorial and Biographical History of Johnson and Hill Counties, Texas* (Chicago: Lewis Publishing Co., 1892), 422–423; Parsons's Report.

43. Sketch of Joseph Lafayette Estes in Mamie Yeary, comp., *Reminiscences of the Boys in Gray 1861–1865* (Dallas: Press of Wilkinson Printing Co., 1912), 215–216; Compiled Service Records of J. S. Turner and J. L. Estes.

44. Compiled Service Record of Samuel A. Higgins.

45. Compiled Service Record of John W. Shropshire; A. J. Byrd, *History and Description of Johnson County, and its Principal Towns . . .* (Marshall, Texas: Jennings Brothers, 1879), 117–118; *Memorial History of Johnson and Hill Counties*, 441, 446.

46. Ibid.

47. Report of William Steele, June 5, 1864, *OR* 34, pt. 1, 625–628; Parsons's Report.

48. Report of Richard Taylor, April 24, 1864, ibid., 580–581; Richard Taylor to W. R. Boggs, June 8, 1864, *OR*, pt. 4, 653–655.

49. William Steele to S. S. Anderson, June 18, 1864, Compiled Service Record of G. W. Carter, Twenty-first Texas Cavalry, Microfilm Rolls 323 : 110–112.

50. Burford wrote that as a private in Good's battery he had won the confidence of his peers, but "as a Regimental commander I have added nothing to the reputation I brought with me from the ranks—without confidence in my capacity to command in the field; and a constant fear of doing something by which our glorious cause might suffer detriment, I can feel no pleasure in my present position." N. M. Burford to S. S. Anderson, May 30, 1864, Compiled Service Record of Nathaniel M. Burford, Nineteenth Texas Cavalry, Microfilm Rolls 323 : 104–106. Comments by William Steele dated May 31, 1864, and John H. Wharton dated June 1, 1864, ibid.

51. Joint Resolution of Congress, June 10, 1864, *OR* 34, pt. 1, 597.

52. Extract from Taylor's address, George W. Ingram to Martha Ingram,

June 12, 1864, in Henry L. Ingram, comp., *Civil War Letters of George W. and Martha F. Ingram 1861–1865* (College Station: Texas A & M Press, 1973), 75–76.

53. Henry Orr to Mary Orr, June 11, 1864, in Anderson, *Campaigning with Parsons' Brigade*, 141–142; General Orders, May 24, 1864, OR 34, pt. 1, 615–616. An original copy of Wharton's order can be found in the Special Order Book of Parsons' Brigade, Collection of Parsons' Brigade Association Texas Cavalry, Sims Library, Waxahachie, Texas.

54. Parsons's Report; Barr, "Texas Losses."

55. Taylor, *Destruction and Reconstruction*, 251.

56. Richard M. McMurry, "The Atlanta Campaign: December 23, 1863 to July 18, 1864" (Ph.D. diss., Emory University, 1967), 323.

57. U. S. Grant, *Personal Memoirs of U. S. Grant*, 2 vols. (New York: Charles L. Webster & Co., 1885), 2 : 519.

58. George W. Ingram to Martha Ingram, June 4, 1864, *Civil War Letters* 74–75.

59. John A. Wharton to J. Bankhead Magruder, June 17, 1864, OR 34, pt. 4, 680–681.

60. Henry Orr to "My Dear Brother," August 26, 1864, in Anderson, *Campaigning with Parsons' Brigade*, 145–146.

61. W. W. Heartsill, *Fourteen Hundred and 91 Days in the Confederate Army*, ed. by Bell Irvin Wiley (1876; reprint, Jackson, Tennessee: McCowat-Mercer Press, 1954), 196, 209, 212–213.

62. J. G. Walker to E. Kirby Smith, August 13, 1864, OR 41, pt. 1, 106; Richard Taylor to E. Kirby Smith, August 18, 1864, ibid., 110–111; W. R. Boggs to S. B. Buckner, August 22, 1864, ibid., 118.

63. Henry Orr to Mary Orr, June 11, 1864, in Anderson, *Campaigning with Parsons' Brigade*, 141–142.

64. George W. Ingram to Martha Ingram, June 12, 1864, *Civil War Letters*, 75–76; Special Orders, June 13, 1864, Special Orders Book of Parsons' Brigade.

65. Heartsill, *Fourteen Hundred and 91 Days*, 216.

66. Ibid., 214.

67. George W. Ingram to Martha Ingram, August 14, 1864, *Civil War Letters*, 76–77.

68. Robert L. Kerby, *Kirby Smith's Confederacy: The Trans-Mississippi South, 1863–1865* (New York: Columbia University Press, 1972), 323–331.

CHAPTER THIRTEEN

1. Richard Taylor, *Destruction and Reconstruction: Personal Experiences of the Late War in the United States* (Edinburgh and London: William Blackwood and Sons, 1879), 254.

2. Robert L. Kerby, *Kirby Smith's Confederacy: The Trans-Mississippi South, 1863–1865* (New York: Columbia University Press, 1972), 335–336.

3. George W. Ingram to Martha Ingram, October 20, 1864, in Henry L. Ingram, comp., *Civil War Letters of George W. and Martha F. Ingram 1861–1865* (College Station: Texas A & M Press, 1973), 77–78.

4. J. B. Magruder to W. R. Boggs, September 10, 1864, U. S. War Department, *The War of the Rebellion; A Compilation of the Official Records of the Union and Confederate Armies* (128 vols., Washington, D.C., 1880–1901), Series I, 41, pt. 3, 917–918 (hereafter cited as *OR;* unless otherwise indicated, all references are to Series I). Also see J. B. Magruder to W. R. Boggs, September 11, 1864, ibid., 922.

5. John A. Wharton to E. Kirby Smith, August 9, 1864, *OR* 41, pt. 2, 1049–1050.

6. In early September Parsons received an order to move to Monticello in southeast Arkansas, where a possible "advance of the enemy from the lower Arkansas is threatened." J. W. Lewis to W. H. Parsons, September 11, 1864, *OR* 41, pt. 3, 923. W. W. Heartsill noted in late October that his detachment was to keep "an eye on the movements of the Pine Bluff garrison." W. W. Heartsill, *Fourteen Hundred and 91 Days in the Confederate Army*, edited by Bell Irvin Wiley (1876; reprint, Jackson, Tenn.: McCowat-Mercer Press, 1954), 220–221.

7. For a complete account of Price's Missouri raid, see Stephen B. Oates, *Confederate Cavalry West of the River* (Austin: University of Texas Press, 1961), 140–154. Report of John B. Clark, December 19, 1864, *OR* 41, pt. 1, 678–685. Pratt's Second Horse Artillery Battalion consisted of his own command, one Arkansas, and two Missouri batteries. Organization of Price's Army, ibid., 641–642; Organization of the Army of the Trans-Mississippi Department, September 30, 1864, *OR* 41, pt. 3, 966–971. In addition, Pratt's tombstone in Oakwood Cemetery, Jefferson, Texas, states that he died of the effects of a gunshot wound received in the Confederate army on October 26, 1864.

8. Report of Frederick W. Benteen, November 3, 1864, *OR* 41, pt. 3, 330–333; Report of Samuel Curtis, January 1865, ibid., 464–523; Report of

Sterling Price, December 28, 1864, ibid., 625–640; Compiled Service Records of John Coffey (Coffee) and William Hewitt, Compiled Military Service Records of Pratt's Battery, Microfilm Roll 323 : 240.

9. George W. Ingram to Martha Ingram, October 20, 1864, in *Civil War Letters*, 77–78.

10. J. C. Morriss to Amanda Morriss, November 6, 1862 [4], in Jakie L. Pruett and Scott Black, eds., *Civil War Letters: 1861–1865. A Glimpse of the War Between the States* (Austin, Texas: Eakin Press, 1985), 47–49.

11. Compiled Service Records of Company G. Compiled Service Records of Confederate Soldiers who Served in Organizations from the State of Texas, Twelfth Texas Cavalry, Microfilm Rolls 323 : 71–74.

12. B. P. Gallaway, *The Ragged Rebel: A Common Soldier in W. H. Parsons' Texas Cavalry, 1861–1865* (Austin: University of Texas Press, 1988), 123–124.

13. Steele reported that he had arrived at Warren and assumed command as directed. Letter from W. H. Steele dated October 19, 1864, Special Order Book of Parsons' Brigade, Collection of Parsons' Brigade Association Texas Cavalry, Sims Library, Waxahachie, Texas. Also see George W. Ingram to Martha Ingram, October 20, 1864, *Civil War Letters*, 77–78.

14. William Steele to E. P. Turner, October 22, 1864, Special Order Book.

15. E. P. Turner to John A. Wharton, October 14, 1864, *OR* 41, pt. 3, 1007–1008; E. P. Turner to John A. Wharton, October 16, 1864, *OR* 41, pt. 4, 998. In the second letter Turner complained to Wharton that headquarters had received a letter from Parsons, who "has been several times instructed from these headquarters to report through you. Will you be kind enough to repeat the instructions from your headquarters."

16. William Steele to John A. Wharton, October 28, 1864, Special Order Book.

17. William Steele to John A. Wharton, October 29, 1864, ibid.

18. J. M. Brandon to B. W. Watson, November 5, 1864, ibid.

19. Burleson's troubles continued for several months. In April, 1865, Captain George Ingram noted: "Jimmy is a witness in the case of Col. Burleson whose trial is on hand at Hempstead and there is no possible chance to get him off." George W. Ingram to Martha Ingram, April 22, 1865, *Civil War Letters*, 81–82. On May 1 Colonel Parsons wrote that he had been called as a witness for the defense at the court-martial. He complained: "There not being a *Field Officer* present for duty in the whole Brigade and I seriously question the power of a Judge Advocate, to summons; a Brigade Commander, without notice to, and ac-

tion by, immediate superiors; which letter was not been taken in this case. The interest of this large command, would certainly be prejudiced by such a summary course." William Henry Parsons to William Steele, May 1, 1865, Special Order Book. For the quote see Henry Orr to "Sister," November 12, 1864, in John Q. Anderson, ed., *Campaigning with Parsons' Texas Cavalry Brigade, CSA: The War Journals and Letters of the Four Orr Brothers, 12th Texas Cavalry Regiment* (Hillsboro, Texas: Hill Junior College Press, 1967), 149–150; Henry Orr to "Father," November 24, 1864, ibid., 151.

20. W. W. Heartsill recorded November 16 that the men had received orders to drill four hours every day in infantry tactics. Heartsill, *Fourteen Hundred and 91 Days*, 223.

21. E. K. Smith to J. B. Magruder, November 18, 1864, OR 41, pt. 4, 1061–1062.

22. Henry Orr to "Sister," November 28, 1864, in Anderson, *Campaigning with Parsons' Brigade*, 151–152.

23. William Steele to J. B. Magruder, November 26, 1864, Special Order Book.

24. George Williamson to J. B. Magruder, November 30, 1864, OR 41, pt. 4, 1084; J. F. Belton to J. B. Magruder, December 1, 1864, ibid., 1090–1091; J. F. Belton to J. G. Walker, December 2, 1864, ibid., 1092; J. B. Magruder to W. R. Boggs, December 9, 1864, ibid., 1104; J. M. Brandon to L. J. Farrar, December 4, 1864, Special Order Book.

25. E. K. Smith to S. B. Buckner, November 29, 1864, OR 41, pt. 4, 1082–1083; W. R. Boggs to J. B. Magruder, December 3, 1864, ibid., 1096; J. B. Magruder to W. R. Boggs, December 9, 1864, ibid., 1104; J. B. Magruder to W. R. Boggs, December 12, 1864, ibid., 1107–1108; E. K. Smith to J. B. Magruder, December 21, 1864, ibid., 1120; J. B. Magruder to W. R. Boggs, December 28, 1864, ibid., 1131; W. R. Boggs to J. G. Walker, December 28, 1864, ibid.; J. F. Belton to J. A. Wharton, January 21, 1865, OR 48, pt. 1, 1337; W. R. Boggs to S. B. Maxey, January 23, 1865, ibid., 1340; J. F. Belton to J. A. Wharton, January 25, 1865, ibid., 1344.

26. J. F. Belton to John A. Wharton, January 25, 1865, ibid., 1344.

27. From Maxey's division Kirby Smith suggested dismounting the regiments of Leonidus M. Martin, Peter Hardeman, John W. Wells, Charles De Morse, Nicholas C. Gould, and James Likens. From Wharton's division Smith suggested the regiments of George W. Baylor and Isham Chisum. In addition, the escort company of D. S. Terry was scheduled to be dismounted. E. Kirby Smith to J. A. Wharton, January 30, 1865, ibid., 1351–1352; E. Kirby Smith to

John G. Walker, January 30, 1865, ibid., 1353; W. R. Boggs to John A. Wharton, February 17, 1865, ibid., 1392–1393; E. Kirby Smith to John A. Wharton, February 22, 1865, ibid., 1396–1397.

28. Organization of Wharton's Cavalry Corps, commanded by Maj. Gen. John A. Wharton, C. S. Army, for March, 1865, ibid., 1458.

29. Philip D. Frazier to "Mother, Brothers, & Sisters," March 2, 1865, Frazier Family Papers, Barker Texas History Center, Austin, Texas.

30. Heartsill, *Fourteen Hundred and 91 Days*, 235.

31. George W. Baylor, "Of a Noted Military Family," *Confederate Veteran* 6 (April 1898), 164–165.

32. George W. Ingram to Martha Ingram, April 7, 1865, in *Civil War Letters*, 78–79.

33. Henry Orr to "Mother," April 7, 1865, in Anderson, *Campaigning with Parsons' Brigade*, 158–159. Brigadier General Hamilton P. Bee replaced Wharton as cavalry commander.

34. Ibid.; George W. Ingram to Martha Ingram, April 7, 1865, in *Civil War Letters*, 78–79.

35. Ibid.

36. Heartsill, *Fourteen Hundred and 91 Days*, 235.

37. *Dallas Herald*, May 18, 1865.

38. Heartsill, *Fourteen Hundred and 91 Days*, 243–244.

39. Ibid., 244–245.

40. Henry Orr to Mollie Orr, May 18, 1862, in Anderson, *Campaigning with Parsons' Brigade*, 43–46.

EPILOGUE

1. E. S. C. Robertson to Mary Robertson, November 14, 1862, Robertson Colony Collection, Special Collections, University of Texas at Arlington Library, Arlington, Texas.

2. Grady McWhiney and Perry D. Jamieson, *Attack and Die: Civil War Military Tactics and the Southern Heritage* (University, Alabama: The University of Alabama Press, 1982), 190.

3. Richard Taylor, *Destruction and Reconstruction: Personal Experiences of the Late War in the United States* (Edinburgh and London: William Blackwood and Sons, 1879), 162.

4. William M. (Buck) Walton, *An Epitome of My Life: Civil War Reminiscences* (Austin: The Waterloo Press, 1965), 54.

5. Although Charles Morgan's command finally reached regimental strength, he never received an official promotion to colonel, and was paroled at Houston in July 1865, at the rank of lieutenant colonel. Around 1867 he married Mary Duval, and they raised six daughters and one son. Sometime after the war he opened a retail store; the census of 1880 as well as the one in 1900 lists him as a grocery merchant. United States Bureau of the Census, Ninth Census of the United States, Bastrop County, and Eleventh Census of the United States, Hill County.

6. According to family records, Parsons apparently went to British Honduras to investigate the possibility of Confederate colonization. William D. Parsons to the author, September 9, 1988. In a letter from W. H. Parsons to B. F. Marchbanks, July 16, 1907, Parsons wrote that he had been "ready to 'accept the situation' as you know I did upon my return from South America just after the War. It takes more courage to stand alone than to battle among your fellows and you recall my stand for reconstruction." Xerox copy in the possession of the author.

7. *Dallas Herald*, May 11, 1865.

8. Ibid., December 10, 1864.

9. Videotape of Mt. Hope Cemetery, recorded by Joe and Ann Cerney, points out that the colonel's tombstone incorrectly gives his date of death as October 2, 1908. A xerox copy of Parsons's death certificate was furnished to the author by Ann Cerney.

10. Carter had arrived in Texas with a Virginia wife and family. After divorcing his wife, he married a second time while in Louisiana—only to divorce again. Carter's third marriage (about the time he left the ministry in 1895) was to a woman from Lynchburg, Virginia. On his application to the Confederate home, he indicated his nearest relative was his daughter Mary who worked as a government clerk in Washington, D.C. At that time Mary Carter lived with her sister Georgi Carr (who had been born in Texas in September 1865). United States Bureau of the Census, Eleventh Census of the United States, District of Columbia; Application for Admission to the Maryland Line Confederate Soldiers' Home and Maryland Line Confederate Soldiers' Home Register, Maryland Historical Society, Baltimore, Maryland; Richardson Dougall and Mary Patricia Chapman, *United States Chiefs of Missions 1778–1973* (Washington, D.C.:

Department of State, 1973), 166; Wanda W. Smith at the Bridwell Library Center for Methodist Studies to the author, October 15, 1986, and October 25, 1986; Fran Amorose to the author, June 25, 1988. Mrs. Amorose is the staff genealogist for Loudon Park Cemetery Company.

11. Charles W. Ramsdell, *Reconstruction in Texas* (1910; reprint, Austin: University of Texas Press, 1970), 115; records of Greenwood Cemetery, Dallas, Texas.

APPENDIX

1. Because of the poor quality of the manuscript records, misspellings may occur. Compiled Service Records of Confederate Soldiers who Served in Organizations from the State of Texas, Twelfth Texas Cavalry, Microfilm Rolls 323 : 71–74 (hereafter cited as Compiled Service Records), National Archives, Washington, D.C. Also see *A Brief and Condensed History of Parsons' Texas Cavalry Brigade Composed of Twelfth, Nineteenth, Twenty-First, Morgan's Battalion, and Pratt's Battery of Artillery of the Confederate States: Together with Roster of the several Commands as far as obtainable—Some Historical Sketches— General Orders and a Memoranda of Parsons' Brigade Association* (Waxahachie, Texas: J. M. Flemister, Printer, 1892), 48.

2. Wier (also spelled Weir) gave Virginia as his birthplace, but his son later claimed it was Mississippi. *A Memorial and Biographical History of Johnson and Hill Counties, Texas* (Chicago: Lewis Publishing Co., 1892), 422–423; Ernest W. Winkler, ed., *Journal of the Secession Convention of Texas, 1861* (Austin: Austin Printing Co., 1912), 177; Mamie Yeary, comp., *Reminiscences of the Boys in Gray, 1861–1865* (Dallas: Press of Wilkinson Printing Co., 1912), 113; Eighth Census of the United States, Hill County, Texas; Muster Roll of the "Hill County Volunteers," Confederate Muster Rolls, No. 1266, Texas State Archives, Austin, Texas; Compiled Service Record of Joseph P. Wier.

3. Ingram, born in North Carolina in 1830, married Martha about 1854–1855. Their letters are valuable not only for the military side of the war, but also because Martha described conditions in Texas. Henry L. Ingram, comp., *Civil War Letters of George W. and Martha F. Ingram 1861–1865* (College Station: Texas A & M Press, 1973), 2–3; Eighth Census of the United States, Hill County, Texas; Muster Roll of the "Hill County Volunteers;" Compiled Service Record of George W. Ingram.

4. Corsicana *Navarro Express*, November 23, 1860; *Ellis County History: The Basic 1892 book (With the Presidents Selection deleted) with Additional Biographies compiled by The Ellis County Historical Museum and Art Gallery, Inc. in Memory of the Courageous Pioneers and Builders of Ellis County* (Fort Worth and Arlington: Historical Publishers, 1972), 138, 664. Eighth Census of the United States, Ellis County, Texas; Muster Roll of the "Ellis Blues," Confederate Muster Rolls, No. 666, Texas State Archives; Compiled Service Record of William J. Stokes.

5. A. J. Byrd, *History and Description of Johnson County, and its Principal Towns* (Marshall, Texas: Jennings Brothers, 1879), 16–17. Byrd served as commissary for Parsons's brigade, but he was also married to Colonel Parsons's sister Mary and was a merchant in Waco. Also see *Ellis County History*, 239, 753–754. Eighth Census of the United States, Ellis County, Texas; Muster Roll of the "Ellis Blues;" Compiled Service Records of J. Em. Hawkins and William M. Campbell. Also see Productions of Agriculture, 1860, Texas State Archives, Austin, Texas.

6. Eighth Census of the United States, Ellis County, Texas; Muster Roll of the "Ellis Grays," Confederate Muster Rolls, No. 1232, Texas State Archives; Compiled Service Record of John C. Brown.

7. John Q. Anderson, ed., *Campaigning with Parsons' Texas Cavalry Brigade, CSA: The War Journals and Letters of the Four Orr Brothers, 12th Texas Cavalry Regiment* (Hillsboro, Texas: Hill Junior College Press, 1967), 2, 3; Muster Roll of the "Ellis Rangers," Confederate Muster Rolls, No. 67, Texas State Archives; Compiled Service Record of William G. Veal; Eighth Census of the United States, Parker County, Texas.

8. Henry Orr to Lafayette Orr, December 21, 1861, in Anderson, *Campaigning with Parsons' Brigade*, 14–17; Henry Orr to "Father, Mother, and Family," April 27, 1864, ibid., 131–134.

9. Fort Worth *Daily Democrat*, December 7, 1878, February 13, 1879, November 7, 1879, October 7, 1880; *Dallas Daily Times Herald*, October 25, 1892; Macum Phelan, *A History of the Expansion of Methodism in Texas 1867–1902* (Dallas: Mathis, Van North & Co., 1937), 150–152. Following the war Veal was very successful mingling business with his ministerial affairs. In June 1876, a woman in Hutchins, Texas, accused him of improper conduct, although a public meeting of the town's citizens passed a resolution vindicating him. The church also investigated and cleared him. Late in November 1878 a

woman in Waxahachie charged him with attempted molestation. Veal nevertheless had a sympathetic following. Although the church expelled him, he continued prominent in public life. In October 1892 Veal was reading resolutions to
his Confederate comrades when Dr. R. H. Jones appeared at the door and shot
him through the head. He died instantly. At the trial the man testified his hatred
of Veal came from an incident ten years earlier involving Veal and the doctor's
wife. But in 1935 Charles L. Woody loyally insisted: "Veal didn't assault Mrs.
Jones. . . . One jury in Dallas County said he did, and two said he did not."
John W. Nix, *A Tale of Two Schools and Springtown, Parker County* (Fort
Worth: Thomason & Morrow, 1945), 50–55.

10. W. J. Neal to William Byrd, June 22, 1861, Volunteers from Johnson
County, Twentieth Brigade, Texas State Archives; Compiled Service Record of
William Jeff Neal; Houston *Tri-Weekly Telegraph* November 14, 1862; Muster
Roll of the "Johnson County Slashers," Confederate Muster Rolls, No. 1646,
Texas State Archives. Unusual for a cavalry captain, the tax roll of 1861 indi-
cated he owned no horses. But by 1862 he had bought two valued at $100 each.
Tax Rolls for Johnson County, 1861, 1862, Texas State Archives. Also see Silas A.
Carpenter to William Byrd, June 24, 1861, and John W. Berry to William Byrd,
July 8, 1861, Volunteers from Johnson County, Texas State Archives.

11. Eighth Census of the United States, Hopkins County, Texas; Houston
Tri-Weekly Telegraph, November 14, 1862.

12. The information on Thomas Franklin Haley comes from photocopies
of the Haley Family records furnished to the author by Mary Christensen of El
Paso, Texas. Also see the Eighth Census of the United States, Johnson County,
Texas; Muster Roll of the "Johnson County Slashers," Texas State Archives;
Compiled Service Record of T. F. Haley.

13. *Memorial History of Johnson and Hill Counties*, 135–136, 550–551;
Eighth Census of the United States, Johnson County, Texas; Muster Roll of the
"Johnson County Slashers"; Compiled Service Record of Benjamin Barnes.

14. Corsicana *Navarro Express*, September 29, 1861; Eighth Census of
the United States, Navarro County; Muster Roll of the "Freestone Boys," Confederate Muster Rolls, No. 1509, Texas State Archives; Compiled Service Record of Appleton M. Maddux.

15. Roy A. Walker, *A History of Limestone County* (Austin, Texas: Von
Boeckmann-Jones, 1959), 43, 51; Eighth Census of the United States, Limestone
County, Texas; Confederate Muster Rolls, No. 1509, Texas State Archives;
Compiled Service Records of A. F. Moss and James P. Brown; Productions of
Agriculture, 1860.

16. This company was also known as the "Bishop Cavalry." M. B. Highsmith Papers, Barker Texas History Center, Austin, Texas; Marcus Wright, comp., *Texas in the War 1861–1865* (Hillsboro, Texas: Hill Junior College Press, 1965), 185–186; Muster Roll of the "Bishop Cavalry Company," Confederate Muster Rolls, No. 1313, Texas State Archives; Compiled Service Record of M. B. Highsmith.

17. Muster Roll of the "Williamson Bowies," Confederate Muster Rolls, No. 509, Texas State Archives; Compiled Service Records of John W. Mullen, Wiley Peace, and J. C. S. Morrow.

18. *History of Texas Together With a Biographical History of Milam, Williamson, Bastrop, Travis, Lee and Burleson Counties* (Chicago: Lewis Publishing Co., 1893), 772–774; Clara Stearns Scarbrough, *Land of Good Waters, Takachue Pouetsu: A Williamson County, Texas, History* (Georgetown, Texas: Williamson County Sun Publishers, 1973), 192–194.

19. Corsicana *Navarro Express*, September 19, 1861; Walter, *History of Limestone County* 50–51; Eighth Census of the United States, Limestone County, Texas; Confederate Muster Rolls, No. 952, Texas State Archives; Compiled Service Record of L. J. Farrar.

20. Kaufman County Historical Commission, *History of Kaufman County*, 2 vols. (Dallas: National Shore Graphics, Inc., 1984), 2 : 43; Muster Roll of the "Kaufman Guards," Confederate Muster Rolls, No. 1421, Texas State Archives; Compiled Service Record of H. W. Kyser.

21. Compiled Service Records, Twenty-first Texas Cavalry, Microfilm Rolls 323 : 110–112.

22. United States Bureau of the Census, Eighth Census of the United States, Goliad and Austin counties, Texas. Macum Phelan, *A History of Early Methodism in Texas* (Dallas: Cokesbury Press, 1924), 404, mentions that Reverend J. W. Kenney gave one of the addresses at the dedication of the cornerstone for the main building at Soule University in 1858.

23. Commission dated October 5, 1861, and signed by all three Methodist ministers—Carter, Wilkes, and Gillespie—authorized Kenney to raise a company for the brigade. M. M. Kenney Papers, Barker Texas History Center, University of Texas, Austin, Texas.

24. William Rust to Pendleton Murrah, June 30, 1864, and William Rust to D. C. Giddings, July 5, 1864, Compiled Service Record of William M. Rust.

25. Walton, born in Mississippi in 1832, moved to Austin in 1853 and became a lawyer. In 1866 he served as attorney general but was removed during Reconstruction. Walton died in 1915. His reminiscences were written in pencil

on a yellow legal-size scratch pad. William M. (Buck) Walton, *An Epitome of My Life: Civil War Reminiscences* (Austin, Texas: The Waterloo Press, 1965), 22–23.

26. Anthony M. Branch, elected to the Confederate Congress in 1863, was a lawyer, Unionist, and owner of four slaves. Thomas B. Alexander and Richard E. Beringer, *The Anatomy of the Confederate Congress: A Study of the Influences of Member Characteristics on Legislative Voting Behavior 1861–1865* (Nashville, Tenn.: Vanderbilt University Press, 1972), 356–357; also see the Eighth Census of the United States, Walker County. In addition, Mary E. Rainey, library associate at the Sam Houston State University, Huntsville, furnished information on G. W. Farris from notes of a conversation with Vernon Farris of Madisonville.

27. Tax Rolls for Brazos County, 1862; Glenna Fourman Brundidge, ed., *Brazos County History: Rich Past—Bright Future* (Bryan, Texas: Newman Printing Co., 1986), 99, 340.

28. Compiled Service Records of T. B. Shannon and R. Sample Howard; Eighth Census of the United States, Montgomery and Anderson counties.

29. Eighth Census of the United States, Travis County; Productions of Agriculture, 1860.

30. Compiled Service Record of W. Hess Jones; Eighth Census of the United States, Gonzales County; Productions of Agriculture, 1860.

31. Compiled Service Record of William M. Harper; Eighth Census of the United States, Lavaca County; Productions of Agriculture, 1860.

32. Eighth Census of the United States, Orange County.

33. Muster Roll dated September, 1861, Confederate Muster Rolls, No. 333, Texas State Archives; Compiled Service Record of J. B. Rocke; Eighth Census of the United States, McLennan County.

34. William Physick Zuber, *My Eighty Years in Texas*, ed. by Janis Boyle Mayfield (Austin: University of Texas Press, 1971), 134; Compiled Service Record of J. R. S. Alston.

35. Compiled Service Records, Nineteenth Texas Cavalry, Microfilm Rolls 323 : 104–106.

36. Ibid., Morgan's Cavalry, Microfilm Rolls 323 : 207–209.

37. Compiled Service Record of S. J. Richardson; Confederate Muster Rolls, No. 1628, Texas State Archives, Austin, Texas; William W. Heartsill, *Fourteen Hundred and 91 Days in the Confederate Army*, ed. by Bell Irvin Wiley (1876; reprint, Jackson, Tenn.: McCowat-Mercer Press, 1954), 2–4.

38. "Yesterday—Marshall in Years Past," Marshall *News Messenger*, December 17, 1954.

39. Richardson was a KGC major and instrumental in organizing castles in Texas. Roy Sylvan Dunn, "The KGC in Texas, 1860–1861," *Southwestern Historical Quarterly* 70 (April 1967), 543–573; also see the *Dallas Herald*, March 28, 1860, quoting the Marshall *Harrison Flag*.

40. Tax Rolls for Harrison County, 1861.

41. Heartsill, *Fourteen Hundred and 91 Days*, 79. Richardson's company began as Company F, 2d Regiment Texas Cavalry, commanded by Colonel John S. Ford, and served the first year of the war on the frontier. Later it was known as Richardson's Mounted Rifles Unattached, and finally Company I, Morgan's Cavalry.

42. Heartsill served in the Army of Tennessee from May until November 1863 and detailed a stirring account of his life east of the Mississippi River. He and his companions left Bragg's army November 7 and arrived at Marshall, Texas, on December 21 after a walk of 736 miles. Also see Special Order No. 19, January 25, 1864, which ordered Richardson to join Morgan. Heartsill, *Fourteen Hundred and 91 Days*, 187, 196.

43. Compiled Service Record of Philip H. Yelton; Heartsill, *Fourteen Hundred and 91 Days*, 142.

44. Compiled Service Records of Drury Connelly and W. A. Thompson; Heartsill, *Fourteen Hundred and 91 Days*, 171.

45. Compiled Service Record of Milton M. Boggess; Garland R. Farmer, *The Realm of Rusk County* (Henderson, Texas: The Henderson *Times*, 1951), 45–49; Dorman H. Winfrey, *A History of Rusk County, Texas* (Waco: Texian Press, 1961), 119; Yeary, *Boys in Gray*, 818–819. Boggess's company began as Company H, 1 (McCulloch's) Texas Cavalry (1 Texas Mounted Riflemen); later it was designated as Company B, Morgan's Cavalry.

46. Compiled Service Record of D. A. Nunn; Thomas A. Mainer, *Houston County in the Civil War* (Crockett, Texas: Houston County Historical Commission, 1981), 44–47, 74; Armistead Albert Aldrich, *The History of Houston County Texas* (San Antonio: The Naylor Co., 1943), 15; Houston County Historical Commission, *History of Houston County, Texas 1687–1979* (Tulsa, Okla.: Heritage Publishing Co., 1979), 514–515; Confederate Muster Rolls, No. 1649, Texas State Archives. This company began as Company L, Twenty-eighth Cavalry Regiment. Nunn's company was detached some time before the regiment was dismounted, but there is no record of a transfer to Morgan.

47. Vontress's company left for Arkansas as an unattached command, then became Company A, Morgan's squadron. Compiled Service Records of Edward H. Vontress and John W. Posey; Eighth Census of the United States, Williamson County; Sketch of J. V. Chism in Yeary, *Boys in Gray*, 135–136. Also see Productions of Agriculture, 1860.

48. *Ellis County History*, 483–485, 502–503, 639; Productions of Agriculture, 1860.

49. Confederate Pension 11207, Texas State Archives, Austin, Texas.

50. Eighth Census of the United States, Cass and Marion counties; Compiled Service Records of F. G. Lemmon and J. N. Scott. Also see Productions of Agriculture, 1860. The company first became Company B, Morgan's squadron but eventually received the designation of Company G in Morgan's cavalry.

51. Eighth Census of the United States, Panola County; Compiled Service Record of Drury Field.

52. William Herbert Beazley had initially joined Company K, Twenty-sixth Texas Cavalry. He also served as dispatch bearer for Commodore W. W. Hunter before assignment as captain of this independent company. Beazley, born in 1837 in Warren County, Mississippi, had come to Texas in 1840 with his family. In 1860 he was living with his father (a physician) at Lynchburg near Houston in Harris County. After the war he also became a doctor and died May 18, 1919. Confederate Pension 30073, Texas State Archives; Eighth Census of the United States, Harris County, Texas.

53. H. Washington to J. B. Magruder, November 12, 1863, Compiled Service Record of W. Herbert Beazley.

54. W. Herbert Beazley to E. P. Turner, November 22, 1863, ibid.

55. This order is scratched across the outside of Beazley's letter dated November 22, 1863, ibid.

56. Compiled Service Records, Thirtieth Texas Cavalry, Microfilm Rolls 323 : 150–152.

57. Ibid. The 1860 Federal census recorded that Gurley, a native of Alabama, claimed $10,000 in personal estate and $20,000 in real estate. Eighth Census of the United States, McLennan County, Texas.

58. J. Bankhead Magruder to S. S. Anderson, December 19, 1862, U. S. War Department, *The War of the Rebellion; A Compilation of the Official Records of the Union and Confederate Armies* (128 vols., Washington, D. C., 1880–1901), Series I, 15, 902 (hereafter cited as *OR*; unless otherwise indicated,

all references are to Series I). Also see J. Bankhead Magruder to S. S. Anderson, January 9, 1863, ibid., 936–937.

59. Compiled Service Records, Thirtieth Texas Cavalry.

60. Smith Bankhead's brigade included Gurley's regiment as well as that of Peter Hardeman and the battery of W. B. Krumbhaar. W. C. Schaumburg to W. R. Boggs, Semi-annual Inspection by the Inspector General's Office, October 26, 1863, *OR* 22, pt. 2, 1049–1053.

61. William Steele to S. S. Anderson, November 9, 1863, ibid., 1064–1065.

62. John Washington Berry to Burton Marchbanks, January 22, 1864, original in the archives of the Layland Museum, Cleburne, Texas. Berry returned to his home in Johnson County, Texas, to recuperate from his illness but died from complications. Marchbanks, also a member of the Thirtieth Texas, was in Texas recovering from a wound received at Honey Springs in July 1863. He also died from complications.

63. Ibid.

64. Smith P. Bankhead to John B. Magruder, September 24, 1863, *OR* 22, pt. 2, 1026.

65. Organization of the Army of the Trans-Mississippi Department, December 31, 1864, *OR* 41, pt. 4, 1141–1146.

66. Organization of Wharton's Cavalry Corps, March, 1865, *OR* 48, pt. 1, 1458–1459.

67. W. H. Parsons to William Steele, April 9, 1865, Special Order Book of Parsons' Brigade, Collection of Parsons' Brigade Association Texas Cavalry, Sims Library, Waxahachie, Texas.

68. P. D. Frazier to "Mother, Brothers & Sisters," March 2, 1865, Frazier Family Papers, Barker Texas History Center, Austin, Texas.

Bibliography

Manuscripts

Henry Boggess Papers. Dallas Historical Society, Dallas, Texas.

Brown, Frank. "Annals of Travis County and the City of Austin." Typescript in Texas State Archives, Austin, Texas.

Compiled Service Records of Confederate Soldiers Who Served in Organizations from the State of Arkansas. Washington, D.C.: National Archives and Records Service.

Compiled Service Records of Confederate Soldiers Who Served in Organizations from the State of Texas. Washington, D.C.: National Archives and Records Service.

Confederate Muster Rolls. Texas State Archives, Austin, Texas.

Confederate Pensions. Texas State Archives, Austin, Texas.

S. W. Farrow Papers. Barker Texas History Center, Austin, Texas.

George R. Feris Papers. Barker Texas History Center, Austin, Texas.

Frazier Family Papers. Barker Texas History Center, Austin, Texas.

Frazier Family Papers. Dallas Historical Society, Dallas, Texas.

George R. Freeman Papers. Barker Texas History Center, Austin, Texas.

D. C. Giddings Papers. Barker Texas History Center, Austin, Texas.

John Hall Papers. Dallas Historical Society, Dallas, Texas.

William P. Head Papers. Barker Texas History Center, Austin, Texas.

M. B. Highsmith Papers. Barker Texas History Center, Austin, Texas.

Martin M. Kenney Papers. Barker Texas History Center, Austin, Texas.

William A. Kirkpatrick Papers. Confederate Research Center, Hillsboro, Texas.

John L. Lane Diary. Confederate Research Center, Hillsboro, Texas.

Lee Family Papers. Barker Texas History Center, Austin, Texas.

Mrs. Charles Mills Papers. Dallas County Historical Society, Dallas, Texas.

W. W. Parks Papers. Barker Texas History Center, Austin, Texas.

William H. Parsons Collection. In the possession of Joe and Ann Cerney, Wichita Falls, Texas.

William H. Parsons Papers. In the possession of William D. Parsons, Lake Forest, Illinois.

Sarah Glenn Riddell Scrapbook. Texas State Archives, Austin, Texas.

E. S. C. Robertson Papers. Robertson Colony Collection, Special Collections, University of Texas at Arlington Library, Arlington, Texas.

Scurlock Family Papers. Copies in possession of Layland Museum, Cleburne, Texas.

Shropshire Letters. Confederate Research Center, Hillsboro, Texas.

William J. Simms Papers. Confederate Research Center, Hillsboro, Texas.

Ashbel Smith Papers. Barker Texas History Center, Austin, Texas.

Thomas B. Smith Diaries. Layland Museum, Cleburne, Texas.

Special Order Book of Parsons' Brigade. Collection of Parsons' Brigade Association Texas Cavalry, Sims Library, Waxahachie, Texas.

Tax Rolls for the State of Texas, Texas State Archives, Austin, Texas.

United States Bureau of the Census. Seventh, Eighth, Eleventh, and Twelfth Census of the United States.

Walter, John F. "Capsule Histories of Arkansas Military Units in the Civil War." Typescript in the Special Collections Department, David W. Mullins Library, University of Arkansas, Fayetteville, Arkansas.

Levi Wight Lamoni Papers. Barker Texas History Center, Austin, Texas.

Winnie Davis Camp Scrapbook. United Confederate Veterans. Sims Library, Waxahachie, Texas.

Printed Primary Sources

A Brief and Condensed History of Parsons' Texas Cavalry Brigade Composed of Twelfth, Nineteenth, Twenty-First, Morgan's Battalion, and Pratt's Battery of Artillery of the Confederate States: Together with Roster of the several Commands as far as obtainable—Some Historical Sketches—General Orders and a Memoranda of Parsons' Brigade Association. Waxahachie, Texas: J. M. Flemister, Printer, 1892.

"Adventures on a Hospital Boat on the Mississippi." *Phillips County Historical Quarterly* 1 (December 1962): 31–42.

Allen, George W. "Civil War Letters of George W. Allen," Edited by Charleen Plumly Pollard. *Southwestern Historical Quarterly* 83 (July 1979): 47–52.

Anderson, John Q., ed. *Brokenburn: The Journal of Kate Stone, 1861–1868.* Baton Rouge: Louisiana State University Press, 1955.

———. *Campaigning with Parsons' Texas Cavalry Brigade, CSA: The War Journals and Letters of the Four Orr Brothers, 12th Texas Cavalry Regiment.* Hillsboro, Texas: Hill Junior College Press, 1967.

Baylor, George. "Of a Noted Military Family." *Confederate Veteran* 6 (April 1898): 164–165.

Bellville [Texas] *Countryman*.

Bishop, S. W. "The Battle of Arkansas Post." *Confederate Veteran* 5 (April 1897): 151–152.

Blessington, J. P. *The Campaigns of Walker's Texas Division.* New York: Lange, Little & Co., 1875.

Brown, Norman D., ed. *Journey to Pleasant Hill: The Civil War Letters of Captain Elijah P. Petty, Walker's Texas Division, C.S.A.* San Antonio: Institute of Texan Cultures, 1982.

———. *One of Cleburne's Command: The Civil War Reminiscences and Diary of*

Captain Samuel T. Foster, Granbury's Texas Brigade, C.S.A. Austin: University of Texas Press, 1980.

Caraway, L. V. "The Battle of Arkansas Post." *Confederate Veteran* 14 (March 1906): 127–128.

Clarksville *Northern Standard.*

Collins, R. M. *Chapters from the Unwritten History of the War Between the States; or, the Incidents in the Life of a Confederate Soldier in Camp, on the March, in the Great Battles, and in Prison.* St. Louis: Nixon-Jones Printing Co., 1983.

Commager, Henry Steele. *The Blue and the Gray: The Story of the Civil War as Told by Participants.* 1950; reprint, New York: The Fairfax Press, 1982.

Condensed History of Parson's Texas Cavalry Brigade 1861–1865: Together with Inside History and Heretofore Unwritten Chapters of the Red River Campaign of 1864. Corsicana, Texas: 1903.

Corsicana *Navarro Express* (also *The Navarro Express*).

Cuthbertson, Gilbert. "Coller of the Sixth Texas: Correspondence of a Texas Infantry Man, 1861–64." *Military History of Texas and the Southwest* 9 (1971): 129–136.

Dallas Daily Times Herald.

Dallas Herald.

Darst, Maury. "Robert Hodges, Jr.: Confederate Soldier." *East Texas Historical Journal* 9 (March 1971): 20–49.

Day, James M., ed. *Senate Journal of the Ninth Legislature of the State of Texas November 4, 1861-January 14, 1862.* Austin: Texas State Library and Historical Commission, 1963.

———. *Texas House Journal, Ninth Regular 1861–1862.* Austin: Texas State Library, 1964.

Debray, X. B. "A Sketch of Debray's Twenty-Sixth Regiment of Texas Cavalry: Paper No. 2." *Southern Historical Society Papers* 13 (January-December 1885): 153–165.

Edwards, John N. *Shelby and His Men; or, The War in the West.* 1867; reprint, Kansas City, Mo.: Hudson-Kimberly Publishing Co., 1897.

Evans, Clement A., ed. *Confederate Military History.* 12 vols. Atlanta: Confederate Publishing Co., 1899.

Fitzhugh, Lester N., ed. *Cannon Smoke: The Letters of Captain John J. Good, Good-Douglas Texas Battery, CSA.* Hillsboro, Texas: Hill Junior College Press, 1971.

Fort Worth *Daily Democrat.*

Fremantle, James A. L. *Three Months in the Southern States April—June 1863.* 1863; reprint, Alexandria, Va.: Time-Life Books Inc., 1984.

Galveston *News* (title varies).

Goodloe, P. H. "Service in the Trans-Mississippi." *Confederate Veteran* 23 (January 1915): 31–32.

Grant, Ulysses S. *The Papers of Ulysses S. Grant.* Edited by John Y. Simon. Carbondale: Southern Illinois University Press, 1967.

———. *Personal Memoirs of U. S. Grant.* 2 vols. New York: Charles L. Webster & Co., 1885.

"Thos. Green to Brother, Sept. 3, 1862." *Chronicles of Smith County, Texas* 6 (Spring 1967), 38–39.

Halleck, Henry W. *Elements of Military Art and Science; or, Course of Instructions in Strategy, Fortification, Tactics of Battles, &c.* New York: D. Appleton & Co., 1846.

Harrison, Jon, ed. "Civil War Letters of John Simmons," *Chronicles of Smith County, Texas* 14 (Summer 1975), 26–57.

Heartsill, W. W. *Fourteen Hundred and 91 Days in the Confederate Army.* Edited by Bell Irvin Wiley. 1876; reprint, Jackson, Tenn.: McCowat-Mercer Press, 1954.

Hicks, Jimmie. "Some Letters Concerning the Knights of the Golden Circle in Texas." *Southwestern Historical Quarterly* 65 (July 1961), 80–86.

History of the Forty-Sixth Regiment Indiana Volunteer Infantry. September, 1861-September, 1865. Logansport: 1888.

Hogan, George H. "Parsons's Brigade of Texas Cavalry." *Confederate Veteran* 32 (January 1925), 17–20.

Houston *Daily Telegraph* (also titled *Houston Daily Telegraph*).

Houston *Tri-Weekly Telegraph.*

Ingram, Henry L., compiler. *Civil War Letters of George W. and Martha F. Ingram 1861–1865.* College Station: Texas A & M Press, 1973.

Itasca [Texas] *Item.*

Jackson, George. *Sixty Years in Texas.* Dallas: Winston Printing Co., 1908.

Jefferson [Texas] *Herald.*

Johnson, Robert U., and Buel, Clarence C., eds. *Battles and Leaders of the Civil War.* 4 vols. New York: Thomas Yoseloff, Inc., 1956.

Johnston, Joseph E. *Narrative of Military Operations Directed During the Late War Between the States.* 1874; reprint, Bloomington: Indiana University Press, 1959.

Jones, James P., and Keuchel, Edward F., eds. *Civil War Marine: A Diary of the Red River Expedition, 1864.* Washington, D.C.: U.S. Government Printing Office, 1975.

Knox, Thomas W. *Camp-Fire and Cotton-field: Southern Adventure in Time of War. Life with the Union Armies, and Residence on a Louisiana Plantation.* New York: Blelock and Co., 1865.

Lawrence, F. Lee, and Glover, Robert W., eds. "Letters of Z. H. Crow." *Chronicles of Smith County, Texas* 4 (Fall 1965): 11–14.

Little Rock *Arkansas State Gazette.*

Little Rock *Arkansas True Democrat*.

Lothrop, Charles Henry. *A History of the First regiment Iowa cavalry veteran volunteers. . . .* Lyons, Iowa: Beers and Eaton, 1890.

Love, William DeLoss. *Wisconsin in the War of the Rebellion*. Chicago: Church & Goodman, and New York: Sheldon & Co., 1866.

Lubbock, Francis R. *Six Decades in Texas: The Memoirs of Francis Richard Lubbock, Governor of Texas in War-Time, 1861–63*. Edited by C. W. Raines. Austin: Ben C. Jones & Co., 1900.

Lupold, Harry F., ed. "An Ohio Doctor Views Campaigning on the White River." *Arkansas Historical Quarterly* 34 (Winter 1975): 333–351.

———. "A Union Medical Officer Views the 'Texians'." *Southwestern Historical Quarterly* 77 (April 1974): 481–486.

Marsh, Bryan. "The Confederate Letters of Bryan Marsh." *Chronicles of Smith County, Texas* 14 (Winter 1975): 9–53.

Marshall *Harrison Flag*.

Marshall *News Messenger*.

Marshall *Texas Republican*.

Millett, E. G. "When General Green Was Killed." *Confederate Veteran* 24 (September 1916): 408–409.

Minutes of the Annual Conferences of the Methodist Episcopal Church, South, for the years 1847–1865. Nashville, Tennessee: Southern Methodist Publishing House, 1848–1870.

Moore, Frank, ed. *The Rebellion Record: A Diary of American Events*. 12 vols. 1861–1868; reprint, New York: Arno Press, 1977.

New Orleans *Daily Picayune*.

North, Thomas. *Five Years in Texas; or, What You Did Not Hear During the War from January 1861 to January 1866. . . .* Cincinnati: Elm Street Printing Co., 1871.

Nott, Charles C. *Sketches in Prison Camps: A Continuation of Sketches of the War*. New York: Anson D. F. Randolph, 1865.

Official. Military History of Kansas Regiments During the War for the Suppression of the Great Rebellion. Leavenworth, Kansas: W. S. Burke, 1870.

Olmsted, Frederick Law. *A Journey through Texas; or, A Saddle-trip on the Southwestern Frontier*. New York: Dix, Edwards & Co., 1857.

Pierson, M. S. "The Diary and Memoirs of Marshall Samuel Pierson, Company C, 17th Reg., Texas Cavalry 1862–1685." Norman C. Delaney, ed. *Military History of Texas and the Southwest* 13 (1976): 23–38.

Pine Bluff *Southern*.

Polley, J. B. *A Soldier's Letters to Charming Nellie*. New York: Neale Publishing

Co., 1908.

Porter, David D. *The Naval History of the Civil War*. New York: The Sherman Publishing Co., 1886.

Porter, Horace. *Campaigning With Grant*. 1897; reprint, Alexandria, Va.: Time-Life Books, Inc. 1981.

Pruett, Jakie, and Black, Scott. *Civil War Letters: 1861–1865. A Glimpse of the War Between the States*. Austin, Texas: Eakin Press, 1985.

Ray, Johnette Highsmith, ed. "Civil War Letters from Parsons' Texas Cavalry Brigade." *Southwestern Historical Quarterly* 69 (October 1965): 210–223.

Reagan, John H. *Memoirs, with Special References to Secession and the Civil War*. 1906; reprint, Austin: The Pemberton Press, 1968.

Report of the Adjutant General of the State of Illinois. Springfield, 1886.

Report of the Adjutant General of the State of Indiana. Indianapolis, 1865.

San Antonio Weekly Herald (also *San Antonio Herald*).

Scott, William Forse. *The Story of a Cavalry Regiment: The Career of the Fourth Iowa Veteran Volunteers From Kansas to Georgia 1861–1865*. New York: G. P. Putnam's Sons, 1893.

Selfridge, Thomas O. *Memoirs of Thomas O. Selfridge. . . .* New York and London: G. P. Putnam's Sons, 1924.

Shaw, W. T. "The Red River Campaign." *Confederate Veteran* 25 (March 1917): 116–118.

Sherman, William T. *Home Letters of General Sherman*. M. A. DeWolfe Howe, ed. New York: Charles Scribner's Sons, 1909.

————. *Personal Memoirs of Gen. W. T. Sherman*. 4th ed. New York: Charles L. Webster & Co., 1891.

Simpson, Harold B., ed. *The Bugle Softly Blows: The Confederate Diary of Benjamin M. Seaton*. Waco: Texian Press, 1965.

Stillwell, Leander. *The Story of a Common Soldier of Army Life in the Civil War 1861–1865*. 1920; reprint, Alexandria, Va.: Time-Life Books, Inc., 1983.

Taylor, Richard. *Destruction and Reconstruction: Personal Experiences of the Late War*. New York: D. Appleton and Company, 1879.

Terrell, Alexander Watkins. *From Texas to Mexico and the Court of Maximilian in 1865*. Dallas: The Book Club of Texas, 1933.

Texas Adjutant General. *Report, November, 1861*. Austin, 1861.

Texas Almanac, 1861–1865. Galveston: D. Richardson & Co., 1861–1865.

U. S. Naval War Records Office. *Official Records of the Union and Confederate Navies in the War of the Rebellion*. 30 vols. Washington, D.C., 1894–1922.

U. S. War Department. *The War of the Rebellion: A Compilation of the Official Records of the Union and Confederate Armies*. 128 vols. Washington, D.C., 1881–1900.

Waco *South West.*

Wallis, J. L., and Hill, L. L., eds. *Sixty Years on the Brazos: The Life and Letters of Dr. John Washington Lockhart 1824–1900.* 1930; reprint, Waco: Texian Press, 1967.

Walton, William M. (Buck). *An Epitome of My Life: Civil War Reminiscences.* Austin: The Waterloo Press, 1965.

Warmoth, Henry Clay. *War, Politics and Reconstruction: Stormy Days in Louisiana.* 1930; reprint, New York: Negro Universities Press, 1970.

Washington [D. C.] *Post.*

West, John C. *A Texan in Search of a Fight.* Waco: J. C. West, 1901.

Wheeler, Joseph. *A Revised System of Cavalry Tactics for Use of the Cavalry and Mounted Infantry, C.S.A.* Mobile, Alabama: S. H. Goetzel & Co., 1863.

Winkler, Ernest W., ed. *Journal of the Secession Convention of Texas, 1861.* Austin: Austin Printing Co., 1912.

Wise, Joe R., ed. "The Letters of Lt. Flavius W. Perry, 17th Texas Cavalry, 1862–1863." *Military History of Texas and the Southwest* 13 (1976): 11–37.

Wynn, W. O. *Biographical Sketch of the Life of an Old Confederate Soldier.* Greenville, Texas: Greenville Printing Co., Inc., 1916.

Yeary, Mamie, compiler. *Reminiscences of the Boys in Gray, 1861–1865.* Dallas: Press of Wilkinson Printing Company, 1912.

Young, Bennett H. *Confederate Wizards of the Saddle: Being Reminiscences and Observations of One Who Rode With Morgan.* 1914; reprint, Kennesaw, Ga.: Continental Book Co., 1958.

Zuber, William Physick. *My Eighty Years in Texas.* Janis Boyle Mayfield, ed. Austin: University of Texas Press, 1971.

Printed Secondary Sources

Aldrich, Armistead Albert. *The History of Houston County Texas.* San Antonio: The Naylor Co., 1943.

Alexander, Thomas B., and Beringer, Richard E. *The Anatomy of the Confederate Congress: A Study of the Influences of Member Characteristics on Legislative Voting Behavior 1861–1865.* Nashville: Vanderbilt University Press, 1972.

A Memorial and Biographical History of Ellis County. Chicago: Lewis Publishing Co., 1892.

A Memorial and Biographical History of Johnson and Hill Counties, Texas. Chicago: Lewis Publishing Co., 1892.

A Memorial and Biographical History of McLennan, Falls, Bell and Coryell Counties, Texas. Chicago: Lewis Publishing Co., 1893.

A Memorial and Biographical History of Navarro, Henderson, Anderson, Limestone, Freestone and Leon Counties, Texas. Chicago: Lewis Publishing Co., 1893.

Anderson, John Q. *A Texas Surgeon in the C.S.A.* Tuscaloosa, Alabama: Confederate Publishing Co., Inc., 1957.

Ashbaugh, Carolyn. *Lucy Parsons, American Revolutionary*. Chicago: Charles H. Kerr Publishing Co., 1976.

Ashcraft, Allen C. *Texas in the Civil War: A Resumé History*. Austin: Texas State Civil War Centennial Commission, 1962.

Avrich, Paul. *The Haymarket Tragedy*. Princeton, N.J.: Princeton University Press, 1984.

Bailey, Ellis. *A History of Hill County, Texas 1838–1965*. Waco, Texas: Library Binding Co., 1966.

Barkley, Mary Starr. *History of Travis County and Austin, 1839–1899*. Waco, Texas: Texian Press, 1963.

Barr, Alwyn. *Polignac's Texas Brigade*. A booklet published by the Texas Gulf Coast Historical Association, November 1964.

——. "Texas Losses in the Red River Campaign." *Texas Military History* 3 (Summer 1963): 103–110.

——. "The Battle of Blair's Landing." *Louisiana Studies* 2 (Winter 1963): 204–212.

"The Battle of Whitney's Lane or The Battle of Searcy." *White County Heritage* 1 (January 1963): 7–10.

Berringer, Richard E.; Hattaway, Herman; Jones, Archer; and Still, William N. Jr. *Why the South Lost the Civil War*. Athens: The University of Georgia Press, 1986.

Bearss, Edwin C. "Marmaduke Attacks Pine Bluff." *Arkansas Historical Quarterly* 23 (Winter 1964): 291–313.

——. "The Battle of Helena, July 4, 1863." *Arkansas Historical Quarterly* 20 (Autumn 1961): 256–297.

——. "The Battle of the Post of Arkansas." *Arkansas Historical Quarterly* 18 (Autumn 1959): 237–279.

——. "The Trans-Mississippi Confederates Attempt to Relieve Vicksburg." *McNeese Review* 15 (1964): 46–70; 16 (1965), 46–67.

——. "The White River Expedition June 10-July 15, 1863." *Arkansas Historical Quarterly* 21 (Winter 1962): 305–362.

Boatner, Mark M. III. *The Civil War Dictionary*. New York: David McKay Co., Inc., 1959.

Bridges, C. A. "The Knights of the Golden Circle: A Filibustering Fantasy." *Southwestern Historical Quarterly* 34 (January 1941): 287–302.

Brown, John Henry. *History of Dallas County*. Dallas: Milligan, Cornett & Farnham, 1887.

——. *History of Texas from 1685 to 1892*. 2 vols. St. Louis: I. E. Daniell, 1892.

Brundidge, Glenna Fourman, ed. *Brazos County History: Rich Past—Bright Future*. Bryan, Texas: Newman Printing Co., 1986.

Byrd, A. J. *History and Description of Johnson County, and its Principal Towns.* Marshall, Texas: Jennings Brothers, 1879.

Campbell, Randolph B. *A Southern Community in Crisis: Harrison County, Texas 1850–1880.* Austin: Texas State Historical Association, 1983.

Campbell, Randolph B., and Lowe, Richard G. *Wealth and Power in Antebellum Texas.* College Station: Texas A & M University Press, 1977.

Carroll, B. H., ed. *Standard History of Houston Texas From a Study of the Original Sources.* Knoxville: H. W. Crow & Co., 1912.

Castel, Albert. *General Sterling Price and the Civil War in the West.* Baton Rouge: Louisiana State University Press, 1968.

———. "The Fort Pillow Massacre." *Civil War History* 4 (March 1958): 37–50.

Cochran, John. *Dallas County: A Record of its Pioneers and Progress.* Dallas: A. S. Mathis Service Publishing Co., 1928.

Cornish, Dudley Taylor. *The Sable Arm: Negro Troops in the Union Army, 1861–1865.* 1956; reprint, W. W. Norton & Co., Inc., 1966.

Crenshaw, Ollinger. "The Knights of the Golden Circle: The Career of George Bickley." *American Historical Review* 47 (October 1941): 23–50.

Crockett, George L. *Two Centuries in East Texas.* Dallas: The Southwest Press, 1932.

Daniel, Larry J., and Gunter, Riley W. *Confederate Cannon Foundries.* Union City, Tenn.: Pioneer Press, 1977.

Daniell, L. E. *Types of Successful Men of Texas.* Austin: Eugene Von Boeckmann, 1890.

Davis, Jackson Beauregard. "The Life of Richard Taylor." Master's thesis, Louisiana State University, 1937.

Dougall, Richardson, and Chapman, Mary Patricia. *United States Chiefs of Missions 1778–1973.* Washington, D.C.: Department of State, 1973.

Dougan, Michael. *Confederate Arkansas: The People and Policies of a Frontier State in Wartime.* University, Alabama: University of Alabama Press, 1976.

———. "The Little Rock Press Goes to War, 1861–1863." *Arkansas Historical Quarterly* 28 (Spring 1969): 14–27.

Dunn, Roy Sylvan. "The KGC in Texas, 1860–1861." *Southwestern Historical Quarterly* 70 (April 1967): 543–573.

Ellis County History: The Basic 1892 book (With the Presidents Selection deleted) with Additional Biographies compiled by the Ellis County Historical Museum and Art Gallery, Inc. in Memory of the Courageous Pioneers and Builders of Ellis County. Fort Worth & Arlington: Historical Publishers, 1972.

Elzner, Jonnie. *Lamplights of Lampasas County Texas.* Austin: Firm Foundation Publishing House, 1951.

Farmer, Garland R. *The Realm of Rusk County.* Henderson, Texas: The Henderson Times, 1951.

Faulk, Odie B. *General Tom Green, Fightin' Texan*. Waco: Texian Press, 1963.

Fiske, John. *The Mississippi Valley in the Civil War*. Boston: Houghton Mifflin and Company, 1900.

Fitzhugh, Lester N., compiler. *Texas Batteries, Battalions, Regiments, Commanders and Field Officers. Confederate States Army 1861–1865*. Midlothian, Texas: Mirror Press, 1959.

———. "Texas Forces in the Red River Campaign." *Texas Military History* 3 (Spring 1963): 15–22.

Foner, Philip S., ed. *The Autobiographies of the Haymarket Martyrs*. New York: Humanities Press, 1969.

Gallaway, B. P. "A Texas Farm Boy Enlists in the 12th Cavalry." *Texas Military History* 8 (1970): 87–95.

———. *The Ragged Rebel: A Common Soldier in W. H. Parsons' Texas Cavalry, 1861–1865*. Austin: University of Texas Press, 1988.

Giles, L. B. *Terry's Texas Rangers*. Privately printed, 1911.

Gleaves, S. R. "The Strategic Use of Cavalry." *Journal of the U. S. Cavalry Association* 18 (July 1907): 9–25.

Griggs, William Clark. *The Elusive Eden: Frank McMullan's Confederate Colony in Brazil*. Austin: University of Texas Press, 1987.

Hall, Roy F., and Hall, Helen Gibbard. *Collin County: Pioneering in North Texas*. Quanah, Texas: Nortex Press, 1975.

Haskew, Corrie Pattison, compiler. *Historical Records of Austin and Waller Counties*. Houston: Premier Printing & Letter Service, Inc., 1969.

Hattaway, Herman, and Jones, Archer. *How the North Won: A Military History of the Civil War*. Urbana, Ill.: University of Illinois Press, 1983.

Henderson, Harry M. *Texas in the Confederacy*. San Antonio: The Naylor Co., 1955.

Herr, John K., and Wallace, Edward S. *The Story of the U. S. Cavalry 1775–1942*. 1953; reprint, New York: Bonanza Books, 1984.

History of Texas Together with a Biographical History of Milam, Williamson, Bastrop, Travis, Lee and Burleson Counties. Chicago: Lewis Publishing Co., 1893.

History of Texas together with a biographical history of Tarrant and Parker Counties. . . . Chicago: Lewis Publishing Co., 1895.

Holder, Anne Thiele. *Tennessee to Texas: Francis Richardson Tannehill, 1825–1864*. Austin: Pemberton Press, 1966.

Holland, G. A. *History of Parker County and the Double Log Cabin*. Weatherford: The Herald Publishing Co., 1937.

Houston County Historical Commission. *History of Houston County, Texas 1687–1979*. Tulsa, Oklahoma: Heritage Publishing Co., 1979.

Huff, Leo E. "Guerillas, Jayhawkers and Bushwackers in Northern Arkansas During the Civil War." *Arkansas Historical Quarterly* 24 (Summer 1965): 127–148.

————. "The Last Duel in Arkansas: The Marmaduke-Walker Duel." *Arkansas Historical Quarterly* 23 (Spring 1964): 36–49.

————. "The Memphis and Little Rock Railroad during the Civil War." *Arkansas Historical Quarterly* 23 (Autumn 1964), 260–270.

————. "The Union Expedition Against Little Rock." *Arkansas Historical Quarterly* 22 (Fall 1963), 224–237.

Huffstot, Robert S. "The Battle of Arkansas Post." A souvenir booklet from the editors of *Civil War Times Illustrated*. Harrisburg, Pa.: Historical Times, Inc., 1969.

Hunsicker, Neva Ingram. "Rayburn the Raider." *Arkansas Historical Quarterly* 7 (Spring 1948): 87–91.

Johnson, Frank W. *A History of Texas and Texans*. 5 vols. Edited by Eugene C. Barker and Ernest William Winkler. Chicago: American Historical Society, 1914.

Johnson, Ludwell H. *Red River Campaign: Politics and Cotton in the Civil War*. Baltimore: The Johns Hopkins Press, 1958.

Johnson, Sid S. *Some Biographies of Old Settlers: Historical, Personal, and Reminiscent*. Tyler, Texas: Sid S. Johnson, publisher, 1900.

Johnson, Sid S., compiler. *Texans Who Wore the Gray*. Tyler: privately printed, 1907.

Jordan, Terry G. "The Imprint of the Upper and Lower South in Mid-nineteenth Century Texas." *Annals of the Association of American Geographers* 57 (December 1967): 667–690.

Kaufman County Historical Commission. *History of Kaufman County*. 2 vols. Dallas: National Shore Graphics, 1984.

Kerby, Robert L. *Kirby Smith's Confederacy: The Trans-Mississippi South, 1863–1865*. New York: Columbia University Press, 1972.

Lindsley, Philip. *A History of Greater Dallas and Vicinity*. Chicago: Lewis Publishing Co., 1909.

McCaffrey, James M. *This Band of Heroes: Granbury's Texas Brigade, C.S.A.* Austin: Eakin Press, 1985.

McMurry, Richard M. "The Atlanta Campaign: December 23, 1863 to July 18, 1864." Ph.D. dissertation, Emory University, 1967.

McWhiney, Grady. *Cracker Culture: Celtic Ways in the Old South*. Tuscaloosa and London: The University of Alabama Press, 1988.

McWhiney, Grady, and Jamieson, Perry D. *Attack and Die: Civil War Military Tactics and the Southern Heritage*. University, Alabama: University of Alabama Press, 1982.

Mainer, Thomas A. *Houston County in the Civil War*. Crockett, Texas: Houston County Historical Commission, 1981.

Memorial and Biographical History of Dallas County, Texas. Chicago: Lewis Publishing Co., 1892.

Muncy, Raymond Lee. *Searcy, Arkansas: A Frontier Town Grows Up With America*.

Searcy: Harding Press, 1976.

Nance, Joseph Milton. *The Early History of Bryan and the Surrounding Area*. Bryan, Texas: Hood's Brigade-Bryan Centennial Committee, 1962.

"The New England and Southern Stock from Whom A. R. Parsons Sprang—Revolutionary Soldiers, Scholars and Honorable Men." *Knights of Labor* (November 1886): 31–32.

Nichols, James L. *The Confederate Quartermaster in the Trans-Mississippi*. Austin: University of Texas Press, 1964.

Nix, John W. *A Tale of Two Schools and Springtown, Parker County*. Fort Worth: Thomason and Morrow, 1945.

Oates, Stephen B. *Confederate Cavalry West of the River*. Austin: University of Texas Press, 1961.

O'Flaherty, Daniel. *General Joe Shelby*. Chapel Hill: The University of North Carolina Press, 1954.

Parks, Joseph Howard. *General Edmund Kirby Smith, C.S.A.* Baton Rouge: Louisiana State University Press, 1954.

Parsons, Lucy E., ed. *Life of Albert R. Parsons*. 1889; reprint, Chicago: Lucy E. Parsons, 1903.

Pennington, Mrs. R. E. *The History of Brenham and Washington County*. Houston: Standard Printing Lithographing Co., 1915.

Phelan, Macum. *A History of Early Methodism in Texas 1817–1866*. Dallas: Cokesbury Press, 1924.

———. *A History of the Expansion of Methodism in Texas 1867–1902*. Dallas: Mathis, Van North & Co., 1937.

Plummer, Alonzo H. *Confederate Victory at Mansfield*. Mansfield, Louisiana: Ideal Printing Co., 1969.

Quarles, Benjamin. *The Negro in the Civil War*. Boston: Little, Brown and Co., 1953.

Rampp, Lary C., and Rampp, Donald L. *The Civil War in the Indian Territory*. Austin: Presidial Press, 1975.

Ramsdell, Charles William. *Reconstruction in Texas*. 1910; reprint, Austin: University of Texas Press, 1970.

Richardson, Rupert N. *The Frontier of Northwest Texas, 1846–1876*. Glendale, Calif.: A. H. Clark Co., 1963.

"Roster of White County's First Company of Southern Soldiers." *White County Heritage* 1 (January 1963): 13.

Sandbo, Anna Irene. "First Session of the Secession Convention of Texas." *Southwestern Historical Quarterly* 18 (October 1914): 162–194.

Scarbrough, Clara Stearns. *Land of Good Waters, Takachue Pouetsu: A Williamson County, Texas, History*. Georgetown: Williamson County Sun Publishers, 1973.

Schmidt, Charles F. *History of Washington County.* San Antonio: The Naylor Co., 1949.

Sibley, Marilyn McAdams. *Lone Stars and State Gazettes; Texas Newspapers before the Civil War.* College Station: Texas A & M Press, 1983.

Smith, W. Broadus. *Pioneers of Brazos County, Texas 1800–1850.* Bryan, Texas: The Scribe Shop, 1962.

Speer, William S., ed. *The Encyclopedia of the New West.* Marshall, Texas: The United States Biographical Publishing Co., 1881.

Spencer, John W. *The Confederate Guns of Navarro County.* Corsicana: The Texas Press, 1986.

Stambaugh, J. Lee, and Stambaugh, Lillian J. *A History of Collin County, Texas.* Austin: The Texas State Historical Association, 1958.

Starr, Stephen Z. *The Union Cavalry in the Civil War.* vol. 3: *The War in the West 1861–1865.* Baton Rouge: Louisiana State University Press, 1985.

Steffen, Randy. "The Civil War Soldiers." In *The United States Cavalry.* Fort Knox, Ky.: Patton Museum of Cavalry and Armor, n. d.

Tarpley, Fred. *Jefferson: Riverport to the Southwest.* Austin: Eakin Press, 1983.

Taylor, Joe Gray. *Louisiana Reconstructed 1863–1877.* Baton Rouge: Louisiana State University Press, 1974.

Vest, D. L. *Watterson Folk of Bastrop County.* Waco: Texian Press, 1963.

Wakelyn, Jon L. *Biographical Dictionary of the Confederacy.* Westport, Connecticut: Greenwood Press, 1977.

Wallace, Ernest. *Texas in Turmoil, 1849–1875.* Austin: Steck-Vaughn Co., 1965.

Walter, Roy A. *A History of Limestone County.* Austin: Von Boeckmann-Jones, 1959.

Warner, Ezra J. *Generals in Blue: Lives of the Union Commanders.* Baton Rouge: Louisiana State University Press, 1964.

———. *Generals in Gray: Lives of the Confederate Commanders.* Baton Rouge: Louisiana State University Press, 1959.

Webb, Walter Prescott, et al. *The Handbook of Texas.* 3 vols. Austin: The Texas State Historical Association, 1952–1976.

Weddle, Robert S. *Plow-Horse Cavalry: The Caney Creek Boys of the Thirty-fourth Texas.* Austin: Madrone Press, Inc., 1974.

Weems, Samuel A. "The Importance of Devalls Bluff, Arkansas, During the Civil War (1861–1865)." Typescript in the possession of the author.

White, Gifford, ed. *The 1840 Census of the Republic of Texas.* Austin: The Pemberton Press, 1966.

Wilbarger, J. W. *Indian Depredations in Texas.* 2d ed. Austin: Hutchings Printing House, 1890.

Wiley, Bell Irvin. *The Life of Johnny Reb: The Common Soldier of the Confederacy,*

1943; reprint, Baton Rouge: Louisiana State University Press, 1978.

Williams, Jack K. *Dueling in the Old South*. College Station: Texas A & M Press, 1980.

Windsor, Bill. *Texas in the Confederacy: Military Installations, Economy and People*. Hillsboro, Texas: Hill Junior College Press, 1978.

Winfrey, Dorman H. *A History of Rusk County, Texas*. Waco: Texian Press, 1961.

Winters, John D. *The Civil War in Louisiana*. Baton Rouge: Louisiana State University Press, 1963.

Wooster, Ralph A. "An Analysis of the Membership of the Texas Secession Convention." *Southwestern Historical Quarterly* 62 (January 1959): 332–335.

Wooten, Dudley G., ed. *A Comprehensive History of Texas 1865 to 1897*. 2 vols. Dallas: William G. Scarff, 1898.

Wright, Marcus J., compiler. *Arkansas in the War, 1861–1865*. Batesville, Arkansas: Independence County Historical Society, 1963.

———. *Texas in the War, 1861–1865*. Hillsboro, Texas: Hill Junior College Press, 1965.

Index

Abney, John: 234
Addison, Oscar M.: 23, 247 n. 20
Alabama Indians: as Confederate soldiers, 233
Alamo: 7
Alexander, Jerome: 91, 273 n. 20
Alexandria, La.: 133, 144, 146, 165–67, 189, 196; Gov. Moore and, 30; during Red River campaign, 181–82, 184–85
Alf Johnson's Spy Co.: *See* Johnson's Spy Co.
Alice Vivian: 170
Allen, Private: 274 n. 30
Alston, John R. S.: 220–21, 223
Alto, Tex.: Carter's Lancers at, 27–28
Alton, Ill.: 92
Anderson, Rufus D.: 269 n. 5
Ankony, Lieutenant: 129
Antietam: Battle of, ix
Arizona: as part of Trans-Mississippi Dept., ix
Arkadelphia, Ark.: 153–54
Arkansas: Arkansas Post, battle at, 100–106: Cotton Plant, battle at, 67–71; Helena, battle at, 150, 296 n.4; L'Anguille River, battle at, 75–81; Little Rock, battle at, 151–53, 298–99 n. 19; as part of Trans-Mississippi Dept., ix; Pine Bluff, battle at, 155–57; Whitney's Lane, battle at, 53–58
Arkansas Post, Ark.: 43, 45, 95, 99, 108, 111, 113–15, 149, 160, 230–32 battle at, 100–106; Confederate surrender of, 105, 106, 250–51 n. 49, 255 n. 27, 279 n. 23, 279–80 n. 25, 280 ns.32 and 34
Arkansas River: action on, 152
Arkansas True Democrat: 48, 52, 60, 79
Army Corps, Federal: XIII, 192; XVI, 166, 186, 188, 192; XVII, 144, 166, 169, 192; XIX, 192
Army of the Mississippi: 101, 107–108
Army of Mississippi: 192
Army of Northern Virginia: x
Army of the Southwest: 49, 62–63, 67
Army of Tennessee: xi, 109, 178, 192, 230–31, 250–51 n. 49
Army of the Tennessee: 167
Army of the Trans-Mississippi: ix, xi, 3

Army of the West: 74
Atlanta, Ga.: Sherman at, 192, 195
Austin, Ark.: 53, 75, 232
Austin City Light Infantry: 219
Austin County, Tex.: 25–26, 219
Austin, Tex.: 7, 9, 18, 58, 207, 211, 217, 220, 222
Ayres, F. H.: 211

Bache, George M.: 172
Bagby, Arthur P.: as commander of brigade, 170
Bailey, Joseph: 184–85
Baker, Conrad: 72
Ball, Fauntleroy R.: 224–25
Baltimore, Md.: 207
Bankhead, Smith P.: as commander of brigade, 237, 323 n. 60
Banks, Nathaniel P.: 146, 149, 245 n. 47; commands Red River expedition, 165–70, 178, 181–86, 188, 192
Barnes, Benjamin: 212–13, 216
Barnes's artillery: 183
Barr, Alwyn: 192
Bastrop Cavalry Company: 55–56, 217
Bastrop, Tex.: 43
Batesville, Ark.: 48, 53, 62, 65
Battle, Nicholas W.: 234, 238
Baton Rouge, La.: 130
Baylor, George W.: as commander of regiment, 313–14 n. 27; kills John Wharton, 201
Bayou Fourche, Ark.: skirmish at, 152
Bayou Metoe, Ark.: battle at, 150, 297 ns. 7 and 10
Bayou Rapides, La.: skirmish at, 185
Beard, Allen: 144, 224–25
Beard's company: 40, 159
Bearss, Edwin C.: 157
Beaumont, Tex.: 25
Beauregard, P. G. T.: 48, 50, 52, 60, 74
Beazley, William H.: 228–29, 233–34, 322 n. 52
Bedford City, Va.: 206
Bee, Hamilton: 183–84, 314 n. 33
Belgian rifles: *See* weapons
Bell, Andrew: 243 n. 29
Bell County, Tex.: 25, 222
Bellville Countryman: 23

214; battle at, 116, 283 n. 13
Galveston Weekly News: 116
Gano, Richard M.: as commander of brigade, 159, 200, 238
Garland, Robert R.: 105, 275 n. 23; as commander of brigade, 104
Gatesville, Tex.: 222
Georgetown, Tex.: 217
Germans: farmers in Texas, 12; as Federal soldiers ("Hessians" or "Dutch Conscripts"), 54, 56–57
Gettysburg: Battle of, ix
Getzendaner, W. H.: 11, 129, 244 n. 32
Giddings, DeWitt Clinton: 29, 31–32, 34, 46, 74, 94, 119–20, 129, 136, 157, 184–85, 218, 220–21, 251 n. 50; capture of, 89–92, 274–75 n. 30; early life, 88
Giddings, Edmund T.: 90, 274 n. 29, 290 n. 19
Giddings, Francis: 88
Giddings, George: 88, 273 n. 22
Giddings, Giles: 88
Giddings, Jabez D.: 88, 273 n. 22
Giddings, James: 88
Gillespie, Clayton C.: 23–24, 29, 31, 34, 99
Gillespie's regiment: *See* Twenty-fifth Texas Cavalry Regiment and Third Texas Lancers
Glorieta Pass, N. M.: battle at, 232
Goliad, Tex.: 219
Good, John Jay: 17, 39, 45
Good, Susan Anna: 17, 39, 40
Goodloe, Harper: 12, 135, 187, 245–46 n. 50, 289 n. 16, 305 n. 49
Goodrich Landing, La.: 138, 143, 145
Good's battery: *See* First Texas Artillery
Goodwin, W. H. B.: 211
Gorman, Michael: 152
Gorman, Willis A.: 108
Gould, Nicholas C.: as commander of regiment, 171–72, 313–14 n. 27
Gould's regiment: *See* Twenty-third Texas Cavalry Regiment
Grady, Dan: 55–56
Graham, Robert: 218
Granbury, H. B.: 250–51 n. 49
Grand Ecore, La.: 167–68, 170, 178, 181

Grant, Ulysses, S.: 99–100, 108, 111, 113, 115, 130–31, 133, 135, 140, 144, 149–50, 166, 192, 194, 206
Gratiot Street Prison (St. Louis): 91
Graves, A. S.: 44–45
Green, Thomas: 71
Green, Tom: 170–72, 175–79, 305 n. 49
Greene, Colton: as commander of brigade, 115, 117, 119, 120–21, 156, 283 n. 10
Greenwood Cemetery: 207
Greer, Elkanah, 168
Grierson, Benjamin H.: 130
Grimes County, Tex.: 222–23
Grinsted, H. L.: 6, 241–42 n. 12
Groce, Colonel: 244 n.33
Grover, J. R.: 211
Gurley, Edward J.: 234–38, 322 n. 57
Gurley's regiment. *See* Thirtieth Texas Cavalry Regiment

Haley, John: 189
Haley, Thomas F.: 189–90, 212–13, 216; as commander of company, 159; as commander of squadron, 185
Halleck, Henry W.: 22, 73, 100, 108, 113, 146, 163, 165–66
Halletsville, Tex.: 222
Hannah, J. H.: 220–22
Hardeman, Peter: as commander of regiment, 313–14 n. 27, 323 n. 60
Hardeman, William P.: as commander of brigade, 200. *See also* Fourth Texas Cavalry Regiment
Harper, William M.: 220–22
Harrell, John M.: 150
Harris, S. S.: as assistant surgeon, 125
Harris, S. S.: as commander of battery, 196
Harrison, Isaac F.: as commander of Louisiana cavalry, 138
Harrison County, Tex.: 45
Hart, William: as commander of battery, 105
Harvard University: 114
Harwood, Alex: 223
Hasbrook, James T.: 224–25
Hastings: 170
Hastings-on-Hudson, New York: 206
Hawes, James M.: 97, 110, 160, 282 n. 56,

The Author

Anne J. Bailey, a native of Cleburne, Texas, was graduated from the University of Texas and holds a Ph.D. from Texas Christian University. She teaches courses on the Civil War and Reconstruction at Georgia Southern College in Statesboro.